HARDPRESS.NET
HOME OF HARD-TO-FIND BOOKS

The Works of Vicesimus Knox, D. D.
by Vicesimus Knox

THE WORKS

OF

VICESIMUS KNOX, D.D.

WITH A

BIOGRAPHICAL PREFACE.

IN SEVEN VOLUMES.

VOL. III.

LONDON:
PRINTED FOR J. MAWMAN,
LUDGATE STREET,
MDCCCXXIV.

WINTER EVENINGS;

OR,

LUCUBRATIONS ON LIFE AND LETTERS.

(CONTINUED.)

EVENING I.

ON RECENT INSTITUTIONS FOR CHARITABLE PURPOSES.

Sui memores alios fecêre merendo.   VIRG.

IF any one should be disposed to censure with uncharitable severity the vicious manners of the present age, I should wish to lead him through the environs of London, and point out to him the modern palaces erected for the poor and afflicted of all denominations. These, I would say, are the trophies of Christianity ; and these, we are taught to hope, will cover a multitude of sins, and plead powerfully in favour of transgressors at the mercy-seat of the Most High.

I was walking one fine morning in St. George's Fields, when the sun, shining delightfully, gilded the spires of the numerous churches in my view, and seemed to smile on the windows of the various public edifices devoted to charity around me ; when I could not help exclaiming, " surely the great Father of us all, when he looks down with indignation on the crying sins of yon great city, will turn with

complacency to these monuments of charity, and
blot out whole pages from the tremendous volume,
where he records the offences of his favourite
creature.

I went on musing on the multitude of charitable
institutions by which this country is honourably
distinguished ; and though former times have many
illustrious examples of munificence to produce, yet
I congratulated myself on being born in an age in
which Christian charity never shone in works of
allowed public utility with greater lustre.

I confined myself, amidst the multitude of noble
examples which occurred, to those which have appeared within a few years, and which have been
seen, in their origin, by the race of mortals now
alive.

`One of the first which was suggested to my me-
mory was that of Mr. Hetherington. I do not recollect that any particular provision had been made
for the necessitous blind, labouring under the additional burden of old age ; though, from the dictates
of common sense and the example of our blessed
Saviour, it might obviously have been concluded
that the blind are in a peculiar manner objects of
Christian charity.

Mr. Hetherington has provided comfort for fifty
of these objects in perpetual succession, by an an-
nuity of ten pounds a year each, during the re-
mainder of their dark pilgrimage. He set a noble
and almost singular example by bestowing his be-
nefaction while he was yet alive, and the example
has been most honourably followed by Mr. Coventry, who has made a similar provision for thirty
more, with a like exemplary bounty during life.

He again has been imitated by a benefactor, who,
choosing to do good clandestinely, has alleviated the

misfortune of an additional thirty, and left it to Heaven only to record his name. Others also have added to the store.

At the very mention of Jonas Hanway, all that is benevolent rises to the recollection. The Marine Society has two effects so important, the providing for the poor vagabond, and the raising of a nursery of seamen, that it is no wonder the name of Hanway, to whom it owes its greatest obligations, is held in high rank among the charitable benefactors to this country.

Who ever ventured to appear the public advocate of the chimney-sweeper but Jonas Hanway? The poor infant of five or six years old, without shoes or stockings, almost naked, almost starved, driven up the narrow flue of a high chimney, driven by the menaces and scourges of an imperious master, and sometimes terrified with flames! Think of this, ye mothers who caress your infants in your laps; and, at the same time, exert your interest and abilities, like Jonas Hanway, in preventing the employment of babes in a work under which the hardened veteran might sink with pain, terror, and fatigue. There was indeed no species of misery which this indefatigable philanthropist did not endeavour to relieve. Happy had his abilities as a writer equalled his zeal as a man. But his excellent plans were sometimes neglected, or contemned, through a deficiency of proper eloquence to recommend them. Yet for what he intended, and what he performed, his name shall be handed down to late posterity, while his bust stands erected by gratitude among the tombs of kings, and greater than kings, those who, though private persons, enlightened the understanding and alleviated the miseries of their fellow-creatures.

Of Mr. Howard's heroic philanthropy the world

wants no monument more honourable than the loud plaudits of his own countrymen.   By a strange forgetfulness, the state of prisons in this and other countries was deplorably neglected, and a degree of punishment was inflicted by the cold, the dampness, the filthiness, the wretched diet and accommodation, and the consequent diseases of the dungeon, far greater than the most rigorous severity of the most sanguinary laws ever intended.   Mr. Howard, by visiting the prisons, by suggesting improvements in them, by causing a sense of shame in the conductors of them, and by raising a general attention to the subject, has already diffused a gleam of comfort through the dark mansion, where misery unutterable sat and pined in hopeless agony.   The prisoner breathed contagion ; and whether he deserved death or not for his crime, he was likely to incur it in the loathsome prison, with all the aggravation of lingering languor.   Great as was his misery, few gave themselves the trouble to notice it.   Many feared infection if they approached to examine, and many, disgusted with the infamy of the guilty, scarcely acknowledged that the wretch in chains, though unconvicted, deserved compassion.   But Mr. Howard, regardless of ease and life, incurred every danger, and almost forgot *their failings in their woe.* `

But it is unnecessary to dwell on Mr. Howard's praise.   Fortunately the public have taken it up ; and there is some danger lest panegyric should be carried to an excess which frustrates its own intent, by creating a sense of excessive plenitude.   I must, however, unite in reproving those who malignantly stigmatise his noble attempts with the name of Quixotism.

The Society for the relief of prisoners confined for

Small Debts deserves to participate Mr. Howard's fame.

Many were the prejudices formed against the society instituted for the recovery of drowned persons; but let any one place himself a moment in the situation of a parent suddenly bereaved of his child, and, if he is not unfeeling in his nature, he will want no argument to induce him to give it every encouragement. Doubts were once entertained of its success, but they may be now removed by ocular demonstration. It is indeed a most affecting sight to behold those who were snatched from the jaws of death walking on the public days in solemn procession, and paying a grateful obedience to their restorers.

The Dispensaries established, and liberally supported, in various parts of the metropolis, are an additional proof of the indefatigable beneficence of the present age.

But many will be ready to detract from the institutors and benefactors, and to say, that these plausible charities are begun and supported by those who mean no more than to gratify their vanity, or promote their interest. There is reason to suspect that this may, in some instances, be true, but not in all; and while so much good is produced, it is narrow and invidious to derogate from the promoters of it, by attributing their activity to selfish incitements.

What can be said of the thousands of unambitious and disinterested persons who eagerly crowd to present their guineas in contribution to every useful mode of beneficence for which their assistance is publicly solicited? It would be no less unreasonable than mean to attribute their bounty to vanity, or any other sinister consideration. To avoid the very suspicion, many give most ample donations and conceal their names; but those who do not, ought in candour to be supposed desirous of diffusing the influence of their example and authority, rather than of seeking the applause of the world and the reputation of generosity.

Of the various hospitals which surround the great city, and form a better defence for it than the strongest fortification, I have said little, because they were chiefly founded in preceding times; and I wished, on the present occasion, to be confined to recent instances, and to such as have occurred within the memory of the rising generation.

From all of them I am led to conclude, that the benevolent virtues are by no means diminished among us, but that they flourish more and more under the guidance of judgment and experience; and may they still flourish, and may every one be anxious to possess a share in them, that he may have something to veil the multitude of his transgressions, when he shall be summoned to give up his account at the tribunal of an omniscient and almighty Judge!

EVENING II.

ON THE EXTENT OF LITERATURE, AND THE SHORTNESS OF TIME FOR ITS CULTIVATION.

WHILE the objects of learning are increased, the time to be spent in pursuit of it is greatly contracted by the modes of modern life. Every year produces some valuable work in some department of science or polite letters, and the accomplished scholar is expected, and cannot but wish, to give it some attention. The art of printing has multiplied books to such a degree, that it is a vain attempt either to collect or to read all that is excellent, much more all that has been published. It becomes necessary, therefore, to read in the classical sense of the word, LEGERE, that is, to *pick out*, to select the most valuable and worthiest objects, not only the best parts of books, but, previously to that selection, to choose, out of an infinite number, the best books, or at least those which are best adapted to the particular pursuit or employment in life.—Without this care there is danger of confusion and distraction, of a vain labour, and of that poverty which arises from superfluity.

The surface of the globe becomes every day more known, enlarges the field of modern history, geography, botany, and furnishes new opportunities for the study of human nature. At the revival of learning, voyages and travels constituted a very small part of the scholar's and philosopher's library ; but at present, in England only, the books of this class are sufficiently numerous to fill a large museum. He who would understand human nature, must inspect them, and will also find it necessary to have recourse to the Dutch and the French travellers. A man might find employment for his life in reading itineraries alone.

The late great improvements in science have multiplied books necessary to be read by the general scholar to a wonderful extent. The volumes of scientifical and literary societies or academies are infinite. The mineral, the vegetable, and the animal kingdoms have been accurately examined, and the result brought to public view, in crowded and bulky tomes. The minutest productions of nature have been described with prolixity ; from the hyssop on the wall to the cedar of Lebanon, from the atom to the mountain, from the mite to man, the whale, and the elephant.

The study of antiquities has added greatly to the number of books. Politics, history, and law, have also crowded the library.

The field of divinity has been most industriously cultivated, and the harvest has been great. The age of Methusalem would be too short to read all the theological works of English divines; to which must be added the excellent productions of France, Holland, and other neighbouring nations. Biblical learning alone, so pregnant is the sacred volume, would occupy a long life, exclusively of all attention to practical theology.

Moral philosophy, both systematical and miscellaneous, is so far extended, that if it is all necessary to the conduct of life, every man must die without knowing how to live; for the longest life would not afford opportunities for its study.

Philology and criticism have appeared in books which equal, or exceed, in number and size, all those original works united, which it was their primary intention to elucidate.

A species of books, unknown to the ancients, and such as are found to attract more readers than any others, has risen in the last century; I mean romances and fictitious histories of private and familiar life, under the name of Novels.

Add to all this a vast quantity of poetry or verse of all kinds, and on all subjects; add tragedies and comedies; add pamphlets in all their variety, fugitive papers, publications of diurnal intelligence; and the sum becomes so great as to lead the general student to a degree of despair.

I have already said, that not only the work to be done has increased upon us, but the time of doing it has decreased, according to the modes of living which now prevail.

Early rising is not in vogue. Breakfast, with all the apparatus of tea-drinking, occupies a long time. The hair must be dressed with taste, or the student will find his learning will not give him admission into the company of people of condition and fashion, nor indeed into any company where decorum is regarded.

The newspapers must be read; or conversation may lose one of its most abundant sources. The coffeehouse perhaps claims an hour. Morning calls must be made, and engraved cards left with servants, or friendship and patronage may be irrecoveraby lost. A morning walk or ride will conduce to an appetite, and the person must be dressed from head to foot, before a genteel student can think of meeting company at dinner. Very little time, it is evident, can be found in the midst of all these necessary occupations for poring over folios. To neglect any of them for his book may cause a man to be called an odd fellow and dismissed to Coventry.

But the morning loss, you will say, may be recovered by the diligence of the afternoon. Impossible; for the hour of dining is the same which in the days of that polite scholar and fine gentleman, sir Philip Sydney, used to be the supper time: and convivial pleasures are so great, as to render him, who should relinquish them for musty books, obnoxious to the imputation of an ascetic or a bookworm. Indeed the mind is unfit for contemplation after a full meal and a generous glass. Various amusements intervene to employ the time till the hour of repose closes the season both of action and contemplation.

While so much is to be done, and so little is the time, how can we expect to find many profoundly learned ? And yet there is as much pretension to learning, and as much volubility upon all subjects of science, as could be expected in the most erudite age. How is this phenomenon accounted for ?

In the first place, *superficial learning*, quite enough to qualify talkers, and to satisfy common hearers, is easily picked up by reading the newspapers and periodical pamphlets, in which little scraps are dealt out, like small wares at a retail shop, for the convenience of the poor; who, though they have no store-room, make shift to live from hand to mouth, and hide their poverty.

In the next and the principle place, a reliance ON GENIUS, as it is called, without application, gives a boldness of utterance and assertion, which often sets off base metal with the glitter of gold. Never was an age when there was so many pretenders TO GENIUS. The great art is, under the confidence of genius, to make the most advantageous display of the little learning you have, to disparage what you have not, to put a good face upon defect, and supply weakness and want of real merit by a noisy confidence and boisterous pretension to *native* powers, above the reach of application. It is not uncommon to throw contempt upon all who show, by their willingness to labour in pursuit of knowledge, a per-suasion that, though a man may be born with powers to acquire knowledge, yet that he is not born with knowledge acquired, with innate science, history, philosophy, and languages.

Knowledge may certainly be acquired by one man sooner than by another, and in much greater abund-ance; but it must be acquired by application, for it is neither innate, nor can be mechanically infused.

Since, then, the field of knowledge is enlarged, and the time to be spent in cultivating it contracted, it is requisite that the student should select a little part of the field only for particular cultivation; and thus, by husbanding his time so as to dig and manure it well, he may carry home a good crop of corn, while others are contented with spontaneous weeds, leaves, thorns, thistles, stubble, chaff, and underwood.

Let him enjoy the prospect of the fine country around as far as the horizon extends; but let him be satisfied with cultivating with his own hands, a little *ferme ornée*, well laid out, prettily diversified, and within a moderate enclosure.

EVENING III.

ON THE UNCOUTH NAMES OFTEN USED BY WRITERS TO EXEMPLIFY CHARACTERS.

SIR,—SOMEBODY, I think, has very properly taken notice of the odd names which Dr. Watts has used to distinguish those characters, which he introduces to illustrate his moral instructions. The characters are commonly grave; but the names are often such as give them something of a ludicrous air. He was a man of learning, judgment, and angelic goodness; but I know not whether his *taste* in literary matters has not been too highly appreciated. I do not recollect the fictitious name which was selected as an instance of absurdity; but in looking for it, I found those of Polonides, Polyramus, Fluvio, and Credonius; all of which are strangely uncouth. Such are also in the same book, Jocander, Positivo, Scitorio, Scintillo, Thebaldino, Niveo, and Plumbinus.

If writers mean to give their characters the appearance of truth, they should not select ancient names for living persons, much less names formed by their own capricious invention, and such as never were given to men of any age or country. We know, indeed, that the name is a mask; but the mask of a respectable character should resemble neither a monster, nor a caricatura. Let all fiction which is intended to please, approach as nearly as possible to reality.

I own I am not pleased with the generality of our dialogue writers, who give their persons Greek and Roman names, though at the same time they make them talk like Englishmen, and allude to modern customs, manners, and places. There is an incongruity in these, which lessens much of the entertainment which the dialogue might otherwise afford.

Why may not modern names be admitted into modern dialogue? You will say perhaps, Palæmon and Philander, Eugenius and Eusebius, have a prettier sound than Smith, Johnson, Walker, Benson, Hudson. The Latin and Greek languages have a prettier sound than the English; and therefore we may, for the same reason, write the whole dialogue in those languages. It is another plea for adopting Greek and Latin names, that, as the Romans did not use the ceremonious salutations of the moderns, a great deal of trouble is avoided by omitting the unmeaning modes of address, Sir, Madam, Your Grace, and My Lord, which some imagine necessary when they introduce a conversation between such personages as Mr. Smith, Mr. Johnson, Mrs. Melville, Lord Clarendon, and the Duke of Kent.

But I think, these ceremonious appellations may be omitted with less violation of probability and propriety, than is caused by introducing Greeks and Romans, talking about the doctrines of Christianity, the laws of our country, and other subjects, on which they could not be made to converse, without a violent anachronism.

When the subject relates entirely to antiquity, ancient names are not improper; indeed, as the ancients may be supposed better acquainted with such subjects than the moderns, the mind is pleased with the propriety of introducing them as the interlocutors.

But while the matter is good, it is not right to cavil at trifles which are no more than forms. Perhaps my remarks are hypercritical: that they may not be tedious, I will here conclude them.

I am, SIR,
to borrow one of Dr. Watts's names,
Your humble Servant,
POLYRAMUS.

SIR,—I am a great lover of learning, but not having had the advantage of a liberal education, I am totally unacquainted with the learned languages; and I lament the defect as a real misfortune. I hear much of their excellence, and you may suppose it a great mortification to me, that I am unable to read those books which have been celebrated as the finest productions of the human intellect. I endeavour to compensate my defect by reading English authors; but I often stumble upon Latin mottos and sentences, which I suppose to contain some jewel, too precious to be exposed to vulgar view, and locked up in a casket of which I have not the key.

But I am not only puzzled and mortified with

mottos and sentences, which I do not understand,
but often with strange names of characters in moral
writers, and of persons who converse in fictitious
dialogues, which, I have no doubt, contain some
significant meaning, which I am at a loss to unriddle.

Dr. More, in his Dialogues, introduces the following persons; Philotheus, Bathynous, Sophron,
Philopolis, Euister, Hylobares, and *Cuphophron.*—
Every one of these is expressive of the character introduced; but I should have been quite in the dark
about them, and have wondered at their oddity, if
the Doctor had not obligingly explained their meaning in one of the first pages of his volume. I wish
the example had been followed by many others,
who introduce me into the company of persons
whose characters I do not know, because I do not
understand the meaning of their crabbed names.

I humbly conceive, that it would be quite as well,
if writers suffered the characters to open themselves
to the reader in the course of the conversation; and
I see no good reason why christian and surnames of
honest Englishmen, may not be given to persons
who come forward to talk on subjects, which they
must understand far better than the wisest of the
ancients; I mean such as Dr. More discusses, the
attributes of God, and his providence in this world;
but in truth, I find, on inquiry, that these names
are not the names of ancients. They occur not in
history, but are compounded of words that seldom
met before, to express ideas which can only be
understood by those who are acquainted with the
learned languages. Such names appear to me to
have no more propriety than some of those which,
in the times of fanaticism, were used by the Puri-
tans, such as, Praise-God Bare-Bones, Make-peace
Heaton, Kill-sin Pimple, and Fly-debate Roberts;

the names of some among the jurymen empannelled in Sussex, during the usurpation of Cromwell.

I acknowledge, however, that the ancient and high-sounding names adopted in English dialogues, give a dignity to the discourse; but I, who am a mere Englishman, wish to see Englishmen introduced, without being ashamed of their names, and do not know why the names of Clarendon, Temple, Raleigh, and a thousand others, equally well sounding, might not answer the purpose as well as names borrowed from Greece and Rome; and, as to the significancy of the above mentioned compound appellations, what should I be the wiser for it without an explanatory table? What must I think of Dr. More's *Cuphophron?* I should not know the sense of the word; and, I am sure, I could not admire the sound. Few Gothic names are of more difficult pronunciation.

But I ought not to judge decisively, as I profess myself no scholar. I only submit to you my complaint, as an English reader. I shall be much obliged to you to desire gentlemen, who may hereafter write dialogues, and introduce uncommon names, as exemplifications of their instruction, either to give modern names, or such as are known in history, or else, always to add an explanatory table.

I am, SIR, Yours, &c.

AN ENGLISH READER.

EVENING IV.

ON CALIGULA'S ATTEMPT TO SUPPRESS THE WORKS OF LIVY AND VIRGIL.

THE tyrants who oppressed Rome in the decline of her empire, were not satisfied with depriving men of their civil rights, but often attempted to chain the mind in servitude, and to domineer with absolute control, where they certainly had no claim to pre-eminence, in the republic of literature. One of the most singular and barbarous attempts upon record was that of Caligula, who formed a design of abolishing the poems of Homer, and had nearly accomplished his purpose of banishing, from all the libraries of his time, the busts and the works of Livy and Virgil. He could not bear, that those noble efforts of genius, breathing a spirit of liberty and virtue, which he could not but hate, should continue to diffuse such sentiments, as must teach all who imbibed them, to detest him as a monster.

The following is the account of this matter given by Suetonius : " Cogitavit etiam de Homeri car- " minibus abolendis. Cur enim sibi non liceret, " dicens, quod Platoni licuisset, qui eum a civitate, " quam constituebat, ejecerit ? Sed Virgilii et " Titi Livii scripta et imagines, paulum abfuit, " quin ex omnibus bibliothecis amoveret ; quorum " alterum ut nullius ingenii, minimæque doctrinæ ; " alterum, ut verbosum, in historiâ negligentem- " que, carpebat."*

Flagitious as was his reign, I know not whether any thing he could have done, would have been

---

* Sueton. Calig. cap. 34.

more injurious, than if he had succeeded in extinguishing these glorious lights. The atrocious malignity of his immoral and tyrannical actions was confined to his own age, but this would have descended to posterity, and continued the effects of his despotism, long after the great teacher, Death, had humbled his pride, by reducing him to the dust, not distinguishable from the poorest wretch whom his insolence despised, and his cruelty persecuted. Indeed his design was impracticable; for, with all his power, he could not have prevented some votary of taste and genius from preserving in secret the noble relics of these illustrious ornaments of human nature.

I have no doubt but the same disposition which could form a wish to abolish Homer, would have rejoiced, if it had been possible, to have extinguished the sun, or to have dried up the ocean. Such tyranny exhibits a melancholy monument of human wickedness, and at the same time furnishes a salutary warning to the world, not to trust enormous power in the hands of a fellow-creature. Human nature retains so much of inherent malignity, that he who possesses power uncontrolled will be in imminent danger of imitating, and nearly resembling the parent of all evil.

But the wicked never want the artifice of giving to their malice some colourable pretence. Caligula alleged that he should be justified in the abolition of Homer by the example of Plato, who banished the poets from his imaginary republic. But what was Plato's motive? a desire to preserve the morals of youth, whose ideas he thought were corrupted and distorted, by an initiation into the strange mysteries of fiction, instead of the knowledge of substantial and practical realities. He did not

mean to abolish their works, or to preclude men,
whose reason was mature, from the study of them.
He only thought, as many others have thought, that
on the minds of young men, the slaves of passion
and fancy, they might operate in the same manner
as novels and romances have been observed to do,
in firing the passions and misleading the imagination. But was Caligula's motive for their expulsion a fear that they might diffuse corruption ?
No such apprehension ever agitated his bosom.
His fear was, lest they should teach a virtue to
which he could never attain, and raise a spirit inimical to his manners, his person, and his tyranny. He
must of known that, among all the persons described
by Homer, he was worthy only to be ranked with
such wretches as Thersites. Before he could shine
he knew that all true glory must be shaded, as the
sun must retire, before the feeble light, which arises
from a foul vapour, can become visible.

But he assigns a reason for the expulsion of Virgil and Livy. Virgil, says he, has no genius, and a
very small share of learning ; and Livy is verbose
in his style, and negligent in his narrative.

Caligula must be excepted against as an incompetent judge both of learning and genius ; for it requires a considerable share of both, to form a just
opinion of the degree in which they are possessed
by a writer. If Virgil had not genius, he would
not, I think, have continued so long the delight
and admiration of all who have read his works with
taste. He has Longinus's criterion of genius, the
united voice of various ages and nations, in his favour. He has Caligula, and a few other men of de-
bauched taste, against him, which is almost as great
an honour as the general approbation.

The truth is, that Virgil has a remarkably happy

union of genius with learning; and a judgment also to guide him in the conduct of both, with that propriety which enables him to delight at once the reason and the fancy. Genius, without learning, often delights the fancy; but the judgment must in the mean time sleep, or the pleasure will be diminished and interrupted.

Whoever has read the works of Virgil, in the excellent edition of Heyne, will want no argument to convince him, that Virgil did not deserve the stigma which Caligula would have fixed on him, that of very little learning; and whoever has sensibility will feel the falsehood of the detracting spirit, that dared to assert of him that he had no genius. It must ever be an honour to suffer detraction from such men as Caligula.

It is very easy to assign a reason for his dislike of Livy. A most arbitrary tyrant, and most profligate man, could not but wish to destroy the works of an historian, who exhibits the assertors of liberty, and the virtuous patriots of a virtuous republic, in such colours, as must at once excite love and lead to imitation. Caligula's charge of verbosity in the style of Livy is utterly groundless. He expresses himself with a noble brevity, and with that concise dignity, which evinced that he had a Roman soul; such a soul, as was adequate to the noble undertaking of a Roman history. The other charge, that of negligence in his account of facts, originated from the malignant wish of the tyrant, to diminish the credit of an historian who related deeds of so bright a splendour, as must render the page in which his own should be recorded foul indeed. Time has unfortunately done much to accomplish the nefarious wish of Caligula, in the destruction of the works of Livy; but enough remains to delight every man of taste, and warm the bosom with magnanimous sentiments, and the generous ardour of public virtue.

It is greatly to be lamented, when princes, instead of patronizing genius, endeavour to repress its aspiring vigour. Such a conduct arises, in such men as Caligula, from envy and malice ; but a neglect of genius is occasioned in others by ignorance, and a total deficiency of taste for works which the world applauds. Even Hadrian, we are told, wished to abolish Homer's works, and substitute in his room the poems of one Antimachus. He thought it was time to leave off admiring old Homer, that he had been admired long enough, and that he should gratify the passion for novelty, by introducing in his place, a modern versifier. He puts one in mind of the rough warrior, who told the captain, to whose care he had consigned some fine pictures which he had taken as spoils, that if they were lost or injured, they should be renewed at the captain's expense.

Men of sense look down upon such emperors, when they dictate in matters of taste, with as much contempt, as the emperors can do on the meanest of their vassals. When learning is diffused throughout a nation, the works of taste and genius flourish and abound independently of the smiles or the frowns of princes.

EVENING V.

ON ERASMUS'S PRAISE OF MARRIAGE.

Among the marks of modern profligacy may be enumerated the reluctance with which young men enter the marriage state. The affections of many are in vain solicited by any charms besides those of lucre. The times seem to be past, when, in the prime of life virtuous love led young men to select a companion, for the amiable qualities of her mind and person, independently of all pecuniary considerations. The loveliest of women may now pine, in hopeless celibacy; for, if they cannot purchase a husband, as they would purchase a gown, with the contents of their purse, they may live and die without one. In vain has nature given them the vermil cheek, and the eye of sensibility, if fortune has refused her more brilliant gifts. Young men gaze at them indeed, like children at the peacock, and turn away without any tenderness of sentiment, or at least, without any wish to possess the beauty which they admire, on honourable conditions.

It is indeed observable, that young men of the present age too often consider marriage as an evil in itself, only to be incurred when the pecuniary advantages attending it afford a compensation. For the sake of the good, it seems, they sometimes condescend to accept the evil. A most insulting opinion, and no less unreasonable and untrue than contumelious; for marriage, prudent and affectionate marriage, is favourable to every virtue that can contribute to the comfort and happiness of the individual, while it most essentially serves the interests of society.

I was thinking on this subject, when I accidentally opened a little book of Erasmus on the Art of Letter Writing. He gives models of letters on various subjects, and, under the appearance of affording hints, in a didactic way, for the use of students, contrives to recommend several most useful things, with great force of argument, and in a very entertaining manner. I happened to open the book in the place where he is writing a persuasive to marriage, and I was so well pleased with several of his topics, that I determined to select a few of them for the consideration of my readers. I mean not literally to translate, or to give the whole of his persuasive. There are parts in it, which one cannot entirely approve; but there are others, which every heart, that is not spoiled by fashion and false philosophy, must admire.

Is there any friendship, says he, among mortals, comparable to that between man and wife? For the love of you, he proceeds, your wife has ceased to value the tenderness of parents, brothers, sisters; to you alone she looks for happiness, on you she depends, with you she wishes to live and die.

Are you rich? you have one who will endeavour to preserve and to increase your property. Are you in narrow circumstances? you have one who will assist you faithfully in the pursuit of gain. If you enjoy prosperity, she will double your happiness; if you are in adversity, she will console you, she will sit by your side, she will wait upon you with all the assiduity of love, and only wish that she could appropriate the misfortune which gives you pain. Is there any pleasure to be compared with an union of hearts like this?

I must add the next passage in his own words.—— " Si domi agis, adest quæ solitudinis tædium depellat; si foris, est quæ discedentem osculo prosequatur, absentem desideret, redeuntem læta excipiat."

She is the sweet companion of your youth, and the pleasant solace of your old age.

What can be more odious than that man, who, as if he were born for himself, lives for himself, heaps up riches for himself, spares for himself, spends for himself, loves no human creature but himself, and is beloved by none?

How will you value your happiness,

> —— Ubi quis tibi parvulus aulâ
> Luserit Æneas,

" qui tuos tuæque conjugis vultus referat, qui te blandâ Balbutie *Patrem* appellitet."

I know, says he, that you will object that all this happiness depends upon the disposition of the wife, more than on the marriage state. A marriage may be thus happy if the wife be good ; but suppose her ill-natured, suppose her unchaste, and suppose the children undutiful. Believe me, the bad husband usually makes the bad wife. You certainly have it in your power to choose a good one ; but what if she should afterwards be spoiled? Erasmus confidently replies, A good wife may indeed be spoiled by a bad husband, but a bad wife is usually reformed by a good one. *Falso uxores accusamus.* Nobody, he assures us (I am afraid too confidently), ever had a bad wife but by his own fault. And with respect to children, good children, says he, are usually born of good parents ; but however they may have been born, they commonly become just such as they are made by education and example.

But why, continues he, do you so anxiously enumerate the inconveniences of marriage, just as if celibacy were totally free from them, or as if any mode of human life were not subject to evil and misfortune. If you would have no inconvenient circumstances in your state, you must leave this life. " Sin intra humanam conditionem animum contineas, nihil est conjugali vita, neque tutius, neque tranquillius, neque jucundius, neque amabilius, neque felicius." But if one can restrain one's desires within the boundaries of happiness which belong to human nature, there is no state safer, more tranquil, pleasanter, lovelier, nor happier, than the conjugal.

Though Erasmus is seeking hints to supply the young letter-writer with matter for his compositions, yet I cannot but think that he spoke his honest sentiments, because he spoke with warmth, and, I believe, meant obliquely to censure those unnatural institutions of the Romish church, which tend to discourage marriage. He is very copious on the subject, and advances many arguments, which I have not room to transcribe, and which indeed will appear to much greater advantage in the original. I must not conceal that, to show his ingenuity, he has written a dissuasive from marriage; but it really contains no argument which is valid, or which is worthy of repetition.

I am of opinion, that the reluctance of many young men of fortune to enter into the state, arises not from any settled conviction of the unreasonableness of the institution, but from profligacy, thoughtlessness, false ideas of pleasure, and a want of rational ideas of human life and the nature of human happiness. But, whatever is the cause, the effect is certainly unhappy both to men and women. Men, indeed, in consequence of their libertinism, gratify their desires in the haunts of vice; and so much the worse, for they thus add sin to misery. Women are often kept in a state of celibacy, for which nature never designed them, and to which, I may say, without attributing to them indecency or immodesty, they are in general not much inclined. It is happy, however, that reserve and virtue so far prevail among them, as, for the most part, to prevent them from forming improper connexions, in consequence of being thus injuriously prevented from making a matrimonial alliance. It is to be hoped, they will still preserve their dignity by preserving their innocence; but their case is hard, and nothing, which a wise legislature can do to alleviate it, should be omitted. Many nations have taken great pains to encourage marriage; but ours places some obstacles in its way, which, though often salutary in the higher classes, are perhaps injurious in the subordinate.

A reformation of manners, among the young men who lead the fashion, would contribute most to the encouragement of marriage; for where libertinism greatly prevails, celibacy, which is favourable to it, will be predominant. Perhaps, if women were instructed in useful as well as ornamental arts, and were less expensive in dress and diversions, the rest might be left to the natural operation of their beauty and agreeable accomplishments. As the small-pox is in great measure defeated, they certainly never appeared more beautiful, than in the present time; and ornamental accomplishments were never pursued by them with more ardour, or advanced to higher perfection.

EVENING VI.

ON NEGLECTING THE PRACTICE OF DRINKING HEALTH AT TABLE.

Tardè Cyathos mihi das; cedò sanè : benè mibi; benè vobis.
PLAUTUS.

SIR,

I LATELY addressed to you a few observations on the omission of grace at table; and I now beg leave to add some remarks on another omission, which fashion seems to recommend, but which is countenanced neither by the examples of the ancients, nor by reason, nor by a sense of propriety. I observed, on my visit to my old friend in London, that the friendly practice of drinking health at dinner was, in most of the fashionable families, very much on the decline, and in many, totally omitted. Indeed the omission arises from a principle which seems very much to prevail in the present age, and which aims at the abolition of all forms and ceremonies, as meaning nothing, and at the same time giving trouble and excluding ease. Forms and ceremonies undoubtedly have their utility, or they would not have been universally retained in every age and nation, which history has recorded. But allowing some forms to be without meaning, I cannot suppose, unless I throw a severer reflection on the friendship and hospitality of modern times than I choose, that the drinking of health is, without exception, a senseless and empty ceremony. A man of a warm and friendly heart usually feels a sentiment of cordial kindness, when he holds the cup of refreshment in his hand, and wishes health and happiness to his friends, who are partaking with him, of the same innocent and necessary pleasure.

The custom prevailed among the Greeks, who carried the elegance which they displayed in the polite arts, to the table and social circle, assembled to enjoy the pleasures of the palate and of discourse. Homer, indeed, has given the model in the first book of the Iliad, who says of the gods at their feast,

Χρυσείος δεπάεσσι
Δειδέχατ' ἀλλήλους.

The manner of drinking to each other resembled what is called among us *pledging*. The person who drank to his friend was said προπίνειν, or to drink first. He drank a part of the cup, and then handed the rest to the friend whom he had named. The words which passed on the occasion were προπίνω σοι καλως, to which the person saluted, λαμβάνω ἀπό σου ηδεως, which may be thus freely translated: I have the honour to drink to you—I pledge you with pleasure.

It was also the custom, after due respect paid to the gods, to drink to absent friends; and, as an emblem of sincerity, it was established as a law never to dilute the wine drunk on this occasion.

I shall not trouble you with various proofs that the custom of drinking health is justified by the example of the politest people of antiquity. It would be easy to collect them from the writers on antiquities; but the instance alleged is sufficient for my purpose, and will serve to confute those, who hint that the custom is unpolite.

There is surely something peculiarly brutal in sitting down to meals without ever thinking of God or man; in neglecting the grace, and omitting the form of wishing health and happiness to those who sit at the same table. We have seen that it is contrary to the practice of antiquity, and of almost all people in the world, who, though they varied in the forms of the table, agreed in the essential points, in giving glory to God on high, and testifying good-will towards men.

Yours, &c.

A RATIONAL FORMALIST.

The omission of drinking health is by no means general; but, as it has been countenanced at the tables of persons of fashion, it may probably descend to their imitators in lower life, and, in time, become universal. My correspondent has therefore very pro-

perly expressed his disapprobation of it. It certainly
displays something of selfishness, and is contrary to
the general sense of the most enlightened and polished
people.   It can only be justified with certain qualifications and restrictions.   It is troublesome, in a
large company, to drink the health of every guest
respectively; and troublesome formalities ought
not to be scrupulously adhered to, when they con-
travene the very purpose of the meeting, which
was certainly to promote cheerfulness, enjoyment,
and ease.

But forms, not evidently and intolerably burthen-
some and foolish, are certainly to be retained, as they
constitute those outworks, which often preserve the
interior parts from assault and destruction.   The
drinking of health is significant of that good-will
which ought to prevail among fellow-creatures, happily enjoying at the same table the bounty of their
common Parent and Creator ; and though it may be
attended with a little trouble, yet there is a great decency and propriety in it, and to bear the trouble
may be considered as an additional exercise of benevolence.

I cannot help expressing a sentiment of pity, or
rather of contempt, for persons who think to recommend themselves as genteel and superior to the
vulgar, merely by such easy means, as the omission
of decent and reasonable ceremonies.   I suppose,
they mean to claim the merit of being superior to prejudice ; but, I think they are under a very silly prejudice, when they think themselves wise enough to
be justified in contradicting the common sense and
common practice of mankind; and when they suppose that singularity alone can give them merit, and
cause them justly to plume themselves on conscious
superiority.

Observe at table that fine lady, and that fine gentleman by her side. How they lift their eyebrows, and smile with ineffable contempt. Heavens! has there been any moral turpitude; or any gross violation of decency committed? None. But, you must know, that yonder gentleman, who is just arrived from the country, where he has resided for a long time, drank to the lady in small beer, and stood up to say grace, and to make a bow to the master of the house. He might have sworn profanely, talked indecently, or drunk intemperately, and if he had shown but the cant of fashion, they who now despise him, would have admired and caressed him as a good man, and as one who had the air and manners of a well-bred man; that air and those manners, which, in the opinion of many, are more estimable than all that virtue ever achieved, wisdom ever taught, or revelation ever discovered. Without that air and those manners, a Solomon would be deemed a fool, and a Socrates voted an intolerably awkward fellow.

EVENING VII.

ON THE UTILITY OF AMUSEMENTS TO OLD AGE.

IT is a natural conclusion from the shortness of life, that none of it should be thrown away; and it is therefore thought wonderful, that there should be many contrivances to abbreviate the duration of what is confessed already to be too much circumscribed. Now pastimes of all kinds are considered as contrivances to wear away time without reflection, and are therefore censured by severe philosophy, as arguing absurdity in man, who is for ever lamenting the brevity of his existence. But, as man is constituted, it must be denied that the time spent in amusement is always thrown away; and, perhaps, time thus spent will be found to lengthen, rather than to abbreviate our duration.

It contributes, when under the restraint of moderation, to confirm health and exhilarate the spirits; both which effects of it not only become causes of long life, but also enable a man to act with vigour and efficacy in the employments of a profession, and in the common duties of society. Thus it not only renders life more comfortable, but more useful.

It is however, true, that in the vigorous seasons of youth and health, some serious and important employment should be engaged in, which may serve society, advance the interests of a family, or elevate the meritorious individual in the ranks of civil life.

But in old age, when these ends shall have been accomplished, and infirmities begin to increase, the active mind will still require an object, and the object ought to be of such a kind, as agitates moderately, not like the storm, but like the gentle breeze of a fine summer evening.

Hobby-horses are very desirable at all ages; but necessary in old age, when the sources of amusement begin to fail. It was this which induced the sensible and experienced Geron to keep an aviary. He had relinquished a busy life, and retired from London to a little country town, where, though there was an agreeable neighbourhood, there were few diversions but those of cards; which, notwithstanding he liked them very well, could not occupy all his time and attention. They are chiefly a winter, and an evening amusement, and he wanted some pastime besides reading, for the summer, and for his mornings. He therefore built a little room in his garden, and fitted it up with admirable contrivance as an aviary. The building of it, the conveniences, and the improvements, which he was continually adding, caused him much pleasure : and it soon became an object of high ambition to breed the most beautiful Canary birds. He succeeded in his attempts, and more than once carried the prize given by a society of bird-fanciers for producing a bird of the finest plumage. He taught bulfinches to pipe a tune, and made them presents to his friends, as instances of singular favour. He reared nightingales from the nest, and attended them with all a parent's solicitude. The delicate, the elegant woodlark was one of his first favourites, and he listened with fresh delight, when his birds warbled their morning melody, which he fancifully considered as songs of gratitude and love to himself in return for food and protection.

But that he might secure variety, which is necessary to add a zest to amusement, he has added several other hobby-horses to this his first favourite. He has acquired a taste for tulips, and prides himself on making a more beautiful display of this gaudy flower in the month of May, than any florist in his vicinity. I called it a gaudy flower, but I speak like an inelegant spectator, when I use a contemptuous epithet in mentioning it : for though to a common eye, a bed of tulips presents only a glare of vivid colours, to a connoisseur it exhibits peculiar elegance as well as finery. Geron views his tulips with the affection and complacency of a lover.

The garden affords him many sources of amusement. He attends not indeed to the olitory, and his strength will not permit him to take an active part in the labours of horticulture, But he has a small green-house, to every part of which he gives a daily attention ; and its various beauty amply repays him, as indeed nothing is more grateful, in return for care and labour, than the tribe of vegetables.

To add to his amusements, he has stocked a fish-pond in a meadow adjoining to his little garden; and, instead of taking out all the fish at once, by emptying the pond or drawing it, which is the usual practice of country gentlemen, he makes a rule that no fish shall be caught out of it but by angling, which he thinks the only fair method of fishing among those who fish for diversion. His strength will not permit him to follow the piscatory sport in the river, as he can neither stand long, nor walk a great way; and he has the sense, wherever he cannot accommodate the nature of the diversion to himself, to submit himself to the nature of the diversion.

He has many little amusements in the house, as well as in the aviary, the garden, and canal. As he is properly disposed in religious matters, the reading of the Scriptures, with a comment, and of pious books of the best characters, fills up agreeably as well as usefully, an hour or two every day; but more especially when the weather is rainy, or in any respect inclement and unpleasant.

Visits and cards in moderation, contribute to enliven his time in an agreeable vicissitude; and the consequence of his wise distribution of his leisure hours, he enjoys a cheerfulness which contributes, perhaps more than any thing else, to health and longevity.

His neighbour Bibo ridicules his amusements as trifling and puerile. Bibo is nearly as old as Geron, but he is not yet free from youthful vanity. He is an old beau, sportsman, gamester, and bottle companion; but his infirmities often prevent him from acting in these characters; and when on a good day, (as he calls it, whenever he is tolerably well) he attempts them, he never acquits himself to his own satisfaction. Old age, and the depredations of time, are his great complaint. He has no resource in himself, and cultivates no taste for domestic and harmless diversions. He mopes over the fire, in the morning, and the bottle, in the afternoon. Melancholy and bodily disease, increased by indolence and excess, accelerate the evils and aggravate the pains of age.

How happy would Bibo have been, if he had condescended to give up the gravity of the gamester, and the affectation of the beau, and adopted a taste for some innocent hobby-horse, which he now despises as too childish and unimportant to deserve his notice.

EVENING VIII.

ON SOME LITTLE ARTIFICES TO GAIN CONSEQUENCE IN VULGAR EYES.

SUCH is the natural pride of the human heart that there is scarcely any trifling distinction which can attract notice, that will not be pursued with eagerness, and fill the possessor's bosom with self-esteem.

One of the easiest, and therefore the commonest methods of drawing attention by trifles, is that of talking loud at all places of public resort. There is something so spirited in it, so charmingly careless, and it gives such an air of superiority, by seeming to despise all the hearers, as if they were no more than stocks and stones, that it seldom fails of exciting not only notice, but some degree of awe and admiration.

I have heard many a fine gentleman and lady, while strutting up and down a crowded walk, question each other on the last night's ball, or their engagements to dinner, in a voice so loud as silenced the rest of the company, and caused a general hum of inquiry, Who are these? Thus the end was answered. The hearers were awestruck and browbeaten, and the happy pair marched off in triumph, like a king and queen of Brentford, till the next morning, when they returned to make new conquests. From their volubility and vehement loudness, they acquired, among many silly listeners, the character of people of infinite sense and spirit, and became the leaders of the Ton.

Another method of gaining notice and admiration, is to swear and swagger at inns, or at any other place, where we are among our inferiors, or are unknown. It is, to be sure, wonderful to observe how respectful a reception a rude fellow meets with, who, with a cockade in his hat judiciously cocked over his eye, with a stick in his hand, and an oath in his mouth, enters an inn and calls about him with a voice like that of the men who cry peas and beans in the streets of London. There have been generals, admirals, colonels, and captains, who never appeared so formidable, nor displayed so much prowess, as in storming an inn in a country town. And the petty gentry, who imitate such heroes, consider themselves as personages of great consequence, when they break the bell wire by the violence of their ringing, frighten the landlady with their fierce looks, send the waiters scampering like men beside themselves, and, with their oaths, set the whole house, yards, and stables, in an uproar.

Knocking vehemently at a door, especially if it be done according to the latest method invented by people of fashion in the squares, adds very considerably to personal importance.

Singularity in dress is one of the commonest modes of seeking distinction; but by singularity I do not mean a deviation from the established fashion, but compliance with it carried to an extreme. An enormous pair of buckles has given many a young man a degree of confidence, which no learning or virtue which he possessed, could ever have supplied. A hat, a coat, a shoe, or a shoestring, of a shape, or size, or colour, exceeding the ordinary mode, have fixed the eyes of a whole assembly, and gratified the ambitious wearer with the most heartfelt satisfaction.

Some, rather than not be noticed at all, will endeavour to draw the eyes of their fellow-creatures upon them by such profusion and expenses, as cause an execution in their houses, and force them to abscond. Hunted by bailiffs and creditors, it is still some consolation to them, that they are the reigning topic. Vices are often practised with a desire of being rendered remarkable; and many plume themselves, as persons of the first consequence, if their profligacy causes them to become the subjects of paragraphs in a newspaper.

Vanity indeed operates with so violent a force, on some minds, that it seems to contradict itself, and defeat its own purpose: for, in pursuit of notice and distinction, it will even industriously seek disgrace.

As the desire of fame, or distinction, seems natural in man, I contend not against it; but I wish it to operate in urging to acts of singular beneficence and social utility, rather than to spend its force in trifles, follies, vanities, and vices.

But of the greater part of these ambitious persons whom I have just described, it may, I believe, be said, that they would act wisely to avoid, instead of seeking distinction, for they seem to be of that character, to which the emphatical words of an elegant political writer may most justly be applied—" a character which will only pass without censure, when it passes without observation."

If men find themselves insensibly impelled, by the ambition of their nature, to seek distinction, let them learn to seek it by arts and virtues which embellish life, and diffuse happiness or convenience through the various ranks of society. If they cannot do this, let them contentedly acquiesce in harmless obscurity.

EVENING IX.

ON THE EXPEDIENCY OF MAKING EXPENSIVE CONNEXIONS TO PROMOTE THE INFERIOR TRADES.

——— Purpura vendit
Causidicum ; vendunt amethystina.   Juv.

In the eye of reason there is certainly no necessary connection between ostentation and excellence. Can the keeping of a chariot be a proof of pre-eminence of knowledge? Certainly not. But such is the world, that the physician on foot stands no chance of being employed, if his rival rides in his chariot.

The preference of the medical professor, who makes a fashionable appearance, to him that does not, has been always remarkable ; so much so, that it is almost a proverbial question, What is a doctor without his chariot? Formerly large wigs, gold-headed canes, full-trimmed coats, and solemn looks, were considered as natural signs of profound knowledge. They are indeed now voluntarily laid aside by the gentlemen themselves; who seem to think it no disadvantage to appear young in person, and easy in manners. But still the appearance of fashionable life, of servants and equipage, is a very powerful recommendation of them to public favour.

A similar unreasonable association of superior excellence to a splendid appearance, seems visible in almost every art, trade, and profession.

And this it is which forms one of the most frequent excuses, in young persons, for launching out a little, as they call it, or living beyond their income.

In the lower orders of mercantile life, a young man begins trade with his little patrimony, or with the gift of a living parent, who, perhaps, distresses himself to raise a sum which, though moderate, might, under proper management, grow, like a handful of seed, to a large quantity. A shop, or rather a warehouse, (for every thing must now have a magnificent name), is hired at a considerable rent. It must be fitted up, not only neatly and conveniently, but elegantly and sumptuously, in the newest taste.

The door-posts are adorned with sculpture, and the name and trade exhibited on a gorgeous tablet adorned with a profusion of gold and colour. The counters, the drawers, the shelves are mahogany; and the master and mistress are every day attired by the most fashionable hair-dresser, and descend (which is but rarely) from the sumptuous dining-room to stand behind the counter, just as if they were going into a drawing-room, or the presence-chamber.

Connexions are sought with the utmost diligence. To promote them, visits are paid and received with all the formality of fashion. The glass in the dining-room is stuck round with gilt cards of invitation to dinners, suppers, balls, and assemblies.

Well; all this is very pleasing; but how goes on business in the shop—(I beg pardon) in the warehouse? O, the scrubs mind that. Mr. and Mrs. Diaper are too much engaged in dressing in the morning and visiting in the afternoon to regard the low concerns of the shop. The clerk, the journey-man, the apprentice, and the porter, are hired pur-posely for that business; but let Mr. and Mrs. Diaper alone; they know what they are about, they are promoting trade, by making connexions and cutting a figure. " There is absolutely no succeeding in the " present days without cutting a figure."

But the misfortune is, every one is cutting a figure, to the utmost extent of their pecuniary abilities; and the connexions which Mr. and Mrs. Diaper make, are themselves making connexions, for the sake of advancing their interest. But none of them have a fund sufficient to support the expenses of the fashionable life which they affect; and, in the course of a few years, they all, in their turn, cut a lamentable figure in the London Gazette.

In higher classes, and in professions and employ-ments, which might justly claim a right to genteel life, it is usual to go beyond the line of moderation and propriety, with the delusive idea, that the greater figure a man makes in the external circum-stances of a fine house, a luxurious table, a splendid equipage, a tribe of servants, the more likely he is to succeed, and to be aggrandized. In the mean time, he himself is sapping the foundation of his own greatness, and the visionary fabric soon falls to rise no more.

These ambitious persons, who hope to raise them-selves by affecting a rank they cannot support, are well described in the celebrated fable of the Frog and the Ox. They and their families, after a short struggle, become ridiculous and pitiable. But the misfortune is not confined to themselves; for though their magnificent appearance gained no credit with their superiors, yet it caused them to be trusted by their inferiors, by poor tradesmen, who supplied them with many articles, both necessary and super-fluous, in the hope of serving themselves and feeding their families. These are usually great sufferers; for being poor and of little consequence, they stand the worst chance of having their demands satisfied. The debts of honour, and the expenses of fashion, must first be paid; but the butcher, the baker, and the brewer, may come in perhaps for sixpence in the pound, when their customers are gone abroad to live genteelly at Lisle or Brussels.

To make that appearance which our rank requires, provided our purse can pay the expense, argues a proper spirit. But it is surely folly, as well as wrong and robbery, in pursuit of a phantom, to expend on luxury and vanity, the property of those who, in the course of their honest callings, have given us con-fidence, and entrusted us with what was necessary to our subsistence, or what we considered as con-ducive to our pleasure and prosperity.

Children brought up to expenses and habits which they cannot support, often rue the folly of parents, who, catching at the shadow of honour or wealth, let go the substance, their own happy and indepen-dent competency.

EVENING X.

ON DIFFIDENCE IN BOYS.

I was once visiting in a family at Christmas, when the eldest son, a fine boy about twelve years old, came home from school for the holidays. As he entered the parlour, which was full of company, in-

stead of paying his compliments to them with the
ease and sufficiency of a master of the ceremonies,
he hung down his head, blushed violently, and
seemed lost in confusion.

Good God! exclaimed his mother, I shall never
be able to endure this. Is this the education of
Mr. Classic's school? I do insist upon it, my dear,
turning to her husband, that Henry shall go no more
to a school where, after three years, he has not
learned how to make his entrance into a room with
tolerable decency! What will become of my poor
child! I shall be ashamed of him—a disgrace, a
downright disgrace to the family!

The boy's confusion, it may readily be conceived,
was not diminished by this passionate and unmo-
therly reception. He burst into tears, and was immediately ordered to leave the room. After a few
remarks on the awkwardness of schoolboys, the
company sat down to whist, and poor Henry was
sent to bed.

I had an opportunity very soon after of inquiring
into the character of the boy, and I found, that so
far from being stupid, as supposed by his mother,
he was the very best scholar in his class, and had
already written one or two pretty copies of Latin
verses in the style of Tibullus.

As I am as fond of making experiments in morals,
as a natural philosopher is in pneumatics, hydro-
statics, or chemistry, I determined to watch the progress of the boy, and to see whether he was likely
to become, as his relations hastily concluded, an
awkward and stupid man. I found he continued to
improve in every accomplishment at his school, for
his removal from it was over-ruled by the advice of
a sensible clergyman, who had great influence in
the family. He went to the university with a great

character, which he supported, and is now a very polite gentleman, an excellent scholar, and a most respectable man.

This event led me to lament the prevalence of an idea, that modesty, diffidence, or bashfulness in boys is a sign of stupidity, and on all accounts, ought to be removed as soon as possible.

The finest rose that ever exhaled fragrance and expanded beauty, was once a rose-bud; and had the bud been torn open with violence in its state of immaturity, would it ever have become a beautiful and perfect flower?

Nature, in a state of imperfection, is not ashamed of blushing. She is conscious of her imbecility, and not afraid to own her diffidence; and while she labours to supply her defects, conceives none to be disgraceful that are unavoidable. Prudence suggests the caution, that we should beware of disturbing nature in her own process, which was undoubtedly prescribed by the God of nature.

That fine sensibility which causes an efflorescence in the cheek of the schoolboy is, I think, a favourable presage of every thing amiable; while that early ripeness which displays a manliness of behaviour at the infantine age, is like every thing premature, of short continuance, and of little solidity.

But fashionable parents are disgusted with manners in their children dissimilar to their own. They are all ease and familiarity. As to diffidence and blushing, some of them had rather be convicted of an atrocious crime. But their children blush and appear awkward in a circle of polite company, that is, of company formed upon the model which happens to be the reigning taste among the rich and idle. Take the boy, they exclaim, from his books and from his masters, if he is thus awkward; for there is no tolerating such an unlicked cub in one's presence.

Have patience, I would take the liberty of saying, the bud will expand in due time, and fruit will appear; but if you touch the bloom, in order to force it open before its time, it is very likely that you destroy the possibility of fruit.

Diffidence wears off when the mind becomes conscious of a sufficient degree of strength to support confidence. With respect to confidence without merit to support it, though often valued in the world, and particularly in the law, I hold it in great dishonour. It may push its way to employment and opulence, but it is scarcely consistent with a good mind; and without a good mind what happiness is to be found in employment and opulence? The vessel must be pure, or the ingredients, however fine, will be corrupted.

People who value themselves on knowing the world, are very apt to insist on effrontery as a necessary virtue to go through the world with success, or rather to recommend it as the substitute and succedaneum of every virtue. But I never hear these persons boasting of their knowledge of the world, and the value of worldly wisdom, but I think of some passages in Scripture, in which they are not held in so high estimation—" The children of this world are wiser in their generation than the children of light;" but it should be remembered, that the wisdom is not that which is from above, but that of the serpent, that of the accursed spirits, originating and terminating in evil under the fair semblance of good.

EVENING XI.

ON THE INFERIORITY OF THE COMPOSITIONS OF SOME PER-
SONS TO THEIR CONVERSATION, AND VICE VERSA.

I HAVE seen men remarkably lively and well informed in conversation, appear to great disadvantage
on committing their thoughts to paper; and others,
who wrote learnedly, elegantly, politely, and acutely,
so dull, and apparently so weak in conversation, as
to be considered as very unpleasant and uninstruc-
tive companions. And I have observed this so
often, as to be led to think, what may appear paradoxical, that a genius for writing, and a genius for
talking, are different in their nature.

It appears to me that superficial men talk most
fluently, and, in mixed companies, most agreeably.
They are usually gay and cheerful, for their spirits
are not exhausted by deep thought, nor drawn from
the things before them by absence. But gaiety and
cheerfulness give them, in the convivial hour, a grace
which the profound scholar, who utters his thoughts
with gravity and hesitation, can seldom display.

A man of a superficial mind and little genius has
no diffidence arising from those delicacies and sensibilities which often cruelly distress men of real
ability. What he thinks, or has read, or heard, he
utters with the confidence of an oracle ; ignorant of
objections and fearless of mistake. His confidence
gives him credit. The company is always disposed
to listen with attention, when any man speaks with
the assurance of undoubting conviction. Attention
gives him additional spirits, and he begins to claim
the greatest share of conversation as his right, and

at length overpowers with volubility and emphasis the silent or gentle diffidence of modest merit.

Ignorant and superficial admirers, finding a voluble speaker just calculated for the meridian of their understandings, are highly delighted with him as a companion, and cry him up as a prodigy of parts and abilities.

Their voices uniting in his favour procure him, perhaps, some professional or official employment in which composition may be necessary. He writes; and the wonder is no more. How are the mighty fallen! Quantum mutatus!

Applauded in the circles of a tavern club, he ventures to publish. A fatal venture! for he who appeared, in conversation, a giant, becomes, when approached in the closet, a pigmy or a Lilliputian.

I wish to prevent the hasty formation of an idea of a man's intellectual talents or genius, solely from his pleasantness or vivacity as a companion. Constant experience proves it to be a fallacious criterion. Men of great thought, solid judgment, and well digested learning, are able indeed to speak to great advantage on great occasions; but they are not sufficiently interested in trifling or ordinary company; and without pride, or any intention to slight, naturally retreat from nonsense and levity to the pleasant indulgence of their own contemplation; therefore they say but little in such company, and that little often from civility, rather than because they are struck with what passes, or impelled to speak by the interesting nature of the question, or the manner in which it is discussed. In the mean time a feather will tickle and excite a fool.

It is wrong therefore, I conclude, to form a decisive opinion of a man's professional abilities from what appears in common conversation. The only true criterion is the exercise of those abilities in some act of his profession. Judge of the companion in company; but of the lawyer's abilities at the bar, or from his written opinion; of the clergyman's from the pulpit, or the press; of the physician's from the repeated success of actual practice; judge of the merchant from his punctuality and payments, from his behaviour and appearance at the Royal Exchange, and not from his volubility at a Mansion-house feast, nor even on the hustings, and in the council-chamber of Guildhall.

It is an erroneous judgment which is often formed of children as well as men, when those are supposed to have the best parts who talk most. Excessive garrulity is certainly incompatible with solid thinking, and a mark of that volatile and superficial turn, which, dwelling upon the surfaces of things, never penetrates deeply enough to make any valuable discoveries. But as no rule is without exceptions, some great thinkers, it must be confessed, have been also great talkers.

No one man can unite in himself every excellence. He who excels, as a pleasant and lively companion, may be deficient in judgment, in accuracy, in a power of attention and labour; and he who excels in these, may want the versatility, the gaiety, the cheerfulness, which are necessary to render the communication of ideas, in a mixed society, agreeable. Men associate, in the convivial hour of leisure from their professional or commercial employment, more for the sake of passing their time with ease, and even mirth, than of being improved or lessoned by the sage remarks of grave and austere philosophy.

Addison, who could write so agreeably on all subjects, was not an entertaining companion, unless the circle was select. Samuel Johnson loved company, because he found himself attended to in it, as an oracle of taste and wisdom; but he could not be said to possess companionable *agrément*. His character insured him respect, previously to his speaking, and what he said justified it; for it was original and solid; his authoritative tone and manner compelled acquiesence, even if conviction was not produced; but, after all, he was not what the world calls a pleasant companion. I could mention some of his contemporaries of far inferior merit, and more circumscribed reputation, who diffused joy and information wherever they went, and were beloved at the same time that they were admired. They also have written books; but their books are not to be compared to Johnson's. Their books were forgotten or despised, even while their conversation was sought and enjoyed by all ranks of people.

But as universal excellence is desirable, it seems right that men should labour to supply every defect, and therefore I wish writers to cultivate the art and habit of conversation, and talkers, on the other hand, to obtain the solidity and accuracy of writers; and thus the advantage derived to hearers and readers will be augmented.

EVENING XII.

LIFE. AN ALLEGORICAL VISION.

A GENTLE ascent led to a lofty eminence, and on the summit was a level plain, of no great extent. The boundaries of it could not indeed easily be ascertained; for, as the ascent, on one side, was easy and gradual, so the slope, on the other, continued almost imperceptible, till it terminated at once in abrupt declivity.

At the first entrance of the hill, I observed great numbers of infants crawling on beds of primroses, or sleeping on pillows formed by the moss. They frequently smiled, and their sweet countenances seemed to express a complacency and joy in the consciousness of their new existence. Many indeed wept and wailed, but their sorrow, though pungent, was short, and the sight of a pretty leaf or flower would cause a smile in the midst of their tears; so that nothing was more common than to see two drops trickling down cheeks which were dimpled with smiles. I was so delighted with the scenes of innocence, that I felt an impulse to go and play with the little tribe, when, just as I was advancing, I felt a wand gently strike my shoulder, and turning my eyes on one side, I beheld a venerable figure, with a white beard, and in a grey mantle elegantly thrown around him.

" My son," said he, " I see your curiosity is raised, and I will gratify it; but you must not move from this place, which is the most advantageous spot for the contemplation of the scene before you.

" Yon hill is the Hill of Life, a pageant which I have raised by the magic influence of this wand, to amuse you with an instructive picture.

" The beauteous innocents, whom you see at the foot of the hill, present you with the idea of angels and cherubs, and of such is the kingdom of Heaven. Simplicity and innocence are their amiable qualities, and the more of them they retain in their ascent, the happier and lovelier shall they be during the whole of their journey.

" But raise your eyes a little. You see a lively train intent to learn, under the sage instructors who accompany them, the easiest and safest way of ascending and descending the hill which lies before them. They often run from the side of their guides, and lose themselves among the shrubs that blossom around them. Some give no ear to instruction, and consequently are continually deviating among thorns, thistles, nettles, and brambles. Their errors are at present retrievable, and few fall in the pitfals with which the hill abounds. Joy illuminates their countenances. Theirs are the ruddy cheek, the sparkling eye, lively spirits, and unwearied activity. They retain a great share of the innocence with which they set out, and therefore they are cheerful. Enviable age, if reason were mature! But folly, wantonness, frowardness of temper, and ignorance, greatly interrupt and spoil their enjoyments. Fruits of delicious taste grow around them, and flowrets of the sweetest scent and most beautiful colour spring beneath their feet. But they soon grow tired of this lower part of the hill, and ambitiously aspire at higher eminences.

" Behold them a few paces higher. They advance with eagerness, and many of them forsake the guides which have conducted them thus far in their ascent. They hasten in their course, nor do they adhere to the direct road, but deviate without scruple. Some indeed return, but the greater part climb the hill by paths of their own choice, full of difficulty and danger. The pitfals, which are placed in every part of the hill, are here very numerous, and not easily to be avoided by those who forsake the high road.— There are indeed no parts of the hill in which a guide is more necessary than here ; nor any in which the travellers are less inclined to seek his assistance.

" You see the beauty of the blossoms. You hear the music of the birds. All nature seems to conspire in affording delight ; but too many of the travellers preserve not that innocence and simplicity, which are necessary to give a taste for the pleasures which are allowed. Instead of plucking the flowers which are known to be safe and salutary, they desire none but such as are poisonous. The aspiring ardour of the travellers urges them to continue the ascent, and by this time, you see, they have reached the level summit, where you observe a prodigious crowd, all busy in pursuit of their several objects. Their faces are clouded with care, and in the eagerness of pursuit they neglect those pleasures which lie before them. Most of them have now lost a great share of their original innocence and simplicity, and many of them have lost it entirely.

"And now they begin to descend. Their cheerfulness and alacrity are greatly abated. Many limp, and some already crawl. The numbers diminish almost every step; for the pitfals are multiplied on this side of the hill, and many of the travellers have neither strength nor sagacity to avoid them. Delightful scenes still remain. Fruit in great abundance grows around them. But the greater part, you may remark, are careless of the obvious and natural pleasures, which they might reach and enjoy, and are eagerly digging in the earth for yellow dust, on which they have placed an imaginary value. Behold one who has just procured a load of it, under which he is ready to sink. He totters along in haste to find a hiding-place for it; but before he has found it, himself is hidden from our eyes, for lo! while I speak, he is dropping into a pitfal. Most of his companions will follow him; but you see no one is alarmed by the example. The descent is become very steep and abrupt, and few there are who will reach the bottom of the hill. Of those few not one advances without stumbling on the edge of the pitfals, from which he can scarcely recover his feeble foot.　Ah! while I speak, they are all gone!"

And is this a picture of life? said I; alas! how little do the possessors of it seem to enjoy it! Surely some error must infatuate them all.　O say, what it is, that I may avoid it, and be happy.

"My son," said my benevolent guide, "do not hastily form an opinion derogatory from the value of life.　It is a glorious opportunity afforded by the Creator for the acquisition of happiness.　Cast your eyes on yonder plain, which lies at the bottom of the hill, and view the horizon."

I looked, and lo! a cloud tinged with purple and gold, parted in the centre, and displayed a scene, at which my eyes were dazzled. I closed them awhile, to recover the power of vision, and when I opened them, I saw a figure of a person in whom majesty and benevolence were awfully united. He sat on a throne with every appearance of triumph, and at his feet lay a cross.　And I heard a voice saying, "Come again, ye children of men."　And lo, the plain opened in more places than I could number, and myriads of myriads started into existence, with bodies beautiful and glorious.　And the voice proceeded, "In my Father's house are many mansions. Ye have all fallen short of the perfection for which ye were created; but some have been less unprofitable servants than others, and to them are allotted the more exalted places of bliss; but there remain mansions appropriated to all the sons of men. I have redeemed the very worst of them from the tyranny of death. Rise therefore to your respective mansions.　Enter into the joy of your Lord." He said; when the sound of instruments sweeter than the unpurged ear ever heard, rang throughout heaven's concave.　And the glorified bodies beneath rose like the sun in the east.

and took their places in the several planets which form what is called our solar system. I was transported with the sight, and was going to fall on my knees, and supplicate to be admitted among the aspiring spirits, when, to my mortification, I thought I was suddenly placed on the side of the hill, where I had to climb a steep ascent. I wept bitterly, when my guide remonstrated with me on the unreasonableness of my tears, since none were to be admitted to glory who had not travelled the journey which I had seen so many others travel. " Keep innocence," said he, " do justice, walk humbly." He said no more, but, preparing to depart, touched me with his rod, and I awoke.

EVENING XIII.

ON BRINGING UP DULL BOYS, IN PREFERENCE TO OTHERS, TO THE CHURCH.

Επιςημη Επιςημων NAZIANZEN.

IF there happen to be a boy in a family unlikely, from deficiency of parts, to make his way in the world, he is commonly selected by his prudent parents for the church; but the idea that little more is requisite to form a clergyman than a black coat and a good living, is so dishonourable to the religious establishment, that I shall think myself very properly employed in controverting its truth.

I acknowledge, that honesty, without learning and abilities, is a better qualification for the sacred profession, than learning and abilities without honesty; but I contend, that they are all three indispensably necessary in every one, who enters the profession, with ideas superior to those of an ensign when he obtains a pair of colours, or a midshipman when he procures a commission ; or indeed of a tradesman, when he hires a shop, or of a mechanic and labourer, when they undertake a job with no other view than to earn the hire.

If, indeed, a man is awkward and unskilful in the practice of a mechanical art, few or none employ him, and himself alone is the only sufferer; but it happens in the church, that he who has neither learning nor abilities, often has the most money, with which himself or his friends purchase an ecclesiastical employment; and they who are immediately concerned in the manner in which he acquits himself in it, have it not in their power to eject him for disability, or to find convenient opportunities of supplying his defects by having recourse to a substitute. They must be contented to be instructed by his precept and example; for, however deficient and erroneous, these are the best they can procure in the legal and regular course.

But if the care of a parish, and that a very large one, be a most important charge, if the moral and spiritual safety of thousands depend on the clergyman's exertions, surely it is criminal in parents to select the least able and promising among their children to fill this office.

But I know it will be urged, and with great appearance of reason, that in this age, when printed sermons abound, it is easy to select proper ones, without danger of detection ; and that, if the clergyman reads them and the prayers audibly and distinctly in the church, and maintains a decent character out of it, he is a no less useful and accomplished parish priest, than if he had the learning and abilities of a Clarke, a Tillotson, a Sherlock, a Secker, or a Jortin.

It is very true, that by reading the pious discourses

of others properly, he may do much good ; but is it likely that he will read them properly, if he is unable to write any himself, that he will enter into the spirit of them, that he will feel and communicate the holy flame of fervent, yet rational devotion? And with respect to his maintaining a decent character out of church ; if he does so, he is so far to be honoured, but if he is destitute of clerical accomplishments, of a taste for books, and a love of learning, there is danger that, from want of proper and professional employment, he will not maintain that decency of character. Having nothing to do but merely to read in the church, he will be idle; and idleness affords many temptations to violate decency of character. Is it not likely, that he may commence a beau, a man of fashion, a man of pleasure, a gamester, a drunkard, or a horse-dealer? When there is no natural turn for the profession, in which a man is placed, and no acquired talents to render him satisfied with himself in the exercise of it, there is great danger of his having recourse to something, either as an employment, or a recreation, very foreign to the decency of character which his profession requires him to support.

But, after all, is mere decency of character sufficient in the teacher of a whole parish, in the comforter of the sick, in the guide to heaven? Decency of character is supported by all his more respectable parishioners, by tradesmen, by mechanics, by servants. Something more is reasonably expected of him who supports the *persona ecclesiæ*, who was anciently called, as an appellation of respect, the *parson*, and who still has the epithet reverend prefixed to his name, as appropriated to his professional character.

He should support a dignity of character as well

as a decency. But no artifice, no external pomp will support it. It must support itself by real superiority. But what superiority is naturally expected as a prime requisite, in a public instructor? Is it not superior knowledge of those things in which he undertakes to give instruction? But can this superior knowledge be acquired without application? And is it likely, that he who was selected by his parent for the church, because he was a dunce, should apply at all, or if he should, that he should apply with success?

A man, who finds himself in a profession, for which he is conscious of his being unqualified, feels himself uneasy. He seeks refuge in amusements unbecoming his profession; and I have no doubt but that it is one reason why many clergymen are seen to take delight in unclerical occupations, that they are selected for a learned profession, without any propensity to learning, and perhaps because they were supposed to be dull of apprehension, and unfit for any thing else.

Nothing is more common, in some places, than to see clergymen devoting the greatest part of their time to hounds and horses, dressing in the extremity of the jockey's or sportsman's prevailing fashion, taking the lead or acting as masters of the ceremonies at assemblies, conspicuously active at horse-races, excessively attached to cards and back-gammon, and foremost in every thing which the more serious part of their congregation considers as vanity.

They may certainly amuse themselves with several of these things, and at the same time be very worthy men; but yet as these things have an appearance of levity, and lead them to associate with loose and profligate characters, they give offence, and prevent them from doing that good, for which alone their profession was instituted. No good can be done by a preacher totally destitute of authority; but authority is founded on opinion, and nothing, except vice, destroys that opinion, so effectually as the appearance of levity.

Though moderate abilities and moderate attainments, with a good heart, and a decent character, may make a very valuable parish-priest, yet I can never allow, that the study of divinity, as some seem to insinuate, requires only moderate abilities and attainments. It certainly affords scope for the greatest talents, and when intended to be carried to any considerable degree of perfection, it requires also profound and extensive erudition.

To be a Christian philosopher, a physician of the soul, it is necessary, in the first place, to have studied the Holy Scriptures with great attention; and, in the second, that wonderful microcosm, the heart of man. As anatomy is necessary to the surgeon, so is the knowledge of the passions, the temper, the propensities, and the alterations which age, prosperity, and adversity, effect in the mind, necessary to him, whose office it is to reduce those who have erred, to afford rational comfort to the afflicted, and hope to the desperate. That he may enforce the doctrines of religion, he must be an orator; he must be furnished with polite learning, and with elegant diction; he must have every assistance which a liberal education can bestow, and which long and attentive reading can obtain. And shall a parent think himself justified in selecting the weakest of his children for an office so important? He who acts so unreasonably, probably renders the child unhappy, while he insults the national religion, and that God, whom it was established to honour.

If the parent thinks he perceives in any of his

boys a remarkable share of abilities, he resolves to
bring him up to the law, and all his worldly-wise
friends commend him for not throwing away so fine
a boy by placing him in the church.   Yet I am
fully convinced, that no department of the law requires the noble faculties of the mind in so great
perfection as the pastoral office.   The law chiefly
requires audacity and sophistry, to both of which the
church is greatly superior.   The law requires the
little wisdom of this world, the wisdom of those
children of the world, who are wiser in their generation than the children of light ; but divinity towers
above such meanness, above lawyers and their sub-
tleties, above every other profession ; for to be a
divine, properly and fully accomplished, is to be all
that philosophy can give, with the addition of the
purest and sublimest religion.

It would afford me much satisfaction if any thing
I can say should induce the serious Christian to
devote the very best of his children to the service
of the God who gave them; and not impiously to
consecrate him to the service of the altar, whom,
from want of parts, he thinks incapable of any
useful service.   I suspect that man to be insincere
in his profession of Christianity who dares to insult
it so grossly.

It is to be wished that the patronage of livings
were chiefly, if not entirely, in the bishops, supposing *translation* prohibited ; for private patronage, in
the present age and system of principles and manners, is highly injurious to the cause of Christianity.
The bishops might sometimes be misled in con-
ferring benefices, by gratitude to their patrons ; but
I am sure they would, for the most part, dispose of
the cure of souls, far better than esquires, who consider the living in their gift, as a mere provision

for some lubberly boy educated as a fox-hunter ; or who, in default of a younger son, put it up to sale, and knock it down with the hammer, like lands, tenements, goods, and chattels.

Nothing surely conduces to injure Christianity so much as a contemptible ministry; and it must of necessity be partially contemptible, when many parishes in a kingdom can exhibit individuals among the laity, more learned and more decent, than the parochial priest, their authorized guide, whom they pay, and whom they ought to revere. The misfortune originates in great measure from the mistaken, but prevailing idea, which I have here endeavoured to explode, *that any thing is good enough to make a parson.* Interest, and a friend at court, are thought sufficient to supply all defect.

EVENING XIV.

ON THE PECULIAR HAPPINESS SUPPOSED TO ATTEND A LIFE OF CONTEMPLATION.

" I no sooner enter my library," says Heinsius, " than I bolt the door, and shut out lust, ambition, and avarice, whose mother is idleness, and whose nurse, ignorance ; and taking my seat among the illustrious spirits around me, I look down with pity on the rich and great, who are strangers to such refined and exalted enjoyments."

If a life of study can produce happiness so pure as Heinsius has described ; if it can exclude lust ambition, and avarice ; if it can give an elevation above the rich and great ; who would not fly from the world and seize that *chief good,* in the recess of his library, which he has vainly toiled for in the road of ambition and avarice ?

But no recess is sufficiently retired, no occupation sufficiently pure, to exclude care and contamination. Man bears within his bosom, wheresoever he conceals himself, and whatsoever he does, the seeds of evil and misery.

Philosophers may describe the happiness of contemplative life, and students flatter themselves that they are out of the reach of corruption; but does experience justify a persuasion that philosophers and students are happier and more innocent than all others? A perusal of their lives will evince the truth, that it is not in man to secure himself from the assaults of passion, and the corruption of vice, by withdrawing his person from the society of the multitude. Volumes have been written on the peculiar misery of the learned, and I wish it could be asserted with truth, that on shutting the doors of their book-rooms, they at the same time shut out desire, avarice, and ambition.

Men of that activity of mind which ranges through all nature and art, see more clearly, and feel more sensibly, than the common tribe whose attention is fixed on frivolity. All the objects of desire, avarice, and ambition, exhibit themselves to their eyes, in the most glowing colours, and in the most engaging forms. Their taste, cultivated and refined by continual exercise of its powers, is enabled to discover charms which escape vulgar notice. Their leisure and freedom from the ordinary cares of life, cause their hearts to fix on what their imaginations have admired. It cannot be wondered at, therefore, if contemplative men, instead of being exempt from the tumults which disturb others, have felt themselves agitated by external things with peculiar force. Their enjoyments have been high, their sufferings keen, and their failings singularly deplorable.

I fear, therefore, that truth must resign those pretensions to that unmolested felicity, which students have sometimes claimed, as the privilege of their learned solitude. In common with all the sons of men they partake of misery; and they are under some peculiar circumstances, which aggravate the woe which it is their destiny to share.

To secure the happiness that is allowed to man, they must, like others, have recourse to virtue and wisdom, not merely to retreat, or to contemplation. With virtue and wisdom, I believe, their employments will be found highly conducive to a most exalted state of sublunary felicity; for their employments are pure and refined, intellectual, and even heavenly, compared with the gross delights of animal sense. He who places his happiness in gluttony and debauchery, must acknowledge, while he boasts of his pleasures, that he is renouncing the most honourable part of his nature, his reason; and that he is assimilating himself, as much as he is able, with the brutes whom he proudly disdains.

I cannot help thinking, that the Platonic philosophy, mixed, as it is, with much folly, deserves more regard than it usually receives. It tends to make man value himself on his *mind*. It teaches to seek enjoyment in the exertions of the discursive faculty, and to aspire at an intellectual excellence, which, though it may never reach, invites by its beautiful appearance, to heights of improvements which it would never otherwise have attained. Platonism, when carried to extremes, like all other doctrines, terminates in nonsense; but under the regulation of reason, it leads the mind to a state of celestial enjoyment and angelic perfection.

Happy would it have been for the contemplative part of mankind, if the honours which are almost universally allowed to Epicurus, had been reserved for Plato. Christian and rational Platonism leads to the perfection of the human soul: nor should the scrupulous be ashamed of uniting with Christianity, a philosophy which, in its nature and tendency, when its extremes are avoided, is all pure, all spiritual, all divine.

If the superior light of Christianity had not irradiated the world, there is no philosophy which the aspirant after excellence would wish to prevail in preference to Platonism, divested of its visionary eccentricities. No philosophy contributes so much to raise man to the exaltation which he may conceive to adorn a spiritual nature. No philosophy exalts him so much above the body, and furnishes him with ideas so congenial to all that we consider as celestial.

But common sense and common experience affirm after all, that whoever attempts to reach undisturbed happiness by flights of contemplation, above the usual ken of mortals, commonly finds himself precipitated at last, like Icarus in the fable.

Superior degrees of happiness are not to be expected solely from a skill in arts and sciences, from study, and from retirement; but chiefly from those virtues, and good qualities, in which even the illiterate find it, from prudence, temperance, justice, fortitude, and contentment. The boast of felicity without these is but the rant of pride, and the rhapsody of inexperienced speculation.

EVENING XV.

ON THE AMUSEMENT OF PUBLIC READINGS.

THERE is a species of entertainment lately introduced, which, being in its nature elegant, in its satisfactions innocently pleasurable, and in its consequences highly improving, deserves great praise and general encouragement : I mean the public reading of excellent passages from the best authors, varied at intervals by the performance of the best music. The understanding, the ear, the judgment, and the fancy, are all agreeably addressed, exercised, and improved by it ; and the politest ages and nations cannot boast a more refined and rational mode than this, of amusing the inhabitants of a great metropolis.

Recitations were a very common amusement among the ancients ; but the ancients do not appear to have always added to the charms of verse the melody of instrumental music. Their recitations constituted their mode of publishing a new piece. The press being unknown, and the methods of writing then in use, tardy and expensive, the poet published his work, in the first instance, by assembling his friends, and reading his production before them, sometimes for their correction, but oftener for their applause.

These recitations became at last a public nuisance. Poets made interest with as much solicitude as a candidate for the honour of an audience. They sometimes paid persons for attendance, that by an appearance of numbers, they might gain the credit of popularity. It must have been greatly mortifying to vanity to hear the excuses which were made by those who wished to avoid the tedious attendance.

No common degree of self-love could have borne them. But the desire of applause originated sometimes in passions more clamourous than vanity, in avarice and ambition. The arts of puffing were practised for their gratification. Hearers were hired at a considerable expense, and placed in commodious corners of the room, to applaud at such places in the poem, as had been previously appointed by the speaker. Complaisance or servility often gave the palm where it was not due. Poetical like civil eminence, was sought by bribery and corruption, and at last, the public recitations became objects of supreme contempt, and were in course relinquished.

But the modern readings, not consisting of original compositions produced by the speaker, are not liable to those evils which the corruption of human nature has always a tendency to introduce. The pieces recited are usually such as have already received the stamp of public approbation. The manner of recital is alone left to the judgment of the audience. If the reader murders his authors, the audience will very justly pronounce sentence of condemnation against him ; for, as they pay for their admission, they have a right to demand a competent degree of excellence in the performance ; and, if their decision should be over-ruled by sinister arts, they can easily punish the delinquent by withdrawing their presence from an entertainment which, under bad management, ceases to afford them that pleasure which they have a right to expect.

Many improvements might be made in this mode of entertainment, which the public seems not disinclined to favour. It has hitherto been in the hands of second or third rate players, of persons of no great repute, very moderately learned, and not

strikingly endowed with the talents of elocution.
There is surely nothing base or disgraceful in the
undertaking, nothing to deter persons of the greatest
abilities, learning, and character, from engaging in
it. On the contrary, as the recital of the best compositions, in the best manner, requires and displays
great taste, great judgment, great eloquence, he who
performs it well, deserves, and will probably receive,
honour as well as emolument for his reward. Men
of the most liberal education might here find a field
for the display of their abilities, with great advantage both pecuniary and reputable. It is certain,
that the entertainment of readings will never possess
the esteem which it deserves, till it shall be conducted by persons of character, by gentlemen and
scholars, at whose feet the learned and the great
may sit and listen, without degradation.

If this entertainment should ever be undertaken
by such men, it might be worth while to erect a
theatre adapted to their purpose. It should, I think,
be in the form of the ancient Odeum, with a stage
or pulpit, and an orchestra for the musicians. A
library might be added for the use of constant sub-
scribers; and a grove or garden might furnish a fine
opportunity for a philosophical or literary promenade.

The expense attending such an institution would
perhaps exceed the revenues. The plan may be
visionary, like Cowley's projected college; but as
this is an enterprising age, such improvements and
modifications of it might be adopted, as would
render it in some degree practicable.

In every mode of entertainment intended for the
public, there must be such a variety as may contribute to the pleasure of a mixed assembly. It
seldom happens that all are sufficiently rational to
be satisfied with the feast of reason. Music is the

best addition that can be made to it. After every recital, an interlude should be introduced, the expression of which should in some degree correspond with the piece which may have been just read; grave or gay, according to the gravity or gaiety of the poetry or prose. Care, however, should be taken to preserve the entertainment distinct from the drama. If it encroaches on the theatrical, it may probably appear, from the want of mechanical decorations, inferior to it, and gradually fall into contempt.

Not but that I believe many persons would listen to a good tragedy or comedy, well read by one person, with more pleasure than they behold it meretriciously drest out with the tricks of the theatre. Fine dresses, painted faces, and gaudy scenes, soon pall upon a sensible mind, which is disagreeably diverted by them from attending to the main business, the merits and beauties of the poem. The finery of a theatre has few charms, but for the illiterate and for children. In the mean time, good poetry, solid reasoning, historical truth, true eloquence, gracefully and properly exhibited at the readings, must always supply the mind with aliment at once pleasant and nutritious.

EVENING XVI.

ON FALLING INTO THE INDOLENCE OF OLD AGE PREMATURELY.

THERE prevails an opinion, that, after a certain age, the mind, like the body, having arrived at its complete size, ceases to admit of that increase which we call improvement. Many appearances seem to justify such an opinion; but I am inclined to believe, that, though the mind at a certain age, may, from several causes, show a tendency to become stationary, yet its tendency may be counteracted by extraordinary efforts and exertion. The machine, by long operation, may have incurred the impediments of excessive friction, or some of the wheels may be nearly worn out; but a little oil judiciously applied, and a few repairs ingeniously made, may restore its motions and augment its force.

One considerable proof, that when the mind has reached the *acmé* of its improvement, it becomes for a little while stationary, and then retrograde, is drawn from observing that the second or third production of an author is often inferior to his first, even though the first were the produce of his juvenile age.

But is it not probable that the exertions of the author may have been remitted after having obtained the distinction which first stimulated his earlier diligence? Success operates on the minds of many like the luxuries of Capua on the soldiers of Hannibal, after the passage of the Alps, and the victory of Cannæ.

When the strength of the body begins to decline, its companion seems to indulge it with a sympathizing indolence. The road that leads to repose is smooth, flowery, and seducing; and many there are who enter it, long before repose is necessary. If they could acquire self-command enough to avoid the charms of the syren, they might still make great advances in climbing the steeps of science and virtue. But it must be allowed that greater efforts are required than the generality of mankind are disposed to make, at any time in their lives, and much less at the period of their decline.

Yet the history of literature affords many animating examples, to prove that great works may be produced after the middle of life. Sophocles and Theophrastus composed excellent works when they were nearly a hundred years old. Our own Milton, whose Paradise Lost is an effort of mental activity equal to any which antiquity can boast, did not begin it till he had arrived at that age when, in the opinion of many, the mind is receding from excellence.

Julius Cæsar Scaliger, who became a prodigy of learning, did not commence the study of Greek till he was nearly forty. He did not even know the Greek characters till about that time; nor did he devote himself entirely to a life of letters till he was forty-seven. His days till then had been spent in an unsettled manner, chiefly in the army, with habits and dispositions unfavourable to study. But he had a mind which, like that of his namesake, the Roman conqueror, was formed to break down all obstacles ; and age, instead of abating his vigour, served but to harden and corroborate the sinews of his intellect.

It seems indeed reasonable to suppose, that works which depend on the warmth and vigour of the imagination, on pathos and sensibility of heart, would always be produced in the greatest perfection at an early period ; but the examples of Sophocles and Milton, who wrote the finest poetry, the one in extreme old age, and the other at a mature age, serve to prove that theories concerning the human mind are too fallacious to be entirely relied on. The defects and failures of nature may be in a great measure supplied or prevented by prudence and perseverance. But laziness and want of spirit suffer them to creep on before nature intended.

Thus is life, in effect, abbreviated. Early old age and early dotage are introduced by an abject dereliction of our own powers. We labour to increase our fortunes, and suffer our faculties to run to ruin without reluctance. But it is surely worth while to contend strenuously for their preservation. Of how little value are the enjoyments of life, when we come to vegetate in stupidity, in the midst of all that should delight our senses, inform our understanding, enrich our memory, and glitter on our imagination! It is worth while to pursue every method which has a tendency to prolong our mental existence. Among these I will venture to enumerate a constant yet moderate exercise of our abilities, a daily accumulation of new ideas, a recollection of the old, a rule over the passions, a temperance in wine and all the pleasures of the glutton and debauchee. We often accuse time and nature for decays which are caused by our own neglect. Instead of immerging ourselves in the pursuit of wealth, which we shall never enjoy, and honours which are empty bubbles, let our desire be to preserve our faculties unimpaired to the last, and to shine as the sun shines, bright through the whole of its progress; and though with abated heat and effulgence at the close of it, yet with a serene and venerable lustre, till it descends to the other hemisphere.

EVENING XVII.

ON THE EFFECT OF LITERARY PRIZES AND FOUNDATIONS FOR LECTURES.

MANY men of generous minds, lovers of learning and desirous of promoting it, have established premiums and pensions to excite exertion, and to allure

modest merit from the shade.   The rewards have
been ample, the honours splendid; but the works
which they have elicited have not often exceeded
the narrow limits of mediocrity.

What is there in our libraries produced in consequence of prizes, or public foundations, which
claims the first rank, and aspires at immortality?
The Miltons, the Shakspeares, the Bacons, the
Newtons, and the Lockes, rose, like the forest tree,
with spontaneous vigour.

The failure of prizes and other similar institutions
to call forth extraordinary and supereminent merit,
is a curious circumstance in the world of letters,
and deserves investigation.

Excitements of this kind operate on two very
strong propensities of human nature, the love of
money and the love of fame.   Rivalry and compe-
tition add a powerful spur to the minds of all men;
and are particularly efficacious among the candidates
for public distinction : but notwithstanding a theoretical probability, that such invitations would produce uncommon excellence, the fact will be un-
controverted, that they have produced only a moderate degree.

It may not be difficult to assign some causes of the
failure.   The mind of man, delighting in liberty,
usually enters on a subject proposed by another with
a frigid and forced attention.   It feels its powers
shackled by authority.   It moves in chains, and
therefore with difficulty.   It is made to resemble a
stream, diverted from its natural channel into a
canal of the inland navigator.   The beautiful mean-
ders disappear, and are changed to a long right line
confined by regular banks, unadorned by spontaneous flowers, willows, and alders, the wild yet
inimitable graces of nature.

Uncertainty of success, where a splendid prize excites a number of competitors, throws a damp on the spirits, or teaches a cold caution, very unfavourable to the noble flights of aspiring genius. It represses those hardy attempts at high excellence which approach to the very verge of a precipice. It causes a solicitude rather to avoid error, than aspire at pre-eminent beauty. A correct composition is the result, where there is nothing to blame, and nothing to commend. The treatise is very fine, says the reader; but take it away, and bring me Shakspeare.

True genius, indeed, does not often engage in competitions excited by gold medals. There is an independent spirit in true genius, a noble pride, and a generous self-esteem, which prevent it from entering the lists, where the prize is oftener conferred on performances without faults, than on striking but unequal excellence. Pecuniary rewards seldom appear alluring to true genius; and the distinction which the obtaining of a paltry prize, against no very distinguished competitors, confers, is too little to rouse the vigour of gigantic powers. The eagle and the lion stoop not to a mean prey. Nothing less than public fame, universal applause, independently of a bauble, or a purse of guineas, can satisfy minds elevated by nature above the common standard of human ability.

Of those who have gained prizes, many have been truly ingenious; but among them we do not see the names of the Drydens, the Popes, and the Grays. Oblivion has already covered most of them in her impenetrable shade. Their success answered the temporary purpose of recommending them to the patronage or employment of cotemporaries; but where are their boasted productions? I search for them in vain in the booksellers' shops; I find them, if I find them at all, in the bundle of waste paper, sold by the pound to the chandlers.

But are prizes useless, and ought they to be discontinued? Certainly not; for they tend to excite a mediocrity of excellence which is found very beneficial among mankind, because it is level to that moderate capacity, which is supposed to predominate. They raise moderate abilities to a pitch, which they would otherwise have never reached. They serve as whips to the dray-horse, though the racer will run with sufficient speed without them; and, in the generosity of his nature, would indignantly spurn at their application to his side.

Does the establishment of lectures on controversial points in divinity promote the cause of Christianity? I think not so much as is sometimes pretended. The effect of arguments is greatly lessened, when an advocate writes for hire, on a subject prescribed by authority. He is supposed to write, not so much the result of his own conviction, as the sentiments of a sect, a party, or a church; and to be actuated, not so much by a sincere zeal for the truth and the cause, as by the desire of gain and reputation. He is supposed to enlist as a mercenary, hired, like the Hessians, to draw the sword for pay, and ready, if he could with decency, to lend his abilities to the opposite side, if they would invite him with greater rewards. And who reads the books which the prizes or lectureships have elicited? A few recluse academics, a few speculative divines. Not the people at large, who require something more popularly written, something with less subtlety and less polemic art, to captivate their attention and convince their understanding. To name particular works or particular writers, though easy, would be tedious; but it would be difficult to point out a single work, among such writings, which has been generally read, or become universally popular, which has silenced the clamour of the infidel, and fixed Christianity on a firmer basis than it stood upon before. They are useful, however, in furnishing exercises for theological students, and employing the time of those who, without such incitements, might have slumbered away their existence in a total inaction.

Perhaps an improvement might be made in the adjudication of literary prizes, and in bestowing the bounty of founders. They might be given as rewards to the best spontaneous work published in the year, in whatever art or science they were originally intended to promote. A committee of judges might be appointed, who should act with the most perfect impartiality. But here would be the difficulty; where shall a tribunal be found among mortals, in which favour and prejudice do not interpose? Not in England; where interest, partiality, party, envy, and malice, too often usurp a dominion in literature, as well as in politics; where a friend in power will supply the want of all desert, and a corrupt vote obtain the lucrative cure of souls and the first prizes in civil and ecclesiastical life.

EVENING XVIII.

ON THE IMPRUDENCE OF URGING INCORRIGIBLE DUNCES TO A LEARNED PROFESSION.

Maxime probavi summum illum doctorem, Alabandensem Apollonium, qui, cum mercede doceret, tamen non patiebatur eos, quos judicabat non posse oratores evadere, *operam apud sese perdere*, et ad quam quemque artem putabat esse aptum, ad eam impellere atque hortari solebat. Satis est enim cæteris artificiis percipiendis, tantummodo similem esse hominis, et id quod tradatur, vel etiam *inculcetur*, siquis fortè sit tardior, posse percipere animo, et memoriâ custodire.   CIC. DE ORAT. Lib. i. Sect. 28.

SECT. I.

OF the multitudes, who are intended for the liberal professions, and furnished with the opportunities of a liberal education, the majority appears to be endowed with only such a share of natural talents as enables them to reach a mediocrity of excellence; and many are so little favoured by nature, as to continue, after much labour and time bestowed in vain, utterly incapable of receiving benefit from literary instruction.

The mediocrists, if I may venture to give them that name, constitute the greater part of mankind, and become very useful and respectable members of society. They are found to undergo labour with patience, and to rise, by care and perseverance, to heights of excellence, which even genius, attended with idleness, cannot attain. Their understandings are not bright and shining; but they are strong and solid: and who does not know that the pick-axe and the spade would be in no respect the better for the acuteness of the razor; and that, in ordinary work, the hammer, the beetle, and the mallet, are as necessary as the keen-edged chisel?

Of the mediocrist I do not at present speak; but of the dunce; of him whom the ancients would have stigmatized with the epithet Bœotian, and of whom they would have said, rather harshly, that his soul was given him only to preserve, like salt, his body from putrefaction.*

Such boys are certainly to be treated with mildness and compassion. Ridiculous as their blunders appear, they ought to be passed over with tacit connivance, or the gentlest reproof. They can no more avoid their stupidity by any efforts of their own, than the blind and deaf can supply the defects of their senses by their own exertion. Their happiness should be consulted by their parents, and by all humane persons who are connected with them; and they should be placed in such situations in life, as may least expose them to contempt, and enable them to act their part with the most decency. The scope of my present attempt is to contribute what can be contributed to their ease and their credit. As to their improvement in learning, he to whom the task of instructing them is allotted, has an employment like the rolling of the rebounding stone, or the filling of the perforated vessel. Pretenders, incited by interested motives, are indeed ready to undertake it with boldness; but honest men, and men of sense, will acknowledge, what they cannot but feel, that it is impossible.

I say, it is the duty of parents to consult the honour and happiness of such boys; but whether to place them at a Latin school, and to confine them there ten or twelve years, and then to send them to college seven more, in order to fix them in a pulpit for life, is to consult their honour and their happiness, is a question to be determined by actual experience

---

* Animum illi pecudi datum pro sale ne putresceret.

CIC. DE FINIBUS.

Dr. South has made use of this idea.

and observation. It appears to me, that such a plan renders them as uneasy as their dull dispositions are capable of being, and at the same time exposes them to insult and ill-usage.

I will endeavour to describe the three states of such unfortunate boys; at school, at college, and in their profession.

At school, the dunce passes the dreary hours, days, and years, from seven to seventeen, under a restraint which, to him, must have all the horrors of imprisonment; for he has no relish for those employments, no desire for that excellence, the pursuit of which might fill the tedious interval. He sits patiently under the rod and cane, at a form, making dogs ears to dirty dictionaries. He is the last in his classes, a mere dead weight, the torment of his instructors, and the laughing-stock of his livelier companions. His ears are stunned with reprimands, and his back (too often) galled with stripes. He paces along, like the mill-horse, always driven on, but never advancing. The school-room is to him a Bastille, or a slave-galley. No bright idea from his books cheers his gloomy way; and if nature had not given him an incrustation of stupidity, like the shell of the oyster or the tortoise, he would be more wretched than the negroes of the West Indies, groaning under an Egyptian bondage. But if his ease is thus secured, it is not so with his honour. He is the standing but of ridicule, the scorn and outcast of the little society.

At length he is emancipated, not in consequence of his attainments, but his age. Too tall for school, he is sent to college. There, indeed, he feels himself at liberty; and soon learns to fill up the vacancies which dogs, horses, and guns leave him, with ale, port, and gentle slumber. He finds no difficulty in procuring from good-natured companions the exercises which are required. He can purchase them of some poor servitor, unless his father has been slack in his remittances. So far well; but there are examinations which must be undergone in person. Here he is miserably exposed; and, if not quite destitute of feeling, wretchedly uneasy from the fear of a disgraceful repulse. After much trouble, he goes through the ordeal by the candour of good-natured judges, who would rather strain a point of conscience, than ruin a young man's interest and expectations; especially as there is a good living purchased for him, that only waits for his acceptance of it. He obtains his degrees and his orders at last; but not without misery and disgrace. Rejoiced at gaining the ultimate object of his education, he mounts his hunter, and turns his back on schools, colleges, libraries, and books, the bane of his happiness, the causes of his dishonour.

He takes possession of his vicarage. He likes the house, the stables, the dog-kennel, the pasture-ground, and the income; but the church and the pulpit are the great drawbacks of his felicity. He has no inclination for clerical or literary employments. He hates the sight of a book, and would as soon think of shooting his best pointer as composing a sermon. He is strict and rigid in collecting his tithes; but when that business is done, he finds his time an intolerable burden; and knows no method of alleviating it, but in such amusements as give offence to the serious part of his parish. He becomes a kind of game-keeper and huntsman to all the esquires around, acts as master of the ceremonies at all the little balls, and plays so keenly at whist (for dunces often excel at cards), that most people are afraid to sit down with him.

He is not unconscious that he is acting out of character. He perceives that he is not respected as a clergyman, though courted by the lower orders of the fox-hunters, as a boon companion. He consoles himself by the consideration, that not himself, but his parents were blameable, who placed him in a profession most repugnant to his nature and inclinations. He feels himself, as a clergyman, like a fish out of water, a dog taught to dance, or a learned pig.

Had he been fixed in a shop, or in any mode of life where learning is not required, he might have been happy and respectable. He would have made a good brewer, grocer, draper, builder, brazier, pewterer, or plumber, though he is but a sorry divine. In his present situation he is as unhappy as his blunt feelings will allow him to be; and as to credit and esteem, he is as little respected as the sexton of his parish, or the organ-blower.

I conclude, therefore, that parents, who bring up dunces to the church, because they are dunces, do not consult the honour and happiness of their children; but expose them to as much misery as their natures are capable of feeling, and to as much disgrace as can be easily incurred without the commission of a crime.

EVENING XIX.

ON THE PROPRIETY OF TRYING DUNCES IN SOME ART UNCONNECTED WITH LETTERS.

SECT. II.

I HAVE introduced an instance from the clerical profession, principally because parents, by a most perverse way of thinking, usually bring up a boy to the church whom they consider as scarcely fit for any thing. It is also certain, that dunces educated for the law and physic, when they find themselves unsuccessful at the bar and the bedside, sometimes seek an asylum in the pulpit. From both these circumstances, it happens that the church is complimented with those, whom the world is supposed to throw aside as refuse. The temple is thus converted into an hospital for incurables.

Dunces at school, are, however, by no means to be considered as refuse, though I must contend that they ought not to be particularly consecrated to the service of the altar. No boy, who does not show some taste for the belles lettres, for oratory, poetry, and history, should be brought up to that, or to any of the learned and liberal professions.

But some boys who are dull in the belles lettres, who never could read or relish the classics, have a turn for mathematics, and all the arts which depend on mechanical contrivance. A reputed dunce should be tried in these studies before he is given up as incorrigible. I have been told of a very able man, who, when a boy, displayed no symptoms of parts till he was tried in Euclid's Elements. They struck him with delight; he studied them with eagerness, grew fond of application, and gradually rose to high eminence as a polite artist.

Others, who make no progress in their books, have a taste for drawing and music. These, indeed, will seldom be sufficient to qualify for employments by which life is to be supported, or a fortune acquired; but, when a dull boy in books appears to be ingenious in these arts, he ought to be allowed to cultivate them at least as amusements, in order to rescue himself from the imputation of a total want of ability.

It should be considered, too, before a boy, who makes little improvement in the classics, is despaired of, that the parts of different boys display themselves at different periods. Many of those who produce fruit of the most durable kind, do not blossom till late in the season.

But yet there are some who show such symptoms of insuperable stupidity in learning, that after a reasonable trial, the limitation of which must be left to the parent's discretion, they ought, as their happiness is valued, to be led to other pursuits in which activity of body is chiefly required.

I have said, that the time of trial should be determined by the parent; for few masters will venture to speak unwelcome truth to their employer, especially on a tender subject, which may affect the whole life of their pupil, and perhaps draw down his bitterest resentment upon them at a more efficient age. The office of deciding whether or not a young man shall proceed in a way of life, pointed out by prudence and by parental authority, is too important to be imposed on a common master. The compensation he usually receives is not sufficient, and the connexion is not close enough to justify the parent in throwing the odium and the burden upon him. The parent himself, after accurate observation, and the opinion of the master, should remove the boy; but not subject him to the mortification and disgrace of being avowedly removed because he was a dunce. Some prudential reason should be assigned to justify the change of plan, and to save the character of the boy. To punish him for the defects of his nature would be savage cruelty. And here, I cannot but observe, that the practice of beating dunces, to make them scholars, is at once egregious folly, and most abominable brutality.

Dunces in books often possess an animal vivacity in the affairs and intercourse of common life, which causes vulgar people, both high and low, to consider them as clever. Indeed, as the whole of their attention is devoted to the body, and to present and palpable objects, they sometimes excel greatly in all bodily exercises and accomplishments, and in every mode and degree of Chesterfieldian grace. External ceremony, dress, and address, are just level to the understanding of a dunce. The worst Latinists and Grecians shine the brightest in the fencing and dancing school. And it is an astonishing circumstance, that blockheads in books show wonderful acuteness and memory in all the fashionable games of chance. Add to this, that they are fond of the small-talk of the day; so that, with all these recommendations, they are usually received, in fashionable circles, as very clever and agreeable fellows.

The army and the navy (I hope the rough compliment will be excused) are the proper spheres for those who are thus furnished with bodily activity, but at the same time deficient in that kind of parts, which are necessary to make a valuable proficiency in polite literature. Dunces not being troubled with any of those fine sensibilities, which form the poet, the philosopher, and the orator, have, in the room of them, a bluntness and callosity, which contribute much to animal courage. Though rejected from the schools of learning, they may shine in the boxing schools, become heroes of the fist, and obtain, by muscular exertion, the patronage of the great and popular. They have usually a strong constitution, unimpaired by thought and sedentary employment, and may therefore bear the hardships of a marine life and a military campaign better than the choicest spirits, which nature has formed of finer clay.

Dunces are also peculiarly sensible of the value of money. It is a good which they can feel and understand perfectly, while they are insensible to the subtle charms of intellectual beauty. They, therefore, seem to be intended by Providence for trade and manufactures. They may shine in the shop, though they disgraced the school; and in time may deride, as they count their stores, the poverty of science and philosophy. I never heard that a man failed of arriving at the dignity of a lord mayor through lack of clergy. Thousands would have worn regimentals, walked the quarter-deck, or stood behind the counter with eclat, who, as divines, physicians, and lawyers, lived uneasy, unhonoured, and unsuccessful.

Agriculture is a very proper employment for boys who show no abilities for the cultivation of science. It is a natural and reputable occupation; and I cannot but regret, that many boys of dull parts, but of good estates, are not brought up to farming their own lands, instead of being thrust violently into schools, inns of court, and universities. Their health and their fortunes would be improved in their patrimonial fields, but in the land of learning, they plow and sow with great labour and expense, and never reap the harvest, either of profit, honour, or internal satisfaction.

EVENING XX.

ON THE PECULIAR IMPRUDENCE OF THE POOR IN BRINGING UP DUNCES TO LEARNING.

SECT. III.

THE remarks which I have hitherto made on the subject of dunces, chiefly refer to persons in easy circumstances; but the propensity to bring up boys of no abilities for learning, to learned professions, is no less frequent in the lowest orders of society.

The well-meaning parent, who has neither fortune nor interest to promote the advancement of his child, resolves to give him, what he calls, a good education. There is a free-school in the parish; and thither the boy is sent to learn Latin, without a moment's consideration on the abilities of the boy, or the chance of his being able to gain his bread independently of manual labour. From the age of four or five to that of fourteen, or perhaps nineteen, he is confined to his book, and flogged through Lilly's Grammar. His health is injured, his spirits dejected, his time lost; for, after all, the parent finds it necessary to employ him in his own trade, in digging and delving, in shoe-making, in the business of a drawer, in the workshop of the smith, the brazier, or the carpenter. The boy has lost some time which might have been usefully spent in learning his handicraft; and has besides acquired, by associating with boys of higher rank, some ideas which teach him to lament the hardship of his lot, to despise his present companions, and the vulgarity, toil, and filthiness of the manufactory: as to the little learning he has gained, it is soon forgotten, and indeed it was scarcely worth preserving, for I am proceeding on the hypothesis that the boy was a dunce. Perhaps he can repeat Propria quæ maribus, Quæ genus, and As in præsenti; but the attainment of these has cost him so many bitter pains, that he wishes to assist his natural tendency to forget them, by total neglect and voluntary oblivion.

I hope not to be misunderstood. I mean only to dissuade traders and labourers from sending their sons to learn Latin, or continuing them in the study of it, when their sons are evidently deficient in natural ability. God forbid that I, or any one, should wish to prevent a poor man, whose son is singularly endowed with the powers of understanding, from giving him every opportunity of improvement, and raising his condition. I know that some of the ablest and best men whom this nation has produced, were the offspring of indigent parents, and educated at free-schools. The founders of those excellent institutions intended them for such as could not be educated but by the aid of eleemosynary endowments. I only meant to discourage the bringing up of dunces to learned professions, whether they are the sons of the rich or the poor. The rich, indeed, can provide for a dunce by interest, or by patrimonial estates; but what can a poor man do for a son whom he has forced into orders, without learning, as well as without borough interest? Even with learning, he would find it extremely difficult to procure a better livelihood for him than a porter, or a menial servant can earn; for distinguished preferment is either sold, or bestowed by interest alone. But without learning, without character, without friends, a young man may live, if he can live at all, to curse the mistaken ambition of his well-meaning parent.

Let a parent then, in the lower rank, be fully convinced by the most indubitable testimony, and not by fatherly fondness and vanity, that his child possesses extraordinary abilities, before he determines to make a scholar of him. He will otherwise neglect the parent's duty, which consists in consulting the real comfort and the credit of his child, without sacrificing solid and substantial good to the fantastic prospects of vanity.

It may be said, that if the poor do not introduce their children to the church, many churches must go unsupplied. I rather think there will always be persons enough in the middle ranks of life, to supply the churches, provided the stipends are such as they ought to be; and where they are not such, the churches should go unsupplied, till they are made such, by those who are concerned to secure their supply. As to the supply of them by dunces, and persons totally unfit for the clerical profession, and unable, by poverty, to preserve even a decent appearance, I do not conceive that such a supply of them can be conducive to the interest of religion. A little distress for persons to supply the churches, might cause an event which has long been most devoutly wished for, an augmentation of the stipends of those who perform the parochial duty. Though the modes of decent life are more than doubly expensive, and provisions and necessaries greatly enhanced in price, yet the stipends of poor vicars and curates continue as they were in the last century. Dr. Bentley says, it was made appear to parliament, that six thousand of the clergy have, at a middle rate, one with another, less than fifty pounds a year; and, I believe, the numerous body of curates was not included in this estimate*. Go now, ye poor parents, and run your lubberly lads' heads against pulpits.

* See Bishop Watson's Letter to the Archbishop of Canterbury.

EVENING XXI.

ON THE NECESSITY OF DELAY AND CAUTION, BEFORE A BOY
IS GIVEN UP AS A DUNCE.

SECT. IV.

BEFORE I leave the subject, I think it necessary to add a caution against a too precipitate decision on the abilities of boys ; a rash removal of them from a life of learning, and a too early condemnation of them as dunces incurable.

There are some natures, and those too of the sublimest kind, which will not submit to the trammels of common discipline, but will thrive with spontaneous vigour, and grow of themselves to a stupendous elevation. Thus the oak of the forest would scorn to be nailed against a wall like the feeble exotic fruit-tree, but will reach the skies when left unmolested in its native soil. Boys of this kind do not display much of their ability at schools and colleges, and often offend those who cannot comprehend their noble natures, by the appearance of a dulness, which, like the mist of the morning, is only the prelude of solar effulgence in a sky unclouded.

The history of literature affords many examples of those who made a disgraceful figure both at school and college, but who afterwards became greater men than their boasted schoolfellows and cotemporary collegians. Scioppius, who wrote a philosophical grammar, would not submit, while at school, to learn the common rules, as he relates of himself ; and Cowley either could not, or, as it is most probable, would not commit to memory those elementary instructions, in which all boys educated at grammar-schools are constantly initiated. There is, in the minutiæ of grammar, as they are taught by some persons, something no less abstruse than logic and metaphysics ; and therefore highly disgustful to boys, whose distinguishing talent is imagination. Very bright boys, therefore, may exhibit, where a proper method of introducing them is deficient, a backwardness in learning grammar, which may cause them to be mistaken by careless observers for dunces.

Our most celebrated schools cannot boast of producing the first-rate poets of this country. Shakspeare, Milton, Pope, and Swift, were not indebted to them. They were educated rather irregularly. They were self taught ; and after all the boasts of classical discipline, the ablest men, diamonds of the first water, stars of the first magnitude, were *automaths*, or instructed by their own persevering diligence. The truth is, that nature, together with the ability, gave them a most ardent inclination for excellence, which advanced them to wonderful heights, and broke through all obstacles. These considerations may answer the purpose-for which they are introduced; that of preventing parents from despairing of their children's proficiency, after the failure of the first trials, or on observing the dulness of early infancy.

But after every trial, and the most patient expectation, some boys will appear, beyond the possibility of error, arrant dunces, in all that concerns what is called book-learning. But even under this unfavourable circumstance, consolation may be derived from reflections of the following nature :

Dunces, it is generally believed, are not the least happy of mankind. Though unable to afford much pleasure to others, they are commonly pleased with themselves in a high degree. A smile of self-applause accompanies all their words and actions. If laughed at by others, they mistake derision for congratulation. The proud man's contumely affects them not. Nothing but real pain gives them real sorrow. They have no imaginary ills, that shadowy train, which haunts the ingenious. They have none of those fine sensibilities which torture the feeling heart with unspeakable agony. Let them have food in abundance, and a sufficiency of raiment and money, and, with a wisdom which philosophers have vainly pretended to, they are perfectly satisfied, and enjoy a fool's paradise.

There is no reason to believe that they will not succeed in the world. Fools, it is proverbially said, have fortune. Some substantial reasons may be assigned to account for the adage. Unfeeling and unreflecting men of dull parts are not hurt by repulses and disappointments. Break their web, and they begin it again with all the patience of a Dutchman. They know no nice scruples of punctilious honour. They have no superabundant delicacy, to prevent their importunity of the great and powerful. They prosecute their claims with exemplary perseverance. A flat refusal, or a downright insult from their patron, strikes them with no more effect than a tennis ball the rock of Gibraltar.

The great and powerful often favour them as servile companions, and, in consequence of familiarity with them, patronize and prefer them. They have no saucy claims of merit. They have no acquired lustre to absorb the glitter of hereditary honour. They are all compliance and servility. They are therefore often elevated to honour and profit, which no brilliancy of envied abilities would ever have reached.

If their success in the world is the object of a parent's first wishes, let him not grieve that his son is a dunce; for experience proves, that the want of literary abilities may be no obstacle to patronage.

But to speak seriously, for many will be disposed to consider such consolatory topics as the sport of a ludicrous irony, it is certain that Providence has adapted advantageous situations in society for all the sons of men, who are not in a state of idiotism or insanity. A thousand departments may be found, which even dunces may fill with credit, comfort, and success. I only contend against the absurdity of educating them, when known to be dunces, for the church, or any other of the liberal professions, where reputation and emolument ought to depend on superior abilities and extensive knowledge.

The mistake of confining dunces to a learned life, arises no less frequently from the duplicity of the master, than from the blindness, vanity, and perverseness of the parent. Many masters are mean enough, for the sake of retaining scholars, to extol a blockhead as a genius, whenever the parent, unable himself to judge, inquires concerning his son's proficiency. It is an artifice among the lower orders of the didactic profession to make every parent imagine that his own son is a prodigy; but it is an artifice not only contemptible in the motive which produces it, but highly injurious in its effects to the scholar, the parent, and society. It is productive of disgrace and disappointment in private life; and in public, of those numerous characters and occupations, which instead of being useful, are an impediment, an encumbrance, a burden, and a pest. The fabric of a well-regulated community is like a fine piece of architecture, where every stone and beam is in its proper place, and where a single derangement would not only destroy the beauty and symmetry, but impair the strength of the pile.

Consolation must be sought under the circumstance of want of parts, as under every other misfortune; but after all, genius is a blessing to be considered as an instance of the favour of Heaven, and an emanation from the Deity. It is devoutly to be wished for, diligently improved, and, when improved, to be devoted to the glory of the giver, or, in other words, to the advancement of human happiness. It is a mean idea which views it only as an instrument of personal aggrandizement, selfish pleasure, and sordid interest. It should, however, be restrained by prudence, and guided by benevolence; and then it will be a source of delight to the possessor, and of a thousand advantages to all who are within the sphere of its powerful influence.

It seems to be the will of Providence that, comparatively speaking, few should possess the glorious endowment in a supereminent degree. All great excellence must indeed be rare, for it would cease to be great excellence if it were common. But let not those to whom genius is denied lament. Genius has its evils, from which they are exempt. It is envied, it is exposed to a thousand pains and penalties from the injuries of those who, not knowing or not regarding the irritable niceties of its sensibility, rudely strike the tremulous fibre whenever they approach it. It is of too fine and subtle a nature for the tumults and agitations of a world madly rushing on in the vulgar pursuits of avarice and ambition. Unguarded by discretion, of which it is often too proud to acknowledge the dominion, it often causes a life of misery, and a premature dissolution.

Let it also be remembered by those who are conscious of inferiority to their fellow-creatures, that all distinctions, whether civil, natural, mental, or corporeal, all but superiority of virtue, will shortly cease; and that it is expressly declared, on the highest authority, that *to whom much has been given, of him much will be required ;* a declaration, which, if duly impressed, might afford comfort to the dunce, and cause the genius to tremble.

EVENING XXII.

ON MORAL PHLEBOTOMY, A MODE OF DISCIPLINE AMONG THE ROMANS.

SIR,—IT was a part of the ancient military discipline among the Romans, to order a delinquent to undergo phlebotomy ; and this was originally intended, as Aulus Gellius seems to think, rather as a remedy than a punishment, " quasi minus sani viderentur omnes qui delinquerent," with an idea that all who misbehaved were therefore to be considered and treated as invalids or unsound.

I was seriously considering this method adopted by the wise Romans, and I could not help thinking, that the remedy might be extended to delinquents in modern times, and in other professions and employments of life, as well as in the military.

Suppose the case of a knowing young man, who is not easy till he has picked a quarrel, or distinguished himself by a nocturnal riot in a college, in Covent Garden, in the lobbies of the theatre, in the rural retreat of Vauxhall, or in a duel in Hyde Park. As his irregularity is usually attributed to the warmth of his blood, I should think the lancet might be used with the greatest probability of success. A few ounces quietly let out in the surgery, might prevent the effusion of great quantities by throwing bottles, by the stroke of the watchman's staff, or the sword of some hot-headed antagonist.

It is usual to call persons who are too eager in

their pursuits, *sanguine ;* for such surely no cure can be so certain and well adapted as phlebotomy.

There is a passion which assumes the name of love, but instead of promoting the happiness of its object, regards neither its peace nor good fame, while it licentiously seeks its own gratification. It has nothing in it of the tenderness, the delicacy, the purity of love, but is very violent, and seems, by the symptoms, to partake the nature of a fever. I believe, in this case, copious bleeding, with a cooling regimen, would not fail of effecting a temporary cure.

There are numerous tribes of schemers, projectors, and garreteer politicians, who pester themselves and the public with their crudities, but who might be brought to their sober senses, if the blood, which flows in too great quantities to the brain, were drawn off by a well-timed and powerful revulsion.

You authors, Sir, excuse my freedom, often stand in great need of phlebotomy. You have a thousand flights, fancies, and vagaries, which can be attributed to nothing but the irregular tide of your blood. You swell with pride and vanity and think to reform the world from your garrets; but the world goes on as it pleases, and you have nothing but your labour for your pains. I think I could lower your pride and vanity by my lancet, and teach you a humility which perhaps you will never learn in the books of philosophy, and which would save you a great deal of needless trouble.

In a word, all poets, religious enthusiasts, balloonists, lottery adventurers, ambitious statesmen, and choleric orators in the British or Irish parliament, may, I am convinced, receive great benefit from the phlebotomising system of morality. I intend soon to offer myself to the universities as a professor of moral phlebotomy. How convenient and expeditious a process will it be! No occasion for preaching, reading, and contemplating; for whatever disorder you labour under, only repair to the artist who shaves for one penny, and bleeds for two, and you may be restored to health. Adieu. I stop short, lest you should think I want bleeding myself.

Yours, &c.

An Ethico-Chirurgical Operator.

Though my correspondent has treated the subject ludicrously, yet I have little doubt but he meant to convey instruction, and I shall take occasion from his letter to recommend bodily temperance, as conducive to the government of the passions and imagination.

The irregularities of youth are oftener caused by excess, than by that natural ebullition of blood which is often alleged in their excuse. But allowing as much as can be required to the impulse of the blood and spirits, yet it will still be true, that extravagances of behaviour will probably be much aggravated by intemperance in wine; for indeed, to add the heat of wine to the heat of youth, what is it but to throw oil upon the fire? Yet at no age do men indulge in wine so freely as when, according to their own confession, their blood is already too much inflamed by its natural fermentation. If, instead of adding to the flame, young men would manage it with discretion, and even damp it sometimes, it would probably continue to burn with a temperate, yet sufficient warmth to extreme old age. But the ardour of youth, raised to a fever by wine, not only urges to acts of folly and madness, but burns the vital stamina which were intended by nature for long duration. I by no means go so far as to recommend either phlebotomy or cathartics to a young man who is under the influence of a violent passion; but I may venture to suggest, that he would find the conquest over himself greatly facilitated by abstinence from wine, and by moderation in diet. His reason might have an opportunity of asserting that ascendancy which she ought to claim, and will probably possess, when the delirium of intemperance is once abated.

The errors of the imagination are very much increased by intemperance. During the fever which it occasions, man is apt to dream, and to mistake his visions for realities. How many lives have been sacrificed to supposed affronts and injuries, to affronts never intended, and injuries never committed! But they appeared, in the hour of convivial excess, not only real, but of the greatest magnitude, and in the most ugly colours. If the offended parties would allow themselves time to cool, and spend the next day in abstinence, or at least, in strict temperance, I think the phantom of imagination, which appeared like a giant, would dwindle to a dwarf, or dissolve into nothing, like a cloud in the azure expanse of heaven, which melts into air and leaves an undisturbed serenity. Temperance would effect what argument attempted in vain; and such influence has the body over the mind, that there is often no method of reducing the peccant humours of the mind so effectual, as that of duly arranging the frail mansion in which it is destined to dwell. It is a most unhappy degradation, when the mind is governed by the body, over which it might, by the exertion of its native powers, exercise, for the most part, an absolute dominion.

To cure the mind through the medium of the body is by no means a new process in mental medicine. The fasts, and the mortification of self-denial, which are recommended in the church, were certainly intended to promote sanctity of life, by purifying the body, which in revelation is so greatly honoured as to be called the Temple of the Holy Spirit. After all our efforts, the humiliating experience of frequent failure must convince every serious man, that he must submit himself to the supreme physician, the physician of souls, who, if he will, can make us clean ; and that he will do so, if we ask as we ought, with sincere faith and piety, there is every reason to hope and believe, from the consideration of that attribute in which he is known chiefly to delight.

EVENING XXIII.

ON RHETORICAL ACTION.

THE ancient rhetoricians understood by *action*, which they so strongly insisted on, not gesture only, but the whole business of pleading a cause ; that is, elocution and gesture united, as they appeared in the Court, the Senate, or the Forum, in the actual delivery of an oration.

Action in this comprehensive sense deserved the high esteem of Demosthenes, who, according to a well-known story of Cicero and Quintillian, being asked what was the first, second, and third requisite of oratory, replied action, action, action. And here action is synonymous with what we call delivery.

But many among the modern speakers seem to think that action is nearly synonymous with activity, and means, in its rhetorical use, the contortions of the arms, hands, legs, eyes, and various features of the face. They imagine that Demosthenes understood by action, gesture only.

An idea thus erroneous, but supported by misunderstanding the prince of orators, has led many into a mode of delivery truly ridiculous. They were determined to display a sufficient quantity of this prime requisite, and have in consequence exhibited the action, or rather agility of a harlequin, when they intended to represent, in their own persons, Cicero and Demosthenes revived. They have made even the pulpit resemble the stage of the mountebank, where a jack-pudding entertains with his *action* the gaping multitude.

It is recorded of a divine, who did not confine his action to the pulpit, that he adorned the following passage in the Psalms with peculiar vivacity of gesture.

The singers go before, the minstrels follow after, in the midst are the damsels playing with the timbrels.

At the words the *singers go before* he reached out both his arms at full length before him, *the minstrels following after* he represented with his finger pointing over his left shoulder, and when he came to— *in the midst are the damsels playing with the timbrels,* he illustrated the passage by playing on the Prayer Book with the fingers of both his hands, just as if he had been touching the keys of a harpsichord.

Gesture in oratory is intended to express the passions and emotions of the mind according to the impulse of nature, and not to display the speaker's abilities in the art of mimicry and pantomime. The imitation of the idea in the mind, by the attitude of the body, should not be very close; because such an imitation is a desertion of the orator's part for the actor's, and turns the attention of the hearer from the subject matter to the agility and mimetic talents of a stage-performer. If the imitation be really good, the spectator is struck and pleased with it, but at the same time loses the proper effect of the speech; if, on the other hand, it be awkward, he laughs, and despises the wretched attempt at an unattained excellence.

Gesture is therefore to be ventured on with great caution, and conducted with nice judgment. It may destroy the effect of a fine composition, and render an orator, who may be in other qualifications respectable, an object of contempt and derision.

This consideration has induced me to express my surprise at the displeasure which many have shown on seeing boys at school, and young men at the university, go through their exercises of declaiming without moving their hands and arms. I have heard the hearers observe on such occasions, that the young man recited with great judgment and propriety; what a pity it was, that he stood motionless as a statue.

This criticism arose from their habit of attending the theatres; where imitation being the professed business of the speakers, mimetic gesture is studied with laudable attention, and without danger of defeating the purpose of the player by too near a resemblance. It is his business to *take off*, as it is well expressed, the external form and manner of those whom he represents as accurately as the wax *takes off* the sculptured figure of the seal, or the paper *takes off* the engraving on the copper-plate.

What Horace said of poetry may be said of gesture in oratory. Mediocrity in it is worse than the total want of it. If it is not excellent in its kind, it is better to omit it entirely. If it is stiff, formal, awkward, or excessive, it will lessen the effect of the finest oration, by mixing with the approbation of the hearer a sentiment of ridicule.

EVENING XXIV.

ON THE INCONSISTENCY OF AFFECTED SENSIBILITY.

THERE seems to be a fashion in virtue as well as in vice. There was a time when learning was the fashion among the ladies at court, and the hours which are now spent by them under the hair-dresser, were devoted to the perusal of Plato in the original language. Chastity was once the pride of all who aimed at the character of people of fashion; and courage, honour, generosity, gravity, and heroism, the ornaments ambitiously pursued by courtiers and fine gentlemen.

The quality chiefly affected of late is sensibility; and the affectation has been greatly increased, if not introduced, by the taste for novels. The sentimental comedies, and the affecting tragedies, in which love and the distresses it occasions when disappointed, are feelingly described, have also contributed greatly to diffuse it.

When it is genuine, and not increased to a degree of weakness and effeminacy, it is certainly amiable. True tenderness, or compassion, is one of the most honourable distinctions of human nature. He who cannot feel as a man, when an object presents itself naturally formed to affect the human heart, displays a disposition not only odious, but such as may lead him to actual and premeditated cruelty.

But while I honour the reality, I must despise the affectation. And there is reason to suspect that much of the sensibility, of which we hear and read, is affected, because it seems to operate partially and ostentatiously. It seems to display itself chiefly in gallantry, and in such acts of bounty as are likely to be known, celebrated, and admired, in the realms of fashion. If any lady or lady-like gentleman can find, at a watering-place, a distress similar to any thing in some fashionable novel, it is surprising with what pathos it will be described, and with what assiduity relieved ; but if a distress equally afflicting occurs in the obscure village, where the mansion-house stands, no notice is taken of it, or no more than a regard to common decency requires. The reason seems to be, a fear that the sensibility which alleviates the village distress will never reach the ears of those who tread the paths of fashionable life.

And if a gross passion, operating in a corrupted heart, prompts to an unlawful amour, it is often obeyed by the parties with little shame, and with a great deal of complacency and self-congratulation on their being possessed of such a sensibility as irresistibly tempts them to say,

Curse on all laws save those which love has made.

. Bad passions, and bad actions, the consequence of them, have always been common, and will continue to be so in the present condition of human nature ; but to boast of them as doing honour to the heart, under the name of lovely and delicate sensibility, is peculiar to the fashionable of the present age. Mr. Sterne and Mrs. Draper have too many imitators. A goat is a personage of as great sensibility and sentiment as most of them.

. If the pretenders to extraordinary sensibility really possess it in a degree which renders its fine impulses utterly irresistible, why does it not appear uniformly, and in other affairs, as well as those of love ? The Christian religion recommends charity and universal benevolence ; but the persons who aim at the epithet fashionable, as the most enviable distinction of humanity, are by no means equally

zealous to obtain the character of good Christians.
Many of them, I believe, affect the character of possessing too much sense to be seduced by any thing
which they call a popular mode of superstition.
When they are at their seats in country villages,
and far from the tribe whose admiration they seek,
do these persons of exquisite sensibility employ their
time in seeking objects of compasssion, in the cot-
tages of poverty and misery ; and their money, in
the diffusion of comfort ? Alas ! they too often take
the opportunity of practising a most rigid œconomy
at home, to the exclusion of all bounty, that they
may have abundance in the next Bath season.
Charitable subscriptions are indeed very common
at Bath, Brighthelmstone, and Tunbridge, and many
are delighted in setting down their names, not for-
getting their titles ; but is there not in the mean
time many a poor family pining in want, near their
houses and estates at home, who never receive any
thing from them, because there is no subscription-
book, no master of the ceremonies, and none of the
fashionable fraternity to observe them ?

Does the sensibility, to which they pretend in
love, display itself towards their husbands, wives,
children, and in all the tender charities of private life?
I rather doubt it, because I observe that Lady ——,
so celebrated for sensibility, is separated from her
husband, and never sees her children ; because Sir
—— never gives a farthing of the fortune he acquired in the East Indies to his poor relations ; because my Lord —— is never at home, where he
has a most amiable wife, who pines in solitude, and
in vain laments his absence. Is it necessary, to the
excitement or gratification of this boasted sensibility,
that the object should be unlawful or clandestine ?
If so, and experience seems to prove it so, it can

have no pretensions to praise; for it is inconsistent with honour and generosity.

True sensibility, equally remote from weakness and affectation, will feel the sentiments of devotion with no less vivacity than those of love. It will, I believe, be oftener warmed with an attachment to virtue than to vice. It will be delicate and reserved, rather than forward, noisy, and ostentatious. But has the sensibility which is assumed at public places, or by the slaves of fashion, any of these characteristics? Is it not, on the contrary, rather inclined to libertinism in religious principle, very far from scrupulous in moral conduct, bold, busy, and conceited? It has indeed every appearance of vanity; and, if there were no danger of confounding it with real sensibility, the honour of our nature, it ought to be universally exploded with ridicule.

That sensibility alone which produces piety to God and benevolence to man has the indisputable mark of genuine excellence. Vice and vanity will produce the other sort, which has every sign of a counterfeit, and like the base coin which, in the hands of the interested, is taught to emulate gold, ought, if possible, to be cried down by public authority. It too often passes current in the world, not without great injury to society: for honour, paid to false virtue, robs the true of its just right, and contributes, by lessening the rewards of truth, to discourage its appearance.

EVENING XXV.

ON AN EXTRAVAGANT ATTACHMENT TO LETTERS.

THE love of letters appears to have operated with a force equal to the most violent passions. Some tempers are indeed so constituted, that whatever attaches them grasps them tenaciously, and holds them firmly, like the roots of the oak fixed in the stubborn clay. Books, horses, dogs, statues, pictures, music, all that is beautiful in art, or in lifeless nature, are found to warm the bosoms of their amateurs with a love equal, and in some instances exceeding, the love of women.

It is related of those deep scholars, Budæus and Turnebus, that they spent their wedding day in a severe prosecution of their usual studies, which were remarkably dry. Their poor ladies, I am afraid, had but little reason to expect much happiness from lovers who could prefer the dreary researches of grammatical and critical learning to the high and innocent delights of nuptial festivity. The bosom which, at such seasons, could have room for any other sentiment than love and joy, must have been too cold for the social duties, and fit only for the damp walls of a monastic cell.

And what did these scholars produce, by an attachment to the severer muses in preference to their wives? Dull tomes of uninteresting erudition, where the worm riots uncontrolled, and the dust accumulates undisturbed by the hand of industry. Such examples are happily not common; and if they were, what would become of philanthrophy?

It is said of St. Jerom, that he filed away his teeth to the very gums, that he might pronounce Hebrew with greater facility.

Joachimus Fortius Ringelbergius advises the student to take great care lest he should lose much time in sleep. He advises him to have an alarum clock by his bedside; but if that is not to be conveniently procured, to lay stones, and bits of wood, on his bed, and under his side, which, though he

will not feel them much at first, may, after an hour
or two, gall him to the quick, and cause him to get
up of his own accord. What an enthusiasm of
application! not content with spending the day in
labour, he wished the student to lose the sweets of
repose, and almost literally to plant thorns upon his
pillow. No pursuit but that of virtue can require
such austerity; and even virtue, in her most rigid
exaction of discipline, listens to reason, and leans to
moderation. When she deserts them, she becomes
fanaticism; and hurries her mistaken votaries to
madness, and to misery.

I never could admire the celebrated, but severe,
discipline of Monsieur Paschal, " He wore," we
are told, " an iron girdle, full of sharp points, next
to his skin, and when any idle thought came into
his head, or when he took any pleasure in the place
he was in, he would give himself blows with his
elbow, to make the prickings of the girdle more
violently painful, and oblige himself, by these means,
to call his duty to remembrance." This practice
appeared to him of such use, that he retained it till
his death, even to those last days of his life, when
perpetual pains afflicted him sufficiently, without
the co-operation of the pungent girdle.

Whoever labours under the mania of excessive
study will, I think, find an effectual cure in reading
Tissot on the Diseases incident to Literary Persons.
Tissot, however, appears to me, to have exaggerated
his descriptions, so as to render them truly terrify
ing, and sufficient to deter most men from the common and moderate employments of literary life. I
mention it only as my opinion, that he has exaggerated his descriptions; and I think so, because I
have known many persons devoted to letters, who
enjoyed remarkably good health, and were instances

of singular longevity. They probably had sense enough to take precautions against the effects of great application ; and to relieve their labours by air and exercise. But Tissot's book may be yet very useful, as it cannot but deter the rational student from excessive application : the evils of which he enumerates so copiously, and paints so formidably, that a man who duly regards his happiness might fall into a bibliophobia from reading it, and fly from a library with as much horror as a mad dog from a pond.

A moderate application is sufficient for the attainment of all necessary and useful knowledge, and the excessive attachment which some men display, is chiefly in trifling pursuits. Not satisfied with the great and essential objects, which answer every purpose of real utility, they pursue their inquiries into matters of mere curiosity, with no other intention, however they may plausibly disguise it, than their own amusement. But time, health, and life, are too precious to be sacrificed to the pleasure of gratifying mere curiosity.

No man comes into the world without many obligations of the moral and social kind. No man can, consistently with his duty, suffer himself to be ingrossed by contemplation. Some sort of social activity is necessary in the most retired scenes, and in professions and modes of life the most distant from commercial and political employment.

Few stand so insulated, as not to be nearly connected with others by friendship or kindred; besides the general connexion with all men, which arises from a participation of the same nature. But how can he, who is immured in his closet, or abstracted by perpetual absence from the busy scene before him, attend to the claims, which others may justly make, on his active beneficence? He will feel as little inclination as ability to serve them. Every call upon his exertions, in their favour, will be considered as an importunate interruption, to be checked by a morose reprimand, rather than listened to with humane condescension. He may, indeed, labour in the recesses of his study; but as his labour terminates in his private gratification, as it produces no external fruits, as it prevents him from taking an active part in society, it is a labour which entitles him to no esteem. He is, in truth, to be numbered among the most selfish of mankind, as he sacrifices all his social duties to the pursuit of his own solitary pleasure.

Providence has taken care that such conduct should bring upon itself its own punishment. For this gloomy, recluse, selfish mode of living never fails to produce dejection of spirits, and the loss of that health and vigour which are necessary to sweeten all enjoyments. Languid, enervated, and feeble, the student who follows his pursuit with unreasonable and excessive ardour, exhibits, when he comes, from the shade of his retirement, into the sunshine of active life, a phantom, pallid as a ghost, and silent as a statue, and excites, in some, horror, and in others, ridicule.

That golden mean, therefore, so celebrated, in the active world, must be observed, with no less reverence, in the contemplative. For man, being a compound of mind and body, departs no less from nature and wisdom, when he devotes himself wholly to the mind, than when he attaches himself exclusively to the body. Till we shall have " shuffled off this mortal coil," we must pay a great attention to our animal nature, in order to preserve the energy of the intellectual, in its due vigour.

There is a passage at the close of Plutarch's Rules for the Preservation of Health, which I beg leave to recommend to the attention of the reader, in the following free translation :

" Men of letters," says he, " must beware of that anxious covetousness, and niggardly attention to matters of study and literature, which leads them to neglect the condition of their bodies, which some of them spare not, even when ready to sink under fatigue ; compelling the mortal part to vie in exertion with the immortal, the earthly body with the spirit which is heavenly.

" The ox said to the camel, who refused to ease him a little of his burden, as they were travelling together, Thou wilt not help me now to bear something of my load ; but very soon shalt thou be forced to carry all that I carry, and me besides ; and so it happened, when the ox shortly after died under the pressure of his burthen.

" Just so it happens to that mind which will not allow the body, its fellow-labourer, rest and repose ; for presently comes a fever, a head-ache, a dizziness of brain, with a dimness of sight, and then she is obliged to give up her books, her discourses, her disputations, and to sympathize with her companion, in all the languor of disease.

" Wisely, therefore, did Plato advise us not to exercise the body without the soul, nor the soul without the body ; but to let them draw together equally, like horses harnessed together in a carriage, paying perpetual attention to the body's welfare, when its vigour is necessary to support the exertions of the mind, and thus producing that fine and lovely state of health, which prevents the body from becoming an impediment to the mind, or the mind to the body, either in action or contemplation."

EVENING XXVI.

ON SUPERFICIAL FINE GENTLEMEN IN THE MILITARY AND OTHER DEPARTMENTS.

THERE is a passage in Menander, frequently noticed by the moderns, which affirms, that the gods themselves cannot make a polite soldier. It has been justly observed, by those who have quoted the passage, that the ideas of the ancients must have differed from those of the moderns on the subject of politeness, or of the military order; for no profession is supposed to be so polite, in modern times, as the military.

But, perhaps, in the present question, the true idea of politeness is not ascertained. If it means the graces of external behaviour only, the soldier of modern times has often a just claim to it; but if it means the polish of a cultivated mind, he will often be found greatly deficient. For, though it be true, that the various company which he may see in the course of his campaigns, or in winter-quarters, may give him a knowledge of the living world, of the prevailing manners, and the fashionable modes of address, yet it cannot give him a knowledge of the history and nature of man, nor such a comprehensive, liberal, and solid turn of thinking as can supply the want of education. As he must live much among strangers, he will find it necessary to make himself agreeable in his manners; for otherwise, he would often want those comforts of hospitality which, in his wandering condition of life, are particularly desirable. But if he had laid in a store of ideas by education, and subsequent reflexion, his company would be more sought, and he would find a satisfaction, from a due degree of rational self esteem, to which, with a mind destitute of literary elegance and philosophy, he must be a stranger.

But though, in consequence of long habit, strong parts, and much observation, he may acquit himself with wonderful success in the ordinary converse of the day, and be esteemed a man of sense in the conduct of business, yet he will discover his defect, his want of education, whenever he is obliged to have recourse to his pen to communicate his knowledge. He will then no longer be able to conceal inelegance and inaccuracy by external grace, nor to compensate the defect of clearness, precision, or argument, by vehemence of action or vociferation. He will often spoil good sense by bad expression, and cause contempt, by blunders occasioned through ignorance of orthography. Nor let it be urged that, in his profession, he will have no occasion to write ; for every gentleman must, in the ordinary affairs of human life, write letters ; and professional men are often obliged to write more formally and exactly on professional and scientific subjects.

It may not indeed be desirable, that soldiers in general should value themselves on learning, or make it their chief ambition to excel in letters. The arts of peace, and the duties of a state of war, are so different in their nature, and require dispositions so different, that it is not easy to excel in the one, without a neglect of the other; though Julius Cæsar, Raleigh, and many others, afford instances to prove that an excellence in both, at the same time, is possible as well as honourable. But in general, it is to be feared, that literary ambition and employments, carried to any great length, might have a tendency to enervate the soldier, to give him a distaste for the hardships which he can scarcely avoid in his profession, and to render a hero by profession effeminate. Letters are only to be pursued collaterally with the grand professional object. They must not rival it, and much less supplant it.

A competent knowledge of letters in the soldier is all that I maintain to be necessary; such a knowledge as enables him to speak and write like a man of liberal education; such a knowledge as enables him to seek and find amusement, in his leisure hours, in polite literature and improvement, in moral philosophy, in the knowledge of himself, and of the various duties arising from the different relations and connexions of social and civil life.

It is to the want of knowledge and taste that much of the improper behaviour of military upstarts is to be attributed. Feeling themselves deficient, and unable to support a conversation on rational subjects, or to acquit themselves with credit in serious and important business, and at the same time very unwilling, from the pride of their profession, to acknowledge inferiority, they find nothing remaining but arrogantly to claim by noise, swaggering, blustering, and bullying, that attention, which they have no other method to secure. They cannot, perhaps, converse rationally, or behave decently; but if you dare to show them that you think so, by the expression of a natural contempt, they can pull your nose, break your head with a candlestick, or run you through with that unhonoured sword, which never knew an enemy, but at a tavern or coffee-house. The less a man excels in intellectual, the more he is inclined to exercise his brute force; but can that part of the profession make peculiar pretensions to politeness, which is ready to give up its claim to rationality, without which there can be no real polish, though there may be a glossy varnish, which, in the eyes of the inexperienced, passes for a genuine lustre?

But though the military profession furnishes many instances of illiterate fine gentlemen, of those who call upon mankind to admire and applaud them for accomplishments and graces merely personal, yet it by no means monopolizes the species. And indeed, in justice to the profession, I must acknowledge, that the reason why so many illiterate persons are found in it, is not that the profession, which, from much leisure in modern times, furnishes peculiar opportunities for improvement, makes them so; but that it finds them so; for who are often selected for the army? They who are blockheads in their books, careless, idle, extravagant, and for that reason said to be fit for nothing else. Add to this, that young men often obtain commissions so early in life as to be weaned from their books too soon, to have a turn of mind given them utterly incompatible with study; and that even those of the best abilities and dispositions are often sent to the regiment before they could possibly have made an advancement in learning, sufficient to continue its effects on the subsequent periods of life.

But illiterate fine gentlemen, I repeat, are by no means confined to the army. There are some to be found in almost every department; though they are not so frequent in this country as they were before the Spectators appeared. At the close of the last century, and the commencement of the present, your very fine gentlemen considered learning as a disgrace, and with fine estates, fine clothes, fine titles, they were content with minds as unfurnished as those of their valets or their chambermaids. They could scarcely write a card or letter on the most common affairs, not even an invitation to a dinner. It was a work and a labour; and when finished, it was hardly legible, from the badness of the hand-writing, and the incorrectness of the spelling ; and, by a strange perverseness, a letter of this kind was supposed to bear the marks of peculiar gentility. Beaux of those days, for of them I speak, were indeed blockheads ; but, as if they were not really ignorant enough, they took pains to display their freedom from what was then contemptuously called clergy, book learning, and pedantry.

The very name of pedantry was artfully contrived, by an association of confederated dunces, to convey ideas of terror ; and, indeed, the scholars in the universities had given too much reason for confounding, learning with pedantry, by their scholastic jargon, and their attention to a philosophy, which was of no use in society, and which, while it prevented men from acquiring the agreeable and disgraceful accomplishments, supplied them with nothing of solid utility to compensate awkwardness and pride.

But the case is now totally different. Men of rank and fortune bring up their children with care, and bestow upon them every improvement which their capacity will receive, and there is often found, in the genteelest and most elevated circles of society, the union of the fine gentleman with the polite and well accomplished scholar. So that the illiterate fine gentleman will not now be kept in countenance, even in the regions of high life, where he once thought himself secure from contempt, and really was so, from the irrational and undistinguishing scorn of pedantry.

If a man be illiterate from misfortune, he is an object of pity, but not of contempt, while he does not give himself airs of superiority, and look round for admiration. But, in the present age, the fop without education, knowlege, taste, and a power of conversing with sense and spirit, must find a so-

ciety of fops equally or more ignorant than himself,
if he would avoid derision, or if he hopes to gratify
his vanity.   He commonly endeavours to supply all
defects by loud talking and overbearing arrogance.

EVENING XXVII.

ON SHEDDING TEARS.

To shed tears is considered, in modern times, as
unmanly; though the greatest men recorded in antiquity are represented, by the poets and historians,
as commonly giving vent to their sorrow by the
fountains of the eyes.

The epithet δακρυχεων, which describes heroes shedding tears, is very frequent in Homer.   Ulysses is
represented by him as excelling all others in understanding; yet Ulysses sheds tears most copiously.
In describing his sorrow in Calypso's island, Homer mentions his tears three times in the course of
seven or eight lines :

Ουδε ποτ'. οσσε

Δακρυοφιν τερσοντο .   .   .   .

Δακρυσι και ςοναχησι και αλγεσι θυμον ερεχθων

Ποντον επ' ατρυγετον δερκεσκετο——δακρυα λειβων.

His eyes from tears
Were never free .   .   .   .
With tears, and sighs, and grief, he pined away.
As o'er the sea he wishful look'd——he wept.

It may then be fairly concluded, that this great
judge of human nature did not consider tears as
disgraceful to the understanding; and that he did not
imagine them derogatory from the character of
courage, may be collected from his causing his
greatest hero, Achilles, to shed tears in profuse abundance.   When Achilles relates the ill usage he had

received from Agamemnon, Homer concludes the recital with

Ὡς φατο δακρυχεων———
Και ρα παροιθ᾽ αυτοιο καθεζετο δακρυχεοντος
———" Τεκνον, τι κλαιεις."———

Thus spoke the weeping hero.
Before him, as he wept, his mother stood.
———" Why weeps my son ?"———

Many other instances might be brought from Homer, from Virgil, and the best poets and historians of antiquity, to prove that they thought the shedding of tears no diminution of their hero's character, either with respect to the understanding, or the heart. If I may be allowed to take an instance from the gospel, as well as from pagan authors, let it be remembered, that " Jesus wept."

It was an observation of ancient wisdom, that " Good men are very apt to shed tears."

Ἀγαθοι ἀριδάκρυες ἄνδρες.

And this epithet was not understood by them in the sense which the French accept it, when they make good synonomous with weak and foolish. There is, indeed, so much misery in the world, that he who does not feel it, and express his feelings as nature intended that he should, must be deficient in some of those organs which are necessary to constitute natural excellence. The strings which should vibrate, are relaxed; the heart that should be penetrated, is petrified.

Vice, luxury, excess, gaming, and a long converse with corrupt company, are found capable of contravening nature, and drying up the lachrymal glands, as the sun-beams scorch the fibres which should give nutriment, verdure, and growth, to the herbage of the meadow. But let not those, in whom this unnatural alteration has taken place, plume themselves on superior sense, courage, fortitude, or philosophy. Their insensibility is defect, not perfection.

Let us take an example of man's natural sympathy, in an actual state of nature. The voyages to the southern hemisphere afford many such examples. There you will observe men, who are ready to face their enemy in the most dangerous battle, weeping with peculiar bitterness of sorrow at every domestic calamity. Look at home for a contrast, and behold a gamester of St. James's, long hackneyed in the pleasurable world, beholding the greatest misfortunes which can befal himself, his family, or the stranger within his gates, with a perfect sang froid ; with eyes which scorn to shed a tear in the most trying circumstances of affliction.

Hardness of heart, and insensibility of temper, conceal themselves under the appellation of manly fortitude. To shed tears, on sorrowful occasions, is no mark of a weak understanding ; but of that tenderness and susceptibility which, as it is the noblest distinction of human nature, is emphatically styled humanity. There is nothing admirable, but rather pitiable, in a heart, which has undergone, by time and collision with the world, a kind of premature ossification ; nor let the most elevated among the sharers of human nature, and of all the evils it is heir to, blush at being seen to give vent to grief by the floodgates of the eyes. The lachrymal glands were intended by Providence for use, as much as any other part of the wonderful mechanism of the human frame.

It must be allowed, that tears have been brought into disrepute by their abuse. Very weak,* and

---

* Vos quibus est virtus, muliebrem tollite luctum.   Hor. Ep.

very artful* people, have rendered them, in many
instances, contemptible and suspicious. There are
those who weep from habit or affectation, on any
and on no occasion; who seem to think a pearly
drop as great an ornament to the cheek, as the
diamond suspended from the ear; who, when they
cannot prevail by argument, have recourse to tears
to excite compassion; who wantonly tamper with
the finest feelings of the heart, and render sorrow
itself ridiculous. Such persons should be watched
with circumspection; for some symptom will appear to an accurate observer, which will betray their
imposture. The usual error of such persons is, to
pass the limits of the occasion; to weep to excess,
to over-act their part, to seek spectators and wit-
nesses of their affected sorrow, instead of retiring, as
nature teaches, to silence and to solitude.

But let not the real mourner refuse to give expression to his feelings by the mode which nature
powerfully recommends, through a fear of being
suspected either of imbecility or artifice. Tears relieve the misery which causes them to flow. When
philosophy, and even religion, have failed to assuage
sorrow, a flood of tears has afforded consolation.
The shower has fallen copiously, the clouds have
immediately been dispelled, and the sky has re-
sumed all its beautiful serenity.

---

* Vidi etiam lachrymas, an est pars fraudis in illis,
  Hæ quoque habent artes, quoque jubentur, eunt.
                                    OVID, AD DEMOPHOONT.

EVENING XXVIII.

ON THE CONTEMPT EXPRESSED BY PROFOUND AUTHORS FOR POPULARITY.

IT has frequently been pretended by some writers that they do not wonder at their own want of popularity, for they never addressed the people, but were contented with the approbation of the wiser few. They judged the vulgar unworthy their attention; and they could not stoop from their own imaginary eminences to hold converse with those who are hidden in the shades of obscurity.

Writers, it is true, in profound philosophy and abstruse science can only address readers of learning; and learned readers are of necessity few, compared with the unlearned and the superficial. But works on morality and religion, subjects which equally concern every mortal, ought to be addressed and accommodated to the taste and understanding of all who possess common sense; and the more popular they are, the more meritorious, because the more useful.

For what is the end proposed by the authors of such writings? To instruct philosophers? but philosophers are able to find instruction in a thousand books already before the public, the very sources from which the modern writer has derived his stream. If pretenders are not able to instruct themselves sufficiently well, yet they usually think themselves able, and the avenues to their bosoms are too often closed by self-conceit. True philosophers are confessedly few; but is it the part of a generous man to wish to confine the benefit he bestows to a few, when great numbers are eager to partake of it who are in immediate want of it? Are the writers whose works are only addressed, and indeed only intelligible, to a few, so valuable and useful as those who have the desire and skill to bring down wisdom from the cloud-topt mountain to reside on the plains below, where myriads are wandering without a guide in the labyrinths of dangerous error? And yet no writers assume an air of greater superiority than those who affirm that they write not to the people, but to the purged ear of a few speculatists, who dream away life, weaving, like the solitary spider, flimsy cobwebs, which a breath can dissipate.

The writings of such men can only conduce to innocent and refined amusement; and they ought to be content with the praise of ingenuity. To extensive utility they can make no just claim; for the utility consists only or chiefly in affording entertainment to a few. Let them possess the praise which is their due, and let them be honoured for the innocence, and the subtlety of their occupations; but let them not assume a superiority over writers who successfully instruct the people at large; that sort of people whom they affect to despise, but who constitute the majority of mankind, who have hearts and understandings capable of happiness and improvement, and who were intended by Providence to be the receivers of benefits from all who are in any respect able to bestow them, either by superior talents or greater opulence.

Our Saviour, who knew the duties of a teacher far better than the proudest of the sophists or philosophers, professedly and particularly preached his Gospel to the poor; that is, to the many, the vulgar, the ignorant, the miserable, those whom worldly grandeur, worldly wisdom, and unsanctified science were, at all times, apt to neglect and despise. The truth is, the approbation of the poor was not calculated to flatter pride, and therefore it was not de-

sired; but he, who sought to do good rather than
to be applauded, addressed his instructions more
immediately to those who had no other means of
receiving it.   He addressed it in a popular way, not
in metaphysical and scientific terms; but in pleasing parables, and in familiar conversation.

And happy are those who are able to communicate good to the minds of men, in humble imitation
of his popular and engaging manner; who use the
talents which they have received, not in seeking or
supplying speculative amusement, not in gratifying
their own and their fellow-students' pride; but in
clothing wisdom in a dress formed to attract the
notice, and captivate the affection, of the erring
multitude.

When I enter a large library, and view the bulky
tomes of dull learning, and abstruse science, the
labours of many painful lives, now standing like useless lumber on dusty shelves, or affording a transient
amusement to a few curious scholars, I cannot help
lamenting that so much industry should have been
exerted with so little advantage to human life. Many
of them indeed were once popular, and did good in
their generation; but more were never intended to
be popular, and never did any good but in affording
work to the ingenious artisan who printed them, or
encouraging manufactures by the consumption of
paper. Their authors and themselves sleep in peace;
but they afford a lesson to the modern metaphysical
and recondite writers, not to over-value their works
on account of their utility; but to pay some respect
to moral writings, which, though despised by them
as trifling, have yet been universally read, and have
diffused virtues and principles, the happy effects of
which have been doubtless great, and not easy to be
defined or ascertained. One hint of practical wisdom

has often preserved a whole life from folly and misery; and thousands and tens of thousands have been benefited as well as delighted by Addison, to every one who has read Malbranche and Locke.

To whatever superiority of understanding the metaphysical sophists may pretend, and whatever contempt they may affect for works which are universally well received by the common people, it is certain that it is not the talent of an ordinary genius to render his works acceptable to the majority of his fellow-creatures. He must have something in his spirit congenial with the better sentiments of human nature; he must have an easy and agreeable mode of conveying his sentiments, a talent by no means contemptible, a talent which those who despise would probably rejoice to possess.

I must distinguish, while I am treating this subject, between temporary and permanent popularity. Temporary popularity is often gained by contemptible arts, and is itself for the most part contemptible. The practice of puffing, as it is called by a ludicrous and cant appellation, often raises a bubble into the air, which bursts, and is annihilated even while the people gaze; but permanent popularity can arise only from a general experience of utility and excellence, and notwithstanding the reasonings of criticism *a priori*, and the arbitrary decisions of reputed judges, the merit of all literary works must be appreciated by their real utility, and their real utility by the extent and duration of their beneficial effect.

Heraclitus is said to have heartily boasted, that one good judge was to him as a multitude, and that the numberless crowds as nobody:

Εις εμοι ανθρωπος τρισμυριοι, οι δ' αναριθμοι
Ουδεις.——

This might be said merely in contempt of some

αμουσοι, tasteless critics, who had censured him without understanding him ; but if he meant to prefer the judgment of any individual to the united opinion of mankind at large, I must dissent from him entirely. All men have hearts and understandings in some degree of excellence ; the general decisions of whole nations must be final ; and I do not believe there is so much difference between one man and another, in the powers of feeling and judging, as the proud imagine, and assert, when they mean to pay themselves the compliment of claiming a place among the wiser few, the select spirits, who from their fancied elevation look down on the multitude wandering in the vale below, just as they behold the reptiles of an ant-hill.

EVENING XXIX.

ON THE LETTERS OF JUNIUS.

WHEN thousands are in search of fame, and desirous to attain it by the hardiest exertions, it seems wonderful that any writer, whose works have already received unbounded applause, should choose to let his name continue in the darkest obscurity. Other reasons, and not the contempt of fame, must have prevented him from claiming the glittering prize. Fear of resentment from the persons whom he may have censured, or a change in the sentiments which he may have advanced with rash confidence, must be the real causes for his preference of concealment to glory. " I am the sole depositary of my own secret," says Junius ; but, unless death has sealed it up for ever, it may be expected, that the secret will burst the bars of its sepulchre, when the danger of its escape shall be removed by time.

But the writings of Junius afford, at this period, more matter for contemplation to the man of taste and literature, than to the politician. Junius will take his place among the first classes of the present age, in the opinion of late posterity. More Attic than Cicero, more florid than Demosthenes, he has reached the desirable point of excellence, where the correct stops short of the jejune, and the ornamented shuns the affected, the diffuse, and the declamatory.

No writings, on political subjects, are to be found, in the English language, comparable in elegance of style and composition to the letters of Junius. Bolingbroke was incorrect and unequal. He has, indeed, many spirited passages in his Patriot King, and some which bear a resemblance to Junius, but which do not equal him. His stream rolls not like a majestic river, with undiminished magnificence; but tumbles on, like a temporary torrent, rushing over fragments of rocks, and stumps of trees, impeded by bushes, clogged with weeds, and often turbid with a muddy commixture.

The periodical papers of the age of Bolingbroke, which attracted much attention during the violence of party attachment, exhibited but few specimens of fine composition. I never found any passages extracted from the Craftsman, Cato's Letters, and the rest of that species, which could pretend to any remarkable elegance of style or manner. Many of them had force of expression, and subtlety of argument; but the best of them seem not to maintain a place among the English classics. They were not formed for duration. They may be compared to the puffs and tartlets of the pastrycook, which are only good immediately after they are drawn from the oven; or to some kinds of perishable fruit, which are no sooner ripe than rotten; which must be eaten immediately, or given to the swine.

Junius, indeed, when he writes on common subjects, writes like common men. He was one of those writers, whose genius is excited by the dignity of his subject, and rises adequately on the occasion. His preface is but of moderate excellence, his Philo-Junius, confessedly written by himself, would not have distinguished him from the herd, and his notes are worthy of little distinetion.

On the disgrace of Lord Mansfield, the Duke of Grafton, the Duke of Bedford, and Sir William Draper, he has reared a column of fame, more durable and beautiful than brass and marble. Those persons were unfortunate in the circumstance of being coeval with such a writer. The hand of genius has disgraced their honours with a cross bar, which neither heraldry nor the mandate of a monarch can remove. The arrow shot from such a bow stuck in their sides never to be extracted. Posterity will read their characters in the Letters of Junius, when friendship and party shall be no longer able to wipe off the colours that have stained them. I enter not into the justice or injustice of his invectives. I believe them often unjust. I only remark that, as it was deemed the highest good fortune to an Achilles to be celebrated by a Homer, so it is the most deplorable fate of these gentlemen to have been stigmatised with infamy by a Junius. The Duke of Bedford might have purchased forbearance of Junius cheaply, at the price of half his enormous fortune, if Junius had been venal. Truth is, indeed, great, and will, in time, prevail; but where, our descendants will ask, are the beneficent actions, the noble achievements recorded, to counterbalance, or invalidate, the representations of Junius ?

The letter to the King, though one of the finest compositions in the volumes, I cannot approve; because it was intended to add pungency to the thorns of a crown. Ministers, and public persons, of all ranks, who are aiming at the rewards of ambition, under the pretence of patriotism, are fair objects of political satire; but a King of England is empowered by the constitution to act so little of himself, that the blame of transactions that pass under his name, cannot, with justice, be imputed to his personal activity. The peculiar nature of the unfortunate illness, which has since afflicted the King, induces every man of common good nature to wish that whatever may have corroded his breast with painful sensations, not absolutely unavoidable, had never been presented to his notice. The pen of Junius was like the steel of Felton. The knife of Margaret Nicholson was a straw to the weapon of Junius.

But on this topic I add no more. I designed to consider Junius only in a literary light. And though, in common with the nation, I admire his Letters, as fine pieces of eloquence of that kind which the ancient rhetoricians denominated the epidictic; though I consider him as the very first of our English classics, in this department; though I admire his terse language, his keen wit, his polished satire; yet I regret, that he did not exercise his talents on subjects of univeral and everlasting concernment; on morals, on letters, on history. He might have produced works which would have not only charmed, but improved an admiring nation. But Sybilline pages on temporary politics seldom have survived their authors to any distant period. Great and important as the men and actions of the present day appear to the present generation, they may not appear great to posterity, who will have their own heroes, of their own day, to form the transient pageant of the hour. The genius of Junius, and nothing but such a genius could do it, will embalm the more trifling topics of his Letters, as straws and flies are preserved in amber. But they will be retained rather in the cabinets of the curious, than diffused among the world at large. Whereas a work of general utility, such as must interest human nature in all times and circumstances, adorned with the graces which he was able to bestow, would have been cherished by mankind with the affection and regard which have preserved to this hour the authors of the age of Pericles and Augustus.

EVENING XXX.

ON A TASTE FOR TREES, AND FOR THE BEAUTIES OF VEGETATION IN GENERAL.

SIR,—There is in the human heart a *philokalia*, or love of beauty, implanted by nature. Wherever the *kalon* appears, whether in things animate or inanimate, natural or artificial, the heart is soothed to complacency by the contemplation of it; unless, indeed, some violent passion or habitual propensity, unless avarice or selfish ambition, gluttony or voluptuousness, have pre-occupied its attachments, and gradually overcome every generous inclination.

I hope I shall never be so entangled by any vice as to lose my taste for the delight arising from the beauties of nature. I have a passion at present, and I confess it to be a very strong one; while at the same time I am confident, that its gratification is attended with pleasure no less innocent than great. Perhaps you will smile, when I tell you, that I have fallen in love with trees, and that my particular favourite at present is the plane-tree. I have many reasons for my attachment to that tree, while I do not deny that I perceive charms in many others, and am indeed, when I am in the forest, a general lover.

But, in my attachment to the plane-tree, I am by no means singular. Herodotus relates, that Xerxes, on a march, happened to find one of remarkable beauty, with which he was so captivated that he presented it with a golden chain, to be twined, I suppose, like a sash around its body, or like a bracelet round one of its arms. Ælian adds, that he also placed at the bottom of it, in token of his passion, his own jewels, and those of his concubines and satraps, and was so smitten with it, as to forget his expedition, and to salute it with the tender names of his love, his darling, and his goddess. When cruel necessity at last compelled him to leave the object of his passion, he caused the figure of the tree to be stamped on a golden medal, which he constantly wore in memory of his love.

This fondness for a tree I consider as doing great honour to a man who might be supposed to be too much elevated with his own grandeur, and fascinated with the pomp of power, to retain a relish for the simple beauties of nature, displayed in the formation of a tree. The circumstances related of his behaving like an enamorato, I consider either as the invention of historians, who were by no means scrupulous in point of veracity, or as mere whimsical sports and frolics, intended for his amusement amidst the toils of war. The fact is curious, and adds something to the many honours of this distinguished tree.

Every scholar knows how greatly the plane-tree was esteemed by the men of elegance and taste among the ancient Greeks and Romans. Homer mentions a sacrifice under a beautiful plane, καλη υπο πλατανιςω. The philosophical conversations of Socrates are represented as passing under its shade, and the academic groves, so celebrated, were formed of it. The Romans delighted in it, and many of them carried their veneration so far as to water it, if I may use the expression, with wine. They thought it not enough, in beautifying their magnificent buildings, to have recourse to architecture, sculpture, and painting; but sought from the hand of nature the chief ornament of their elegant recesses, the lofty and diffusive plane-tree.

Nor have the moderns been wanting in respect to it, if it be true, as I have somewhere read, that the French once prohibited all persons from planting the tree who were under the rank of noblemen; and even exacted a fine from every plebeian who aspired to the honour of sitting in its shade.

A tree distinguished by the admiration of philosophers, poets, nobles, kings, and in the politest ages and countries of the world, cannot but be interesting to the modern observer, if it were only considered as a curiosity. The man of classical taste will view it with sentiments similar to those which he feels in the contemplation of antique vases, urns, medals, statues, the relics of ancient taste, and the monuments of oriental magnificence. But even in England, a cold northern country, where I imagine its growth is impeded by an uncongenial climate, the plane appears with a degree of beauty which seems to justify the admiration of the ancients. Its ample foliage, of a vivid and durable verdure, its pleasing outline, formed by the extremity of the branches, and its tall and stately stem, distinguish it most honourably in those modern plantations of England, where every goodly tree that will vegetate is sure to find a place. In our country, shade, to afford which this tree seems to have been formed by benignant nature, is not, during any long time, in any part of the day or year, necessary to indulgence. It is therefore less valued here than in warmer climates, where it united, in a high degree, embellishment and utility. I never could learn that it was of much use as timber; and, honoured as I wish it to be in the pleasure-ground and park, I hope it will not supersede the oak in the forest.

The oak itself is, indeed, a first-rate beauty, when it grows in rude magnificence, unembarrased by other trees too near to admit its expansion. It is itself a noble image, and if we associate the idea of strength with grace, it is difficult not to be enamoured with the *tout ensemble*, like the eastern prince with his plane-tree.

To a man of taste in trees, there is scarcely a native of the forest which has not charms to captivate. And why should not a taste for trees be cultivated as well as for flowers, birds, shells, or any other production of nature? It is equally pleasing when once formed, and it has something in it more sublime and elevating, as an oak and cedar are grander objects than the tulip, the ranunculus, or the carnation.

But, say the men of business and gravity, is it worth while to bestow any great degree of attention on any of these objects, which, as matters of mere contemplation, are trifling and of little use? I answer, that as God has placed man in a theatre, with faculties to perceive beauty, and with beauty to be perceived, it would be a sullen stupidity and ingratitude not to look and be delighted. Man, it is true, has many serious duties to perform, and many evils to suffer; and it was for this reason that so many refreshments were placed by a kind Providence within his reach. And, indeed, it has always and justly been said, that few things are so conducive to piety as the contemplation of nature, that knowledge which Solomon possessed, who knew every tree and plant, from the cedar to the hyssop on the wall.

A great part of mankind come into the world surrounded by opulence, and really have so little to do of necessity, that if they do not form a taste for science in general, and for a knowledge of nature in particular, they will be strongly tempted to do nothing, or something worse than nothing, to seek in vice a refuge from the pain of inaction. But when a man has once become an elegant spectator of the vegetable world, of trees in particular, which every where occur, he will be able to gratify his taste, without trouble, without expense, without danger of corruption, and with a probability of moral and religious improvement, arising from reflexion.

The mere man of this world, the votary of avarice and ambition, sees more charms in 'Change-Alley, or at a levee of a great man, than nature throughout all her works is able to display. But surely his pleasures are alloyed by anxiety and disappointment; and he might take more delight even in them, if they were diversified by a taste for the delights of nature exhibited on the mountain, or in the forest; and indeed in the garden, as it is now laid out in England, with a close imitation of the inventress of all real horticultural beauty, majestic yet simple Nature. I pity the man from my heart, who cannot, like Xerxes, forget a while pomp, power, and riches, and fall in love with a tree. Adieu.

EVENING XXXI.

ON WRITING MODERN BOOKS IN THE LATIN LANGUAGE.

BOCCACE and Petrarch wrote Italian with such purity, and advanced its elegances to such a degree of classical perfection, that a party was formed in Italy, soon after their appearance, to supersede the practice of writing the Latin language.

That men should utter their ideas, on all occasions, in their own country, in the language which they learn from their parents, is the dictate of nature; and it seems, at first sight, as improper to lay it aside for the sake of using a dead language, as to amputate one's legs in order to wear a pair of wooden ones, or to part with one's natural teeth to be supplied with a set by Messrs. Spence and Ruspini.

But the practice of writing in Latin has always found powerful advocates; and there are certainly many reasons which formerly rendered it highly proper, and may now cause it to be sometimes retained.

If an author's native language is rude, harsh, unmusical in sound, and scanty in signification, he will naturally wish to find a better, that the fruits of his study and reflexion may not lose their value in the eyes of those for whom they are designed, by the meanness of the vehicle in which they are conveyed and presented. What Dædalus would work in bone, in preference to ivory; with brick, rather than with marble?

Latin has long been the universal language of the learned. Whatever is communicated by it, is immediately understood by all the literati in the more enlightened nations of the world: and, if it is of consequence enough to deserve the labour, they translate it into their several vernacular languages, for the benefit of the unlearned. A light is thus held up, which scatters its radiance far and wide, and by which the most distant countries may illume their own torches, and shed a splendour over the remotest and the darkest corners; but if the original light had been so placed as to be visible to one country only, its diffusion would certainly have been retarded, and possibly circumscribed within the narrow boundaries, in which it first appeared. The writing in Latin has, therefore, contributed greatly to extend and facilitate the acquisition of science throughout Europe.

He, who writes in Latin, not only consults the diffusion of his works, but their duration. He builds his edifice with marble, he forms his statue of gold, and they consequently possess a value, and a strength, which no time can depreciate or corrode. But had he written in Dutch, Welsh, or even in English, as it appeared a few centuries ago; his work would have fallen to decay, like a hovel of wood, or have crumbled into dust, like an image of clay.

The practice of writing in Latin contributes greatly to preserve the national attention to that noble language, and to the fine authors in it, which a kind Providence has snatched from the wreck of time. How much the improvement of the human mind depends upon preserving a taste for them, let experience determine. When they were neglected, every one knows how dark a night of ignorance overshadowed the world; when they were recalled from their concealments, a cheerful, a glorious sun arose in the horizon, and at once chased away the gloom of ignorance, and the phantoms of superstition. Liberty and science reared their heads; and religion herself was not ashamed to own great obligations to the writings of Greece and Rome. If they should be neglected again, though I will not say a similar darkness would ensue ; yet I may venture to express an apprehension, that the love of liberty, sound learning, and rational piety, would be in danger of a decline. As an academical exercise, the practice of writing Latin should be carefully retained ; and some works, such as I shall hereafter mention, should, even now, be written in Latin, not only without incurring the imputation of pedantry, but with the praise of prudence.

The best judges have allowed, that an imitation of the fine writers of antiquity contributes greatly, in every country, to excellence in vernacular composition. Taste is improved by it ; and taste, once well regulated, will extend its influence to every part of a student's productions. He who can write well in Latin will be able, by transferring his attention to the best models of his own country, to select and imitate their beauties, and to write equally well in his native language. He who writes a language not natural to him, must write with great attention and care, to write it well ; and thus he gains a habit of correctness, which will not fail to operate upon him whenever he sits down to compose in any language.

But it must be allowed, that the principal cause of writing in Latin, the unfitness of modern languages for elegant composition, no longer exists. A general ardour for improvements of language has pervaded Europe. The love of reading has demanded books without number, in the respective dialects of the several nations of Europe ; and vernacular writers, emulous of excellence, have laboured with unwearied diligence, both in the selection and structure of their own language.

But though the necessity of writing in Latin is happily removed, yet the expediency of it, in several cases, remains to this period unaltered, because it is founded in reason.

All new philosophical and theological opinions, which, though they have the appearance of probability, are yet far from being indubitably established, might, with great propriety, be published in Latin, and locked up from those injudicious and half learned persons, who may pervert them to their own essential injury.

Controversies in divinity often divulge doctrines and doubts, which the unbelieving and the malignant eagerly embrace, and zealously disseminate. When they appear in English, the lowest of the people acquaint themselves with them imperfectly, either in the books themselves, or in the extracts which the press liberally multiplies, in a free country. As these persons are not duly prepared by education, or previous reading, it is probable that they will misunderstand them, and ignorantly fall into all the errors of infidelity. But if they were retained among the learned by a language known only to the learned, such parts of them alone might be communicated to the public, as were likely to be beneficial. The old distinction of esoteric and exoteric doctrines was founded in sound policy.

Medical books and cases might, with great propriety, be written in Latin, both that the information they convey might be immediately diffused over foreign nations, and also, that invalids of little learning and judgment might not be tempted to tamper with their constitutions, and to imagine themselves afflicted with every disease whose causes and symptoms they read and adopt, in their hours of morbid dejection. Some inconvenience might, indeed, arise from the ignorance of the inferior practitioners in medicine; but this would, in time, operate in causing more care to be taken in their classical education.

All communications to the public, which concern foreign nations as much as the native country of the author, and which are of so delicate a kind as to endanger the happiness of the illiterate or injudicious reader, might, without the imputation of pedantry or labour ill bestowed, be presented to the world in the universal language of the learned.

But I am aware that those who pretend to peculiar liberality will be ready to object to my doctrine, as favouring of papal tyranny, and as having a tendency to retain the vulgar in an ignorance which may facilitate the deception of them, for mercenary and political purposes. I have no such design; but mean to prevent the errors of those who are not qualified to judge of many important points for themselves; but who are tempted to read, and to form opinions from books obtruded on their notice, and inviting their attention, by the circumstance of appearing in their native language. There is certainly a sort and degree of ignorance, which conduces to happiness; and a knowledge so imperfect, yet so bold, as to increase misery, by increasing error and temerity.

But though I think, that many scientific, philosophical, and theological, and medical treatises, might, with great propriety, appear among us in Latin; yet, I know, that there is little probability of their being often produced in any other than the mother tongue. There is a confirmed neglect of Latin composition in both readers and writers; and the venders of books will be naturally disinclined to encourage the production of commodities which can find but a partial and confined acceptance.

EVENING XXXII.

ON ASPIRING TO THE CHARACTER OF LEARNING WITHOUT
ANY JUST PRETENSIONS TO IT.

ALL kinds of deceit and affectation deserve to be
detected and exposed to censure, if it were only that
truth may not be overborne and discouraged by their
prevalence. It is certainly injurious to society, that
a composition should be sold for diamonds, and the
counterfeit of Birmingham pass in currency for the
coin of the Mint in the Tower.

Among a variety of arts practised by many of the
vain and superficial in the present age, who make it
their first object to be admired by the company
into which they happen to fall, is that of endeavouring to shine as men of skill in science, as well as in
the art of pleasing, and of a taste in books as well
as in buckles. Unfortunately, their attention to
trifles in their youth has prevented them for acquiring a store of real learning, and they are therefore obliged to have recourse to hooks and baits in
fishing for literary praise.

They take as much care as they can to give the
conversation a literary tone, only when they are
sure the company makes no pretensions to excellence in literature. If there be a scholar among
them, they are shy of it, and introduce subjects
connected with the gay world, and slily throw contempt on learning as pedantry.

I have sometimes been diverted with hearing one
of these gentlemen harangue in a semicircle of ladies
and beaux on the character of the classics, talk of
the beauty of the oriental languages (in which he
comprehended the Greek and Roman), and admire
the original Latin of Homer, and the fine Greek of
Virgil, though, as I had been credibly informed, he

never could proceed at the grammar-school beyond Cordery's Colloquies, with Clarke's translation, and had been removed thence to a shop, where he had served behind a counter seven years, without looking into any other book than Kent's Directory. But he had come to a fortune lately, and having been already a beau, had been led, by making out as well as he could the meaning of Chesterfield's Letters, to attempt to please in all companies, and to affect the character of all-accomplished. From reading the pamphlets and papers of the day, he had picked up a few phrases, which he hardly understood, on most subjects ; and, I assure you, was considered by the party, in which he displayed his talents, not only as a very agreeable man, but also as a very good scholar, happily uniting in himself, to the confusion of pedants, solid sense with graceful accomplishments. He was a great quoter of verses ; not that his stock was very large. I believe he might have learned by heart a hundred lines in all, from various poets, on various subjects ; and by well timing his quotations, he passed for a man not only of singular taste in poetry, but of a prodigious memory.

This artifice of quoting is often practised by those who, without being coxcombs, like the above-mentioned gentleman, in dress and the graces, wish to obtain an esteem and reputation as men of letters, to which they possess no just claim. I know a man who has read a little, but is by no means distinguished for his learning or genius, and who having committed about forty lines of Homer to his memory, when a schoolboy, contrives to introduce a few sounding verses in all strange company, with such address as to put himself off for a wonderful classic ; whereas, in truth, he now never reads any thing but Hoyle, the Court Calendar, and the newspapers.

Quoters are indeed very numerous, and I must acknowledge, that they are often very entertaining; but they must not, however, steal away the palm of learning by legerdemain, or a *deceptio visus*, which too often succeeds with common company. It is very easy for any man, who does not employ his studious hours in a better way, to commit to memory, like a schoolboy's task, a number of beautiful passages, in prose and verse, on subjects likely to occur in the course of various conversations. And though I give the quoters the praise of pleasant companions, provided they are not too prolix, yet they should not be suffered to impose on mankind so much, as to assume a superiority over real scholars, who have been treasuring up original ideas, while the quoters have been imitating parrots or professed spouters, in committing words only to memory, purposely for the sake of ostentation.

There are many who assume the office and authority of critics in all literature who have no pretension to judgment beyond the cut of a coat, the neatness of a shoe, the style of hair-dressing, a minuet, or the dress of an actor or actress on the stage. They have caught a kind of technical phraseology from periodical and newspaper criticisms, and they utter their opinions, like oracles, in the little audience which has learned to look up to them as to dictators. A new book is for the most part severely handled by them, especially if it happens to take with the public, and is really a good one. It argues a wonderful perspicacity in them to be able to find out defects in works which the million are fools enough to buy and admire. They do not, indeed, make a point of reading the books they condemn or praise. They are furnished with vague terms of general praise and censure, and can give laws to their subjects, like the tyrant who said, My will stands for my reason.

The using of long words, derived from the Greek or Latin, commonly called hard words, has long been an artifice of those who wished for the praise of learning and knowledge, without giving themselves the trouble to acquire them. Apothecaries are often ridiculed for their use of medical terms, which they often misunderstand and misapply; but when they use them among the illiterate to raise opinion, their " *ampullæ et sesquipedalia verba*" may have a good effect; for whatever contributes to increase confidence in the medical practitioner, contributes, at the same time, to the cure of many distempers. By the way, I must repeatedly inculcate, how desirable it is that apothecaries, to whom the first application is made in the greatest distresses of human nature, had a more liberal education than can fall to the lot of those who, at the age of fourteen, or earlier, are bound to a long state of mechanical servitude.

Freethinkers, libertines, infidels, prating disputants in divinity and morality, with little learning and no principle, are very apt to add an authority to their conversation, by using expressions which they do not understand, and citing books which they never read, or totally misunderstood. Their affectation deserves not only ridicule, but all the severity of satire, all the insult of contempt. They produce false or mistaken authorities as genuine, which mislead hearers, who might be proof against the nonsense of their sophistry, if it were unembellished by the pomp of unintelligible words, and unsupported by the appearance of a solid and profound erudition.

With respect to the mere pretender to learning, who attempts not to corrupt or mislead his simple

admirers, though his affectation is ridiculous, yet it is
certainly less culpable in conversation than scandal
or indecency.   One may freely pardon one who, in
order to appear a man of science and philosophy,
reads on the temporary topic, previously to his entering into company ; as I remember a gentleman
who always made it his practice, on the appearance
of an eclipse, a comet, or the rumour of an earth-
quake, to retail an article from Chambers's Dictionary
on the subject, in all the various companies into
which he fell, so as to raise a very exalted opinion
of his learning, and an idea that he was as well acquainted with all parts of science as with these,
though in fact he understood nothing perfectly but
the first four rules of arithmetic.

The evil of this affectation is, that it is a deceit,
and no deceit should be in general tolerated in
conversation, because it diminishes the confidence of
society ; that it often overbears the modest scholar,
for ignorance is bold and vehement ; and that it
diffuses error, by asserting things without knowledge, and without examination, as truths confirmed
and indisputable.

I do not condemn the principle which stimulates
men to wish for the esteem which is due to science ;
it is often a laudable, and always an innocent principle ; but I wish it to operate in another manner,
in exciting a degree of industry which may enable
men to acquire that knowledge of which they soli-
citously seek the appearance.   The trouble often
taken to support the false glitter, might obtain a
considerable portion of the solid gold ; and would
probably improve the mind in the research, so as to
be superior to all the little arts of empty ostentation ;
arts which fail of their design, and cause a contempt
of those who might pass unobserved, or even be

honourably noticed, if they were contented with their own plumes. Nobody ridiculed the poor daw, till he attempted to deck himself in the feathers of the peacock.

EVENING XXXIII.

ON THE BOASTED SUPERIORITY OF ANCIENT TO MODERN ELOQUENCE.

It is impossible to read the accounts of ancient orators without being struck with the strong expressions with which their eloquence is characterised. It is frequently compared to thunder and lightning, to a storm, a tempest, and a torrent, forcing all before it with irresistible impetuosity.

Now some of the most celebrated orations, of which so much is said, have fortunately descended to modern times, in a state of perfect integrity. Yet let them be read, or pronounced from memory, by the most accomplished speakers of modern times, and, I believe, no such violent effects will be experienced, as can justify the strong expressions in which they have been commended. They will, indeed, be approved and admired ; but approbation is a cold sentiment, and even admiration itself is far removed from the enthusiastical extasy in which the rhetoricians praise the ancient orators.

The subjects of the ancient orations, it may be said, are now no longer interesting, and the language neither so well pronounced, nor so perfectly understood, as by those to whom it was the mother tongue. This consideration will certainly account, in some degree, though, I think, not entirely, for the indifference with which passages are received, which are said to have set whole nations in a flame, and to have produced revolutions of empire.

But I am of opinion, that the principal reason why orations had more effect in ancient times than in the present, is, that the art of multiplying books being unknown, men could not gratify their curiosity, or inform their understandings on the subject of politics, but by the oral communications of some distinguished statesman or eloquent demagogue.

It was scarcely possible, when books were so scarce as they must have been before the invention of printing, that the multitude could be able to improve their minds, and to derive information from reading. When they wished to gratify their thirst for knowledge, they could not, like the modern inhabitants of a great city, run to a coffee-house, or send for a pamphlet, and read the speeches of great men in their closets, but were obliged to crowd the forum, or public place of assembly. There they listened to the orator as to an oracle. A moderate degree of excellence would delight them; because it conveyed those ideas, or that information, which they in vain sought from any other source; but when to information was added the charm of real elegance, and the force and fire of true genius, they were then at last ravished and enraptured.

In a country where books were extremely uncommon among the vulgar, and yet, at the same time, where the great had easy access to them; and, by their examples and improvements, had diffused a taste for literary exertions, and particularly for eloquence, the effect of oratory on the common people must have been great, for this among other reasons: their feelings were not worn and jaded by an excessive application, as is too much the case in modern times, when men are so much in the habit of reading all kinds of books, addressed to all the passions and powers of the mind, that at last they cease, from mere satiety, to be affected with any extraordinary emotions, even where the excellence of a speech might otherwise justly excite them. They acquire so general a knowledge, that few things retain the grace of novelty. But in an assembly of the common people at Athens and Rome, almost every thing which came from the mouth of the orators was new to the ears of the people, affected them with the liveliest impressions, and raised their astonishment, while it inflamed their passions, and gratified their curiosity.

The common people in England, who have not anticipated the subjects on which an orator is to speak, by their own reflexions, and by reading, are much more affected, and more violently moved with what they hear, than the delicate, the refined, the enlightened student. They remember a speech longer, and entertain a much higher opinion of the speaker. But the majority of a Roman and Grecian audience, in an assembly of the people at large, consisted of those who were totally unacquainted with books, and whose minds were so open and disengaged, as to afford ample scope for the whole force of art and genius combined in the subtle and accomplished orator.

Whether the old Romans and Athenians had tempers more susceptible than the moderns may admit of doubt. It appears to me rather unphilosophical, to attribute so much influence as to suppose intellectual perfection to depend entirely upon it; or at least, to imagine, that the same influence which the climate of Greece and Rome possessed in ages of antiquity should not operate at present; which, I believe, it does not, as the modern Greeks and Romans by no means prove, by their public exertions, any just claim to mental supe-

riority, over the present inhabitants of France,
Britain, and Ireland, the barbarians of antiquity.
. There have been those who have predicted, that
the time will yet come, when some modern genius,
furnished by nature with every gift, and by art with
every improvement, will arise and astonish the
world with the effects of an eloquence similar in
kind, and superior in degree, to all the celebrated
oratory of Greece and Rome. None can confidently divine how far human excellence may advance ; but whether eloquence, oral eloquence, is
so beneficial in modern times, as it was in ancient,
I will not determine. I think its necessity is greatly
lessened since the invention of printing. For what
can the most excellent oral eloquence effect in comparison with the productions of the press ? Oral
eloquence is naturally circumscribed within the
compass of a human voice, which can reach only to
few ears compared with the rest of mankind ; who,
if they could all be supposed present in one place,
would not be able to imbibe the sound emitted by
the loudest organs of utterance. But oral eloquence
is not only confined to the limits of the voice, but,
for the most part, to a room, a hall, a court, or a
senate-house. If its effects were not confined in
extent, they are, of necessity, limited, as far as they
depend on actual delivery, within the bounds of a
very short duration. A few hours of vehement
exertion will fatigue the most powerful speaker, and
silence him by the infirmity of his body, even
though the powers and resources of his mind should
continue unexhausted.

Oral eloquence, as displayed in public harangues,
is, therefore, of much less value to the public, than
the eloquence of written composition. It serves,
indeed, many temporary and valuable purposes,

promotes private interest, raises friends, fortune, characters, and is therefore greatly to be esteemed, and studiously cultivated; but, after all, it is not, since books have abounded, indispensably essential to the welfare of society, nor absolutely necessary to the improvement of human nature. These grand purposes may be more effectually and more extensively accomplished by the able writer.

It is certain, that an eloquence, which, like that of the ancients, is said to astonish like thunder, and carry all before it, like lightning, and a torrent, may be used in effecting bad purposes as well as good, in hurting as well as in serving society ; and, therefore, its value must depend upon the honesty and good principles of those who possess it in perfection. In the possession of bad men, it is always to be suspected. In the possession of good men, it cannot do so much good as a written discourse, sent into the wide world by the operation of that providential discovery, the typographical art, the most important in effect which the world ever received.

There is, however, no danger lest oral eloquence should want cultivation. It is necessary at the bar, and the senate ; and, by serving temporary and political purposes, contributes more than any thing else to gratify the importunate cravings of ambition.

By the term oral eloquence, I for the most part mean, in this paper, public harangues in the senate, in the council, in the field, and in the tribunal ; I do not comprehend under it the eloquence of conversation, which is always of high value ; and deserves to be cultivated with assiduity, by all who wish to taste some of the highest and purest pleasures of their existence.

EVENING XXXIV.

ON THE MANNERS PREVALENT AT SOME PUBLIC SCHOOLS.

SIR,—I am aware that the dispute concerning the preference of private schools to public, or of public to private, is as trite as the common observations on the weather. I mean not to trouble you with comparisons, but to acquaint you with my own case, and leave you to form your own opinion.

I am confident, that I derived some of the greatest vices and misfortunes of my life from a fashionable school. I was placed there when I was but an infant, and lived as a *fag* under a state of oppression, from my school-fellows, unknown to any slave in the plantations. Many hardships I suffered by day; but I would have borne them without complaint, if I had been permitted to repose at night, and enjoy those sweet slumbers which my fatigue and my age invited : but several nights in a week I was disturbed, at various hours, from the mere wantonness of cruelty, thrust out of bed, and, in the coldest weather, stript of the clothes. My health and my growth, I have no doubt, were injured by the ill usage I suffered, and the constant fear in which I spent my infant days. I was beaten by the senior boys without the least reason, and often robbed of the little solace I had sought, by expending my pocket allowance with the old apple woman. It would be tedious to enumerate the various hardships I underwent before I was twelve years old. Let it be sufficient to say, that in the age of innocence, I suffered in mind and body more than many adult criminals who are convicted of flagrant violations of the laws of their country. My instructors, in the mean time, were mild, and my parents, affectionate; but the wanton tyranny of my school-fellows prevented me from enjoying either ease from clemency, or delight from the tenderness of parental love.

As I grew older, I was emancipated from the slavery, and perhaps became a tyrant in my turn, though I believe I had learned compassion from my own misery. But I was delivered from one kind of slavery only to relapse into another; for, as I mixed among great boys, it became necessary, as I thought, to adopt their manners and their vices.

One of the first bad propensities I acquired was, to a profusion of expense, and to the supply of my pecuniary deficiencies by running in debt, wherever I could gain credit, either in purchasing my indulgences or in borrowing money. I had, indeed, in common with several others of my class, some very expensive habits; for I went daily to a pastry-cook's or the coffee-house, and very often to the play clandestinely. My pocket allowance was one shilling a week; a mere trifle, and by no means commensurate to my out-goings; in consequence of which I learned to take the methods practised by many others, which were to pawn at some distant house, known by the sign of the three golden balls, whatever I had possession of, either from the indulgence of relations, or as a necessary apparatus of a scholar. My watch has been in pawn a hundred times before I was fifteen. My books were sold as soon as I moved into a higher class, where they were not immediately wanted, and pawned, whenever I had an opportunity of supplying their place, on the day we were to read them, by borrowing others of some boy whom I could beat into compliance. A thousand other tricks were played to raise money, many of which had a tendency to destroy, in the very bud,

all principles of real honour and common honesty.
And the intemperance, both in eating and drinking,
which the money we received from our friends, and
raised by our wits, enabled us to indulge in, I am
convinced, laid the foundation for many chronical
distempers, which, at the very moment while I am
writing, render my existence painful, and will probably abbreviate it.

There prevailed an opinion, not only among the
boys, but among some parents, that to be mischievous
and wicked was a sign of spirit and genius; and our
sallies were often encouraged by smiles of approbation, though corrected by the official discipline of
the masters whenever they were discovered. It was
thought an honour to suffer in a good cause, and we
despised the rod, while we were talked of as heroes
by the poor people whom we injured, by the little
boys who admired us, and by *quondam* scholars, who
used frequently to say, that they were quite as bad,
or worse than we, when they were at school. I am
ashamed to relate the cruel and unjust feats, which we
performed; but we were admired, and the more we
distinguished ourselves in these ways, the more likely
we were thought to become, one day, ministers of
state, archbishops, or lord chancellors.

Just before we went to college, we concluded that
we were men, and rushed into vices which naturally
and unavoidably produced loathsome diseases; but
even these we considered as feathers in our caps,
and as manly distinctions. It may be thought extraordinary, but it is true, that few of us deemed
ourselves sufficiently qualified for college till we had
run deeply in debt with a surgeon.

In the midst of such cares and employments, it
cannot be supposed that we paid much attention to
the object of education, the improvement of our-

selves in valuable and polite knowledge. Indeed, we were not anxious on that subject; if we could but prove our parts, and excite the admiration of young noblemen, as great geniuses, by our vicious exploits. The grand purpose was to display parts and spirit; and we had often heard that the only way to be a great man, was to be a libertine. I am sorry to say, that even our parents, many of whom had been at the school before us, did not discourage our irregularities as they ought to have done, but laughed at them with apparent complacency.

I have found since, that we were not sent to school so much to acquire learning as to make connexions; that is, to make ourselves agreeable sycophants, or humble companions to some great man, who might take us by the hand, as it is called, and place us hereafter on the episcopal or judicial bench. Alas! the end, supposing it is likely to be accomplished, was not worth the means! The means were such as tended to destroy every purpose, and every end for which a good man wishes to live. Health, learning, fame, fortune, conscience, fell an early sacrifice. I censure not the schools themselves, nor the masters, who were, I fear, unable to stem the foul and rapid torrent of fashion, ignorance, impudence, and folly united.

But I condemn parents, who cannot but see these things, and yet will not co-operate with masters in the restoration of salutary discipline; who, for the mere chance of a fortunate connexion, risque every thing that is rationally valuable; who talk of their children's flagrant enormities as harmless and laughable frolics, puerile levities, fine ebullitions of spirit, which mark a sprightliness of parts, and promise future eminence. I cannot help, at the same time, despising those persons who are always boasting, before boys, and others, of their own foolish feats at school, and endeavouring to make it appear that they were as mischievous, wicked, and malicious, as a truly diabolical spirit could render them, at an age when every lovely quality is the natural growth of the unpolluted mind. Much of the ill conduct of boys, and young men, arises from the conversation of those silly triflers, and I have reason to lament that I ever heard it.

Your's, &c.
SERO SAPIENS.

EVENING XXXV.

ON PROLOGUES AND EPILOGUES.

A PROLOGUE is a prefatory address to the spectators in a theatre, containing either an apology for the poet, a recommendation of the plot, or a brief narration of whatever concerns either the story or the composition of the piece. It is not properly an essential part of the drama, but merely accessary.

It has been divided by the critics into two sorts: the *monoprosopos*, or that which is spoken by one person; and the *diprosopos*, or that which is spoken by two. The former kind is the most usual; though there are instances of the latter both among the ancients and the moderns. Thus Plautus introduces his *Trinummus*, with a dialogue between *Luxury* and *Poverty*; in the prologue to the *Rivals*, Mr. Sheridan has formed a dialogue between a sergeant at law and an attorney; and Mr. Garrick's epilogue to the *English Merchant*, consists of a conversation between Lady Alton and Spatter.

It is curious to observe the hard names which the pedantry of criticism has given to the various sorts of prologues. They tell us there are three sorts; the *hypothetic*, the *systatic*, and the *anaphoric*. The hypothetic, contains the argument of the piece; the systatic, recommends the fable or the poet to the people; and the anaphoric, refutes objections, recriminates opposers, or returns thanks to the audience. But these terms seem only contrived by literary pride to give an air of importance to trifles, and an appearance of learned obscurity to things sufficiently obvious to common sense.

The prologues and epilogues of modern times differ much from those of the ancient drama. They were dull, heavy, spiritless, and uninteresting; and when contrasted with the lively turn of modern prologues, they are scarcely better than dead small-beer compared to Champaigne, or water-gruel to Madeira.

The modern prologues and epilogues (for I unite them, as they are similar) are so totally different from the models afforded by antiquity, that I am induced to consider them as *poematia sui generis*, and of modern invention. As to rules for them, which the old critics were fond of prescribing for all kinds of poetry, they are so little subject to control, as hardly to be conformable to any rules, but those which are obviously suggested by that best of criticism, the criticism of common sense.

The style which they chiefly require is evidently the colloquial or epigrammatic. They are so Proteus-like in their form, that they may be either as comical as a farce, or as serious as a sermon. In the hands of Addison, Johnson, and Pope, they sometimes resemble the satires of Juvenal; in those of Foote and Garrick, they have all the lively urbanity of Horace.

Many excellent examples of both kinds are extant, and may constitute a general division of the prologue and epilogue style into the serious and the comical.

So great a latitude do these little essays claim, that they are found to have been well received, when they have had scarcely any connexion with the dramas to which they have been prefixed or appended. Their general object has been to put the audience in good humour; and this they have accomplished the better, by their oddity and eccentricity. Any whimsical idea, pursued in familiar verse for a few minutes, has served the purpose of amusement, and raised the wished-for smile.

As their end is to conciliate favour, and avert displeasure, they should certainly be respectful, though not mean; supplicatory, though not abject. They will indeed seldom obtain their end by supplication without wit; but there is a decorum in their assuming the air of a petition. They may even approach with the tone of a sturdy beggar, provided that they display humour and ingenuity to keep their audacity in countenance.

In the days of Shakspeare, prologues and epilogues seem to have been in their infantine state. Shakspeare's plays wanted not so slight a recommendation, and it must be owned, they have it not. Nothing can be quainter, and more uncouth, than the greater part of Shakspeare's prologues and epilogues. They were not much in fashion, and he did not exert the vigour of his genius to produce what was not demanded with eagerness.

Dryden was the most celebrated writer of prologues and epilogues of any recorded in the history of the English drama. His nervous lines were well adapted to the purpose. Wit, satire, force, and fire, give his compositions of this kind a decided superiority over all the flimsy, flippant rhymes of the modern poetasters. His are like solid surloin, theirs like whipt syllabub.

It has become much the fashion of the times, among the mob of gentlemen who write with ease, to aim at a sprig of bays, by writing prologues and epilogues. Too lazy, or too weak, to attempt a dramatic piece, they hope to share the poet's fame, and become talked of in the circles of fashion, by scribbling a few pert rhymes, by way of prologue or epilogue. The poet is glad of a fashionable name to give him a little countenance among people of ton, and admits compositions as harbingers, or followers, of his pieces, which, it is probable, he could greatly excel, if he chose to compose his own prologue and epilogue.

It might, however, be useful to hint to some of the fine gentlemen, that pertness is not wit, nor rhyme poetry. Coxcombs, and men of ton, should confine themselves to their proper sphere, their toilettes, their stables, and their race-grounds. They may plume themselves on their boots, buckles, and head-dresses; but should not wish to divide the praise of the real poet, by a trifling copy of verses, in which they might be outdone by many a schoolboy, and many a rhyming lady. But their vanity would en-gross all kinds of praise; and steal even the laurel from the poor poet's brow, who has no other pro-tection but its shade; and a cold shade it is, if we may form a judgment of it from boxes, pit, and gal-leries, thinly filled with orders; and from the copy-money of dramas that scarcely repay the expenses of their publication.

EVENING XXXVI.

ON THE LITERARY CHARACTER OF ARCHBISHOP SECKER.

THE foundation of that singular eminence and dignity to which archbishop Secker arrived, was laid at the academy of Mr. Jones, a dissenting teacher of Gloucester, who had the honour to educate another most excellent divine, that shining ornament of the church and nation, bishop Butler.

It may reasonably be concluded, that the person who trained two characters so distinguished, was himself respectable ; and he certainly deserves the esteem of posterity, if it were only that two such lights of the church as Secker and Butler derived from his lamp their early lustre.

The character of Mr. Jones could not, I imagine, have been perfectly known to the biographers of the archbishop, Dr. Porteus and Dr. Stinton, whose reputed benevolence and liberality forbid one to believe that they would have spoken rather slightingly of Mr. Jones, if they had known how much he was esteemed by the archbishop, and how well he appears to have deserved the most honourable mention. Their words are—" The archbishop received his education at several private schools and academies in the country. . . . . In one or other of these seminaries he had the good fortune to meet, and to form an acquaintance, with several persons of great abilities. Among the rest, in the academy of *one Mr. Jones,* kept first at Gloucester, then at Tewkesbury, he laid the foundation of a strict friendship with Mr. Joseph Butler, afterwards bishop of Durham."

They say nothing of improvements made at *one* Mr. Jones's academy, but only of a connexion which he had the good fortune to make there. I am convinced, from their characters, that they could not intend to undervalue Mr. Jones merely because he was a dissenter, and his academy was not honoured with the distinctions of the two *Almæ Matres.* But I believe, they might not have seen Mr. Secker's pleasing letter concerning Mr. Jones, not many years ago presented to the public by that good Christian, Dr. Gibbons, in his life of Dr. Watts.

Let us hear the exemplary youth, for such he appears to have been, thus speaking of his preceptor, the Rev. Mr. Samuel Jones.

" Mr. Jones," says he, in a letter to Dr. Watts, " I take to be a man of real piety, great learning, and an agreeable temper ; one who is very diligent in instructing all under his care, very well qualified to give instructions, and whose well-managed familiarity will always make him respected. He is very strict in keeping good order, and will effectually preserve his pupils from negligence and immorality. And accordingly I believe, there are not many academies freer, in general, from those vices than we are, . . . We shall have gone through our course in about four years time, which I believe nobody that once knows Mr. Jones will think too long. . . . . We pass our time very agreeably betwixt study and conversation with our tutor, who is always ready to discourse freely of any thing that is useful, and allows us, either then or at lecture, all imaginable liberty of making objections against his opinion, and prosecuting them as far as we can. In this and every thing else he shows himself so much a gentleman, and manifests so great an affection and tenderness for his pupils, as cannot but command respect and love."

The future archbishop gives a short account of Mr. Jones, and his plan, in the sequel ; and it is impossible not to think highly of the preceptor, and to lament that he should be spoken of as an obscure person, scarcely worthy of mention in the life of his scholar, afterwards the most distinguished primate of his time in Christendom.

I believe it to have been a very happy circumstance, for Mr. Secker, that he was educated in a dissenting academy, and under so good a tutor. I attribute much of his future eminence to this circumstance, as well as to the connexion he fortunately formed there; that purity, that dignity, that decency of character which enabled him to fill the great offices of the church with singular weight and efficacy. There may have been deeper scholars, or greater divines, but there has seldom been a prelate of more personal authority, and in whom ecclesiastical dignity shone with brighter effulgence.

He was not without enemies, and many prejudices were formed against him; but this is no new phenomenon in the moral world. I also once considered him as a worldly politician, who depended chiefly on external appearance, on distance or dissimulation, for the attainment of respect. I thought him an artificial character; but, though he might not be without pride, and might assume something of a behaviour rather affected and reserved, yet, upon a review of his life and works, both literary and moral, he appears to be one of those whom posterity will consider as a truly great man. His charity, and his industry, were singularly great. But I refer my reader to his biographers for his general character, while I amuse myself with the contemplation of him chiefly as a man of letters.

Educated in the dissenting persuasion, and under dissenting tutors, he had paid less attention to polite letters, and more to divinity, than is usually bestowed

by students in the universities. Young men in
Oxford and Cambridge frequently arrive at an age
for orders, and become successful candidates for
them, who have studied scarcely any other divinity
than such as is to be found in Ovid's Metamorphosis,
and Tooke's Pantheon. Hebrew they usually neglect, as partaking but little of classic elegance; but
Mr. Secker, at the age of eighteen, says, speaking
of Mr. Jones's method, " I began to learn Hebrew
as soon as I came hither, and find myself able
now to construe, and give some grammatical account
of about twenty verses in the easier parts of the Bible,
after less than an hour's preparation. We read every
day two verses a-piece in the Hebrew Bible, which
we turn into Greek, no one knowing which his verses
shall be, though at first it was otherwise."

"By the time he was three and twenty," his
biographers relate, " he had read over carefully a
great part of the Scriptures, particularly the New
Testament in the original, and the best comments
upon it, Eusebius's Ecclesiastical History, the apos-
tolical Fathers, Whiston's Primitive Christianity,
and the principal writers for and against ministerial
and lay conformity, with many others of the most
esteemed treatises in theology."

Few regularly bred divines, as they are termed, apply themselves to divinity at so early an age; and, indeed, through the defect of a knowledge, and of a taste
for it in youth, many, after obtaining orders, still continue to study, if they study at all, the theology of
Athens and Rome. But the dissenters study divinity
at an early age, and if they had united the study of
the belles lettres with it in a due proportion, I believe their divines would have made a still more
honourable appearance than they have done, though
they are, and ever have been, highly respectable.

The belles lettres enable a man to adorn his knowledge, and recommend his writings to general notice. If Dr. Secker had united a little more polite learning to his theology, I think his writings would have been more popular. They want the graces of a beautiful style and diction.

But it will be said, that he was a very popular preacher; and how could he become so great a favourite if his language were not elegant, nor his style of eloquence adorned by the captivating graces of classical beauty? I answer, by the solidity of his reasoning, united with the authority of his person, the gravity of his manner, and the sanctity of his character.

" Quid isthoc erat eloquentiæ admirabilis," says Dr. John Burton, " quod a plerisque tam magnificè prædicatum accepimus? Non sanè in sententiis δεινοτης Demosthenica, non dictionis ardor splendorque, non ingenii exultantis lusus, non rhetoricorum pigmenta, et quæ aures delinire solet, periordi decurrentis clausula numerosa et canora; verum erat in sententiis αχριβολογια planè Aristotelica, stylique penitus castigata luxuries, nihil operosè elaboratum, nihil temerè effusum: pro re natâ sine fuco, sine ornatu dictionis, casta simplicitas: quicquid illud erat, verbis inerat το τις ον et in popularium aures animosque influebat mitis oratio: gustûs decori gratia, et in vultu placida severitas, singula commendavit; imo et dictis quasi Fideæ imperavit ipsa dicentis authoritas. Quod erat philosophi et theologi, satis habuit distinctè, graviter dicere; quod vero erat rhetorum, ornatè dicere, ille non tam nescivit, quam ultrò neglexit. Quid multa? Orator hic noster sine dicendi artificio veram eloquentiæ laudem consecutus videbatur."

" Ornatè dicere," says Dr. Burton, " ultro neglexit;" but Dr. Burton, on this occasion, is a professed panegyrist, displaying his own eloquence in the encomiastic style. If Dr. Secker had been a polite writer, he would have sometimes shown the graces of fine composition without intending it. Many of his writings are addressed to the learned, to whom *ornatè dicere* would not have been improper. Few who possess a beautiful style choose to conceal their talent on all occasions, though before hearers of ordinary capacities, and coarse taste, they may either think that it is not worth while to produce any thing elaborate, or that the plainer and less adorned their style, the more intelligible and effectual will be their discourse; but Dr. Secker preached most of his sermons before the politest congregation in England; and the graces of diction would not have failed to have been tasted by those who frequented St. James's church. In the vicinity of a court, it could not be said, when he displayed the beauties of language, that he was casting pearls before swine.

But it is candid to suppose, that he was influenced by the example of St. Paul, who glories that his preaching was not with enticing words of man's wisdom, not as pleasing men, but God, who trieth the heart. It has been said, *Cujuscunque orationem vides politam et solicitam, scito animum in pusillis occupatum.* But perhaps this doctrine is chiefly inculcated by those who revile the excellence which they cannot reach. Why should eloquence, which serves all other causes most essentially, be prohibited from becoming the handmaid of divinity?

If however his composition is not elegant, what rendered him popular? His elocution, the grace and dignity of his person, the earnestness and gravity with which he enforced his solid doctrines.

It has not yet been considered duly whether his style is Attic. I think it is not; as it appears to me rather to approach to the dry and the jejune. They who affect atticism in antiquity frequently fell into the dull. The attic style may be compared to the dress of the Quakers. It is neatness without finery, and without superfluity. But the dry style may rather be said to resemble the Sunday dress of a country hind. It is clean; it has no splendour indeed, but at the same time it has no grace. It has no attraction from shape or colour; perhaps it rather disgusts by its meanness and poverty. The jejune style suggests not the idea of a healthy living body, but of a body dried by art for the purpose of the anatomist.

There is a great difference in the discourses of Dr. Secker. Some are, if it is possible, too plain, unless they were formed for the congregation of Cuddesden, a little village near Oxford, where Dr. Secker, when bishop of that see, long resided and officiated as a parish-priest. If he thus adapted his discourses to his audience, he is worthy of more praise than any excellence of style can procure. And there is reason to think he did, as his Act Sermon before the university of Oxford, and several others, are written in a very pleasing and correct style, and such as may perhaps justly deserve the name of the attic. Though, after all, the style is not the excellence on which any of his sermons are chiefly to be valued.

They all abound in good sense, and solid observations, collected by a cautious judgment, from remarks on real life and experience. They abound in fruit; while many rhetorical declamations, much more popular in the great city, have little to recommend them but transitory and barren blossoms.

The cool, dispassionate style of Dr. Secker is the style of truth and good sense; and it is to be wished, that all hearers and readers had good sense enough to give it due attention. But, in order to this, they must be all rational; they must be that already which it is the design of sermons to render them; so that, for the purpose of attaching the minds of a mixed multitude, the passions and imagination must be sometimes addressed. But too great an attention to these leads to a false glare, an unsubstantial eloquence, that glitters indeed like base metal, when new, but soon loses its lustre, and possesses neither the beauty nor the value of pure gold.

I do not know whether the style of Secker's sermons is to be recommended as a model; but I am sure their good sense, their candour, their dispassionate manner, are such as must be approved by all who unite a sound judgment with their zeal for religion. There are few pieces of didactic divinity more excellent than the catechetical lectures. They are at once rational and pious, learned and familiar. His charges to the clergy are given in a style of authority becoming a great prelate, and contain such admonition as, if followed, cannot fail to render the clerical function the most honourable in fact, as it is in idea, of all that supply the various wants of a well-regulated society.

EVENING XXXVII.

ON DRYDEN'S CELEBRATED ODE ON ST. CECILIA'S DAY.

If a foreigner were to ask an Englishman for the best specimen of lyric poety in the English language, I have no doubt but that he would be presented with Dryden's Ode on St. Cecilia's Day.   This celebrated piece is supposed to have reached the pinnacle of excellence, to have surpassed Horace, and rivalled Pindar.

An ode could never have been so universally renowned, without intrinsic and extraordinary merit. Its beauties have been felt as well as understood. The heart and the ear have decided in its favour, previously to the determination of the judgment. I acknowledge and admire its excellence; but I must be so far guilty of critical detraction as to say, that its merit appears to me to have been over-rated, and that, in my opinion, it is not the best Ode in the language.

There are blemishes in it, which sully the lustre of its beauties; there are lownesses in it, which degrade its sublimity; there are vulgarities of expression, which at once destroy its elegance, and debilitate its pathos.

The plan is excellent, the spirit noble; and my chief objection is to the choice of words, which, according to all the rules of criticism, and the dictates of natural taste, should be peculiarly delicate in the Ode.

The word "belyed," in the line,

A dragon's fiery form *belyed* the God,

is beneath the dignity of the serious lyric, and inconsistent with the sublime idea of the God of heaven and earth metamorphosed to the fiery form of a dragon.

His "stamping an image of himself," as he was then in the image of a dragon, conveys to a careless reader the idea of his having stamped a dragon.

Bacchus is represented, at least to the mind of a

mere English reader, in a manner unknown to classical antiquity :

> Flush'd with a purple grace
> He shows his honest face.

These lines exhibit the picture of a drunken sot, with bloated cheeks and a red nose; though the poet himself has just described the God, as " Ever fair and ever young." The line, " He shows his honest face," is in a style so familiar and colloquial as to militate against the dignity and matron-like decorum of the lyric muse. Honest, indeed, in its truly classical signification, is a very elegant expression, synonymous with beautiful ; but not one English reader in a hundred understands the epithet any otherwise than as it is often applied to a drunkard, or *bon vivant*, when he is called an honest fellow; that is, a jolly Bacchanalian. It was a reason against Dryden's using this epithet, even if he intended it in its classical sense, that it was sure to be misunderstood by the majority of his readers. Virgil, speaking of Bacchus, says,

> Quocunque Deus caput egit honestum.

And Dryden probably had this very line in view ; but "honest," in this classical sense, is not yet naturalized in England, and therefore it was injudicious in Dryden to use it. " Honest," conveys the idea of a mere good-humoured plumpness of face, a broad grinning mirth ; whereas the old classics speak of Bacchus, as remarkable for the delicacy of his countenance. They attribute to him the *virginea forma et virgineum caput :* not the immutable rubicundity, and stupid fatness, of a brandy-faced landlady.

Dryden was a remarkably good classic, and could

not but know the mode in which Bacchus is delineated by the poets; therefore there is every reason to think, that he chose the epithet "honest," intending to display his classical knowledge and
taste; and, had he written to none but classical
scholars, his epithet would have been applauded
without one dissentient voice: but, to the common
reader, it gives an image very different from that
which existed in the poet's mind. It exhibits such
a Bacchus as we see dangling from a country sign-
post, astride on a tun. It disgraces the Ode, and
renders it, in this part, little superior to the song of
an Alexander Stevens, roared by a club of sots in
an alehouse. The other lines,

> *Drinking* joys did first ordain,
> *Drinking* is the soldier's pleasure;

are coarsely expressed, and more characteristic of
Tom D'Urfey, than of Pindar.

The greater part of the subsequent stanzas is
either truly pathetic, or sublime. Yet I cannot
admire, in an Ode said to equal, or surpass, every
thing in lyric sublimity and grace, such lines as

> Thus, long ago,
> Ere heaving *bellows* learned to blow.

The bellows being a culinary machine, strikes the
ear with a vulgar sound, and the mind with a vulgar idea. The poet should have spoken of the bellows by an elegant periphrasis, or some name removed from plebian use. The bellows, in this
place, if I may be allowed a frigid joke, blows out
much of the poetic fire.

That creeping, sluggish Alexandrine,

> With nature's mother-wit and arts unknown before,

is flat and prosaic. "Mother-wit," is a term which

the sublime muse of the lyre, in her better judgment, would not have adopted.

But I recollect the censure that has justly fallen on Zoilus, and on all the race of hypercritics : I recollect also the trite idea of finding spots in the sun. I must therefore apologize to the reader, for the liberty I have taken with this celebrated Ode, by declaring that I do not mean to deny that it possesses a very high rank; but only to controvert its claim to the highest rank among the lyric poems of England.

Gray, as a poet of the lyre, appears to me to be more uniformly grand and majestic. The mind is elevated by him to ethereal regions, and soars with eagle flight, without being forced to fall from its eminence, like the son of Dædalus. Gray wins his way on high like a glorious luminary, all stately, all regulary magnificent; Dryden rises like an air balloon, which now and then breaks, and tumbles precipitately down, contrary to the intention of the conductor of it, and to the great mortification of the gaping spectators.

The above strictures may expose me to the anger of the irritable sons of Aristarchus. I shall only observe, that on literary subjects like these, though there may be reason for dissent, I cannot see any occasion for the bitterness of malice.

EVENING XXXVIII.

ON INSCRIPTIONS AND THE LAPIDARY STYLE.

As the space on monuments, columns, and sepulchres, which admits of inscription, is usually too little to contain many words; it is necessary that the words which its limits are capable of receiving

should be expressive of as much meaning as words
are able to convey, and be couched in a style as
forcible as rhetoric can devise.

The smallness of the space devoted to the writing,
and the trouble and difficulty of writing on stone,
marble, and brass, were the reasons why abbrevia-
tions abounded on the ancient inscriptions, and, indeed, furnish the principle of that rule which pre-
scribes for them a laconic brevity of style.   Convenience or necessity are the foundation of all rules
which are worth observation.

Indeed, if these causes for brevity had not existed,
it would have been still very desirable, since inscriptions were to be read by the passenger as he jour-
nied on his way, to whom it might not be convenient to be detained ; and since, also it was
to be wished, that they might be remembered as
well as read, brevity certainly facilitated this desirable purpose.

But brevity alone would be a poor recommendation of the lapidary style.   It admits of point,
antithesis, harmony, and sublimity.   It is a style,
participating of prose and poetry ; in a due mixture
of which consists its peculiar character.   The cold,
the dull, the humble, and the mean, it rejects with
contempt.   Whatever is noble in sentiment, or
forcible in expression, whatever is lively, animated,
nervous, and emphatic, forms an essential ingredient
in the lapidary style.

The churches, and church-yards of England, furnish many examples of sepulchral inscriptions, which
would do honour to the best ages of antiquity.   At
the same time they exhibit others, which excite sentiments very unnatural in a church or church-yard ;
those arising from the absurd and the laughable.

For the credit of the country, in the eyes of

foreigners as well as natives, I therefore think it would be right, if the rectors and vicars of parishes were to claim the privilege of revising and correcting the epitaphs which are to be consigned to posterity by the faithful marble. It might, indeed, be considered as an infringement of liberty, if they were to assume a right to dictate the matter of an epitaph; but to reform the style, and to prevent the appearance of ridiculous and ungrammatical inscriptions, would be to consult the honour of the defunct, and of the surviving friend. Every epitaph, at least from the meaner people, should be submitted, in manuscript, to the clergyman of the parish, before it is given to the stone-cutter to be indelibly engraved. Travellers would then visit the repositories of the dead with improvement and rational pleasure; I say rational pleasure, for the pleasure which they often derive from laughing at the absurdity of the tomb-stone, is such as reason cannot approve.

Westminster Abbey affords many fine models; but it would have afforded more, if many of the epitaphs had not been merely historical. Monuments intended to perpetuate characters, which might afford topics for the sublime and pathetic, present a tedious detail of dates, as little affecting the heart as a common paragraph in a newspaper announcing a death, or an article in the parish register. It appears, indeed, that much more reliance is placed on the sculptor of the tomb, than on the writer of the epitaph; whereas, a very plain tablet, with a fine inscription, would redound more to the fame of the departed and of his family, than the mausoleum of a monarch, or the most exquisite chiseling of a Bacon or Roubilliac.

It is a question, whether epitaphs on extraor-

dinary persons should be in Latin or in English?
Attached, as I acknowledge myself, to the elegance
of the Latin language in the lapidary style, I rather
give a preference to the English, for the obvious
reason of its greater intelligibility.　We find many
excellent epitaphs in Latin, in country churches and
church-yards, where scarcely any one enters once in
seven years who understands Latin, save the minister of the parish.　Nothing, in such cases, is usually
known of the party, by the common parishioner,
but his name.　The principal end of the monument
is therefore defeated, by the writing in an unknown
tongue.　And, indeed, in churches more frequented
by scholars than rural places of worship, why should
not the epitaphs be equally obvious to all?　The
English language is able to express every idea of
the human mind with force and beauty; and there
are examples of epitaphs in English cemeteries which
equal, in every excellence of style, the best inscriptions of ancient Greece and Rome.

Latin is, indeed, confessedly well adapted to the
style of inscriptions; but that it is not intelligible
to all who may wish to read the epitaph, is a sufficient reason for its rejection from the greater part
of monumental inscriptions.　The best reason for
its use is, that it enables foreigners, unacquainted
with English, to read them; but though foreigners
may frequently visit Westminster-Abbey, yet their
presence in country churches is too rare to require
such a piece of complaisance, as, while it accommodates them, must be inconvenient to the natives,
the neighbours, and the parishioners.

Epitaphs are either in verse or prose; and it
may admit of inquiry, whether verse or prose is
to be preferred? Verse is more easily remembered,
and there are certainly many very fine ones in

verse; but yet I rather prefer a measured prose. I think the best epitaphs, both in Latin and English, are in that sort of prose, which, though it is not confined to metre, is formed by the rules of a rhythm, highly gratifying to the ear, and capable of exhibiting the most striking beauties of splendid composition.

But the lapidary style, though most frequently used in sepulchral inscriptions, is not confined to them. It is required on statues, obelisks, and public buildings; and many fine pieces of art are disgraced by the tablet which gives the history of the person, event, or foundation, intended to be honoured by it. Artists, founders, and public societies should bestow as much pains on the style of the inscription, as on sculpturing the block, polishing the surface, or adorning the pile by architectural embellishments.

I cannot quit the subject without remarking, that there is now a prevailing mode of cutting the letters on the tablet, which injures the inscription, by rendering its real beauties less obvious to the reader. For the sake of gaining room, the lines are not separately inscribed as they were written, but joined together with tasteless continuity. Thus the rhythm that was judiciously marked by the writer, is confounded; and not easily to be developed, but by eyes and ears more delicate and critical than usually belong to the majority of passengers, or the common readers of monumental inscriptions.

EVENING XXXIX.

ON THE IDEA OF THE ANCIENTS CONCERNING THE CRIME OF PERJURY.

An apprehension has been expressed by good and wise men, that the religion of an oath is, in the

present age, less and less regarded. Indeed, the
infidel principles which have been recently diffused
with uncommon industry and art, have an immediate tendency to produce, in a reading age, this
shocking corruption.

Sunt qui in Fortunæ jam casibus omnia ponunt
Et nullo credunt, mundum rectore moveri,
Naturâ volvente vices et lucis et anni,
Atque ideo intrepidè quæcunque altaria tangunt.

JUVENAL.

Those writers who call themselves philosophical
philanthropists, and who, in the calm retreat of their
museums, indulge their vanity by composing treatises against religion, would do well to consider a
moment, that they are opening a door for villains
to enter and break down every salutary restraint of
law and equity. If such writers really have that
regard which they profess for mankind, let them
prove it, not by disseminating ideas which introduce
confusion and every evil work, but by adding force
to those awful sanctions which are found by experience to increase confidence between man and man,
and to facilitate intercourse, by rendering contracts
inviolable and testimony credible.

But the general subject of oaths and their violation has been amply discussed by divines and casu-
ists, and common sense must see at once the sad
effects of prevailing perjury.

I shall present the reader with a few ideas of
the ancient heathens on oaths, and the punishment due to the violation of them. Those who
unfortunately neglect Christianity, and the admo-
nitions of the Christian divine, may, perhaps, pay
some attention to the opinions of men who were
guided merely by their reason in stigmatizing this
atrocious offence.

Agamemnon, in Homer, swears, that he delivers up Chryseis inviolate, by the furies who punish the perjured, not only here, but ΥΠΟ ΓΑΙΑΝ, under the earth :

———Εριννυες, αι δ᾽ υπο γαιαν
Ανθρωπους τιννυνlαι, ὁτις κ᾽ επιορκον ομοσση.

And he concludes with solemnly wishing, that if he had sworn falsely, he might suffer all those many sorrows which the gods award to him who offends them by perjury.

Ει δε τι των δ᾽ επιορκον, εμοι θεα ΑΛΓΕΑ δοιεν
ΠΟΛΛΑ ΜΑΛ᾽, ὁσσα διδουσιν, ὁτις σφ᾽ αλιτηlαι ομοσσας.

Hesiod affords reason to believe that the creed of his age respecting perjury was, that the sin of the perjured father was visited on the children as well as on himself.

Ος δε και μαρτυριησιν εκων επιορκον ομοσσας
Ψευσεται, εν δε δικην ελαψας, ΝΗΚΕΣΤΟΝ ΛΑΣΘΗ.
Του δε τ᾽ αμαυροτερη γενεη μετοπισθε λελειπται.

" Whoever willingly swears a false oath in giving his evidence, and injures justice, inflicts on himself an injury without remedy, and his generation after him shall fall to decay."

In the idea of the ancients, every false oath was an imprecation of vengeance on the head of him who swore ; and it was common for the hearers to call down the wrath of heaven on the violator. In the covenant between Menelaus and Paris, previously to the single combat, after the slaughter of the lambs, and the libation of the wine, the people said with one accord,

" Most glorious and almighty Jove and the other immortal gods, whoever first shall violate his oath, may their brains be shed on the ground like this wine, both theirs and their children's; and may their wives be ravished."

Ζευ κυδιςε, μεγιςε, και αθανατοι Θεοι αλλοι,
Οππoτεροι προτεροι υπερ ὁρκια πημηνειαν,
Ωδε σ' εγκεφαλος χαμαδις ρεοι ὡς ὁδε οινος,
Αυτων, και τεκεων· αλοχοι δ' αλλοισι μιγειεν.

Here also prevails an idea that the punishment of perjury was to be extended to posterity; an idea never entertained but when the crime was considered of a most flagitious nature.

The epithet ορκιος was applied to Jupiter in particular, by which was intended to be signified, that to him belonged vengeance for violated oaths. The general idea was, that the crime was of such magnitude as not to be punished sufficiently by human laws, and that Heaven itself visited the perjured with peculiar misfortunes. Hesiod represents the Furies going their circuit, every fifth day of the month, to haunt the bosom of the perjured wretch.

Εν πεμπλη γαρ φασιν Εριννυας αμφιπολευειν
Ορκον τιννυμενας.———

In the *Bouleuterion*, or Council Chamber of Olympia, there was a menacing statue of Jupiter, with a thunderbolt in each hand, and an inscription on the base, denouncing woe to him who should call the god a witness to a falsehood.

In some countries, the punishment by human law was death, and in others, that kind and degree of penalty, whatever it might be, which the culprit, whom the false witness endeavoured to injure, would have undergone if the perjury had been believed.

I cannot help thinking, while I am on this subject, of the solemn words in our communion service. If we take the sacrament (which is a solemn oath) unworthily, "We kindle God's wrath against us, we provoke him to plague us with divers diseases, and sundry kinds of death." I wish those who are capable of perjury would apply these dreadful words to the commission of that crime. The ancients certainly did believe that such would be the consequence of it.

They seem also to have had an imperfect idea of that law in which it is awfully said, " I the Lord thy God am a jealous God, and visit the sins of the fathers upon the children unto the third and fourth generation of them that hate me, and show mercy unto thousands in them that love me and keep my commandments." For their doctrine is, on one hand, that

> In natum dilata ruunt perjuria patris,
> Et pœnam merito filius ore luit.   CLAUDIAN.

and on the other, that

> Ανδρος δ' ευορκον γενεη μετοπισθεν αμεινων.

The idea was universal among them that the punishment, though tardy, was certain and dreadful, and that the progeny of the perjured was involved in the punishment.

Similar opinions occur in Ecclesiasticus. " A man that uses much swearing shall be filled with iniquity, and ' the plague shall never depart from his house.' If he shall offend, his sin shall be upon him ; and if he swears falsely, ' his house shall be full of calamities.'"

What was the cause of the destruction of Troy, but perjury ? The violated oath of Laomedon and its effects, in this instance, though but a fable, show the sentiments of the ancients on its dreadful criminality.

Diodorus Siculus relates that perjury was punished with death among the Egyptians, as a crime which at once violated the piety due to the gods, and destroyed confidence among men, the strongest bond of human society. A milder sentence prevailed afterwards, according to the celebrated law of the Twelve Tables,—" Let the divine punishment of perjury be destruction; and the human, disgrace—Perjurii pœna divina, exitium; humana, dedecus;" accordingly, with us it is punished with the pillory.

Strabo says, that the crime was capital among the Scythians; and, among the Indians, punished by cutting off the fingers and toes; and I believe there are countries where the tongue, as the offending member, was amputated by the public executioner.

From every inquiry, it appears that the heathens considered the crime of false-swearing as most offensive to God and man. To the gods its punishment was in great part left, with a full persuasion that vengeance would be taken, though not immediately, yet severely and dreadfully. In this particular, Christians surely have much greater reason to stand in awe, and sin not. I omit passages from Scripture on the subject, as they are obvious, and as I intended only to produce the opinions and practices of those who could not be influenced by Christianity.

But if the crime becomes more frequent among us than it was formerly, it is incumbent on the rulers of the nation to investigate and rescind the causes, and to encourage religion and its professors by their countenance and example.

The multiplication of oaths in petty offices, in law business of small consequence, and in commercial transactions, as at the Custom-house in particular, conduces greatly to lessen the veneration due to an oath, and to increase perjury.

On the frequency of oaths, hear the heathen philosophers. " Avoid oaths entirely, if possible," says

Epictetus; "if not, as much as you can." And Simplicius adds, that swearing should be utterly declined unless on occasions of the highest moment. "Some," says Eusebius, in a passage quoted by Stobœus, "advise men to take care that what they swear is the truth; but I advise them not to swear at all, if they can easily avoid it." The words of Hierocles are remarkable:

Εν τη συνεχεια του ομνυειν ραδιως αν μεταπεσοι τις εις επιορκιαν—Ουτω γαρ αν τηρησαιμεν το αει ευορκειν, ει μη καταχρησοιμεθα τοις ορκοις.

"In the frequency of oaths any man may easily fall into perjury. We may preserve ourselves free from perjury, if we do not use oaths frequently and unnecessarily."

What would these sensible and pious ancients have said, if they had heard the oaths administered at public offices, in courts of justice, and other places, on trifling occasions, by attornies, clerks, and cryers, who read the most awful forms just as if they were running over a lease, or galloping through lands, messuages, tenements, and hereditaments? But this haste and indecency is unavoidable, say they, because it is necessary for the dispatch of business.—Of business, Sir, says the clerk in office, or the attorney, knitting his brow, and looking with all the air of self importance.—And what business? Is it such as will justify endangering the peace of mind, and the everlasting happiness of ourselves and our fellow-creatures? O, Sir, no preaching, says the clerk, or attorney, for the justices or commissioners are just come—here, take the book, five or six of ye, and swear away—there, there—very well—kiss the book—you kiss your thumb—kiss the book, I say—there—So help you God.—Call the rest—come, make haste—here is room for more thumbs upon the book.

—We cannot stay here all day—swear away, I say—So help you God—*tactis sacrosanctis Christi Evangeliis!*

How must the awe which the common people entertain for God and magistracy be diminished, by proceedings thus hasty and irreverent, in the midst of noise, riot, and confusion! Government must lay in more timber for pillories, if oaths are thus administered, and if infidelity is encouraged by the example of the Great.

Let modern experience determine whether the opinion of the ancient is not true, when he says,

Φυεται εκ πολιορκιας Ψευδορκια.   PHILO.

" False swearing is the natural consequence of much swearing."

EVENING XL.

ON THE POSSIBILITY OF ADVANCING SACRED POETRY TO GREAT PERFECTION.

Sir,

THERE is, I think, a prejudice against sacred poetry which cannot be justified. To praise God with the voice of pious gratitude, and to celebrate him with that genius which he gave, is the noblest employment of the mind of man. I wish, indeed, that more men of genius had undertaken this office. But men of genius have been seduced by the world. They wished very naturally for praise ; and they thought sacred poetry not likely to confer it in the same degree as profane. If Shakspeare, Dryden, and Pope, had directed their powers to it, great would have been the effect! If they had struck the Davidean lyre, what multitudes would have joined in the song, and have been led by melody to the altar, and from the altar of the church to the choir of heaven,

It has been concluded from the rarity of excellence in sacred poetry, that it is scarcely attainable; that there is some insurmountable obstacle to perfection in its very nature; that sacred subjects are already so exalted that poetry cannot raise them any higher. It is true, that moderate poetry cannot raise them; but what think you of Milton's muse? Cowley very justly says, " none but a good artist will know how to do it : neither must we think to cut and polish diamonds with so little pains and skill as we do marble : for if any man design to compose a sacred poem, by only turning a story of the Scripture, like Mr. Quarles, or some other godly matter, like Mr. Haywood of Angels, into rhyme, he is so far from elevating of poesie that he only abases divinity. He who can write a profane poem well, may write a divine one better; but he who can do that but ill, will do this much worse."

Divinity has been too often debased in England by bad poetry : but even that bad poetry has had a good effect on corresponding readers. It has pleased and informed those who were bad critics, though good men. Youth and ignorance have been induced by rhymes and metre to learn by heart valuable instruction. Minds that could not rise to the elevation of Milton have been nourished by the humble poetry of the good Watts. That saint (for he has a better title to the name than many in the Calendar) often sung sweetly; but there was something wanting to make his songs generally acceptable to the lovers of classical poetry. " His devotional poetry," says Johnson, " is, like that of others, unsatisfactory. The paucity of its topics enforces perpetual repetition, and the sanctity of the matter rejects the ornaments of figurative diction."

Johnson's judgment of Watts as a poet appears to

be just.   But if he means to affirm of sacred poetry,
that its topics are few, and that it rejects the ornaments of figurative diction, I think his opinion liable
to controversy.   There is no subject of morality,
copious as it is, which will not admit of being spi-
ritualised.   Heaven, hell, earth, and sea, abound
with topics for sacred poetry.   But the critic says,
" the sanctity of the matter rejects the ornaments
of figurative diction: " an opinion formed with less
deliberation than most of the decisions of this judicious writer; for is not the model of all sacred
poetry, that of the Bible, more figurative than any
other?   Figures are no where more abundant, nor
more lively, than in Isaiah, the Psalms, and the
Song of Solomon.   If the ornaments of figurative
diction are not frequent in Watts, there is reason to
believe the poet voluntarily sunk himself in the devotee.   In the preface to his imitation of the Psalms,
he says, " I am sensible I have often subdued my
style below the esteem of the critics, because I
would neither indulge any bold metaphors, nor admit of hard words, nor tempt an ignorant worshipper
to sing without understanding."   In his preface to
his Hymns, he says, " The metaphors are generally
sunk to the level of vulgar capacities. . . . Some of
the beauties of poesie are neglected, and some wil-
fully defaced. . . . I have given an alloy to my
verse, lest a more exalted turn of thought or language should disturb the devotion."

An estimate, therefore, of what may be done in
sacred poetry must not be formed from what has
been done by Watts; for he professedly lowered
his genius, and wrote below his own standard, for
the sake of accommodating his readers in humble
life, who were not judges of poetry, but who, in the
offices of devotion, stood most in need of assist-

ance. That singular virtue can never be sufficiently esteemed, which mortified the pride of human nature, by sacrificing the love of praise to the desire of doing good among those whose esteem is too often little valued, the poor and the uninstructed.

But there are many in whom exalted piety and refined taste are happily combined. From these a higher style of devotional poetry is justly required; and therefore I cannot help wishing that some of the greatest poets had exerted themselves in sacred poetry, and produced works of prime merit and value, and fit to be placed among the first classics of our country.

It cannot be said that nothing is extant of this kind. Milton's works are very much in the style of sacred poetry. Cowley's Davideis indeed is not esteemed a fortunate attempt. Pope's Universal Prayer and Messiah show what he could have done if he had chosen to bend the force of his genius to it. Addison had a turn for it, and succeeded well in his imitation of the Psalms. Young has deserved the reputation he has gained on sacred subjects, by his sublimity and originality.

Authors of inferior genius have abounded in the walk of sacred poetry. Mrs. Rowe has delighted many readers. Merrick's genius was formed for sacred verse. But a multitude of poems and divine songs have had nothing about them divine but the epithet in the title-page. The great numbers of rhymers pretending to sacred poetry evince that there is a great love of the subject. It is a fertile field, from which, when the sun of true genius shall shine upon it, a fine crop of fruits, and a beautiful display of flowers, may reasonably be expected.

Mr. Seaton's prizes at Cambridge were laudably intended to turn the attention to sacred poetry.

But, as I have elsewhere observed, though prizes excite a great deal of useful and elegant mediocrity,
they have seldom called forth the display of first-
rate genius.   They have raised meteors, but not
created suns.   The Seatonian poems have however
to boast a Smart and a * Porteus, and many others,
who, if not equally known to fame, have singular
merit.   Free-born genius seems to stand too much
in awe of those who are to examine her pretensions,
and decree the prize.   In that servile state, the
noble freedom of genius seems lost in a timidity
which debilitates the mind.   Yet I do not know a
collection of poems, on divine subjects, more laudable
than those of the Seatonian poets, Bally, Glyn, Scot,
Hey, Jenner, and other successful candidates for
the prize.   The classical reader, of a serious and
religious turn, will rejoice to find in them a happy
union of classical elegance with pious sentiments.   I
wish this institution was more encouraged by public
notice, that the poet's emulation might be excited,
and a taste for poems which tend to inspire piety in
a most agreeable manner, rendered more prevailing.

If poets of the first-rate genius had dedicated
their talents to the sublimest subject, the great God
of heaven and earth, by hymns of gratitude, by celebrating his works, and recommending every moral
and religious duty of obedience to his will, with all
the charms of numbers, and in all the colours of a
fine imagination, they would have converted many
to Christianity, and inspired those with the love of
virtue who are now often seduced by the licentious
muse to vice and scepticism.   Let then men of genius enter this field ; and, lest they should think

---

* See his fine lines on *War*, in his Poem on Death, inserted in
" *Elegant Extracts.*"

the province does not belong to them, let them recollect that the example of composing hymns was
set by their great predecessors Homer and Callima-
chus; and that Milton derived from sacred subjects
a style of poetry which all the enlightened world
agree to admire.

EVENING XLI.

ON THE IMPROPRIETY OF SUBSTITUTING THE SACRED LATIN POETS IN THE PLACE OF THE LATIN CLASSICS AT SCHOOL.

It has been much the fashion among sceptical
writers to extol Julian the apostate. They are desirous of attributing to him every excellence, and
particularly the liberality of an enlightened philosopher. I leave it to the reader to judge how liberal
he was, when he prohibited all Christians the study
and attainment of Grecian literature. He meanly
hoped, by keeping them in ignorance, to be able to
effect that ruin, which all his power, and all the
wisdom and insolence of his adherents, was unable
to accomplish. He could not trust to a fair engagement in the controversial war; but interposed his
imperial authority to take the arms out of the hands
of his opponents, in order to oppress them with ineffectual resistance.

It was during this disgraceful prohibition of the
Greek authors that Apollinaris, to supply the Christians with classics of their own, wrote the history
and antiquities of the Hebrews to the reign of Saul, in
twenty-four books, and in a professed imitation of
Homer. Aspiring to supply the want of the classics
in all respects, he also imitated Menander in comedy,
Euripides in tragedy, and Pindar in lyric poetry.

It was a pious and a spirited design; but I cannot

help considering it as rather ridiculous, that a man should think it so easy a thing to supply, on an emergency, the loss of the finest writers in the world, by the substitution of his own hasty effusions. There is something mechanical in the idea. An artisan of the press might properly say, on hearing that books were destroyed or prohibited, " Regard it not, we can easily make others ;" but to sit down with as much coolness as you sit down to write a letter, to write such books as might supply the want of Homer, Menander, Euripides, and Pindar, argues either too high an opinion of the writer's own, or too low a one of their excellence.

The man undoubtedly meant well, and his works would have been valuable, as curiosities, if they had all descended to posterity. Sozomen, who probably speaks with the warmth of zeal, affirms that the imitations of Apollinaris equalled the originals.

As his Hebrew antiquities were intended for schools, whence the classics were at that time tyranically excluded, they might be truly useful. They might contribute greatly to diffuse a knowledge of Jewish history among the early Christians and converts from heathenism.

Many modern writers have, like Apollinaris, expressed a wish that the Christian classics were introduced into classical schools ; but I fear their zeal has exceeded their judgment.

The pious Monro, in his burning zeal to promote Christian education, says, " What can be more surprising than to find the Christian books so far discarded, that very few, if any of them, are to be found in our grammar schools ? . . . One need not scruple to say that Nonnus's metrical paraphrase of the Gospel of St. John is infinitely more fit to be put into the hands of Christian youth than Homer's

Iliads; and Macarius's Homilies than any part of the writings of the blasphemous Lucian. And certainly the very elegant and polite Orations of Muretus may be useful to the Christian youth on several accounts. And why should not the excellent poems of Prudentius, Nazianzen, Palingenius, Sedulius, and Textor, together with a great many more, both ancient and modern, Christian poets, particularly the several elegant Latin versions of the Psalms of David, as also the noble Greek paraphrase of the same divine book done in heroic verse by the celebrated Apollinaris, bishop of Laodicea, and designed originally for the benefit of the Christian youth; why should not, I say, the poems of such eminent and learned Christians, at least in Christian schools, be preferred before those of Ovid, Horace, or Martial, before Hesiod or Theocritus, or any other of the Pagan writers?"

With a spirit of fervent piety, the author proceeds to recommend the use of Christian poets in Christian schools. His persuasion will, however, be ineffectual; and indeed it must be owned, that what he says militates against a classical education in general; for whatever may be urged by such zealots, Homer, Virgil, Horace, and the other fine writers of the better ages, will never find equivalent substitutes in Apollinaris, Prudentius, Palingenius, Nazianzen, Sedulius, and Textor. A boy will not acquire classical taste from those who possess not classical beauty; and as to piety, he might probably learn the elements of it at least *as well* in prose and in his vernacular language.

The classics, in my opinion, should be cleared for the use of schools of all corrupting ideas and passages; and then they will not only not be hurtful, but highly improving both to morals and taste; for the morality in which they abound has the great advantage of being impressed on the mind with all the force of eloquence, and the captivating graces of polished language. Many of the Christian poets, whom the zeal of well-meaning persons would substitute in the place of the classics, have as little of poetry or elegance as they have of good sense.

Prudentius is esteemed the best among the Christian classics; and though I cannot think, with Sidonius Apollinaris, that he is to be compared to Horace, yet I have observed many passages which have such a degree of excellence as entitles them to the epithet, *pretty*. Prudentius was called by the old literati Amænus, as if it were his proper name.

The following passage from the *Hymnus Epiphaniæ* has been much and justly admired. The subject is, a congratulation of the Innocents massacred by Herod. It is quoted in Dr. Edward Sparke's *Scintilla Altaris*, or Primitive Devotion, and afterwards by Dr. Horne, in his Sermon on Innocents' day.

> Salvete, flores Martyrum,
> Quos lucis ipso in limine,
> Christi insecutor sustulit,
> Ceu turbo nascentes rosas.
> Vos, primæ, Christi victimæ,
> Grex immolatorum tener,
> Aram ante ipsam, simplices,
> Palmâ et coronis luditis.

Pious readers may find a good deal of amusement in the perusal of Prudentius; but then they must not read him as a classic of the first rank, to which elevation zealous devotees wish to raise him, and, in the very attempt to exalt, debase him.

The most esteemed poem, according to Crenius, is the tenth hymn of the Cathemeron, " in exequiis defunctorum." The eleventh of the same book, " octavo calendas Januarias," is extolled in high terms by Buckner, who calls it, " egregium ac plane divinum ; cui neque ad dictionis elegantiam nec concinnitatem numerorum tum inventionis acumen atque ingenium, quidquam deest."

Aurelius Prudentius Clemens was born in Spain about the year 348, and flourished in the reign of Theodosius the Great.

He first studied the law, and pleaded at the bar, and was afterwards promoted in the army and in civil rank, which is chiefly collected from his own verses:

> Frænos nobilium reximus urbium
> Jus civile bonis reddidimus, reos
> Tandem terruimus militiæ gradu
> Evectum pietas principis extulit.

There is but little known of his private life ; but it is generally believed that, after a life of civil honours, he died in old age.

In poetical excellence he rose greatly above the Christian poets of his time, though, after all, he cannot be said to have often surpassed the line of mediocrity. It is a great defect in him, as he does not compensate it by sublimity, that he scruples not to violate the common rules of prosody. A false quantity appears to him a venial poetic licence. Among many others, I select only the instance of γιδωλον, *Idolon*, the penultima of which he makes a short syllable.

He is not without his zealous encomiast. Barthius calls him a treasury of elegance, and a poet not to be passed over like one of a vulgar and common genius. He honours him with the name of the Divine Pindar.

In the *Scaligerana*, he is called not only a good but a very elegant poet. General praise however is little to be depended on.

Like a Christian, he speaks humbly of himself on all occasions, and by no means in the style of Horace's "Sublimi feriam carmine sydera."

Prudentius, valuing the praise of poetry less than of piety, remarks in a lowly strain :—

——————— loquendi
Cura de sanctis vitiosa non est,
Nec rudis unquam

He comforts himself with adding in another place,—

Adprobat tamen Deus
Pedestre Carmen et benignus audit.
Attamen vel infimam
Deo obsequelam præstitisse prodest
Quicquid illud accidet,
Juvabit ore personasse Christum.

It is common among all pious writers to declare, that they voluntarily renounce the elegances, the graces, the beauties of style and composition as beneath their dignity. It is certainly an ill-judged renunciation ; for why should not sacred subjects have a dress corresponding to their dignity, and why should profane and licentious compositions have advantages over them which will never fail to draw the attention of mankind, and frequently cause a majority of votes in their favour ?

EVENING XLII.

ON SOME OF THE SACRED POEMS OF VIDA AND OTHERS.

LATER poets have approached much nearer to Augustan elegance and purity, than those early Christians who wrote about the age of Prudentius, and who seem to have neither admired nor studied the best models of poetic diction. Their first object was the expression of devotional sentiment. So far they were indeed right; but as they thought it proper to express their piety in verse, it was surely worth while to render that verse agreeable to the reader, by the graces of a fine style. I am sure the cause of religion would have been greatly promoted by an union with elegance. They disgraced piety as far as they were able, by clothing her in a mean dress; and those who admired their sentiment could not but despise their diction.

Not so Marcus Hieronymus Vida. He drank at the Virgilian fountain; and borrowed the beauties of Pagan poetry to decorate the sentiments of Christian devotion.

> Sat ludo scenæque datum.
> Carmina nunc mutanda; novo nunc ore canendum
> Jamque alias Sylvas, alios accedere fontes
> Edico: jam nunc, polluto calle relicto,
> Hâc iter esto.———
> Quo rapior? quo vota trahunt? quæ tanta cupido
> Sevocat abductam mortali a corpore mentem
> Ignotasque vias laté jubet ire patentis
> Ætheris et liquido mihi sedem figere cœlo?
> Terra, vale; curæque humiles hominesque, valete. . .
> Tollor homo, totusque levem propé vertor in auram,
> Aeriasque plagas superare et linquere nubes
> Sub pedibus, rapidoque viam conjungere soli,
> Dulce mihi, summoque in vertice sistere mundi.

He goes on in a manner similar to this in a hymn to God the Father, of near one thousand lines, in which, lamenting his inability to do justice to his subject, he says,

> Sint ideo potius tibi nostra silentia laudi,
> O Deus, O jubar æternum! inviolabile lumen.

Which appears to me to have been imitated in Thomson's Hymn:

> ——— But I lose
> Myself in Him, in light ineffable.
> Come then, expressive Silence, muse his praise.

A similar fire from the altar glows with fervent heat through the hymns to the Son and Holy Ghost. If there is any fault, it is one which does honour to his invention, a too great exuberance, or even prolixity. There are many most animated passages in the hymn to the Holy Ghost; a fine subject for the sublimest genius.

An Deus in nobis?————
                   ———— Deus insidet ipse,
Intus agit Deus, et nostro se pectore versat. . . . .
Fallor? an ille ruit calor? ecce mihi artubus ardor
Ingruit; ante oculos lux en! mihi plurima oberrat.
———— Sancte, veni; penitus te mentibus insere nostris
Aura potens, amor omnipotens, cœli aurea flamma.

The whole volume of *Hymni de Rebus Divinis* breathes the spirit of divine love, and exhibits a great share of Virgilian grace. These qualities are the great *desiderata* in sacred poetry.

In his hymn on the Eucharist, speaking of the bread and wine, he very injudiciously calls one Ceres, and the other the draughts of Bacchus:

                   ———— nec crede sapori
Dum gustu exploras Cererem laticesque Lyæos.

But no wonder at any absurdities, when he was describing the transubstantiation.

Allowance must be made in reading Vida for many Popish errors, and some absurdities which arose from his desire of describing the doctrines of Christianity in the language of heathen mythology. Oil and vinegar would coalesce as soon as the polytheistical fictions of Greece and Rome with the pure religion of Jesus Christ.

I am aware that Julius Scaliger says of the hymns and eclogues, "Puerilia sunt et plebeia. Catulli venerum dum vult assequi, delicias lenociniis plebeias fecit." De Poet. lib. 6. But Julius Scaliger is a literary tyrant, and of his arbitrary dictation it may be said, " stat pro ratione voluntas."

As I have given a specimen of Prudentius on the subject of the Innocents, I will cite another from Vida on the same subject. Prudentius for once, perhaps, has the advantage.

> Beatæ animulæ, parvuli integelluli,
> Quos hausit immanissimi regis furor
> Ab ubere abreptos, parentium ab sinu,
> Dum perdere fimul autumat, regno cavens,
> Incognitum sibi aureum puellulum,
> Quem nuntiabat siderum præsentia,
> Regem universis nuper ortum gentibus.
> Vos vere veluti gemmulæ, quas primulo
> Adussit albicans pruina primulas,
> Ætatulæ ipso concidistis flosculo.
> Pro illo ante vobis contigit pulchrè mori
> Qui pro omnium vitâ immolandus venerat;
> Beatæ animulæ, flosculi cœlestium.

Vida's Christiad, though founded on a most sublime subject, is generally thought to possess but moderate merit. There is in it a deficiency of fire. But the poet was evidently awed by the grandeur of his enterprise ; and his genius sunk under his apprehensions of failure. I cite the following specimen on the Resurrection, a theme which might inspire the dullest of bards :

> Ibunt aligeri juvenes, cœlumque profundum
> Horrifico sonitu implebunt, atque ære recurvo
> Quatuor a ventis excibunt undique gentes:
> Judicis ad solium properabitur æthere toto :
> Ipse alte effultus, montisque in vertice summo,
> Arbiter effulgens circumferet ora tremenda,
> Secernetque pios, dextraque in parte locabit.

There is in this, and throughout the whole poem, an even tenor of elegant versification ; but there is too little of the *mens divinior*, and the *ignea vis.*

Perhaps the critics have expected too much in this poem; and, as it commonly happens, have in consequence of a disappointment of unreasonable hope, revenged themselves by a contempt equally unreasonable.

Vida is less known and read in Great Britain than the two Latin translators of the Psalms, George Buchanan and Arthur Jonston. But I consider Buchanan as one of the most illustrious ornaments of Scottish literature. He was born in 1506, and died in 1582. His works consist of a Dialogue de jure regni apud Scotos; the Grammatical Rudiments of Linacre, translated from English into Latin; the History of Scottish Affairs; a poetical paraphrase of David's Psalms; and a collection of miscellaneous Poems. Joseph Scaliger, in a complimentary copy of verses to Buchanan, says,

> Namque ad supremum perducta poetica culmen
>   In te stat, nec quo progrediatur, habet.
> Imperii fuerat Romani Scotia finis;
>   Romani eloquii Scotia finis erit.

He is extolled in the highest terms as an historian; but at present I am to consider him as the poetical paraphrast of the Psalms.

The ninth and tenth verses of the eighteenth Psalm are universally admired, even in the production of Thomas Sternhold : but as they are trite, I should not quote them but for the purpose of contrasting them with other translations.

> The Lord descended from above,
>   And bowed the heavens high,
> And underneath his feet he cast
>   The darkness of the sky.
> On Cherubs and on Cherubim
>   Full royally he rode,
> And on the wings of mighty winds
>   Came flying all abroad.

Merrick has given them thus :

> Incumbent on the bending sky,
> The Lord descended from on high,
> And bade the darkness of the pole
> Beneath his feet tremendous roll.
> The Cherub to his car he join'd,
> And on the wings of mightiest wind,
> As down to earth his journey lay,
> Resistless urged his rapid way.

Let us compare Buchanan's Translation.

> Utque suum Dominum terræ demittat in orbem
> Leniter inclinat jussum fastigia cœlum :
> Succedunt pedibus fuscæ caliginis umbræ ;
> Ille vehens curru volucri, cui flammeus ales
> Lora tenens levibus ventorum adremigat alis
> Se circum furvo nebularum involvit amictu
> Prætenditque cavis piceas in nubibus undas.

This is well paraphrased ; except perhaps that there is an unpardonable cacophony in terminating two succeeding lines with words so similar in sound as ales and alis. But this I confess is not the most favourable specimen of Buchanan ; and I by no means think it equals the admired sublimity of Sternhold, which probably was accidental.

It may not be disagreeable to present the same passage to the reader in the words of Arthur Jonston :

> Æthere depresso, solio descendit ab alto,
> Nubila sidereos implicuére pedes.
> Ventorum volucres humeris circumdedit alas
> Scandit et ætherei flammea terga chori.

The twenty-third Psalm is one of the most popular :

> The Lord my pasture shall prepare,
> And feed me with a shepherd's care, &c.

Buchanan translates it thus :

> Sicut pastor ovem me Dominus regit :
> Nil deerit penitus mihi.

Per campi viridis mitia pabula,
Quæ veris teneri pingit amænitas,
Nunc pascor placidè, nunc saturum latus
    Fessus molliter explico.
Puræ rivus aquæ leniter adstrepens
Membris restituit robora languidis
Et blando recreat fomite spiritus
    .   Solis sub face torridâ.

I subjoin the version of Jonston :

Blandus ut upilio, me pascit conditor orbis,
  Ne mihi quid desit, providus ille cavet.
Dat satur ut recubem pratorum in gramine molli ;
  Ducit et ad rivos lenè sonantis aquæ.

It is to be lamented that Jonston versified all the
Psalms in the elegiac measure, however different
their subject or style. His verses are pretty and
correct ; but he does not appear to reach the sub-
limer strains of David's lyre. But, lest I weary my
reader with Latin citations, I will conclude with a
short extract from a poetical paraphrase of the
twenty-third Psalm by Dr. Jortin.

Me tuos inter numerare, pastor
Summe, dignaris, quibus ipse virgâ
Aureâ ductor reseras beati
    Ruris honores.
Pascimur campis, ubi lene ridet
Florido natura decora cultu
Fonsque vitales saliente rivo
    Sufficit auras.

Such comparisons as these form one of the amusements of polite letters ; and though they are made
with ease, furnish good opportunities for the improvement of taste.

EVENING XLIII.

ON A PASSAGE FROM ARISTOTLE, WHICH SCALIGER ADMIRED,
AS EXPRESSIVE OF DIVINE INFLUENCE ON THE HUMAN MIND.

I LATELY met with the following quotation from Aristotle in the works of Dr. Henry More, which I cannot but consider as remarkable.

Τίς ἡ τῆς κινήσεως ἀρχὴ ἐν τῇ ψυχῇ; Δῆλον δε ὥσπερ ἐν τω ὅλω, ΘΕΟΣ, και πᾶν ἐκείνω; κινεῖ γαρ πῶς πάντα ΤΟ ΕΝ ἩΜΙΝ ΘΕΙΟΝ· λογου δ᾽ ἀρχὴ ὀυ ΔΟΓΟΣ ἀλλά ΤΙ ΚΡΕΙΤΤΟΝ. τί ὀυν ἂν κρεῖτΐον κὶ ἐπιςημης πλὴν ΘΕΟΣ; "What is the beginning of motion in the soul? It is evident that it is, as in the universe, God himself, and all in him. For it is the same *numen* in us, that moves all things in some sort or other; and the beginning of reason is not reason, but something which is better; but what can be better than science, but God* ?"

This passage from Aristotle is well worth the attention of every student in divinity. Scaliger, on reading it, could not repress the warm sentiments which it excited, but burst into the following exclamation :

Quid ais, divine vir? Estne in nobis aliquid divinum quod sit præstantius ipsa ratione? An tibi quoque noti fuerunt ipsi radii spiritus sancti? " What sayest thou, O thou divine Philosopher? Is there any thing within us of a celestial nature, and more excellent than reason? Were then the irradiations of the Holy Ghost known to thee?"

TO EN HMIN ΘΕΙΟΝ. " The divinity within us !" An idea which approaches very nearly to the sublime doctrines of the Christian religion, respect-

---

* Translated by Dr. Henry More.

ing the existence and operation of the third person
in the Holy Trinity :

Est Deus in nobis, agitante calescimus illo.

There is, indeed, every reason to believe, that the
Deity vouchsafed to bestow a considerable degree
of religious illumination on the minds of the wiser
Heathens.   The soul of man, whether Heathen or
Christian, purified and exalted by knowledge, virtue, and benevolence, could not but be a beloved
object to the Father of all Truth, Goodness, and
mercy.   God saw that it was good, comparatively
good ; and, as the emanation of his love, indulged
it with the view of celestial truths*.   But this revelation was partial and confined, till, in the wonderful dispensation of Divine Wisdom, it seemed good
to God to send Him who brought life and immortality to light through the gospel.

How does the doctrine of grace, taught us by
this heavenly instructor, elevate and aggrandize humanity !   A particle of the Divinity, we learn, condescends to unite itself most intimately with our
spiritual essence ; and not only so; but our very
bodies are rendered the temples of the Divine Per-

---

* Thus the Platonists, by tradition or illumination, had acquired
an idea of the Trinity, 1st, το εν, τ'αγαθον,—2d, Νους or Λογος,—who
was also the Δημιουργος,—3d, Ψυχη :—that is, 1st, the One absolutely
good.—2d, The Mind or Word, the Maker.—3d, Ψυχη, the Soul or
Spirit.

Seneca's words are remarkable : " Quisquis formator universi
fuit sive ille DEUS est potens omnium, sive incorporalis Ratio, ingen-
tium operum artifex, sive divinus spiritus, per omnia, maxima, minima,
æquali intentione diffusus."   Whoever was the former of the universe,
whether God Almighty, whether incorporeal Reason, whether the
divine Spirit, diffused equally through all things, the greatest and the
least, he adds " sive Fatum."   See Jortin's Discourses on the Christian Religion.

son. These poor frail habitations of the soul are not thought unworthy of being made the mansions of one person in the Godhead. Mysterious, yet comfortable and animating truth! And let us never incur the danger of losing the association of this Sanctifier, Illuminator, and Comforter, by disbelieving, with presumptuous audacity, the reality of his existence, or doubting his actual operation on the minds of good men.

I know that nothing is more common than to attribute all the operations of the Holy Sprit to imagination and enthusiasm; and that they who, at any time, have made pretensions to any species or degree of influence of this supernatural kind, have been treated, by wicked and worldly men, as well as by proud philosophers, with contempt and resentment as fanatical impostors, or foolish devotees. He who undertakes to maintain the reality of it is considered, by the vain and superficial pretenders to singular wisdom, as little different from a fool or a hypocrite. I fear, however, that persons thus disposed to ridicule all idea of supernatural influence on the mind of man, by the operation of the Holy Ghost, are in a deplorable condition. They seem to be among those whose hearts are rendered insensible, and whose eyes are darkened, because they have perversely and presumptuously refused to receive the truth as it is in Jesus with due faith and humility.

It is by no means inconsistent with the sublimest philosophy, independently of religion, to believe that the Supreme Being is able to act on the human mind by an invisible and supernatural influence. The most celebrated philosophers of antiquity have given reason to conclude, that they thought a very intimate connexion subsisted between the soul of man and the essence of the Divinity: nor did it appear in the least contradictory to nature and possibility, that he who made both the soul and body, in a most wonderful manner, should be able to act upon them secretly, yet powerfully, and in a manner scarcely less wonderful than their original creation.

I must confess I cannot help considering the doctrine of the Holy Ghost, and its operation on the human mind, as at once the sublimest and most comfortable doctrine of the gospel.

How little happiness and perfection can I reach by my own poor efforts. I struggle, but am defeated; I climb, but I fall. All is weakness, all is misery. But the evil is not without a remedy. God Almighty has promised to strengthen my weakness and comfort my sorrow, by actually participating in my nature, if I endeavour to render myself not unworthy of the merciful condescension.

The Scripture expresses the entrance of the Holy Ghost into the heart of man in strong and lively language. We are born again. We are become new creatures. Glorious advancement to felicity and perfection! Here is scope for ambition. By this union we become truly ennobled. How sordid, how mean, how base do the distinctions on which men pride themselves appear, on the comparison! The true Christian, whom God has blessed with the influence of his Holy Spirit, is the only character which deserves the appellation of *great*. All other pretensions to greatness appear, on comparison, childish and ridiculous. The *Palingenesia*, or regeneration, can alone aggrandize fallen man.

Professed wits and professed philosophers, both of the minute species, will treat this subject with ridicule. They are ready to denominate whatever is advanced on the subject of supernatural influence, the mere rant of enthusiasm. Abuse, however, proves nothing but the levity or anger of him who has recourse to it. Let it be remembered by him who feels himself disposed to deride the doctrine of supernatural influence on the human mind, that it is not merely the doctrine of any mortal, but of the Holy Scriptures; and that its truth has been confirmed by the actual experience of many good and pious men, whose reason was in too great a degree of perfection to be easily deceived, and whose hearts would not permit them to deceive others. Is it more difficult to believe that the Spirit of God can operate on the human soul, than that a piece of stone or iron, where there is no influence or effluence visible or tangible, should be able to attract a needle?

It is difficult, indeed, to maintain this truly scriptural doctrine, without incurring, in a sceptical age, the charge of methodism. But if such a charge should be brought against the writer of this paper, he will bear it with fortitude, while he denies its justice with perfect confidence. It is, however, hardly worth while to contend against the misapprehensions and misrepresentations of anonymous ignorance and malice.

EVENING XLIV.

ON CARELESSNESS RESPECTING RELIGION.

MAN has so natural a tendency to religion, that few would be irreligious without the intervention of circumstances produced by pride and wickedness, and operating against the natural sentiments of the human mind. The prevalence of vice, at an early age, conduces greatly to the diffusion of infidelity; for when a young man has lost his innocence, and the satisfaction of a quiet conscience, he is much disposed to listen to any doctrine which pretends to make him easy, and at the same time allows him to be vicious. He admits doubts and scruples in this case, which he would otherwise reject on intuition.

But it seems to be acknowledged, that young men, in the present age, are admitted into the world, or introduced into life, as it is called, much earlier than at any former period. Imagining themselves men, before they have reached maturity of judgment, they fall into vices, which, they think, give them a manly appearance. The next step is to justify themselves, if possible; and this is attempted by renouncing, or doubting the truth of Christianity.

In thus deluding themselves, they will never be at a loss for aid, as books abound well calculated to diffuse infidelity, by presenting it under the veil of wit and elegance.

Writers possessed of ingenuity and taste, but, unfortunately, destitute of sound wisdom and of goodness of heart, have, in modern times, remarkably abounded; and as, from the agreeable dress in which their sophistry appears, they amuse and entertain, it is no wonder that they have gained a numerous train of readers, admirers, and votaries. Their writings are particularly addressed to the rising generation; and what, therefore, can be expected, in process of time, but a deluge of infidelity?

It is particularly unfortunate, that those who read the writings of modern philosophers, seldom inspect those of solid divines; that they are disgusted with the dullness and gravity of both style and subjects of those who, despising tinsel and paint, have laboured only to procure the substance and solidity of truth.

Add to this, that a religious education among young men of fortune and fashion is become uncommon. There prevails an idea, that to teach young men the principles of religion according to the ideas of their grandfathers, is to confine them unfairly in the trammels of superstition, to render their minds narrow and contracted, and to preclude an attention to things at that age far more in character, and far more useful.

I have seen many parents anxious on the subject of their children's education. They would spare no expense for the acquisition of languages, dancing, fencing, music, and every attainment which can render their sons agreeable in company, and skilful in a profession. They wished to see them qualified as orators, and all-accomplished as fine gentlemen, but they have displayed no remarkable solicitude on their attainment of religious ideas, and have even hinted an opinion that religion might be postponed to a maturer period. They have not, indeed, objected to a few formalities, such as a regular and decent attendance at a church, or the learning of a short catechism ; but they have not seriously and anxiously laboured the point like persons sincerely desirous that it might be pursued with ardour and success.

But the example of indifference in religion, exhibited by a parent, must always militate strongly against all that is taught in a school or by a private preceptor.

Whoever is acquainted with the manners of our ancestors will acknowledge, that more regard was formerly paid to the religious instruction of children, in high as well as in the middle and lower ranks, than in the present times. Example, parental example, did more than the best instruction alone can ever effect.

The general omission of family devotion has contributed as much as any cause to the diffusion of an

indifference to all religious concerns. The houses
of our nobility have chapels in them, and service
used to be performed there regularly; but how few
retain the practice? The example had a salutary
influence on the subordinate ranks, when almost
all families of respectable character were observed
to preserve family worship with pious constancy.
Fashionable amusements and dissipation have now
scarcely left time for it, even if the tendencies remained undiminished, which it were an excess of
candour to suppose. The consequence is, that not
only masters and mistresses of families, but the children and domestic servants, live from day to day
without being reminded of their great Benefactor,
and without being warned of the approach of death,
of all the evils to which life is exposed, and the
consolation under them.

The assembling at church is also neglected as a
necessary consequence of increasing indifference;
or if an attendance is kept up, it is often more in
compliance with custom and decency, than from the
warm impulse of a voluntary devotion.

Religious books, both doctrinal and practical,
abound, but who will spend his leisure hours in
reading them, when he is not duly impressed with
the importance of the subjects; and when he is
more powerfully solicited by novels and seducing
publications, which flatter his vices, and, by pleasing,
corrupt his imagination?

From all these causes it happens that infidelity,
or an indifference scarcely less culpable and pernicious, increases more and more; and the inference
which the clergy and all sincere Christians must
draw is, that there is a necessity for peculiar exertion to stem the torrent. But who is able to succeed in so vast an enterprise? The consolation is,

that each acquits his own conscience, by exerting himself to the best of his power, and that the blessing of God frequently gives success to causes apparently inadequate.

EVENING XLV.

ON THE CONCERN WHICH EVERY MAN HAS IN THEOLOGY.

Every superficial talker is ready to object prejudice against the serious professors of religion. But can there be any prejudice equal to that of him who considers theology as a matter foreign to himself, fit only for bigoted and superannuated devotees, and for those who, from their office and profession, find it a source of lucre? Such an opinion is equally narrow and malignant, and no less unphilosophical than irreligious.

Theology is every man's concern, and it is his duty to study it according to his abilities and opportunities. If we are all the sons of one Father, and all bound to do his will, it is certainly the duty of all to endeavour to discover it. As all regard their happiness, it is incumbent on all to seek to please him in whom is the sole disposal of good and evil. And though a religion is *revealed,* yet it requires the attention of its professors to be able to receive the revelation according to the will of the Bestower of it. And what is this attention but the study of theology? Let it not be confined to the cloisters of monks, or to the sacred profession alone, since it is every man's most important business to know as much of it as he can; to study it amidst his secular employments, and to seek consolation from it in adversity, and security in the most prosperous state.

It will be readily allowed that every man, the Jew and Turk as well as Christian, is concerned in what is called practical divinity, by which little more is understood than moral practice. With such divinity a man may be a heathen, and yet a practical divine. A great part of practical ethics he may certainly learn without hearing of Christianity.

But I urge, that it is incumbent on every man to know something of his religion speculatively as well as practically. I do not mean that he should enter into controversial points. A little learning of this kind is a dangerous thing. " It puffeth up, and destroyeth charity." It commonly leads also to doubt, and ends in licentious infidelity. But if he reads and reflects at all, will he not, as a man pretending to reason, read and reflect on that which claims to be of the first importance ? on that which gives a peace which the world cannot give, in this state, and in the next, life everlasting ? Let us weigh these things duly, and not suffer the words to pass without notice or effect from the frequency of their occurrence.

People of fortune and condition are anxious to improve their sons in all fashionable accomplishments, and are desirous that they should be learned in such arts as tend to their advancement in life. The law is studied with uncommon ardour as opening a road to the highest honours in civil life ; but as to divinity, says Sir Phaeton Hunter, leave that, Tom, to the parsons.

But both Sir Phaeton and Tom are as much concerned in divinity as the parsons, so far as relates to their own spiritual state. But, exclaims the man of fashion and pleasure, I have no relish for these things. And why ? Because you understand them not, and because you have never given your mind to the consideration of them. It is an old saying,

Ignoti nulla cupido,—There can be no wish for that of which we know nothing. The concerns of the man of pleasure, which he considers of so much importance, his politics, his wit, his gaming, appear nonsenical to the plain country man, who understands them not, but who is wise, like Horace's Ofellus, without rule, *abnormis sapiens;* wise by the dictates of common sense, and illuminated by the light which God has placed in his bosom, and by the sun of gospel revelation.

Many others who pretend to wisdom and philosophy will study every thing but theology. They will digest Newton; but never think of Him who made both Newton and the orbs, whose path he pointed out, and whose motions he explained. Yet Newton himself, the greatest of all modern philosophers, unlike many among his minute successors, studied theology together with philosophy, and, while he made a revelation of nature, loved, revered, and faithfully believed, the revelation of grace.

EVENING XLVI.

ON THE CHARACTER OF BISHOP WILSON, BISHOP OF SODOR AND MAN.

If one were desired to exhibit to sceptics or infidels a specimen of human excellence produced by the influence of Christianity, I know not whether it would be easy to find a more finished model than Bishop Wilson. His whole life appears to have been an uniform tenor of goodness, unequalled, and unrivalled, by any of the philosophers who are the pride of antiquity, and who are cited as instances by modern sophists, when they wish to extol reason and depreciate revelation.

His piety, charity, diligence, and vigilance were truly apostolic; and I make no doubt but that he deserved to be canonized better than many of the holiest saints in the calendar, the marble steps before whose shrines are worn by the knees of adoring pilgrims.

He rendered the beauty of holiness eminently conspicuous; and I think no man of sensibility can read his life without being charmed with the lovely picture. Indeed he must be confirmed in wickedness to a most deplorable degree, if he does not find his heart meliorated by it. Such a life, since example is confessedly more efficacious than precept, might possibly convert the wicked and unbelieving from their errors more certainly and expeditiously than any oral or written instruction. I recommend it to the attention of all, as likely to promote their Christian improvement more effectually than any other piece of biography which I can at present recollect. Many great divines have adorned this country by their lives no less than their learning, but there have been few who have not devoted a considerable portion of their time and abilities to mere erudition, to controversy, or to politics; but Bishop Wilson was entirely a Christian, aspiring at no honour or happiness but that which arose from the diffusion of good, and the performance of his duty, as the servant of Jesus Christ.

There is no doubt but that he could have written with an ostentation of learning, and in a style adapted to the taste of refined hearers; but he was superior to the arts of seeking human applause, and nobly relinquished all claim to elegance, for the sake of simplifying his writings, and adapting them to the understandings of those to whom they were immediately addressed, — the poor Manks, rude rustics, and converted Indians. Elegance would have been very proper, if he had written or preached to the learned and polite. But his generous condescension to the poor argues unquestionable sincerity, and reflects greater honour on a Christian preacher than any fame which could have been obtained by emulating the graces of Pagan eloquence.

Though his sermons have none of the rhetorical graces, they are yet eloquent, for they are persuasive : and they are persuasive, because the character of the writer is such as gives them the stamp of truth, the greatest charm in the composition of sermons. It reflected honour on the ancient rhetoricians, that, as a primary requisite to successful oratory, they required the orator to be a good man. They knew that an esteem of the orator has more weight in the mind of a thinking hearer, than ingenuity of argument, which an hypocrite is often as well able to invent and utter as an honest man. They knew that the best arguments would avail little from the tongue of him who was known to have no principle, and consequently who was ready to defend or recommend any thing which the exigency required, in opposition to truth and to his own conviction. They therefore laid peculiar stress on the moral qualification of unaffected goodness in the accomplished orator. A poor composition, with this quality in the orator, would tend more to produce persuasion, or conviction, than the finest words and sentiments which were ever combined without it ; and it is to the goodness of Bishop Wilson's life that his plain discourses are principally indebted for their power over the hearer and reader.

I must acknowledge that they display no marks

of genius either in the expression or invention, and that nothing would enable them to produce a powerful effect over a learned and elegant audience but the appearance of sincerity. At the same time, I think them judiciously adapted to the use of those, who, for want of other opportunities, stand most in need of instruction from the pulpit, the plain Christians who compose the majority of a rural congregation.

The goodness of his heart gives indeed the chief recommendation to all his works; though, at the same time, it must be allowed, that perspicuity and plainness are beauties not always so easy as they appear to be, not only because it requires some effort to express ideas so as to be perfectly intelligible to the meanest intellect, but also because it is difficult to conquer that pride of heart which leads to a contempt of whatever is familiar, and an affectation of abstruseness and sublimity; difficult to restrain that self-love which leads the preacher and writer rather to display his own taste, learning, or acuteness, than to labour faithfully in the improvement of his disciples.

The instruction for the Indians, and the little treatise on the Lord's Supper, have done more good in the world than the finest compositions formed in the schools of eloquence. How little is the merit of pleasing the imagination and taste, compared to that of purifying the heart, and rendering that temple of the Holy Spirit fit for his reception?

If there were many instances of Christian perfection equally conspicuous with Dr. Wilson's, I believe, the amiableness of their appearance would make many proselytes to the Christian faith, and do more to engage the careless and the sceptical than the most laboured argumentation. Providence raises from time to time such examples of human excellence, and causes them to shine like lights in the firmament; and happy they who are favoured with grace to assist them in following the guidance. Happy they who feel comfort from such plain books of piety as those of Bishop Wilson, and whose devotional taste finds a pleasure where their classical taste can receive no gratification. Happy they who catch the pure and gentle flame of such a man's devotion, and imitate him in piety to God and beneficence to man.

Greatly as I esteem the good Bishop, I cannot bestow a general panegyric on him, as if I approved his errors, for errors he had; and was he not a man? I think his favourite topic of inflicting the punishments of ecclesiastical discipline, in frequent and common cases, argues something of an intemperate zeal, and of a severity rather wonderful in a man of his exemplary benevolence. He appears to me to be mistaken in this point, whether I consider the subject of penance in a political or a Christian light. Tyranny will never increase the number of converts in a free country; and men will readily desert a church where the mere infirmities of human nature may expose them to great suffering and public infamy; and I believe it will be difficult to point out any passage in the gospel that will justify the severity of ecclesiastical punishment; but the Bishop meant well, and was, I believe, free from any evil passion, when he strenuously recommended the infliction of penance. His error was in his judgment, not in his heart; for I believe his heart was incapable of error, if it is possible to be so in the present state of human nature.

EVENING XLVII.

ON THE MOTIVES FOR PUBLICATION AND TACITURNITY.

GREAT are the dangers attending publication.
An author exposes himself to the shafts of all those
enemies whom, in the wonderful events of human
life, he may have raised either with or without
deserving their displeasure. His works may contain opinions adverse to the interest or prejudices
of many whom he never knew, but who will gratify
their resentment by the severest animadversion.
The path of life which leads through the vale of
obscurity is certainly the safest; but, at the same
time, it must be allowed, that if men contented themselves with safety, they would achieve but little
worthy of praise.

It is not easy to form a true judgment of our own
opinions, and to decide whether or not they are
worthy of communication. It is well known that
Milton and several other very eminent writers were
greatly mistaken in the estimate which they formed
of their works. The public only can decide with
certainty. Even a friend may err in his decision,
though qualified with every kind of learning, and
sufficiently furnished with the natural powers of
judgment. The works of many which were censured or praised in manuscript have been differently
received when offered to the public eye. The literary republic is remarkable for its liberty, and every
member of it has a right to appeal from private
judgment to the people.

He who steps forward advances at his own hazard.
He incurs the danger of severe censure and of general contempt. The danger is so great, as to require

the force of several motives of no little power to oppose it. The love of fame and the desire of profit are the two great incitements. A desire to promote the public good is indeed the usual pretext ; but, in the present imperfect state of humanity, it is to be feared that it is much less frequently the true motive than ambition and interest.

The love of fame contributes so much to keep alive a spirit of activity, to entertain and to benefit the world, that it certainly ought not to be repressed with excessive severity. When it displays itself in pride and vanity, it deserves both ridicule and censure ; but when it seeks its gratification in liberal employments and useful productions, it ought to be encouraged by all who wish to promote the public happiness.

The love of fame too often operates in the production of mischief. There are many who had rather be distinguished by doing injury, than to remain in the inglorious shade of obscurity. Thus, for instance, the disturbers of the public tranquillity, by diffusing false alarms, and the violators of that peace and comfort which a belief in religion affords, often mean little more than to distinguish themselves and to become famous, though all who are so unfortunate as to receive their doctrines, are likely to be injured in consequence of their credulity. All works produced by a love of fame operating in opposition to benevolence and decency ought to be censured, or at least suffered by neglect to sink into oblivion.

But if the love of fame instigates an author to publish what he conceives may be generally useful, either to arts, to science, or morality, though he should not possess a genius, and therefore should be able to produce, after his best efforts, nothing but a feeble and insipid performance, he will not be justly held up to ridicule.   His spirit of adventure will deserve encouragement, and his honest intention should not only shield him from violent attacks, but secure to him a share of the public esteem.   Nothing but vice and ridiculous vanity can deserve that asperity of censure, which some very harmless authors have been so unfortunate as to have incurred in consequence of their unsuccessful lucubrations. Weak and tasteless performances can never do much injury, nor continue long to excite attention, even if they should have been able to excite it at all by personal influence or the grace of novelty.

The love of profit is perhaps a much more universal motive for publication than the love of fame. Literature in this case becomes a species of commerce; and those to whom the commodity is offered have a right to examine it with the most scrupulous attention, and to censure with severity, if they are defrauded by promises and pretensions unperformed. It cannot be denied that many frauds are committed in the humbler walks of literature by the unprincipled and the necessitous.   It is therefore right that there should be literary journals and critiques to give the public notice of all attempts upon their purses, and to put them upon their guard against *Bibliopolian* deceptions, fabricated without principle, and merely for the sake of lucre.

But as it is not easy to discover motives with certainty, it becomes every critic to exercise his judgment and authority with caution and candour.

My subject leads me to consider the communication of ideas, not only by letters, but by conversation.   Much is said by the ancients in praise of taciturnity; but it is not greatly admired by the moderns.   And, indeed, when we consider that it is often the effect of dullness and pride, it may admit some doubt whether it is worthy of praise.

There are various motives for taciturnity. Some persons are afraid of exposing themselves to danger, and others to contempt. It is certain that a man who communicates his thoughts with little reserve is very likely to say something which he may wish in vain to retract. A word once uttered can never be recalled; "and many an one," says an ancient, "has repented of having spoken, but scarcely one of having kept silence."

But this regard for safety may certainly be carried too far. The extreme selfishness from which reserve often proceeds is by no means amiable. Caution is certainly necessary in what we utter, but it does not follow that the same caution should deter us from uttering at all. Neither our words nor our affairs usually make that impression on others which our vanity is apt to conceive. If we are of such consequence as that our companions may find their interest in studying every part of our conversation and action, it will then become necessary to be oracular, or silent. Or, if we are so unfortunate as to have chosen our companions among the base and treacherous, it will certainly be right to keep our mouths as it were with a bridle. But in this case the best advice that can be given is, to abandon the company in which we cannot confide. In general we may conclude, that there is not so much danger in speaking, if we take care to regulate our words by prudence, as to justify taciturnity.

Another cause of taciturnity is an excessive diffidence: and this quality is often found in men of the most amiable tempers and dispositions. Their feelings are so delicate, and their modesty so invincible, that though they are often the best qualified to make a good appearance in conversation, they give up all pretensions to excellence, and content themselves with becoming hearers only.

This weakness, though excusable in itself, is yet injurious to society, as it prevents the communication of many ideas and opinions which are calculated to improve mankind, and to sweeten the pleasures of friendly association.

But pride is a no less frequent cause of taciturnity than diffidence. There are many persons who think the company which they keep for the sake of ceremony, or in compliance with form, not worthy the honour of hearing the communication of their sapient cogitations. They observe also, that silence gives the appearance of wisdom; and they are conscious that they possess no method of acquiring the character of wisdom so easily as by silence. This requires no exertion of ingenuity or invention, but is often the natural result of sullen pride and subtle artifice.

Pride is so often united with ill-nature, that they may, I believe, be called inseparable companions; and it is undoubtedly true, that taciturnity is frequently caused by ill-nature; but let not moroseness and sullenness, expressed by a haughty and contemptuous silence, pass for wisdom, virtue, and erudition.

Stupidity is among the principal causes of taciturnity. If a subject arises which requires knowledge and elegance in its discussion, many persons are condemned to an involuntary silence. And indeed taciturnity, in this case, is the only quality which can appear to advantage; for to prate on subjects which we do not understand, evinces at once our vanity and our ignorance. A modest attempt, however, to take a part in such conversation cannot but deserve praise and encouragement. Questions may be asked with great advantage to the inquirer, and without the least violation of decorum.

Upon the whole, I think it appears that taciturnity is by no means amiable or justifiable, except in cases of particular importance, in which judgment and common sense must ever dictate the proper behaviour.

In early youth indeed, silence is not only becoming, but the means of deriving improvement. He who is always talking in the company of his elders, fills up that time with his own superficial remarks which might otherwise be employed in listening to the lessons of wisdom. In general, it may be prescribed as a rule, that we ought not to communicate our ideas, till we have reason to entertain a modest confidence that they are worthy of acceptance; but how shall we be able to judge whether our ideas are acceptable or not, without making some probationary efforts, without trying experiments on our hearers' attention? These experiments must, however, be made with modesty and delicacy. We must not talk long at a time, nor frequently. With such cautions there is no doubt but that talkativeness is greatly to be preferred to taciturnity, both for our own and others' pleasure and improvement.

EVENING XLVIII.

ON ADAPTING SERMONS TO CONGREGATIONS.

SIR,—I constantly attend my parish-church, and hope not without improvement. The rector, who preaches every Sunday, is not only a very learned man, but humane, charitable, good-natured, and, as far as I am able to judge, a living image of the virtues which he recommends from the pulpit.   He is both beloved and respected by all who make just pretensions to a character of decency and religion.

It happens that the parish contains several families of distinction, and gentlemen of the professions ; whose education and habits of reading have given them a taste for elegance of style.   They esteem the minister greatly ; but they cannot help lamenting that his sermons, though learned and pious, abound in language which has not the least appearance of elegance or beauty, but indeed is frequently disgraced by the coarse and obsolete expressions of the last century.

Now, Sir, if the congregation consisted of rustics only, or chiefly, there could be no reasonable objection to a rustic style ; but as it is polite and learned, I think the language in which the minister addresses them, should be conformable to their taste, or, at least, not such as can give them offence.

I do not complain from fastidiousness, or a desire to be pleased and amused by a fine literary composition ; but because I am convinced, that the want of elegance in our preacher prevents much of that good, which his sermons are calculated to produce on a polite audience.

If you will take this subject under your consideration, you will oblige your correspondent,

ATHENÆUS.

———————————

SIR,—I am a plain and regular man, of a character which the fine folks might perhaps stigmatize with the epithet old-fashioned ; but I regard the approbation of my own conscience much more than the opinion of the world.   I am a constant attendant at my parish-church, though I cannot say that I entirely approve the preacher. I think the constant attendance at one's parish-church affords a good example, and therefore I sacrifice something of my own pleasure and improvement to the benefit of others, to whom my age and station may render me a model.

My complaint, which however I offer with all due humility, is against the language of our preacher. He is a very polite man in his manners, and no less so in his composition; but he abounds so much in long words of foreign extraction, and in polished periods, that his congregation is often deprived of Christian doctrine for the sake of displaying the graces of an elegant style. He seems to be almost afraid of introducing a passage from scripture, and totally rejects those old words which convey religious ideas with peculiar precision, but often without any elegance.

I am almost certain, that half the congregation understand no more of his sermons than if they were written in Latin or Greek. The consequence is, that a great part of the parishioners have deserted the church, and attend an illiterate enthusiast, who harangues in a neighbouring barn; and the rest either fall asleep, or divert themselves with reviewing the dress of the rural belles who make a figure with their best ribbons every Sunday. Upon the whole, the church service, as it is now conducted in our village, contributes so little to excite devotion, or to instruct in the duties of Christianity, that I am clearly of opinion, it might be entirely neglected with very little injury to the cause of religion.

You will oblige me by taking this letter into your consideration, and perhaps a hint from you may induce our vicar to suit his doctrines and his language to the understandings of his homespun hearers.

I am, Sir, your's, &c.

CORYDON.

I wish it was in my power to exchange the livings of the two clergymen of whom my correspondents complain ; for the style of Corydon's minister would exactly correspond with the taste of an enlightened congregation ; and the rustics would be delighted with the plain language of a plain preacher.

I have often lamented that, in the present confused state of human affairs, it is not easy to adapt the preacher to the congregation. The patrons of livings bestow them as benefits to the preacher, without having an opportunity of consulting the peculiar advantage of the parishioners. Thus it often happens, that a learned divine, who is qualified to shine in the schools of an university, is appointed the religious instructor of a congregation of mere farmers, who can hardly read and write, while another of very moderate attainments is fixed in some capital town, where the congregation is intelligent, and capable of improving by the ablest and most elegant discourses from the pulpit.

But it is perhaps in the power of any clergyman to descend, if not to ascend, to the intellects of his audience. Taste must not interfere so far as to exclude plain and ordinary words from a sermon ; for plain and ordinary men, of whom the greater part of rural congregations consist, can attend to no other with advantage. A scholar unacquainted with the living world, can hardly form a just idea how difficult it is to render every word in a sermon intelligent to the majority of a rustic audience. Words, which are commonly esteemed easy in the middle ranks, are in the lower quite unintelligible.

Moliere, as it is well known, used to read his comedies to an old woman, who had no advantages of education, that he might judge by the manner in which she was affected, how his wit and humour would be received by the public. I believe a clergyman might read his sermon to some aged matron, or to his parish-clerk, and derive equal advantage from observing the effect which it should produce.

On the other hand, it is certainly right to use every means which taste and eloquence can devise, in attracting the attention of a politer congregation. Many have been allured by the elegance of the preacher to listen with attention; and, though they began to attend like mere heathen critics, have ended in receiving a very strong conviction of the truth of Christianity, and the propriety of many moral actions which they had once derided.

Let taste be sanctified by becoming the handmaid of virtue and religion. She has often been engaged in the service of vice, and served the cause of infidelity much more effectually than any reason or argument.

Much has been said on the subject of pulpit eloquence, and great pains are bestowed in acquiring the graces of style and delivery; but, after all, it must be acknowledged, that the plainest manner with a very loud voice, but without any studied graces, is often the best calculated to convey sound instruction to the rustic villager.

The first object in the preacher's mind should be, to speak in such a manner as is most likely to convince and affect the mind of his hearer. Different classes of hearers require different modes of address. However learned a clergyman may be, and however well qualified to expatiate on profound and metaphysical subjects, he will do right to descend from his own eminences, and stoop to such sentiments and language as are familiar and intelligible to the persons over whose spiritual state he is appointed to watch.   The church is not to be considered as a school of eloquence, neither ought any one to ascend the pulpit as he would the stage, merely to display his own talents, and to amuse an audience.

Instruction is the first object.   It is right to adopt the style and manner which conveys it most effectually ; but the plainest and the least studied, the mere colloquial, are often the best for this purpose. In a word, the preacher who possesses sufficient judgment and abilities, will rise or fall in his eloquence according to the standard of his hearers' taste and knowledge.

A man of learning and abilities is often afraid to descend in his style, lest he should expose himself to one or two hearers who may be superior to the rest, or who may accidentally enter the church. His character requires the support of constant endeavours for the acquisition of excellence ; and if, for the sake of accommodating his discourse to his hearers, he should write or preach in a style below himself, he fears that he may incur neglect or contempt from the judges of literary excellence.   But he should divest himself of all such considerations, and, like a faithful servant and soldier of Jesus Christ, bear with alacrity every indignity and injury which may arise in the conscientious discharge of his duty. Hearers, on the other hand, should not be hasty in their censures, but, when they examine the merits of the preacher, consider the state and condition of his audience,

EVENING XLIX.

ON SUPERIOR ADVANTAGES OF MEN OF THE WORLD OVER SCHOLARS AND PHILOSOPHERS IN SOME RESPECTS.

Principibus placuisse viris non ultima laus est. Hor.

MEN of the world have many advantages over the scholar and philosopher, if advancement to civil honours and to lucrative preferment are the grand objects of human ambition, and the most valuable purposes of life. They are not prevented from the prosecution of their interested designs by study and application to science; neither are they embarrassed with those delicacies which often confine men of genius and learning to the shade of studious retirement. While the scholar is busy in the search of wisdom, in turning over the volumes of antiquity, and tracing the labyrinths of science, the man of the world is knocking at the great man's door, distributing his cards of address, or bowing at a levee. He obtains a promise in some favourable moment, in the *mollia tempora fandi*, and in consequence of it is advanced to honour and emolument, while the student is neglected and forgotten in the obscurity of his closet.

But when young men observe that honours are bestowed on characters which they remember to have had no pretensions to solid merit, and that the learned and the virtuous are paid only with the scanty pittance of reluctant praise, they lay aside their books, and relax the strictness of their morals, that they may learn the manners of the world, and acquire those superficial graces which they find to be the most successful recommendation to modern patronage.

The following letter of my correspondent suggested my remarks on this subject:

SIR,—I am one of those persons whom the world calls disappointed men. I own I have been disap-

pointed : and you will do right to suffer this circumstance to have its due weight in considering
the justice or injustice of my complaints and my
observations.

My friends congratulated, and assured me that
there was no doubt of my succeeding in the church,
as my pupil's father was a man of great interest,
having two boroughs of his own. Indeed I thought
myself certain of a living at least, though I was not
sanguine enough to promise myself a dignity.

Having always supported a decent character both
for morals and literature, at my school and college,
I was honoured with the appointment of tutor to a
young nobleman soon after I had taken holy orders.
I succeeded very well in my attempts to improve
my pupil, and gave universal satisfaction.

It was not my *forte* to be a boon companion. I
could neither sing, drink, or game. I was not indeed
very fond of company, especially that mixed sort
which was often assembled at his lordship's table.
If there was a possibility of being excused, I was sure
to be absent, and make an apology. Study was my
delight ; and I really found that the dissipation of
much company totally disqualified me for reading
and reflexion. I am not conscious of having been
querulous or morose ; but I found that I was not
very eager to be admitted into the numerous parties
which often assembled at his lordship's house, so
neither was I very anxiously solicited.

It happened that, at his lordship's country-resi-
dence, the vicar of the parish, a cousin of a neighbouring esquire, was, what was called in that country,
a very good kind of fellow ; that is, he was totally
destitute of all learning, and of all pretensions to it.
He threw off all formality, so as not to be distinguished from a jockey in any other respect than by

a light grey striped coat. He kept a fine hunter, a pair of pointers, a greyhound, and a terrier. He loved company, and could entertain his companions with many songs, and histories of hares and foxes. These qualifications and this character rendered him extremely agreeable to my lord; and he was constantly invited to dinner after every hunt, and on every extraordinary occasion.

I saw very plainly that I possessed but a small share in the affections of my patron, in comparison with my rival. However, I will do my lord the justice to say, that he paid me regularly during my employment, and made me a present of ten guineas on my final dismission.

I retired to a very good curacy in a country town, where I have resided many years, studying, praying, and preaching, but totally unnoticed by my pupil and his father. I have had a hint indeed, that my lady was displeased with my unpolished manners, and that to this day she attributes the stooping of her son to my requiring him to read and write too much while I had the honour to be his tutor.

My rival, as I called him, did not undertake to supply my place as tutor to the noble pupil, but he became his constant companion, to the great delight of my lord and lady. To evince their gratitude to him for having taught the young gentleman to shoot flying, and to cry " *Tally ho!*" with a good grace, they have already bestowed on him a rectory of four hundred a year, promised him the next vacant prebend, and given him reason to believe, if his lordship should come again into place, that he shall have one of the best English bishoprics, because his father influences a borough.

I think I have some reason to complain; but I will not trouble you any farther. I will only inform you, that I am not in want ; and that, with the assistance of Christian philosophy, I bear my disappointment without repining.

I am, Sir, your's, &c.

I cannot help thinking it injurious to the cause of religion, that young men of no qualification, except that which enables them to shoot, should be patronised by lay-patrons, to the exclusion of learned and respectable clergymen. The right of presentation to a living, or of appointment to an ecclesiastical dignity, is a sacred trust. Thousands may be most essentially concerned in a proper choice of an incumbent or a dignitary ; but patrons and men in power are too apt to consider only the pecuniary value of the preferment, and to bestow it on a friend or dependant, merely as an emolument to the person preferred, without considering the duties of the office, or the influence of the example. With respect to qualifications for preferments, it was said by some worldly-minded man, that every one is qualified for what he can get in this world. This maxim seems to have been practically received by many patrons and by many preferment-hunters. But every serious, sensible, and conscientious man will consider the consequences of an appointment to those whom the duties of it are to influence. To bestow the cure of souls on a man little better qualified in morals or learning than a common groom or game-keeper, is a deed which a good man would be sorry to answer for, either at the tribunal of God or his own conscience.

There is another, and a very different kind of men, who often obtain preferment and promotion in this age with very little merit. They assume all those appearances of merit which can be assumed without the reality, and which tend to delude the superficial.

They are most accurate in their dress, and in the punctilios of ceremony and behaviour. They wear large wigs, or their hair most sprucely dressed, they speak with oily tongues, they never contradict, they bow low, and they talk learnedly before the ignorant. They spend their time in calling upon every body to whom they can procure the slightest introduction. They throw away no time on musty books. At a general election they are very active, and by means of dress and address, commonly prevail with the weak to vote for their patron, who they hope will recommend them to the prime minister, or lord chancellor. They usually succeed, for their varnish is of so excellent and beautiful a kind, that not one in twenty can see the poverty of the materials which it covers. When they are elevated to the highest ranks, and become patrons instead of dependants, they take care to show no regard to real merit, and for this good reason—they are conscious that they are under no obligations to it for their own advancement. In bestowing favours they are influenced and governed by interest, by applications from greater men than themselves, whom they still look up to with an eye of adoration, like a dog waiting for a bone.

It is very certain that many are possessed of wealth and power who are not capable of judging of real merit, or who, if they were, have not liberality enough to be influenced by it in the distribution of their favours. The evil, therefore, can seldom be prevented where the patrons are in a private station. But public authority might interfere to prevent such abuses in public officers and in statesmen, who are elevated, not merely that they may fill their own pockets and those of every servile instrument of their power, but that they may encourage merit in the community, by rewarding it with honour and emolument. Ecclesiastical patronage exerted for the purposes of parliamentary corruption, is an abuse which contributes to undermine the foundation of both Church and State, and at once inconsistent with common honesty and sincere Christianity.

It is no wonder that public establishments of religion should lose the public esteem, when the Church is used to corrupt the State.

EVENING L.

ON THE WISDOM OF SEEKING CHEAP OBVIOUS AND INNOCENT PLEASURES.

THERE can be no doubt but that it is the most important interest of every man to enjoy his existence. The only question is, in what manner he shall seek and find this valuable end. It has been the inquiry of all philosophers, from the earliest ages to the present, in what the chief good of man consists. They have never been unanimous, but have differed so much as to induce those who attended to them to entertain a mean opinion of all philosophy.

" I hate the philosopher," said an ancient, " who is not wise for himself;" that is, whose philosophy has no tendency to make himself happier. Opinions, however ingenious, which conduce not to sweeten the pleasures of society, or to regulate the conduct of individuals, are of little value.

After all the subtle disputes of philosophers, it is evident that cheerfulness, arising from real benevolence of heart and conscious rectitude, is the quality which contributes most to the enjoyment of life. It diffuses a perpetual sunshine over every thing around us. Whether prosperity or adversity be our lot, this quality calms the storm, and converts it to an universal serenity, like that of a fine summer evening.

Innocence is the first requisite to cheerfulness. Guilt can only affect external gaiety. Health is also essentially necessary to secure the possession. But as none of us are perfectly innocent, but find, on a review of our lives, much to lament, it will be necessary to restore by religion what we may have lost by depravity. Exercise and temperance will usually secure the blessing of health. When these two leading qualities, innocence and health, are secured, we may then seek for amusement. Amusement in this life is one of the best means of promoting our happiness, after the conscientious performance of our necessary duty.

It is certainly very desirable to preserve the mind in a state capable of being pleased with those ordinary circumstances which are frequently stigmatised and despised as trifles. A good conscience is necessary to produce this disposition. He who is under the influence of malignant passions cannot be easy; and without ease there can be no cheerfulness, and no placid and substantial enjoyment.

Many of the common occurrences of life are trifles when they are weighed in the balance of reason. But he who resolves not to be entertained by them as they arise, will rescind a copious source of soothing satisfaction. The art of trifling agreeably and innocently, after long and laborious exertions, has been called wisdom. But it must be remembered, that trifles must not occupy the time and attention which are more justly appropriated to the serious duties of life.

In fine weather, few pleasures are greater to an

uncorrupted mind than walking or riding amidst the
beauties of rural scenery   It is wonderful that they
who profess to be the votaries of pleasure should
confine themselves to hot rooms and card-tables,
when the zephyr invites them to survey the beauties
of Flora, and to taste the delights of nature, on
hills, in vales, in woods and groves, by the sides
of rivers, and in the paradise of a cultivated garden.
The air of an assembly-room in the months of July
and August must be foul and unwholesome to such a
degree, as cannot fail of being injurious to beauty, as
well as inconsistent with enjoyment.   The smoke of
candles, exhalations of perfumes, and other effluvia,
added to the heat of the weather, must be particularly disgustful to those whose organs of sensation
are not rendered dull and obtuse by habitual relaxation.   And yet the life of those who are engaged in
scenes like these is named, by way of eminence, a
life of pleasure ; and habit often renders it necessary.
   The great object of him who wishes to render his
life truly pleasurable, according to his own ideas of
enjoyment, and not according to those of a capricious fashion, is to preserve his heart in a general
state of tranquillity.   In this happy state he is able
to enjoy all that is rationally desirable, and to judge
clearly and properly of every thing which falls under
his notice, and demands his attention as a man, a
Christian, and a member of civil society.   The state
itself, like that of health, is a state of constant pleasure. But there is one amusement among the fashionable which is peculiarly destructive of tranquillity.
I mean the amusement of deep play. Nothing
agitates the mind so violently as gaming. Game-
sters indeed affect a coolness, and often appear with
a composed countenance ; but this very composure
is the result of study, it is deceitful, it is a mask ;

and the emotions of the heart are often the more painful from the restraint under which they are kept by that artifice, which renders a placid countenance essentially necessary to the character of a skilful gamester.

Some degree of variety and novelty appears to be essentially requisite to a continued state of enjoyment. Travelling is found to gratify the passion for novelty and vicissitude, more agreeably than any other mode of amusement. Journies in our own country, without danger of the sea, and without the inconvenience of distance from domestic connexions, afford great delight, and render home more agreeable, by changing the scene. It has of late indeed become a frequent practice to make an autumnal excursion to the north, and to view Nature in her fine uncultivated forms, as she sits on the rocks and mountains of the less frequented parts of this island. The folly of visiting foreign climes, with a total ignorance of our own fine country, seems to be now acknowledged. In the order of travelling, it is certainly right to begin with viewing the beauties in our vicinity, before we extend our prospects to remoter regions.

But, indeed, change of place is but a poor resource for happiness. The best expedient is to keep the mind in a state of self-government, to subdue the passions, and to restrain that extravagant love of variety which leads to discontent in our present circumstances and situation.

After all the boasted amusements and pleasures of dissipated life, there is nothing which can so sweetly compose the troubled spirit of man, nothing which can so effectually smooth the rugged path of life, and strew it with flowers, as piety and charity. A perfect confidence in God is a firm foundation for the fabric of felicity, which no storms and tempests can shake, much less overturn ; and no ingredient in the cup of life can sweeten it like benevolence.

EVENING LI.

ON THE CHARACTERS OF THEOPHRASTUS AND OTHER WRITERS OF CHARACTERS.

IF the artist whose pencil represents the features with fidelity is greatly esteemed, it is surely reasonable to appreciate highly the skill of him who can paint the manners to the life. The moral painter must be furnished with a taste equal to that of any manual artist, and he must also possess a peculiar penetration. He must know mankind, not only in a theoretical view, but also from actual experience, and in the common transactions of human intercourse. He must be accustomed to watch those minute circumstances of conversation and behaviour, which escape the notice of a superficial observer. He must trace words and actions to their motives. He must, in a word, possess a sagacity with which few are distinguished ; and he must have had many opportunities for its exertion.

The ancient critics refer every thing to Homer. They affirm that Homer was the first who wrote characters, and that the characteristical writers derived the idea of their works from him. Casaubon introduces, in his preface, a fine quotation from the thirteenth book of the Iliad ;* a specimen which seems to justify the opinion. It is a very lively picture of the coward, and of the brave man. But Homer every where discriminates his characters, and blends

---

* Lib. xiii. ver. 278.

beautiful epithets, which mark his heroes with peculiar distinction. It is on all sides confessed, that in this respect he is greatly superior to Virgil.

Theophrastus is the earliest author extant who has professedly written characters. Varro wrote a book περι χαρακτηρων, or concerning characters, but his work is not preserved, and it is imagined that he treated on the characters, or discriminating marks of style and composition. Others think it was on the different kinds of eloquence.

Theophrastus flourished in the time of Alexander the Great, and about three hundred years before the Christian æra. His name was Tyrtamus; but Aristotle changed it to Theophrastus; because his elocution had something in it of divine, and the word expresses that idea.* He was celebrated as a natural philosopher, and his school was frequented by four thousand scholars. He lived to the age of one hundred and seven, and wrote a multitude of treatises.

But I must not deviate from the present object, which is the consideration of Theophrastus as the delineator of moral characters.

His book contains twenty-six chapters, in each of which a character is delineated. There is no doubt but that much of the work is lost, something interpolated, and a great deal transposed. It is but a fragment; yet, like the fragment of a diamond, curious and valuable.

Menander is said to have been the scholar of Theophrastus; and Theophrastus has been therefore called the Father of Comedy. The characters certainly contain many touches of such comic humour as might adorn the stage.

---

* Θεοφραςος προτερον εκαλειτο Τυρταμος· Δια δε το θειως φραζειν, υπο Αριςοτελης εκληθη Ευφραςος, ειτα Θεοφραςος. SUIDAS.

They begin with a formality which would induce one to expect rather a dry and philosophical treatise on the subjects proposed, than a comic picture. The definition of the abstract and concrete resembles the dry and methodical style of Aristotle; but the reader is agreeably surprised to find the careless ease and lively painting of Horace.

It must be owned that Theophrastus appears not to have been possessed of any great delicacy. He pursues his subject so far, as frequently to lead his readers to uncleanly scenes. But the ancients, with all their improvements, were inferior to the moderns in that purity of taste which excludes whatever is offensive to the senses or imagination. What can be more indelicate than the writings of Aristophanes, which the refined Athenians greatly admired?

To judge of Theophrastus, a reader must divest himself of that narrowness of mind, which leads to suppose no state of manners right or tolerable but its own. The French have often displayed that fastidious delicacy which has prevented them from perceiving pleasure in the most celebrated works of antiquity. Even Homer was once too gross for the literary beaux of Paris.

Theophrastus, there is little doubt, represented the Athenians as he found them; and it is a very curious set of pictures which he has bequeathed to posterity. We find, what indeed might reasonably be expected, that men's manners were, three hundred years before the Christian æra, much like those in our own century. Men were then dissemblers, they were misers, they were triflers, they were lovers of novelty to excess; they had a thousand other failings, in every respect resembling those of modern times in modern Europe.

He must possess good sense, and some knowledge

of the world, who can relish Theophrastus. To a mere scholar, the work must appear defective and disgustful. It has nothing in it of system. The method in each character is often confused, probably from the injuries of time, and possibly from the age of the author; for Theophrastus was no less than ninety-nine years when he composed it, as he informs us himself, though Laertius and some of the critics pretend to know better. One might naturally have expected more regularity in a disciple of the Stagirite.

Casaubon published a most excellent edition of Theophrastus. Casaubon being an admirable scholar, his notes are very instructive and entertaining. That he fully entered into the spirit of his author I much doubt. I am certain he often misunderstood him; but, at the same time, his notes are valuable. Theophrastus requires not a profusion of learned notes; but, nevertheless, he has had commentators remarkably prolix. Needham's edition is tediously dull, and in no great estimation. Newton's is, I think, the best adapted to young persons. Newton has made the author easy to be understood, and has explained many passages, and many single expressions, with great ingenuity.

But I must not enter into the extensive subject of editions. I mean rather to point out the merits of the authors themselves, or to mention any little circumstances respecting them which may interest the student of polite letters.

Bruyere stands next in general estimation to the ancient Theophrastus. His work has been much admired, and consequently produced many bad imitators. The characters which he draws are supposed to be personal; yet most of them are capable of general application. There is a great deal of singular sagacity in them, and much knowledge of the world may be derived from them. Whatever knowledge of the world can be acquired without mixing too much in its follies, is certainly desirable ; but the wisdom bought by actual experience usually costs too high a price. The translation of Theophrastus, which Bruyere has prefixed, is by no means masterly. Indeed, I rather consider the addition of Theophrastus as a screen to hide the personalities included in the author's own characters. He wished to have his work introduced to the reader's notice as an imitation of Theophrastus. But it is not so : it is a work greatly superior. It has exactness and force. It has wit and satire. It has elegance. But, with all its excellencies, there are few books which sooner tire the reader. The mind loves a connexion of thought, at least for a page or two, when its attention is once secured. It delights in roving for a short time; but it soon grows weary, and seeks satisfaction in confining its attention to a more regular series of ideas.

Chesterfield has strongly recommended Bruyere, and indeed his book conduces greatly to the good purpose of habituating young minds to make observations on men and manners. The substance of much of the more valuable part of Chesterfield's advice will be found in Bruyere.

Bruyere well describes the effects of the external graces in the following passage :—" La politesse n' inspire pas toujours la bonté, l'equité, la complaisance, la gratitude ; elle en donne du moins les apparences, et fait paroître l'homme au dehors comme il devroit être interieurement."

I think I can discover a similarity of style, as well as sentiment, in the writings of Chesterfield and Bruyere ; and there is every reason to believe that Chesterfield had been an attentive student of Bruyere.

An author of our own country, in a book entitled Maxims and Characters, has imitated Bruyere with good success. It is lively and witty. There is, at the same time, an inequality in the work, and several of the descriptions are already antiquated.

Pope is an admirable delineator of characters; nothing was ever more highly finished than his character of Atticus. Addison is also particularly distinguished for his talent of moral painting. Fielding yields to few in the description of manners; and if Smollet had tempered his fertile genius with a regard to decorum, there is no doubt but he would have been one of the first in this kind of excellence.

If the knowledge of human nature is valuable, the power of delineating manners with fidelity is justly held in high esteem. Nothing can contribute more to communicate a knowledge of the human heart, and of the sentiments and conduct probable in any given situation, than such representations faithfully exhibited. One circumstance has prevented so much good from being derived from the painting of characters as might have been, and has even caused it to be productive of evil. This is no other than a proneness to personal satire and invective. Moral paintings have too often been little else but severe caricatures of excellent persons whose virtues excited envy.

EVENING LII.

ON MULTIPLYING BOOKS BY THE PUBLICATION OF TRIFLING AND USELESS WORKS.

MAJORAGIUS, abounding in leisure, and abusing that happy circumstance, is said to have written an oration in praise of mud or clay; Puteanus, in the same situation, celebrated an egg; one has written a panegyric on drunkenness; and others on a louse, a flea, the itch, and the ague. They might, it is certain, write what they pleased, and it is happy for us that there is no compulsion to read what they have thus wantonly composed.

There are already more books than can be used by any man, or to any good purpose. To increase their number by writing mere nonsense and insipid bagatelle, is certainly improper. And it is to be wished that they who are so fond of scribbling to spoil paper, without the least idea of advantage to science or morals, would be contented with the amusement they derive from the employ, and forbear publication.

The love of novelty is indeed so powerful, that it will often recommend to notice books which have nothing else to recommend them. But it is to be wished, that as the love of novelty may certainly as well be gratified by good performances as by bad ones, it would give itself the trouble to exercise the powers of judgment and selection.

The most trifling compositions of the present age are novels, poems, and miscellanies.

There are, however, many novels of real and substantial value, such as appear to have owed their origin to true genius and to classical taste. Wherever they exhibit genuine pictures of life and manners; and wherever they furnish matter for reflection, they certainly constitute some of the most useful books for the instruction of young persons. They are so pleasing, that the mind is gradually allured by them to virtue and wisdom, which it would perhaps never have duly considered and fully adopted had they been recommended solely by dull argumentation.

But it is a misfortune, that among the great variety and multitude of novels with which the world abounds, very few are capable of teaching morality. Their authors are found, for the most part, to lean to the side of vice; or if any begin with a sincere purpose of instructing the rising generation in real goodness, they are so injudicious in the conduct of their work, as to enter into such warm descriptions and narratives, as to conduce rather to inflame than to allay the fury of the passions.

There are three kinds of novels; those which are really good, and have nothing in them of a corrupting nature; those which are extremely excellent, considered only as compositions, but of a bad tendency; and those which are almost insipid, which possess nothing striking in the story, nor elegant in the language, but are formed merely to amuse minds of an effeminate and inconsiderate turn.

The first sort ought to be read in youth, as they are peculiarly fitted to improve the mind. They are such as Don Quixote, if any such can be found. The second are certainly to be laid aside till the student has passed the dangerous age of early youth. The last are never to be read at all, but to be classed with Majoragius *De Luto*.

Poems, without any pretensions to poetry beyond a smoothness of versification and good rhymes, greatly abound in the present age. Every newspaper has its poet's corner. Now, as Horace has justly said, and as thousands have said since Horace, there is no possibility of tolerating mediocrity in poetry. Poetry is not one of the necessaries of life. The information it conveys may be conveyed in prose. It is sought only as an excellence, a refinement, an elegance. If therefore it is not excellent, refined, and elegant, it may be dispensed with. We shall be better pleased with a plain good dinner, than with a dessert of pretended sweetmeats, in which there is nothing truly delicious. Almost all the versification which obtrudes itself on the public eye in public papers, is useless and superfluous. It proceeds from those who, with little learning or genius, are smitten by the sweets of poetical fame, and are desirous of making an appeal to the world, and trying whether or not they shall be judged worthy of the laurel. Among the trifling and useless poetry may certainly be classed all rebuses and acrosties, and most of the modern pastorals.

It will perhaps be said, if these silly sports of ingenuity amuse the idle innocently, they are useful. But I ask whether, if the idle were to lay aside such unimproving works, they might not probably find more pleasure, together with improvement, in works of sound judgment, taste, and knowledge.

The books which abound in modern languages, under the title of Miscellanies, are often of no other value than as they serve to promote the paper manufacture, and to employ the ingenious persons who labour in the typographical art. They are often posthumous; such as the author never intended to publish, though he preserved them among his papers, from a parental partiality for all his literary progeny. They are often mere juvenilities, exercises, or preludes to greater performances, and ought no more to be presented to the public eye, than the rehearsals which actors go through previously to their actual appearance on the stage.

The miscellanies of a writer really possessed of abilities, and published by himself, or with his approbation, and under his immediate inspection, may certainly be very valuable. But those crowds of books which are obtruded upon us under this form, by those whose only intention is to make a saleable commodity, might certainly, as far as the interests of literature are concerned, be spared. Yet they are not to be severely condemned, as they are often highly beneficial to youth, and, in a commercial view, to the community. It is very equitable that a tradesman should reap his emolument in the fair exercise of his trade, whatever may be the intrinsic value of the commodity which he produces. If his book is ill composed, nobody is compelled to buy it; and if any are so deficient in taste as to admire what is not excellent, the mistake is by no means such as should exasperate the mind of an observer. Many parts of literature are merely amusing; and, though errors should frequently prevail, yet in forming a judgment of them, it is not worth while to be very angry. It would be miserable, if readers in general, like Bentley and Warburton, were of a disposition to draw daggers for differences on subjects of little importance.

Old persons, who cease to aspire at improvement in learning, or persons retired from mercantile business, or those who are only capable of seeking an innocent pastime in books, are justifiable in taking up whatever is capable of fixing their attention in the short time which they devote to reading; but I think it a misfortune to have contracted a trifling taste at an early age, and when a young man ought to be preparing his mind to act a manly part in some honourable employment. For such a purpose he cannot possibly acquire too great a share of ideas. He should therefore read original authors, and those

who comprise a great deal in a little. He should
aim at the attainment of a solid judgment and of real
knowledge. He should be armed against deception
of every sort, and therefore should be exercised in
improving his judgment, and chiefly conversant in
such authors as require close attention, and will
abide the test of a rational, though candid, scrutiny.

EVENING LIII.

ON MR. POPE'S CLAIM TO THE CHARACTER OF A REAL POET.

THERE are some minds which seem to possess an
universality of talents, and I believe the mind of
Mr. Pope to have been one of these. " But no,"
says a cavilling critic, " I cannot conceive any reason for such an opinion; for did Mr. Pope write
any thing in dramatic poetry?" He certainly did
not; but I know not that it is just to conclude that
he could not, if he had chosen to undertake the task.
But the truth is, life is too short for the display of
abilities in all kinds of composition. He translated
Homer's works, a most fatiguing undertaking; he
wrote a great many miscellanies; and of the short
period allotted to man, he did not reach the utmost
boundary. There are passages in all his poems,
which evince that he did not want a poetical genius
for any kind of poem to which he might have directed its powers.

A very ingenious and elegant critic, for whose
knowledge and opinions in polite literature great
respect is certainly due, has exerted himself, in his
first volume, to prove that we hold Mr. Pope in too
high estimation as a poet, and that he is entitled
to little other praise than that of a good satirist and
correct versifier.

In his preface, he rather unfairly selects a passage from a moral epistle, and turns it into prose, as a proof that it has no claim to poetry beyond the rhyme. He says, that you cannot select ten lines out of the Iliad, Paradise Lost, or Georgics of Virgil, and reduce them by any process of critical chemistry to prose. But surely it is not equitable to compare a moral epistle, in the Horatian manner, with epic poems, or with a didactic poem written in Virgil's most embellished style. Yet, allowing this to be right, I cannot allow the assertion to be well founded. I am certain that from either of these poems, but especially from Milton, many a passage of ten lines may be reduced to prose, by taking the words which constitute the music of blank verse out of their inverted order. I know not that the first lines, to go no farther, of Paradise Lost, have any title to poetry but from the harmony of the verse.

This ingenious critic seems to think Mr. Pope deficient in the first requisites of a poet, pathos and sublimity.

But the censure will include Horace; for the greater part of his writings is evidently prosaic. It would however, be extremely unfair to collect from this circumstance that Horace is not a poet, but only a moralist or satirist. He has given evident proof of his ability as a poet in his odes. He has exhibited both pathos and sublimity. But in his satires and epistles he has voluntarily fallen from the heights which he ascended. And why may not the same be said of Mr. Pope? Mr. Pope exhibited many instances of the sublime in his Opuscula, and many also of the pathetic. What shall we say of many lines in his Sacred Pastoral, in his Windsor Forest, in his Ode on St. Cecilia, and in his Uni-

versal Prayer? Can any thing be more empas-
sioned than the Epistle from Eloisa to Abelard?
And there are strokes of the pathetic in the Elegy on
an Unfortunate Lady, fully sufficient to prove that he
was capable of excelling in the pathetic if he had
chosen it. As to Dr. Johnson's reasonings on the
propriety or impropriety of celebrating a lady in the
circumstances described, I cannot help thinking they
might have been omitted, for poetry will overlook a
multitude of personal failings ; and though in a moral
sense the subject should be censurable, yet the poem
may be excellent. A reader may find passages in
the Iliad of Pope which evince his ability to equal
any of our English poets in pathos and sublimity.

One is concerned to see ingenuity and learning
employed in detracting from such reputation as is
established by the concurring opinions of the best
judges during a long time. It usually argues something of envy in the detractor ; and if any are
made converts to his opinion, they are generally
precipitated beyond the just limits of equitable judgment, and appear to derive a pleasure from censuring with unbounded severity those whom the
world has agreed to admire.

Envy, however, cannot possibly be the motive
which induced the essayist on the genius and
writings of Pope to depreciate his merits. Indeed,
I cannot help thinking that the critic entered upon
the work with ideas much more derogatory from
him than those with which he concluded. For, in
the second volume, he allows him a place in the next
rank to Spenser, Shakspeare, and Milton. This is
a very honourable place. There is reason to believe,
that where either of these poets is read once, Mr. Pope
is read twice, which is, after all that critics may advance, the truest honour, and the best test of real merit.

EVENING LIV.

ON THE MODERN COMEDIES OF THE ENGLISH STAGE.

THAT kind of entertainment which the English call Farce is the true ancient comedy, as it appears in Plautus and Aristophanes. Serious comedy is indeed almost a contradiction in terms. Terence's comedies are confessedly too serious. The language is elegant, the sentiments beautiful; but there is not a sufficient quantity of comic force.

To recreate, by exciting laughter, and to instruct, by exhibiting foibles and faults as objects of ridicule, is the final cause of comedy. I know that philosophical critics, or rather logicians and metaphysicians, give very subtle definitions of comedy; but I am inclined to view it rather in a popular light, as it appears to a crowded theatre, or is perused by the common reader, than as it is contemplated in the schools of spider-like metaphysicians. If I were to appeal to an audience assembled at Covent Garden or Drury Lane theatres, I believe they would cordially agree with me, that a truly excellent comedy is that which causes them to shake their sides most frequently with the drollery of its scenes, and the wit and humour of its conversation.

A perplexed and involved plot is disagreeable to the majority. It employs their attention in a painful complication of events, while it ought to be easily and pleasantly amused by the dialogue. The greater part of an audience assemble at a theatre after the toils of the day, to be innocently amused. They are not desirous of that laborious exercise of the memory and understanding which is sometimes necessary to comprehend the plot of a modern comedy. I think it would be an improvement in the dramatic line, if the plots of plays were more remarkable for simplicity; but many comedies are in the greatest esteem which are singularly perplexed in their story.

Sentimental comedies have been greatly admired; and it seems to argue a great delicacy of taste and purity of morals when a whole people are delighted with them. But it may be said of them with great truth, that they encroach on the province of tragedy. A sentimental comedy chiefly endeavours to excite emotions of pity; and cannot this purpose be more effectually accomplished by tragedy?

Let us suppose a person intending to amuse his evening by the sight of a play. At one theatre a comedy is to be exhibited, at another, a tragedy. He debates the point with himself to which he shall go; and finds that his mind is in a disposition to be diverted with ludicrous representation. He resolves therefore to see the comedy. Unacquainted with the piece, he enters the theatre in expectation of mirth; but the comedians, after a great deal of delicate, refined, and serious converse, begin to weep. The spectator can scarcely believe that he has not made a mistake. He finds the distress of tragedy, under the deceitful title of comedy. He is dejected and disappointed; and indeed has a right to complain of a feast little corresponding with the bill of fare.

I argue, from the just displeasure of a spectator so disappointed, that sentimental comedy should be distinguished by some name appropriated to its nature. I have read several sentimental comedies which exhibited beautiful language, and were, on many accounts, very pleasing in the closet, though they did not excite laughter on the stage. Terence is certainly the model of sentimental comedy; but his imitators ought to remember, that the best judges, among whom was Julius Cæsar, disapproved his want of wit and humour.

The pleasure which wit and humour are capable of affording the human mind is exquisite, and was intended by a benign Providence to mitigate the ills of life. It is therefore desirable that comedy should preserve her genuine excellence, and not lose the power of exciting mirth by being confounded with a serious and pathetic species of composition.

There are indeed restraints under which the comic muse ought to be confined. She has often transgressed the bounds of decency and nature. Her sallies have transported her to eccentricities which judgment must condemn, though the gaiety of thoughtless merriment may seem to have approved, by joining in the laughter which they excited in a theatre. Indeed the ancients are more culpable than the moderns in this respect; for where is the modern who in obscene and filthy ideas can be compared with Plautus and Aristophanes? The excellent Collier did great service to society by satirizing the indecencies of the English stage in the last age; and indecency is certainly not the fault of the present comedy.

The fault of the present comedy is rather an insipidity. The language is usually elegant, and the plot well laid, but the comic force is not often sufficient to command universal laughter, independently of the grimace and theatrical tricks of the actor. It is, as I have more than once already hinted, much more like Terence than Plautus. To say this, is to pay it a greater compliment than perhaps it deserves; for Plautus has never been estimated at the same value with Terence. Plautus has mingled many coarse jokes and many indecent allusions with his wit, which cannot but lower his merit, and lessen the praise which would otherwise be liberally bestowed upon him.

If a writer should arise with all the drollery and humour of Plautus and Aristophanes, yet without their ribaldry, I think he would find universal approbation. We have many excellent comedies in the English language, but the most witty of them are disgraced by indecency.

The morals of a people must of necessity be much corrupted by the profligacy of comic writers, for they have the laugh in their favour, which, with the herd of mankind, is a far more convincing proof of excellence than any argument. The pulpit menaces in vain when the stage points its batteries against it. Vice has many advocates on her side within our own bosoms, and when she finds wit and ridicule called in as her auxiliaries, she no longer hides her head in shame, but walks in the broad sunshine, and haughtily triumphs over the modesty of virtue.

Preaching indeed and moralizing with severity would be out of place in a comedy. They would lose much of their dignity and beauty by appearing in a garb of levity ; but a medium might surely be found to direct the comic writer, so as that his comedies should neither on the one hand become dull moralities, nor, on the other, corrupting farces.

The best purpose of comedy is to render vice ridiculous ; but it has been too often employed in rendering virtue so. The French comedy is far purer than the English. Let it no longer be said with truth ; for a gross taste in works of wit and humour will suggest a suspicion that we are really inferior in true politeness, as well as in external grace, to our rival neighbours.

EVENING LV.

ON VANITY AS A MOTIVE OF AUTHORS, AND THE DISAGREEMENT OF THEIR CONDUCT AND DOCTRINE.

IF the love of fame is not, as Dr. Young asserted, the universal passion, it certainly operates on a very large majority of the human race. It conceals itself under ten thousand forms, but may yet be discovered in most of them by a sagacious observer.

Fame indeed conveys an idea rather more extensive than I mean in this place to convey. It implies that renown which arises from public celebrity. But the passion which is found to be almost universal, is rather a love of distinction among those in whose view we act, and with whom we are connected. I believe it will be difficult to find a single instance of a human creature possessing the use of his faculties, and at the same time undesirous of distinction.

Authors appear to be peculiarly under the influence of this desire. They usually affirm, in the prefaces and introductions to their works, that they are actuated by the pure motives of communicating knowledge, or reforming manners. But what does their conduct imply? When a man publishes his opinions, may he not be understood to say, Come hither, ye who want instruction? I am able to afford it you. I understand the art or science which you cultivate, or the art of life, better than you do, and am desirous of contributing to your improvement. Is not this tacitly to say, I am wiser than you?

Such indeed appears to be the construction which may possibly be put upon his conduct, in stepping forward from the privacy of his study, and holding up his volume to the public eye: and it is no violation of charity to impute the greater part of publications to the influence of vanity.

Vanity, or a desire of distinction, though often a ridiculous infirmity, is often the cause of meritorious conduct. At least, it will be allowed, that it produces advantage, though itself should have no just claim to merit.

Let us imagine all men destitute of vanity, or, as it may be more candidly denominated, a desire of being distinguished. What a torpid state ensues, The world is on a sudden sunk in a deep sleep; for though there is no doubt that many virtuous persons would continue to do good from generous principles, yet that universal activity which now keeps alive a public spirit in all orders would disappear. The number of those who are so far improved as to do good from principle alone, without the least regard to the opinion of their fellow-creatures, is small in comparison with that of those who do good from an united motive, a desire of performing a duty, and of obtaining the esteem and regard of those who are influenced by the performance of it, or who observe and admire it.

And what shall we say of the author who gives advice which he does not follow ?

A moral essayist recommends some particular virtue. He recommends it sincerely, though he is not remarkable for it himself. Is he a hypocrite ? Does he wish to persuade men that he is possessed of every excellence which he describes and enforces? Possibly not. Whence arises the incongruity of his life and writings ? From the imbecility of human nature, and the corruption of the world. He writes what he thinks and feels in his better moments, when his reason is able to operate without the bias of passion. But, in his intercourse with the world, he is under the influence of those passions which ever did and ever will draw all men in some degree from the right line of acknowledged duty.

However vain an author may be, or however unequal his conduct and practice to his advice and doctrine, yet if his advice and doctrine are in themselves valuable, they ought not to lose their value from the personal folly, wickedness, or weakness of their author. A reader should remember that an author is, like himself, a man; improved probably in intellectual abilities and attainments, but still retaining that propensity to evil which belongs to his nature; and which, though it may be lessened, cannot be entirely removed by any improvement of human reason.

Religion only can perfect what reason begins. All our laboured books, and all our boasted wisdom and philosophy, are but trifles, nonsense, shadows, compared to the influence of that grace which the God of all goodness vouchsafes to the pious and devout believer.

EVENING LVI.

ON SUPPORTING A CHARACTER OF LEARNING AND DIGNITY BY ARTIFICE AND GRIMACE.

THERE is a sort of persons in the world too indolent to study, and perhaps too deficient in parts to make any great improvement, who yet see the advantage of a literary reputation, and assume the airs of decisive critics, without having ever produced any certificate of their qualification. It does not appear that they read much, and it is probable that they have written little; it is certain that they are very shy of producing what they know to public view, either in the pulpit, at the bar, in the senate,

or any where else.   Their character is entirely supported by artifice and caution; it often deceives
those who know not how to distinguish gilding from
gold; it shines with particular splendour among the
vulgar, who commonly associate knowledge with a
great wig, a precise air, a grave countenance, and
the robes of a profession or office.

The possession of a good library, or at least of a
numerous collection of well-gilt folios, gives to many
the confidence and the credit of learning, especially
when the possessor has read enough of the gilt letters
on the back, to be able to talk of them fluently
whenever he is in company with the ignorant and
superficial.   If you walk into the library, or, as it
is now called, the book-room of one of these pretenders, you see the ranks in the utmost order, and
not a book misplaced, except perhaps a Poly-
glott lying open on the reading table.   If you wish
to see the place which the student really devotes to
contemplation, you must enter his dressing-room.   It
is there that he practises *gnothi seauton,* or the rule of
studying himself, there he inspects the mirror, and
indulges himself in the most pleasing reflexions.

Preciseness of dress and address, and great caution
in all that they say, is a principal artifice in passing
for men of erudition.   Thus, if the subject is literary,
they are by no means eager to speak their opinion,
unless indeed the company is known by them to
be unqualified to judge; but content themselves with
a reserve which excites respect, and gives an air of
dignity.   The owl looks grave, and passes for the
bird of wisdom.   The utmost length they will venture to go among men of sense and knowledge, is
to make grimaces, to lift up the eye-brows, turn up
the nose, shrug the shoulders, move their hands and
eyes, or walk off with an air of fastidious contempt.

The company give them credit for superior judgment, and doubt not, if they had thought it worth their while to open before such inconsiderable hearers as themselves, or on topics which to them must appear trifling, they would have communicated something which the hearers might have deposited in the treasury of their memory for life. When the mountain was in labour, and gave such awful throes, the spectators were dumb with the expectation of some production which should become the wonder of the world : and if the mouse had not crept out, they would have still supposed that the mountain teemed with something of a most stupendous magnitude. The men I am describing are wiser than this celebrated mountain, and take special care, when judicious spectators are present, not to let out their mouse.

I have known one pass for a man of great learning and a critic by dint of a pair of spectacles, and a gold headed cane, with a silk string and tassels. He said little among judges of the subject, according to the general maxim of the pretenders. But his manner was, to elevate his chin, project his lips, fix his eyes on the ceiling, place both his hands on the head of his cane, with the string round his wrist, and pretend absence of thought. Young company was awestruck, and either said nothing on learned subjects, or expressed themselves with the utmost diffidence, referring all to the decision of the gentleman in the spectacles.

I was lately diverted with one of the swindlers of literary reputation, who is a man of considerable connexions in high life, and consequently pretty well taken care of, as the phrase is, in the church, where men of rank and power meanly provide for their old tutors, dependants, and relations, without expense to themselves. The subject introduced was the literary character of Dr. Johnson. As the swindler wore a great feather top and full-bottomed peruke, and a short cassock, every one was solicitous to hear his opinions. He fought shy, as the cock-fighters say, a long time, but he was so much pressed by importunity that he could not persevere. " To tell you truth," said he, stroking his chin, " I have no opinion of the man. I have endeavoured to read his Ramblers, but neither I, nor Dean ————, nor Archdeacon ————, nor, I believe, Bishop ————, could get through them."

" But, Sir," said a sensible young man, who had hitherto sat silent, " you must allow him to be a friend to religion and morality, a warm friend to the church ; and for that reason surely, if no other, worthy the esteem and praise of yourself and the other dignitaries whom you have mentioned."

The doctor was silent near a minute, when, after taking snuff, and twisting his features into a variety of contortions, he said, " Sir, Doctor Johnson was a bookseller's author. His morality I know little of; but his religion was superstition. Sir, he was not a man of learning. He knew little of theology as a science. But indeed, Sir, I do not undertake to characterise Dr. Johnson, as I profess myself no great reader of essayists or superficial writers of any denomination.—The Fathers—"

The young gentleman was too well bred to dwell on a topic which his opponent seemed to decline. And the rector of the parish coming in with a brace of pointers, the subject gave place to the history of that day's shooting, which was universally relished, and the conversation terminated with a game at backgammon. I could evidently observe that the company thought the doctor an oracle of learning and criticism, though, with respect to his ability to judge of Dr. Johnson's works, I rather doubt it, as I found he was not possessed of any part of them, and as I knew he seldom read any thing but the Court Calendar, a ministerial newspaper, and Ecton's Thesaurus. He was a good man, as to his morals, but rather weak of understanding, and yet vain enough to wish to pass for a great scholar. I believe he had persuaded himself, and the little circle of his own family and friends, that he was deep indeed.

There are many others who, with good sense and competent learning, are yet inclined to destroy that reputation which they have been unable to reach; unwilling, through laziness, to seek fame with constancy in the laborious mode of obtaining by deserving it. The artifices used by these gentlemen are full of malignity. The first requisite is to exalt themselves to consequence, that their dictatorial edicts may be issued out with authority.

" Pray, Sir, what do you think of the new poem?" says some modest inquirer. " Moderate, very moderate," replies the critic. " I am sorry the young man should have put his name to it."——" Why, Sir, it has a rapid sale."——" O, to be sure, it is calculated for the meridian of the mob. The vulgar admire what good judges cannot approve. Popularity, in my estimation, is never a test of merit. Such trifles, indeed, are not worth my attention; I, for my part, chuse to dwell with authors of a better age than the present. Literature is sadly degenerated. Nothing but trash and rubbish in the market."

He then talks of some old author whose name he has found in a catalogue, or whose title-page he may have read at a bookseller's. The young man thinks him another Aristarchus, though those who know him are convinced that he has as little value as taste for letters, any otherwise than as the reputation of learning may gratify his pride or promote his interest. He is none of your amateurs who love literary excellence,

Præmia si tollas.

Let him take off his great wig and gown, as combatants strip when they fight, and I believe he would be unable to carry the prize from many an undergraduate, and even schoolboy.

These men might be laughed at and let alone, if they did not frequently do mischief; but they hesitate not to rob the deserving of the only reward of their labours, an honest fame.

————— Detrahere ausi
Hærentem capiti multâ cum laude coronam.   Hor.

As impostors and deceivers, they deserve also the punishment of derision. Counterfeit coin ought to be cried down and stopt in its circulation, lest they who, in the honesty of their hearts, take it as lawful currency, should suffer a loss which they have not merited.

EVENING LVII.

ON A SUNDAY EVENING LECTURE AT SCHOOL.

Honoured Sir,—I send you, as you desired, a copy of our master's introductory Sunday lecture, as nearly exact as I can remember it.

"I am," said he, "truly sensible of the important trust reposed in me, and cannot but feel a solicitude to discharge it with propriety. I will not say that the pecuniary emolument arising from it is by any means indifferent to me. No man would sacrifice his ease, and enter into an anxious employment, without a desire of those rewards which are allotted to industry. And it is equitable that he who is willing to step forward and render himself extensively useful to others, should derive such advantages from his exertions as may render his old age easy and respected, or provide for the wants of a rising family. But I must declare, on the other hand, that the satisfaction proceeding from a consciousness of performing the duty incumbent on me, and rendering a service equivalent to the recompence, sweetens every labour, and gives additional value to the pecuniary compensation.

" You are placed here for two purposes; the improvement of the understanding, and the formation of virtuous principles for the guidance of your moral conduct.

" Improvement of the understanding is apparently the first object in your entrance at school; but it cannot be doubted but that improvement of the heart is really esteemed, by those to whom you are most dear, at a higher price than the finest accomplishment of the most cultivated intellect.

" It is your business to unite these estimable objects, and to suffer your hearts and understandings to vie with each other in the pursuit of excellence.

" Of these lectures which I have instituted as a laudable method of employing a Sunday evening, the principal purpose is to promote the knowledge and the practice of the Christian religion; and in the performance of this purpose, I shall of necessity be led to recommend the purest system of morality. Ethics, improved and exalted by the Christian religion, become the guides to real wisdom and solid happiness, to which they could never attain when taught only in the schools of heathen philosophy.

" In the religious part of your education, it is not expected that you should be engaged in the profound disquisitions of theology. The plain doctrines of the religion which you have been taught to profess must be explained to you; but the principal business is to open your hearts for the reception of those sentiments and precepts which conduce to the direction of your actions in the employments and engagements of your subsequent life.

" In the first place, I must then remind you of the necessity of reading the Scriptures; that is, of drinking the sacred waters at the fountain.

" But to read the Scriptures with advantage, judgment is necessary; and as judgment at your age is not mature, you must seek and follow the directions of your instructors. At your age the plainest and most perspicuous passages will best deserve and reward your attention. The historical parts of the Old Testament will entertain you, if you consider them only in a classical view, as valuable passages of ancient history; but I chiefly refer you to the books which more immediately conduce to moral instruction, such as the Proverbs, the Book of Ecclesiastes, the Wisdom of the Son of Sirach, and the admirable Book entitled Ecclesiasticus. I must indeed lament that this fine remain of ancient wisdom is not inserted in the common editions of the Bible.

" The prophetical books will not at present afford you much instruction; because they cannot be understood without a larger share of preparatory learning than you can be supposed to possess at your age. But I advise you to read several of them for the poetical beauties which they confessedly display. Isaiah abounds with such beauties, and Jeremiah is by no means deficient in them. Many of you have read Mr. Pope's Messiah, and could not but have observed that some of its most pleasing beauties were taken from Isaiah. The learned Dr. Lowth has displayed, with great accuracy and taste, the beauties of sacred poetry in the lectures which he read as Professor of Poetry in the university of Oxford.

" If you read the Old Testament with a taste for its beauties, you will accomplish two important purposes at the same time. You will acquire a knowledge of the Holy Bible, which is your duty ; and you will improve your taste and judgment in Oriental poetry, which is a part of your business as students in the course of a polite education.

" The New Testament requires the peculiar attention of every one who professes himself a Christian. But here also judgment is necessary to direct the student in the mode of his study. To one who has not the requisite share of introductory knowledge, the Gospel will appear to contain many difficulties. As you cannot yet engage in theological studies, I must recommend it to you to take up the Testament with that humility which becomes all human creatures, but more particularly persons so young as you are, and so destitute of all that knowledge which can enable you to form a decisive opinion in divinity. You will do right to pay particular attention to the sermon on the mount, and to that admirable epitome of all moral philosophy, the rule of doing to others as we wish them to do to us. If you give due obedience to this precept, you will never hesitate in determining what part you shall act whenever difficulties occur.

" It will however be proper that you should at an early age familiarise to your mind the language of the Scriptures, in all their parts, though you should not be able fully to comprehend it. You will thus treasure up passages in your memory, which, on many occasions in the course of your lives, may be useful. A very early acquaintance with the words

of the Old Testament, even before any adequate
ideas of their meaning have been obtained, has been
found useful in subsequent life to the professed divine.

" And here I cannot but animadvert on the prevalent neglect of the Holy Scriptures; a neglect
which too plainly indicates a faint belief in the doctrines which they contain, and which ought to animate every parent and instructor in the business of
infusing religious sentiments and a reverence for the
Bible while the mind is most susceptible of deep impressions. You, who constitute a part of the rising
generation, will exert yourselves in removing an evil
which menaces the ruin of the national morals and
prosperity. They indeed among you who are capable of a sentiment so enlarged as this, exhibit a manliness of mind, which is the more honourable to them
as it is uncommon at their age.

" In the religious part of your education it would
be a disgraceful omission to neglect the catechism.
The catechism of the Church of England is concise,
yet, as a catechism, sufficiently instructive. It is
plain and unadorned, and for that reason the more
excellent. I know it has enemies, who complain
that it is too short, and that it teaches doctrines
which they do not admit or understand. I recommend it to you as a useful, though humble guide, and
I wish to warn you against that pride of heart which
induces some persons to slight it.; and against that
spirit of censoriousness which causes in others a
violent antipathy to all that contradicts their own
peculiar persuasion. Be ready to receive valuable
instruction from whatever party or sect it may proceed; but, unless there is some real and solid objection to the mode in which your fathers have been
instructed, I wish you to adhere to it with a dutiful
veneration unmixed with bigotry.

" Archbishop Secker's lectures on the catechism are very useful explanations. They are plain in the style, and purposely adapted to the understandings of the simple. You will not inspect them for the graces of language, or the figures of rhetoric, but for information in the principles of Christianity.

" From the Scriptures themselves, the catechism, and Secker's lectures, you will derive as much knowledge in the department of religion as you can reasonably be expected to acquire at your school. Let these constitute a foundation, on which you will be constantly making some addition, either theoretical or practical, during the future course of your lives.

" But all this will avail but little, unless you add your prayers and praises. Make it then a rule never to be violated, to pray night and morning. It is indeed true that in this and other schools it is usual to read prayers at the commencement and at the close of the day ; but, I am sorry to say, that these are often considered as mere formalities. You will pay attention to these, and you will also repeat private prayers at lying down on your pillow or rising from it.

" You will in vain expect success in your studies unless you implore a blessing on them from heaven ; or, if you should be permitted by Providence to make a proficiency in knowledge for the sake of others, you will not derive from your acquisition that degree of happiness which you would otherwise enjoy. You must ask the Giver of every good gift for the very valuable gift of literary improvement, and the comforts that flow from it.

" You are apt at your age to be thoughtless. You enjoy health and spirits. You are strangers to the cares of the world. Cheerfulness indeed becomes you ; but let me prevail with you, when I entreat you to consider the value of time, and the importance of making a good use of it.

" Consider your parents. Form an idea of the anxiety which they feel on your account. You must have observed how eagerly they wish for your improvement. They feel a laudable ambition, which prompts them to desire that you may arrive at eminence in whatever profession or employment you may hereafter be engaged by Providence. To them it would be a painful sight to see you contemptible and unsuccessful. But nothing can vindicate you from contempt, or insure your success so effectually, as personal merit, or the qualities of a good disposition adorned with a competent share of human learning and accomplishments.

" Your parents do all that lies in their power to promote your improvement; but, after all, they cannot but know that it remains with yourselves to give efficacy and final good success to their endeavours. The mind is not like a vessel, into which may be poured any quantity of whatever the teacher chuses to infuse. It is rather like a plant, which, by the operation of its own internal powers, imbibes the nutriment afforded by the earth.

" But, not to dwell on similes, it is certain that your instructors can serve you only in conjunction with your own efforts.

" Let me then entreat you to exert yourselves, if you have any regard for your parents, whose happiness entirely depends on your conduct; if you have any regard for your own honour, success, and comfort; if you desire to be useful and respected in society."

———

I hope I shall be wise enough to consult my own happiness by following the advice contained in the above lecture, and in those many affectionate letters, in which your paternal tenderness softens all the severity of wisdom, and tempers discipline with indulgence.

I am, honored Sir,
Your's most dutifully,
PIUS FILIUS.

EVENING LVIII.

ON THE DANGER AND FOLLY OF INNOVATION.

SIR,

I AM the tenant of an old stone mansion, very firmly built, and supported by massy buttresses; but inconvenient though spacious, ugly though magnificent, and unhealthy though in a fine situation.

A few alterations would render it a most desirable residence; but the proprietor, old Lady Alma Mater, bears as great an antipathy to innovation of any kind as a mad dog to water. Indeed I think her antipathy is so violent and so unreasonable, that it may be justly deemed a disease; and I have accordingly given it the name of the *Neophobia*. It is, I fear, an incurable malady.

The windows of the Gothic house I live in are in the shape of a lancet, and scarcely larger. The panes of glass are cut in diamonds, and not above three inches square. The iron bars are so thick as to obscure the sun-beams, which shine in vain upon the cold and damp walls. Our rooms have scarcely any fresh air, and not light enough to see distinctly to read. The old Roman catholic paintings in the best parlour window, added to the smallness of the panes, the quantity of the lead, and the thickness, make it as gloomy as a charnel house. There is a most delightful prospect from the windows of every room, but they are placed so high, that you cannot look out of them without the assistance of a chair or a pair of steps.

The door-way is so low, that a person in the modern dress cannot enter without stooping; and so narrow, that you are necessitated to enter sideways.

The rooms are hung with green cloth, faded tapestry, matting, and some frightful old portraits. The floors have been penetrated by rats, worm-eaten in every part, and are become uneven from the sinking of the joists and girders. The ceilings are cracked, yellow with smoke, and decayed by damp. Yet the original dimensions are good, and every room might be rendered not only comfortable but elegant, if the landlady would admit of a little alteration. But she shakes her head whenever it is mentioned to her, and vows it to be her firm belief, that whenever a single improvement shall be made, the whole fabric will be in danger of falling down. The toothless old lady declares she will have no such doings, not she.

A surveyor came to see us not long ago, and, with the most disinterested intention, sketched a plan of alterations that, at a very little expense, would have made the mansion the pride and envy of the whole country. He presented his papers to the proprietrix, who no sooner had perused them than she fell into a violent rage, threw the plan into the fire, lifted up her cane, and threatened that, if the innovator came near her premises, she would cause him to be taken up as a dangerous and designing person.

Thus we are reduced to the necessity of bearing the inconveniences of the antiquated seat, though it is so very uncomfortable that hardly any one would come to see us, if we did not keep a good table and cellar, and if the great antiquity and magnificence of the place did not render it, in some degree, fashionable to resort to it. The needy and the idle flock to us; but if our residence were a little accommodated to the improved taste of the times, there is no doubt but many of the most respectable people in the nation would take up their abode with us during some part of the year.

I remonstrated on the subject to the good old dame. She sat silent a good while, till at last she mumbled out the following declaration :

" Look ye, Mr. Innovator, I consider myself as the best judge of fitness and propriety ; and shall not be dictated to by any one. Old age brings wisdom. I know you think me in my dotage ; but remember the adage, young folk think old folk fools ; while old folk know young ones to be so. I have had very good tenants for time immemorial; they paid their rents well, enjoyed their ease, and seldom complained. I am for keeping up the good old ways. Innovation is a most dangerous thing : nobody knows where it will end. You are for enlarging the windows and widening the doors; another, perhaps, will desire to have new floors and ceiling ; a third will pull down the buttresses, because they are ugly forsooth—and then down goes the whole pile. No, no, Sir : innovation is a dangerous thing ; and I would sooner see the whole building covered with moss and filth ; nay, overrun with rats and vermin of every kind, than suffer a nail, a hinge, a stone, or a tile to be displaced ; because, when innovation begins, you do not know where it will end."

I perceived the old lady was desirous of going on with her harangue ; but for want of argument was obliged to run into tautology, and to repeat, as well as her decayed organs of utterance would permit her, " Innovation is a dangerous thing ; when you

begin, you do not know where it will end." She
harped continually upon the same string, and sung
the same notes to it, like the cuckoo.

My patience being exhausted, I begged leave to
interrupt her garrulity. "Lady Alma," said I, "I
wish to pay you every respect that is due to age; but
there is a point of mental decrepitude at which contempt would take place, if pity did not intervene.
To adopt the language of Lord Chatham, 'Age may
justly become contemptible, if the opportunities
which it has brought have past away without improvement. The wretch who, after having seen the
consequences of a thousand errors, continues to
blunder, and whose age has only added obstinacy
to stupidity, is surely an object either of abhorrence
or contempt, and deserves not that his grey hairs
should secure him from insult.'*

" Innovation, Madam, is a term used by the indolent and the artful merely as a bugbear. Dismiss it,
and adopt improvement in its place; for I would
have no innovation which is not, after mature deliberation, clearly shown to be an improvement. Place
the word improvement in the room of innovation in
your favourite apophthegm; will you say that improvement is a dangerous thing? Will you say that
improvement leads to ruin? You might as well say,
that to cure a disease is to hasten death; to stop the
leaking of a ship, to cause it to founder.

" To enlarge your doors and windows would be
to admit more sun and air. Would the admission
of sun and air cause the timbers to decay, or injure
the health of the inhabitants? To address you on a
topic more interesting to your sex—A new garment
is an innovation; but would you, Lady Alma, refuse

* An nihil in melius tot rerum proficis usu?   JUV.

to purchase a new gown, when by length of time
your old grogram was worn to tatters, or grown so
unfashionable as to excite ridicule in the very boys
as you go to church ? If there were an art which
could restore efflorescence and plumpness to those
pale withered cheeks of yours, or rekindle the fire
of those dim orbs, would you not have recourse to it
without fear of dangerous innovation ? If those grey
locks could be changed to the auburn tresses which
flowed down your shoulders in the days of your
youth, would you not deem the innovation an improvement devoutly to be wished ? Or could those
toothless gums be re-adorned with their native ivory,
instead of a few rotten stumps, would you condemn
the restorative art as a dangerous innovation ?"

While I was putting these questions, I perceived
that the old lady sat uneasy on her chair. The little
blood that she had left boiled up into her nose and
cheeks; and at last, by the help of her stick, she
rose from her elbow-chair, tottered to the bell, and
muttering curses as she went, gave it a violent pull
with her thin, bony, veiny, palsied hand, and ordered her steward, on his entering, to see me to the
door, and serve me immediately with an ejectment
from the mansion-house which I had tenanted. She
then went to the closet, applied the brandy-bottle to
her mouth, and wrapping herself up in her old purple velvet cloak, took a nap in her great chair, and
forgot all that had passed.

I retired with complacency; happy to quit a residence so very incommodious, so wretchedly uncomfortable, so damp and so dark ; especially as I
plainly saw that my landlady was too far gone in
her dotage to admit of any improvements. Time,
however, will at last destroy the edifice, and then
probably it may be rebuilt with all the beauty and

convenience of modern ages; for, to adopt the expression of Mr. Brown, there certainly are great capabilities. The foundation of such a building did honour to the nation and to human nature; and if it were from time to time repaired, and accommodated to the improvements of succeeding ages, it would continue to be one of the most useful and ornamental fabrics in the universe.

EVENING LIX.

ON THE MISERY OF THE LOWER CLASSES, CAUSED BY PASSION AND GROSS IGNORANCE OF RELIGION.

SIR,

THE weather was remarkably serene, and I resolved to leave my book-room to enjoy the vernal season. I walked carelessly from field to field, regaled with the sweet smells which arose from the new-mown hay, and cheered by every appearance of plenty and tranquillity. External objects have a powerful effect in soothing the mind of man. I found myself sympathising with the appearance of happiness round me. Every ruder passion was lulled to rest, my heart glowed with benevolence, and I enjoyed for a short time a state of perfect felicity.

As I roamed without any settled purpose, my feet carried me to the city. Curiosity led me with the crowd to an execution; and as I had just left a beautiful scene, in which all was peace, I could not but be particularly struck with the contrast of the present noise, tumult, and dreadful spectacle.

I hastily left the place, when, to my mortification, I found that I had been robbed of my watch and handkerchief. While I was lamenting my loss, and encouraging some sentiments perhaps rather too unfavourable to my species, I was suddenly involved in a crowd, collected with eager curiosity to see two hackney-coachmen terminate a dispute by the exertion of their strength in single combat. The parties were nearly equal, and terrible was the conflict. The blows resounded at a great distance, and presently I beheld them both covered with blood and dirt; shocking figures to the imagination. The spectators expressed no wish that the combatants might be separated; but seemed delighted when a violent blow took place, and disappointed when it was spent in air. I wished to interfere and promote an amicable adjustment of the matter in dispute; but I found my efforts ineffectual. I ventured to propose the separation of the poor creatures who were thus cruelly bruising each other, to a jolly butcher, six feet high and three feet broad, but he gave me an indignant look, and threatened to knock me down if I dared to interpose. I found, indeed, that the combat afforded exquisite pleasure to the crowd. Some rubbed their hands with glee, some silently grinned, while others vociferated words of encouragement, and others skipped for joy. Great pleasures are, however, of no long duration, and this amusement was terminated by one of the combatants ceasing to rise, on receiving a violent blow on his left temple. Down he fell, and the ground shook under him; and though he attempted three times to rise, he was unable to effect his purpose; and the whole circle agreed that he was beaten within an inch of his life. The conqueror had only lost three of his fore teeth and one eye, and all agreed that he had acquitted himself like a man. The crowd, which had been so much delighted with the fray, no sooner saw it concluded, than, with looks of disappointment, they began to disperse. I took the opportunity of examining the state of the vanquished party,

and found him still alive, though almost in need of
the means which are used by the Humane Society
to accomplish his complete revival. An officious
acquaintance hastened to his assistance with a dram
of brandy, which contributed greatly to accelerate
his recovery. He no sooner rose than he poured
forth a volley of dreadful imprecations on his limbs,
which had already suffered extremely. Instead of
thanking me or any of the spectators who had endeavoured to restore him, he swore, in a muttering
tone, that if we did not stand out of his way, he
would fell us to the ground. We readily receded,
when the hero, putting on his clothes, walked
away, turned down an alley, and was seen by us
no more.

My reflexions on this scene were such as tended
to the degradation of my species; and not being in
very good spirits, I determined to enter a coffee-
house, and seek amusement by a perusal of the newspapers. I sat down, and happened to cast my eye
over the last column, which consisted of nothing but
narratives of rapes, robberies, and murders. Though
I knew that this was not at all uncommon, and that
every day's paper of intelligence could furnish something of a similar history ; yet, being in a melancholy
mood, I was particularly struck by it; and hastily
laying down the paper, and paying for my dish of
coffee, I put on my hat, and resolved to walk to my
little rural retirement about four miles from this
turbulent scene.

As I walked along, I could not help calling to
mind, with sentiments of extreme regret, the pleasing ideas with which I had set out in the morning.
All was then tranquillity and benevolence. But I
have seen, in the space of a few hours only, such
pictures of human misery and perverseness as

could not but occasion uneasiness in a mind not utterly destitute of sympathy.

Surely, said I, nature, or the God of nature, never intended that man should be so degraded. It is passion which deforms the beauty of the moral world; it is wickedness and the neglect of religion which renders man more miserable than the brute, who is happy in his insensibility. What then can I think of those writers who argue in defence of immorality, and against revelation? What of those governors of the world, who bestow no attention in preserving the morals of the common people, and encouraging the teachers of such doctrines as conduce to the raising of the reptile man from the voluntary abasement in which his evil inclinations are able to involve him? Let the magistrates, the clergy, the rich and powerful of every occupation, whose example is irresistible, exert themselves in diffusing virtuous principles and practices among the people at large. Such benevolence, more beneficial than all pecuniary bounty, considered only as preventing temporal misery, causes man to approach nearer to his benignant Maker than any other conduct. To that Maker, said I, let those who have charity apply themselves in prayer for the diminution of evil of all kinds, and the extension of happiness and peace.

I was musing on such subjects when I found myself at the door of my little cottage. The evening was beautiful. The clouds in the west were variegated with colours, such as no pencil has yet been able to imitate. My garden breathed odours, and displayed the bloom of shrubs, such as might adorn the Elysian fields of the poets. All conspired to restore the tranquillity of the morning; and when I retired to rest, my spirits being composed, I soon sunk into a sweet sleep, pleasingly interrupted in the morning by a dream, which, as it appeared to have some connexion with the ideas which I had entertained in the day, I shall relate.

I thought I was on a large plain covered over with flocks of innumerable sheep. They appeared to straggle without a guide. Many had their fleeces torn by brambles, some were lost in a barren wilderness, others were pursued by wolves, and not a few were constantly engaged in annoying each other with their horns. There was a general bleating in a tone expressive of great distress. I pitied the poor creatures, but saw no hopes of affording them relief, till I turned my eyes to the eastern part of the plain, when I beheld a venerable shepherd with his crook inviting the sheep into a fold, through which ran a delightful stream of clear water. Many rushed in, and began to drink with avidity. The alteration in their appearance was in the highest degree pleasing. The lambs played about without any fear of the wolf, and the sheep lay and basked in the sunshine, or sought refreshment in the cool shade. The shepherd's looks were benevolent beyond expression. He made use of every inticement to bring the sheep into the fold, but many would not hear his voice, and some seemed to hear it, but perversely ran away from him. I saw those who were so unhappy as to refuse to enter, perish miserably by falling from rocks, by famine, by the violence of the wolf, and by disease. I turned from the painful prospect to see the good shepherd and his fold ; and I thought at the close of the day he led the sheep into a green pasture, the verdure and fertility of which was increased by the gentle river which flowed through the middle of it.

I was so delighted with the scene, that I was going to call out to the shepherd in an ecstacy of joy, when I awoke.

I could not but lament the absence of so pleasing a vision; but the avocations and necessities of life called me from my bed, which I left with resolutions of devoting the rest of my life to the alleviation of evil wherever I should find it, and to the securing of his favour who can lead me from the vale of misery to the waters of comfort and the fountain of life.

I am, Sir, your's, &c.
A CONTEMPLATIVE RAMBLER.

EVENING LX.

ON THE SIMPLICITY AND HONESTY OF MEN OF TRUE GENIUS.

MEN of genius see a beauty (TO KAΛON), unknown to others in the subjects which they contemplate. They become enamoured with the form of ideal beauty, and, like other lovers, regard but little many things which solicit the notice and attach the heart of the multitude.

Joseph Scaliger has said, " Jamais homme ne fut poete, ou aima la lecture des poetes, qui n' eut la cœur assis en bon lieu." And Horace said before him,

—— Levis hæc insania quantas
Virtutes habeat sic collige ; vatis avarus
Non temere est animus ; versus amat, hoc studet unum.

Poets and men of genius are frequently no one's enemies but their own. From their contempt of riches they too often fall into poverty, and live in an ignorance of that humble kind of wisdom, which, though it makes no conspicuous figure, contributes much to comfort. They become the dupes of designing men ; of little minds that grovel in the mire; of men who, though they cannot see far above the earth, yet see their interest with great acuteness, and pursue it with artifice that seldom fails of good success, and who look upon persons employing their time in making verses, pictures, or in reading books, as simpletons easily to be deceived; as much their natural prey, as the pigeon is to the kite.

It is therefore to be wished that, in obedience to the scriptural rule, men of genius would endeavour to unite the wisdom of the serpent with the innocence of the dove.

But as to this dove-like innocence, there are who controvert with powerful arguments its peculiar prevalence in poets and men of genius. I rather think there is a tendency to it in them; but, as it happens in most general rules, there are many exceptions.

Horace says, a poet is seldom avaricious; but proofs to the contrary may be brought: yet the assertion is, in general, true; for there are many more proofs of their want of thrift, and their contempt of riches.

The instance of Pindar, in the second Isthmian ode, suggesting a hint of his wants to Xenocrates of Agrigentum whom he was celebrating, is cited as an instance of poetical meanness and avarice.

In distress he might make such an application without being avaricious. The very want, which drove him to so disagreeable a necessity, might be occasioned by his contempt of money.

Mr. Pope was, I believe, strongly attached to money, and knew both how to gain and keep it. But not so Spenser, nor Shakspeare, nor Dryden, nor Otway.

It is to be wished that poets, and artists of genius, would add discretion to their taste and skill; for it is lamentable that they who give so much pleasure to others should make themselves miserable.

There is, after all, something amiable in their simplicity and generosity. It preserves them from base actions. You may, in general, make a safe agreement with a man of genius ; I mean, of true genius ; for as to the mere pretenders to genius, many of them are remarkable for duplicity and knavery

But if poets and men of genius are free from avarice, they have shown themselves prone to other passions equally or more detrimental. They have been voluptuaries in the extreme ; and, upon the whole, they do not appear to have surpassed the rest of mankind in happiness so much as in talents.

The pleasures of genius, in its exertions, are certainly exquisite ; but the horrors of a gaol, and of want, or disease, must greatly lessen, if not totally destroy them; and the applause and renown bestowed upon them, however flattering to the human heart, are but a poor recompense for the aggravated distresses of private life, which often involve a wife and family. Since genius must be supposed to have been bestowed as a gift conducive to the happiness of him who possesses it, let him take care to add to it discretion, and that useful but humble kind of wisdom called common sense.

EVENING LXI.

ON THE CONTEMPT THROWN ON POETRY BY THE SORDID.

NOTHING contributes more to prove the spirituality of man, than the exalted delight which he is able to derive from the operations of his intellect or his fancy. The pleasures of sense have indeed too much seductive influence on us all; but we are all ready to acknowledge that they are transient and unsatisfactory. The pleasures of the intellect, on the contrary, increase with indulgence, and give a delight no less exalted than pure, and far more permanent than the gratifications of sensuality.

The soul is charmed with the creations of a true poet. Visions of bliss are excited, and the enraptured reader enjoys in fancy all the happiness of Elysium. Language embellished with art and harmony introduces ideas of bliss into the mind with irresistible force, and the reader or composer is raised, in the hour of retirement, above this orb, to roam in fields of delight.

But his excursion is transitory. His natural wants, and his social connexions, draw him down again to the earth. Yet the soul, conscious of her kindred to heaven, will still be striving to escape, and eyes the golden sun, like an eagle confined in a cage. God has given it as a privilege to pure minds uncontaminated by intemperance and vice, to escape from the body, and soar to their native climes.

Ambition and avarice, and the necessary business of the world, require so much time and attention, that but little is left for the delightful flights of fancy. Indeed, the men of business are so warmly attached to their own pursuits and modes of life, that they affect to despise the pleasures of poetry as trifling and nonsensical. O blind and stupid ! ye rob yourselves of one of the sweetest alleviations of your toils; the pleasant pastime which Providence has allotted man, to brighten his prospects, and to mitigate his sorrows. Your souls are locked up in the iron chests with your guineas, or confined in their flights to the regions of 'Change Alley and your accompting houses. If your dull toils are necessary, as society now exists, which I fear I must allow, be content with the profits and the honours of them, but do not throw contempt on poesy, whose origin is divine.

The contempt in which the poet's art is held by the men of business is easily accounted for. They do not understand it. They know not its nature; they have never experienced its effect in themselves, and therefore they are unable to estimate its power on the bosoms of others. One thing they clearly see, and it gives them a dislike to it. They see that it has no tendency to enrich or aggrandize; and they have heard, or observed, that the most ingenious poets have been remarkable for indigence. This alone is sufficient to make them both hate and despise even a Homer, a Virgil, and a Milton. What nonsense to be measuring syllables, and talking of purling streams, shady groves, and mossy banks, to a man who has no taste for any thing but newspapers, and who is constantly engaged in contemplating the sublime subject of the consols, scrip, annuities, and lottery tickets! Such an one considers himself as a Solomon, when he compares himself with a man of rhymes; for so he would call a Dryden, a Pope, and a Gray.

The majority of those who are the slaves of covetousness and pride, carry their contempt for poetry and its admirers to the utmost extent; yet, after all, their contempt recoils upon themselves, for it arises from their ignorance and insensibility.

But many will say, that the love of poetry is incompatible with prudence; and it must be confessed and lamented, that a very warm attachment to it is apt, like all other passions, to engross the attention entirely.

The calls of a wife and children, and indeed of a man's own personal wants, are so importunate, and at the same time so just, that they must be satisfied before particular attention can be paid to any mere amusement. But there are few situations in life where business is so urgent as not to allow some leisure.

Poetry, and the other fine arts, are admirably adapted
to fill such intervals innocently and pleasurably.

Let a distinction be made between reading and
composing.   They who are from choice or necessity
engaged in the affairs of the world should be content
with reading poetry, and never think of composing
it.   Others, whose fortunes are easy and secure, may
very safely and honourably obey the impulse of their
genius and inclination in writing verse.

All I mean to contend for is the honour of the art.
It has been sadly degraded by the votaries of Plutus.
It is far above any pursuits of which a narrow and
mercenary mind is capable.   This nation is mercantile, and if wealth is to engross honour, what is to
become of the arts of whom honour is the nurse ?
The arts should be encouraged in a mercantile people,
because they open, enlarge, and refine the human
mind, so as to enable it to enjoy that wealth for
which merchandize is instituted.   Does the accumulation of money and the increase of property always contribute to happiness and the dignity of
human nature ?   Experience evinces that a man may
be superlatively rich, and at the same time very
mean and very unhappy.   It is the improvement of
the mind, it is the exaltation of the ideas which,
next to religion and morality, tend most to human
happiness and perfection.

Let poets therefore be held in high honour.   By
poets I mean not trivial rhymers and common-place
versifiers, but men to whom nature has given such a
degree of sense and sensibility as enables them to
transport their readers with every passion or fancy
which they mean to excite.   Such do not abound.
Indeed, the first rate appear but once in an age, perhaps in many ages.   There are, however, in the second rank considerable numbers, to whom every

enlightened and liberal mind will be happy in giving honour, as to the improvers and soothers of the human bosom in the soft hour of prosperous leisure, and also in the time of tribulation.

I cannot, on this occasion, deny myself the pleasure of remarking, that a beautiful vein of originality pervades the poems of our contemporary, Mr. Cowper. He exhibits also a virtuous freedom of sentiment, and a manly force of expression, which render him worthy to be deemed the Juvenal of his age. Possessed of genius and spirit, he stands forth an avowed and powerful champion of moral and religious reformation; and while he admonishes with all the rigour of censorial discipline, he charms with the luminous language and vivid colouring of descriptive poetry.

EVENING LXII.

ON THE SAVAGE MANNERS OF THE SOUTH SEA ISLANDERS, AND THE BEST MEANS OF IMPROVING THEM.

It is impossible to read the voyages to the South Seas without great delight; but the delight is interrupted too frequently by sentiments of horror and of painful sympathy. Our newly-discovered fellow-creatures appear in many amiable points of view; they are generous, sensible, and friendly. Their hearts seem to be peculiarly susceptible of pleasure and of pain; but they are guided too implicitly by their lively sensations, and their reason appears to be universally overpowered by the violence of their passions. Though by no means cruel and ferocious in their natural temper, they exhibit, under the operation of revenge and superstition, the most horrid instances of savage barbarity.

Much has been written on the subject of Anthro-

pophagi or Cannibals ; and many entertained a suspicion that they did not at present exist, if it were
true that they ever existed.   But the late voyages
have rendered that truth, disgraceful as it is to human nature, indubitable. It is a circumstance which
aggravates, instead of extenuating, the malignity of
their practice, that it arises not from hunger and necessity, but from a diabolical sentiment of revenge.
That passion, uncontrolled by religion and philosophy, is not to be gratified completely but by the destruction of the unhappy object of it, and even by
tearing it in pieces, and devouring it with a canine
ferocity.   Is it not easy to perceive, in practices so
malignant, the interference of an Evil Spirit ?

.The accounts of our late circumnavigators are un-
questionably true, and they evince the necessity of
endeavouring, by the very first opportunity, to call
the strangers from the error of their ways, and to ini-
tiate them in the benevolent doctrines of Christianity.

Superstition also exhibits a scene in the South
Seas not less shocking than revenge.   To sacrifice a
fellow-creature in order to please a benignant Deity,
is a design which the Evil Spirit only could infuse
into the heart of man.   The practice is by no means
peculiar to the Islanders of the Southern Main ; it
prevailed among the ancient Ægyptians, Phœnicians,
and Canaanites ; and even Abraham, mistaking the
real will of God, would have sacrificed his son Isaac,
if the hand of Heaven had not, for the correction of
this fatal mistake, interposed, and supplied one of
the bestial train as a more acceptable offering. Philo,
indeed, detracts from the merit of Abraham's faith
and intention, by asserting, that many kings and
nations accustomed themselves to sacrifice their first-
born sons, for the sake of propitiating an angry Deity.
There is a passage in the close of the third chapter

of the second book of Kings, which fully confirms the idea that Abraham's was not a single instance—— " And when the King of Moab saw that the battle was too sore for him, he took with him seven hundred men that drew swords, to break through even unto the Kingdom of Edom; but they could not. Then he took his eldest son, that should have reigned in his stead, and offered him for a burnt-offering upon the wall." It is shocking beyond expression that a father should immolate a son; but what deed is so nefarious of which the natural man, unassisted by the grace of God, is not capable? Aristotle says, that it was usual among the Trebatti for a son to sacrifice a father.* I make no comment on deeds which carry with them their own immediate condemnation.

But I cannot but be struck with the wonderful similarity observable in the manners and superstitions of savage men throughout the world, and in all ages. The idea of propitiating the Deity by bloodshed, or the sacrifice of some living creatures, either human or bestial, is almost universal. The sacrifice of animals began with Abel, and it is probable that the tradition of its being acceptable to God was handed down from him to the days of Noah. Noah himself exhibited an example of it to all posterity, for, on his departure from the ark, we read, that he " builded an altar unto the Lord, and took of every clean beast, and of every clean fowl, and offered burnt-offerings on the altar; and the Lord smelled a sweet savour; and the Lord said in his heart, I will not again curse the ground any more for man's sake."

It seems probable, that as men were dispersed through various parts of the world from the ark of

---

* In Topicis, lib. ii. cap. ult.

Noah, they carried with them the example of sacrificing animals, and diffused the idea that God was
pleased with them, as indications of faith and sincerity.

There is, I think, no doubt but that they were
types, or faint adumbrations of the great sacrifice
that was to be made by the Lamb of God for the sins
of the whole world. It is to be attributed to a well-
meaning, but superstitious excess, that in the place
of irrational animals, the nations at length sacrificed
human creatures. This is to account for it by the
most candid conjecture; but I believe it will be
consistent with reason and Scripture to suppose,
that it was the Evil Being who tempted man to
break one of the first laws of God, which says, Thou
shalt do no murder.

It is certain, that God cannot behold such deeds
with any other sentiments but those of extreme displeasure. "Whoso sheddeth man's blood, by man
shall his blood be shed," was the edict of Him who
made man, and who alone possesses a right to dispose
of him. "Will I eat the flesh of bulls, or drink the
blood of goats?" saith the Lord. Much less can he
delight in the blood of his favourite creature.

Can any man then of common humanity, in the
civilised countries of Europe, avoid most earnestly
wishing, that these poor children of nature in the
Pacific Ocean might learn what that means, "I will
have mercy, and not sacrifice?"

The exposing or murdering of infants is another
savage practice, which disgraces all those virtues and
amiable dispositions which are represented as existing in a remarkable degree among these Islanders.
This practice, like the others which I have mentioned,
prevailed also among the ancients before the Christian
æra. Moses was exposed, as were Romulus and
Remus among the Romans, and Oedipus among the

Greeks. But the Greeks and Romans used to place with the exposed infant some valuable things, which might induce the traveller who should find it to take care of it, if it were alive, and to bury it, if dead. I do not indeed recollect any country in which, like Otaheite, there seemed to be a combination of the rich and powerful to destroy their offspring. Poverty, indeed, and shame, frequently causes such acts of extreme barbarity among individuals in civilised nations; but they were never tolerated or countenanced, but, on the contrary, severely punished, wherever Christianity has been introduced. The Foundling Hospital in England, while it does honour to human nature as a charitable institution, reflects some disgrace upon it, since it proves that parents abound in England who are ready to relinquish their offspring for ever. Indeed, the prevailing practice of putting children out to nurse, even when the mother is healthy, and able to afford it the nourishment which nature gave, is not very honourable to the sentimental affections of those who at the same time pretend to an uncommon share of sympathetic refinement.

This neglect, however, though culpable, is not in the smallest degree comparable to the cruelty of the Islanders with whom our navigators have lately made the world acquainted. Christianity would not permit such abominable practices, and therefore it is incumbent upon those rulers who have caused the discovery of these people, to take care that they shall be instructed, as soon as they can be made capable of receiving instruction, in the truths of the religion of Jesus Christ. Was Omiah baptised? or was he in any respect prepared to improve the spiritual state of his countrymen? If not, I cannot help lamenting that the zeal for the propagation of Christianity, that is (as Christians must deem it), a zeal

T 2

for the diffusion of happiness, is greatly relaxed among us.

I say nothing of the theft and lust, and other evil practices and habits which prevail remarkably among these Islanders, since they are trifling faults, however heinous in themselves, when contrasted with the atrocious crimes of which I have already spoken. When greater evils are corrected, the more inconsiderable will soon be removed.

I cannot help expressing the pleasure I felt in reading the last voyages, at that passage, which relates that the Spaniards had set up a cross, with the inscription, *Christus Vincit*. It is an honour to that nation to have first introduced the name of Christ into these islands. There is in this enlightened age, and in the benevolent temper of the present times, no danger lest they should be guilty of cruelty in carrying on the conquests of Jesus Christ. The olive branch, and not the sword, is now borne under his banners.

I wish our own nation had paid some regard to this noble object, as well as to the observation of the transit of Venus, to botany, to longitude and latitude, and to other matters which belong to us only as inhabitants of this little planet. What a glorious voyage that will be, and Heaven grant that it may not be distant, when pious men shall carry the cross on the prows of their vessels, and triumphantly enter the havens of the Pacific Isles, announcing the good tidings of peace, joy, and immortality.

EVENING LXIII.

ON STUDYING THE ART OF SPEAKING WITHOUT PREVIOUS CONTEMPLATION.

It is one reason why eloquence among the ancients had more effect than among the moderns, that they had not the art of printing, and that the most diffusive method of communicating ideas in the age of Demosthenes and Cicero was oral utterance. The modes of transcribing written copies were slow, and the opportunities of distributing them few and incommodious. All, therefore, who wished to raise themselves to importance, or to benefit the public by their knowledge or their wisdom, studied to accomplish themselves in the arts of oratory.

But in modern times, and especially in England, there is nothing which cannot be communicated in a a few hours to larger multitudes than ever were assembled in an auditory, or than could possibly hear the voice of the loudest orator. Among us, every day, and almost every hour of the day, teems with newspapers; but when the Athenians desired to hear something new, it was necessary to ask for intelligence of strangers as they arrived in the port, or to listen to the popular rhetoricians in the public assemblies.

But not only from newspapers, but from books also and pamphlets, the moderns are able to draw information, and to catch the fire of public virtue or sedition, perhaps more effectually than it was ever diffused by the harangue of the speaker.

The art of printing, the wonderful dispatch with which it is practised, the expeditious modes of publication, and the general love of reading whatever comes recommended by the grace of novelty, have rendered the art of speaking, or artificial rhetoric, far less requisite in modern times than in the ages of antiquity. Yet it is still sufficiently useful and ornamental to justify great care in its cultivation.

But there have arisen teachers who have laboured to persuade the world, that the art of speaking ought to be considered as the very first accomplishment of human nature. Every opprobrious epithet is bestowed on the dead languages, and they who have devoted their lives to the study of them are represented as the slaves of prejudice. I cannot help thinking that their zeal in favour of an art which they have studied has carried them far beyond the limits of good sense and propriety.

Their precepts tend to make men declaimers in common conversation; than which character few can be less agreeable. Let us suppose every man who sits in a social circle, talking only to distinguish himself for his powers of oratory. All would be speakers, and none hearers. Such speakers ought to hire an audience to listen to them at so much an hour. The sight of such a meeting would be ludicrous and entertaining; but the ears would be disgusted by jargon and dissonance. The ease and the simplicity of natural conversation would be lost amidst the efforts of art. Men of sense, to whom nature has given the organs of utterance without defect, will never be at a loss to express themselves with propriety, and with sufficient grace, though they should never have cultivated the art of speaking in the arrogant schools of modern rhetoricians.

Much is said on the defective state of pulpit elocution. There are certainly defects in it; but I am not convinced that the precepts or examples of theatrical teachers will introduce a species of pulpit oratory in every respect to be approved. It has long been agreed, that the elocution and action which become the stage are unfit for the pulpit.

For what reason? Certainly because they display too much art, or rather artifice, to appear with grace or dignity in him who is to speak the truth, as it is in Jesus, with all sincerity and simplicity. Some preachers are careless and indifferent, and on that account greatly reprehensible; but it is difficult to believe that men of sense and liberal education, if they are earnestly devout, and willing to exert themselves, cannot deliver their harangues from the pulpit without the instructions of a player. I believe there is reason to think that most players might receive instruction, even in their own favourite art of speaking, from a clergyman of sound sense, regularly and duly cultivated; but men of this character have usually learned, with their other virtues, the virtue of modesty. One hint of advice to them on the art of speaking will, if followed, become more serviceable than all the instructions of a mercenary declaimer. Let them speak sufficiently loud, distinctly, and earnestly. Nature and truth will prevail over the hearts of their hearers, when trick and artifice shall assault in vain.

I beg leave to ask the pretending orators, whether the theatric manner would be tolerated at the bar? Judge, jury, plaintiff, and defendant, would unite in disapproving it. They would feel sentiments of anger and contempt at it. They would suppose themselves to be insulted by it. And the advocate would immediately see the necessity of unlearning that part of his preparation for the eloquence of the bar which he had acquired in the school of the theatre.

In what department then is this sort of oratory which the players recommend really useful? Not in conversation, not in the pulpit, not at the bar. It must, therefore, be remanded to the place whence it came, to the stage.

And however warmly the patrons of the art of speaking may declaim against my doctrine, I shall not be afraid to maintain, that it is infinitely more advantageous to cultivate the art of thinking than the art of speaking. A store of various knowledge, acquired by a good education, with an improved judgment, and with but a transient attention to the art of speaking, as it is systematically taught, will furnish a man possessed of a natural good ear and voice with sufficient eloquence. The mind, the source from which all true eloquence must flow, is first to be adorned. A man should learn, like the disciples of Pythagoras, to be silent a considerable time, that he may be able to fix his attention on books. Great talkers are but little thinkers. One might indeed suppose, that where there are many words there must also be many ideas; but experience evinces the possibility of talking long, loudly, and even rhetorically, without knowledge, without judgment, and without common sense.

Does not reason suggest, that the solid qualities should be studied before the ornamental? On what is the ornament to be fixed, if there is no substantial support beneath it? The beauties of the Corinthian capital rest on a solid shaft. Does not reason prescribe the necessity of accumulating a stock of materials, before we venture on expense and consumption? How can the water flow in the pipes of conveyance, if there is none in the reservoir? How shall he be a speaker who, having attended only or chiefly to utterance, has neglected to provide a store of materials? Sense, knowledge, judgment, I repeat, are first to be sought, and when they are acquired, a very little attention to rules and practice will make an orator, competently skilled for all the good purposes of his profession. It must be remembered, that a good man will not qualify himself merely from vanity, for ostentatious purposes, but to do good, and to become really respectable by solid merit. But will words, however smoothly and affectedly uttered, stand in the place of deeds, or of habitual and well-confirmed skill in an art, science, or profession ?

Indeed, this is a wordy age, and speaking has done much more injury to the public than benefit. Public business is impeded, doubts and difficulties unnecessarily raised, and faction and sedition fostered, by pretenders to oratory. Let not the next generation be educated, according to the earnest advice of some instructors, merely as praters. An age of praters ! What a misfortune to those whose situation condemns them to be hearers of them ! Indeed, the nation at large, and the cause of learning and virtue, must suffer greatly whenever the taste for speaking supersedes the love of reading and reflection. True wisdom is the child of contemplation. Orators amuse the vulgar, and mislead them. Orators, when they are only orators, that is, men who, possessing a flow of words, have acquired by habit an artificial method of lavishing them on all occasions, with little meaning, and without sincerity, are the bane of business, and the pest of society. If Englishmen had been more active and less talkative in the last war,* the national grandeur would not have been disgracefully diminished.

The theatrical, declamatory, or sophistical mode of instructing the rising generation in the art of speaking, is no less hurtful to true eloquence, as an art, and as a matter of taste, than it would be injurious to the commonwealth, if it were universal. The best judges acknowledge, that eloquence was

---

* The first American War.

ruined after it began to be taught by sophists and
grammarians in the schools. Of speaking, as well as
writing, good sense is the source, "Sapere est prin-
cipium et fons." Without knowledge and sense, the
finest elocution is but as a sounding brass and a tink-
ling cymbal; and distant be the day when Englishmen, among whom true eloquence has often appeared
in defence of liberty, shall be led to sacrifice manly
sense to empty sound, the language of truth and nature to the tricks of the sophist, to the declamation of
schoolboy rhetoric, and to the tedious yet delusive
trash of trading politicians and mercenary pleaders.

EVENING LXIV.

ON PRESERVING THE DIGNITY OF THE LITERARY REPUBLIC.

ALL human arts are found to flourish or decay,
according to the degree of esteem or of contempt in
which they are held by the general opinion. Poetry,
eloquence, and whatever constitutes polite literature,
cannot exist under the chilling influence of neglect.
The sunshine of favour is necessary to expand their
blossoms and mature their fruit. Excellence in any
art requires considerable application as well as a
natural capacity; but there are few who will apply
their abilities with constancy to such subjects as are
attended with no honour, and at the same time with
little advantage.

It is therefore of consequence to literature, and to
the improvement of the human mind, that the dignity of the literary republic should be supported.
In that republic, as well as in the political, the
brightest and most lasting lustre of character must
be derived from the merit of the constituent members; but in both there are extrinsic circumstances
which cannot but produce a very powerful effect.

One of the most injurious events that can happen in the learned state, unlike the civil in this instance, is a general disposition in its members to trade with their produce. A mercenary author by profession is not likely to consider the truth or propriety of things, but to comply with the reigning taste and principles, in whatever subject he adopts for his discussion. Immorality, infidelity, and false taste in the fine arts will be recommended, even against conviction, by him who, with little principle, turns the honourable profession of letters to a craft, and renders its first object, not the advancement of learning, but the acquisition of lucre.

The public, though deceived for a time, will be at last disabused; and, finding error and folly propagated by the books it has admired, will lose much of its regard for books in general, and for universal literature. The good authors will be confounded with the bad, and their numbers will, in course, be diminished. They, who would otherwise have shone with lustre in the schools of philosophy and the arts, will be tempted to shun the studies from which no honour redounds, and to join the vulgar throng in the pursuit of gold.

> Nam si Pieriâ quadrans tibi nullus in umbrâ
> Ostendatur, ames nomen victumque Machaerae
> Et vendas, &c.   Juv.

Venality has an immediate tendency to impair genius. It draws off its attention from the sublime and beautiful objects of art and nature, diminishes the love of truth and liberty, and confines the mind to the narrow contemplation of profit and loss, the price of the funds, and the premiums of usury.

I divide the members of the literary republic into two sorts, writers and readers; and I venture to affirm, that the excellence of writers depends greatly

on the judgment of readers.   If the taste of readers
is capricious or erroneous, the popular writer, who
aims at applause, will be under strong temptations
to conform his writings to it in opposition to his
better judgment.   For instance, if the rage had continued for that kind of writing which is denominated
the *Shandean*, many men of parts and abilities would
have endeavoured to imitate it, though confessedly
irregular and indefensible by the best laws both of
right reason and sound criticism.   If the style of our
British Ossian had been universally approved, there
is little doubt but that our poets would have copied
it, though it is not conformable to true taste, nor to
any one of those classical models, in the admiration
of which the various ages and nations of the world
have so long been united.   Nothing is so irregular
and anomalous, but it may become fashionable; and,
when it is once fashionable, it will be made a model.

The dignity of the republic of letters is much lowered by the publication of many novels, pamphlets,
and newspapers.   Newspapers are not contented to
treat on the prevailing topic, the news of the day,
and the state of the nation; but they enter into
philosophy, criticism, and theology.   They do not
express themselves on these important subjects with
diffidence, but determine with that air of superiority
which real merit alone can claim, but which ignorance and vanity is aptest to assume.   Illiterate
readers are easily misled by them.   No books can
counteract their effects; for where one book is introduced and read, ten thousand newspapers have
had the advantage of a previous perusal.

I do not intend to insinuate, that the papers are
always culpable and delusive: but, from the frequency of their appearance, and the quantity which
they are obliged to furnish, it will happen that trash

and falsehood will often occupy an ample space in the best among them.

If trifling publications convey no improper sentiments and ideas, yet they are still injurious to letters, because they engross that time which would otherwise be bestowed on books of established character, and subjects of incontestible importance. Books, as they cease to be wanted, cease also to be valued. The majority of readers, in consequence of their depraved taste and deficient knowledge, become incapable of forming an adequate idea of works profoundly learned, and eminently well composed.

Dictionaries, compilations, and works distributed in weekly numbers, being intended solely to serve the purposes of interest, often appear in a mean yet ostentatious form, and detract from that respect which is due to real knowledge and original compositions. They multiply books without adding any thing to the store of science; and this also contributes to lower the general value of books, and the reputation of their compilers.

A great quantity of any thing valuable naturally depreciates it. A market overstocked reduces the price of the commodity. Gold would soon lose its value, if every stream resembled the Tagus or Pactolus. When the dispensers of science, wisdom, and taste, were but few, they were honoured extravagantly. Others, who may possess the same degree of science, wisdom, and taste, will be less honoured, because they succeed those who were first in time, and because they publish their inventions when books were multiplied.

Vanity, or the love of praise, would alone produce a great number of books; but avarice produces many more. Vanity, however, aims at excellence for the sake of applause; but avarice condescends to prostitution for the sake of gain. The public is distracted with the number of publications, and the ignorant and injudicious often purchase, at a considerable price, that which is of no value. In consequence of frequent disappointment and injury, many cease to procure books even of allowed merit, and sit down with a prejudice that the literary republic abounds with fraud.

When this is the case, where is the dignity of learning? True merit is confounded with false pretensions; and, in consequence of general contempt, is much diminished.

It is certainly an object of great concern to human happiness, that good letters and solid science should be duly honoured. When they have decayed, not only states, but the dignity and welfare of human nature, have been involved in their decline.

It is self-evident, that one of the most obvious and necessary means of raising the estimation of modern literature, is to take care that whatever is offered to the public shall have a sufficient degree of intrinsic merit, to deserve and to repay its notice. Let none be writers who have not first been readers; or, to speak more plainly, who are not qualified both by natural abilities and acquired attainments to afford pleasure and information. But who shall enforce this law? Human affairs will in many respects take their own course, and defy control. And perhaps it would be wrong to restrain the efforts of enterprising poverty, or even to refuse the pleasure which attends the indulgence of innocent vanity.

Those writers, indeed, who, for the sake of a name, or for lucre, publish works which militate against learning and religion, can be excused by no apology. They are not only the disgrace of the literary republic, but of all society, and of the human race.

EVENING LXV.

ON ŒCONOMICS, AS A SCIENCE.

That logic, ethics, physics, and metaphysics, should claim the dignity of liberal arts or sciences, excites no surprise; but that the art of managing a house and family should be placed on a level with them appears rather wonderful. Yet it is certain that œconomics were taught as a scholastic science by the ancient philosophers; and there still remains a very curious book, in which Xenophon has recorded the doctrines of Socrates on the subject of œconomy. At first sight, one is apt to imagine that philosophy has departed from her province when she enters on domestic management; and that it would be ridiculous to send a housekeeper or a husbandman to Socrates for the improvement of good housewifery or agriculture; yet it must be confessed, that there is in the work of Xenophon nothing of impertinence, but a great deal of good sense most elegantly expressed.

Notwithstanding the air of superiority which is assumed by logic, physics, and metaphysics, yet, considering the influence on human happiness, the greatest value should be placed on œconomics; for the others, as they are treated in the schools are little more than speculations, and have but a very limited influence either on the regulation or the enjoyment of life.

But the true *paterfamilias*, or master of a family, is one of the most respectable characters in society, and the science which directs his conduct, or reforms his mistakes, is entitled to peculiar esteem. Such is that of œconomics; and though it be true that the wisdom obtained by experience is the least fallible, yet it often costs so dearly that the intrinsic value scarcely compensates the price. Whatever science is able to anticipate it, certainly deserves attention; and there is nothing in which human industry and happiness are greatly conversant which may not be improved by those who consider it with the dispassionate attention of sound philosophy.

Much of the misery which prevails at present in the world is justly to be imputed to the want of œconomy. But the word œconomy is usually misunderstood. It is confined in its meaning to parsimony, though it undoubtedly comprehends every thing which relates to the conduct of a family. Frugality is indeed a very considerable part of it; but not the whole. It is the judicious government of a little community inhabiting one house, and usually allied by all the soft bands of affinity and consanguinity. The person who executes such a government should be eminently furnished with prudence and benevolence.

The rage for fashionable levities, which has pervaded even the lower ranks, is singularly adverse to the knowledge and the virtues which domestic life demands. Dress occupies the greater part both of the time and attention of many; and the consequence is too often ruin in polite life, bankruptcy in the commercial, and misery and disgrace in all.

It might be attended with great advantage to the community, and to the happiness of particular persons, if some part of the time and attention bestowed on the ornamental parts of education were transferred to those arts which teach the prudent management of domestic concerns. The conduct of children in the age of infancy requires considerable skill, as well as tenderness; and how should she know how to enter upon it whose whole time has been spent in learning the polite accomplishments, which, though they add much to gracefulness, make no pretensions to utility? She must be guided by servants, nurses, and medical practitioners; but surely it would be safer and pleasanter to possess such a skill as should prevent her from lying entirely at the mercy of ignorance, vanity, officiousness, and presumption.

As to music, which ladies spend so much time in learning, it is well known that they seldom practise it when they have entered into the married state. Many other feminine accomplishments there are, which cease to attract attention when once their possessors are engaged in the care of a family. It is therefore probable, that the time consumed in the acquisition of things which are confessedly of no use to them, might be employed in acquiring such knowledge as would enable them to contribute greatly to the happiness of the man to whom they should give their hands and hearts, and of the children which might be the pledges of their conjugal love.

I by no means refer them to Xenophon or Socrates for instruction in domestic management. Their own parents should communicate the result of their experience and observation on the subject. Above all, they should inspire them with a love of home, and the pleasures and virtues of an affectionate family association.

Complaints have been made that, in the present age, marriage is not sufficiently prevalent, or, at least, that good husbands are not numerous. The men who appear to be insensible to female charms, allege, in excuse for their not soliciting some lady in marriage, that such are the expensive manners, dress, and amusements of the fashionable part of the sex, so little their skill in conducting a family, and such their ignorance of œconomy, that to be married is often to be ruined, even in the midst of affluence. The viciousness of many among the sex enables vicious men to gratify their desires at a small expense. All the meaner part of mankind, of which perhaps consists the greater number, are unwilling to incur the danger of dissipating their fortunes in supporting a woman who can contribute nothing to the alleviation of their cares by domestic prudence and discreet œconomy.

In every view it appears most clearly, that nothing would contribute more to the happiness of females, and indeed of men and families in general, than a cultivation of that unostentatious knowledge which is in hourly request, and without which there can be little permanent security in the most exalted rank and most abundant affluence. Socrates judged wisely, therefore, in ranking œconomics among the most useful and honourable of the arts and sciences.

EVENING LXVI.

ON MILTON'S DEFENCES.

FROM all who are happy enough to have a taste for poetry, and a love of liberty, whatever work is descending to future ages with the name of Milton on the title-page, cannot fail to attract a reverential regard. The vigour of his mind, and the depth of his learning, mark his prosaic works with strong features, with vigour and variety of style, with solidity and extent of knowledge.

His History of England is perhaps an exception. This subject, which one would have thought likely to kindle the fire of his genius, seems to be unaccountably deficient in his usual spirit. It is really dull. But his " Defence of the People of England," his " Second Defence," and his " Defence of himself," display all the fire, the nervous, the masculine eloquence of the apologist, in a diction of classical beauty.

It is at the same time matter of astonishment and regret, that a mind so elegant, a genius so pre-eminently sublime as Milton's, should descend to the very lowest vulgarity of personal abuse. His " Defensiones" abound in jokes and sarcasms, which, though sometimes severe and ingenious, are often puerile and scurrilous. His susceptible temper seems to have been heated too intensely by contest, and he became unable to discuss the subject with the dispassionate coolness of a philosopher. That fervid glow which in poetry produced a due degree of animation, kindled a flame in his political writings, which renders them too violent to be always reconcilable to the just decisions of sober reason.

I mean not to be understood as entering into the merits of any political questions discussed in the " Defensiones ;" but as considering them merely in a critical and historical view, and as curious pieces of controversial composition.

That fine piece of soft melancholy, the " Icon Basilike," raised an universal sympathy for the misfortunes of the prince whose undisguised feelings it was supposed to display with fidelity. The tide of popular fury seemed, on its publication, to flow impetuously against the regicides. Milton was supposed by his partisans the best able, and was therefore called upon by them, and urged by his own inclination, to vilify this favourite book, and, if possible, to diminish its popularity. As the king's book was entitled, " The Image of the King," Milton called his answer, " Iconoclastes," or The Image Breaker.

On the other side, the son of the unfortunate king, and his adherents, were no less solicitous to defend the royal cause, and to represent the conduct of the

regicides in the blackest colours of vindictive rhetoric. Salmasius, a professor in the university of
Leyden, enjoyed the reputation of being the most
accomplished scholar of his time; and, in consequence of his fame, was employed by the exiled
prince to write a defence of his father. Salmasius
undertook the cause, and rapidly produced, for he
was a most rapid writer, a prolix treatise in Latin,
to which he gave the title of " Defensio Regia pro
Carolo primo."

In this work it was not easy to do justice to his
subject, without animadverting on the author of the
" Iconoclastes." He roused a lion. Milton arose
with the gigantic arm of genius, and crushed his
antagonist.

The title of his defence was " Joannis Miltoni An-
gli Defensio, contra Claudii anonymi alias Salmasii,
defensionem regiam." The contempt with which he
treats Salmasius is beyond all bounds and example;
and such as was by no means deserved; for Salmasius was a scholar of uncommon learning, and if he
feebly maintained the cause which he was employed
to espouse, he preserved a due regard to decency and
moderation, both which were neglected by Milton.

Among other unbecoming levities, Milton condescends to the very low wit of playing upon names.
He awkwardly compares Salmasius, from the similarity of sound, to the fountain Salmacis in Caria,
which had the fabulous property of depriving those
who bathed in it of half their virility, as the effeminate doctrine of Salmasius tended, in Milton's opinion, to deprive men of their rights as men, that is,
of the privileges of a republic. In another book, he
ridicules his supposed opponent More, by alluding
to *Moros* the Greek for a fool, to *Morus* a mulberry-
tree, and to *sycamorus*, a sycamore.

Milton is said to have received a thousand pounds for his " Defensio pro Populo Anglicano," It was succeeded by his " Defensio Secunda," a piece of still more virulence, excited by new provocation. The idea of his being paid detracts greatly from the honour of his zeal, but I do not believe it.

There appeared in the midst of this controversy a book entitled, " The Cry of the King's Blood to Heaven against the English Parricides." It was attributed to Alexander More, a Scotchman, whose character Milton paints in the most odious colours. The rage with which Milton attacks him evinces that the " The Cry to Heaven" was well calculated to raise the popular resentment against the regicides. He would not have exerted himself so vigorously against a feeble adversary, who had thrown only a weak and pointless weapon. Milton had possessed himself of some scandalous anecdotes against More, and enlarges on them with all the triumph of vindictive glee. After all, More was not the author. The book was written by Peter du Moulin, afterwards prebendary of Canterbury, who, for the sake of avoiding the odium which it might occasion, had engaged More to own it, and had industriously reported that More was the writer. More had cause to repent of his acquiescence when it was too late; for Milton caused him to smart severely both in his " Defensio Secunda," and his " Defensio pro se." This man is delineated in a shape so ugly as raises at once both hatred and contempt. When he who drew Death, Sin, and Satan, in a style so unparalleled, undertook to draw the caricatura of an antagonist, it will readily be imagined that luckless was the wight who sat for the picture.

The " Defensio Secunda" must be commended as a fine piece of eloquence. There is in it the *vis ignea* of genius.   There is even a glimmering of that light which was to burst forth in all its majesty in the Paradise Lost.   I wish the dignity of the sentiments had uniformly accorded with the magnificence of the expression.   But this noble genius, this ardent lover of freedom, often descends from the towering heights of eloquence, to grovel in the miry ways of spiteful and plebeian obloquy.   The vulgarity of his appel- lations is a little concealed by the veil of an ancient language, the sound of which even when it conveys ribaldry, retains its dignity in a modern ear; but, if it were properly translated, it would seem to an English reader the language of a porter, rather than of the man to whom nature had given

> Mens sublimior atque os
> Magna sonaturum;

and who was formed with powers to penetrate

> ——Extra flammantia mœnia mundi.

Milton, ashamed to have displayed so much ran- cour on a mistaken object, did not believe, or at least pretended not to believe, but that More was the author of " The Cry to Heaven."   He therefore wrote a Third Defence, which he entitled " Auctoris pro se Defensio contra Alexandrum Morum."   In this there is the same vein of satire as in the other; the same bitterness, and the same elegance.   Notwith- standing the unjust acrimony abounding in many parts of them, these three memorable Defences are among the finest Philippics of modern ages; they unite in them the beauty of Ciceronian copiousness and the penetrating vehemence of Demosthenic force.

Every Muse must weep, that so much fire and so much eloquence, that the genius which could de- scribe the delicious groves of Eden, should be wasted on a temporary subject, which, however interesting

when the parties were violent, is now suffered to
sleep in neglect, if not in oblivion. The finest writing on temporary politics can scarcely confer immortality. When persons are dead, and things forgotten which gave rise to the controversy, the elegance of the composition will only be attended to by
those who delight in fine writing as a curiosity,
like the medalist in coins which cease to be current.
The common people prefer a halfpenny to an antique otho.

In taste, Milton had an indisputable superiority
over all his antagonists. Salmasius, the greatest of
them, though a most respectable scholar, had no just
claim to singular genius, or peculiar refinement of
taste. It might have been supposed that he would
have been accurate in his Latinity. But Milton censures him severely for the use of the word *Persona*
in a sense unclassical. Salmasius had said, in his
preface to the " Defensio Regia;" " Horribilis nuper
nuntius aures nostros atroci vulnere, sed magis-
mentes, perculit, de parricidio apud Anglos in *Persona*
Regis, sacrilegorum hominum nefaria conspiratione,
admisso." Milton asks in the tone of a schoolmaster,
after ridiculing this pompous passage, which is certainly not well written, " Quid, quæso, est parrici-
dium in persona regis admittere? Quid in *persona*
regis? Quæ unquam Latinitas sic locuta est."

Dr. Johnson rather defends Salmasius's use of the
word Persona, and cites in support of it the passage
from Juvenal :

> Cum fædior omni
> Crimine persoua est.

But Juvenal himself did not write the purest Latin,
such at least as would have been approved in the age
of Augustus, the model of Milton; and Dr. Johnson

was not so good a judge of Latin words as of English; for in his few Latin poematia there are many unclassical modes of expression. Persona, however, is by no means indefensible.

The sagacious biographer, who, on this occasion, is not partial to Milton, accuses him of a solecism in the words which he insultingly addresses to Salmasius, immediately after having chastised him for the impropriety of Persona. Milton says, " Vapulandum te propino grammatistis tuis." *Vapulo* being a neuter verb, every schoolboy in the head-classes will observe, that it is not easy to find in it the future in *dus*. But Dr. Johnson should have acknowledged, if he knew it, that he was not the first who discovered this error. It was noticed long before by Vavassor de Epigrammate, by Crenius in his Animadversiones Philologicæ, and by Ker in his Observations on the Latin Tongue. In that part of Ker's work which relates to barbarous and vicious modes of expression, speaking of *vapulandum*, he says, in reference to it, " Pinguis solœcismus Miltono excidit; ubi Salmasium ob solœcismum exagitavit." This lapse of Milton was the less to be excused, because it happened while he was censuring a disputable error in Salmasius with an air of haughty triumph and unrelenting severity. Milton, though well acquainted with the purity and accuracy of the Latin, was not so scrupulously cautious as not to suffer, in the precipitation of passion, many words and phrases to escape him, which grammarians and critics might justly reprehend.*

What a loss to the admirers of polite letters, that he who could write " L'Allegro," " Il Penseroso," the

---

* Thus he says, " Populus assentitus est"—and " res nostras hallucinante."

Battles of Angels, and the Loves of Adam and Eve, should suffer his life to waste away in disgraceful and importunate controversy, in rough and uncultivated fields, where briars and nettles flourished, instead of flowers and laurels.

One cannot but deplore the temper of both writers. Salmasius attributes, with triumph, the loss of Milton's sight to the labour of the controversy; and Milton, to the disgrace of humanity, is said to have expressed some complacency in the idea, that his severity shortened the days of poor Salmasius.

Some had considered the blindness of Milton as a judgment on him for defending the crime of the Regicides, or for some other atrocious offence.

Milton was thought by many, in his controversial defence of rebellion, to have resembled too much his own fallen angel, for he also had a powerful and seducing eloquence, and could make the worse appear the better cause. This censure of Milton is too severe; but they who attack others with severity must expect retaliation.

EVENING LXVII.

ON SALMASIUS, THE ANTAGONIST OF MILTON.

CLAUDE DE SAUMAISE, the great antagonist of Milton, or Claudius Salmasius, as he is called by his latinised name, was born at Dijon in France, in the year 1596. He was one among the numerous instances of early genius and proficiency. When he was scarcely fourteen, he was the editor of a book on the primacy of the pope: and in the succeeding year, published Florus, with notes, dedicated to Johannes Gruter.

His principal works, at a maturer age, were: Commentarii in Augustam Historiam; Exercitationes Plinianæ in Solinum; Apparatus Sacer; Tractatus de Annis climactericis; Libri de Usuris, modo Usurarum et Fœnore Trapezitico; Defensio Regia pro Carolo primo, et Liber de Transubstantiatione, &c.

He was held in high esteem by his contemporaries. The Venetians offered him a very considerable pecuniary reward, if he would consent to read three annual lectures in public. He refused the offer, from motives of diffidence and modesty. The Dutch judged him worthy to succeed the great Scaliger at Leyden. As a divine, a lawyer, a physician, a philosopher, and philologist, he maintained a distinguished place in the opinions of those of his age who were best enabled to form a judgment. He died in the year 1652, not without leaving an opinion in the minds of many that his life had been shortened by poison. After his death, his manuscripts were burned by his wife, in pursuance of his own request.

His learning was profound and extensive. To his knowledge of the learned and European languages, he added that of the Arabic, Coptic, Persic, and Chinese. He was sometimes called the walking library, and the miracle of his age. The most celebrated scholars of his own time, and of that which succeeded it, speak in high terms of his learning. The great Grotius says of him, " That he had rather pass over in silence the consummate learning of Claudius Salmasius, than lower his praises through the defect of his own genius." Vossius, Joseph Scaliger, and Isaac Casaubon, competent judges, are warm in the praise of Claudius Salmasius.

Such is the writer whom Milton has reviled, in his " Defence of the People of England," in the most contemptuous terms, as a reptile beneath contempt. He who should derive his ideas of Salmasius from

Milton's book, must consider him as a mere pretender to learning, a petty grammarian, and a character unworthy, not only of esteem, but even of notice.

Of his character, indeed, it is affirmed that he was irritable and resentful ; that he had the pride of learning, and the confidence of conscious superiority. Those who felt the weight of his merit, who were scorched by his lustre, or who dissented from him in religious and political principles, did not hesitate to load him with censure. But none of his enemies proceeded to such extremities as the great ornament of English poetry, John Milton.

The truth is, that our ardent champion for the rights of mankind was exasperated beyond measure, by Salmasius's book in defence of King Charles, which could not but reflect severely on the party which had brought that unfortunate monarch to the scaffold. But Milton's confutation of that work would have carried with it more weight, if it had been more argumentative and moderate. It was the sudden effusion of a violent party spirit ; and proceeded less from judgment than from downright anger.

The " Defensio Regia" is acknowledged, even by the friends to the cause, to be unequal to the expectations formed of the author. It is confused and prolix. Salmasius's idea of a king seems to be that a despotic potentate. He considered not duly the different degrees of kingly power. He had no right idea of a limited monarchy. But an author, by no means partial to Salmasius, cannot help expressing himself thus unfavourably of Milton's answer, or Defensio pro populo Anglicano : " Excepit eum mordax scriptor Miltonus, sed in quo desideres prudentiam et equitatem judicii ; in sarcasmo est artifex, unde petulans ejus ingenium satis se prodidit."

HERMAN. CONRING. DE REGN. ANG.

Salmasius was one of those writers who seem more ambitious of becoming voluminous than of writing a few works of finished excellence. He wrote with great haste, but he was qualified to do so, as his memory was richly furnished. The materials, though hastily produced, were generally of intrinsic value; and he did not often give himself the trouble to transcribe his composition, but sent it to the press as it teemed from his prolific mind and memory.

He has confessedly more learning than original invention. As a work of great erudition, I admire the " Plinianæ Exercitationes in Solinum." Solinus himself is an author of little value. His work entitled Polyhistor, and dedicated to Adventus, is chiefly geographical, and, like our modern geographical grammars, gives something of the history, and relates the curiosities of the countries which it describes. Solinus's work fills not more than sixty-three folio pages; but Salmasius's Exercitationes upon it, take up near a thousand, printed closely in columns. Salmasius did not esteem Solinus's book, though he made use of it as a subject on which to write almost as many annotations as crowd the pages of two large folios. Salmasius calls Solinus " mirum nugatorem; merum miscellionem; omnia turbantem et confundentem simium." Scaliger characterises him as a most futile author. It is certain that he often quotes the words of Pliny, and applies them in a different meaning from that in which they were intended. Salmasius knew the defects of Solinus, and therefore his choice of his work for the purpose of a comment is no disgrace to his knowledge, though it may be to his judgment. The Exercitationes of Salmasius are justly held in high esteem. They furnish a great variety and quantity of information; and Hugo Grotius calls them *immensæ frugis opus.*

In justice to a very respectable author, I have mentioned these circumstances concerning his character, and the estimation in which he was held by the learned of his own age. Milton's severity of censure has rendered him an object of hatred and contempt in our country : but now, at last, when the rage of party fury is no more, justice must hold the balance, and in weighing the merits of Milton and Salmasius, must allot to Milton the praise of uncommon genius and learning united ; and to Salmasius, not indeed the praise of Milton's genius, but of learning, equal to Milton's, if not superior.

The following parallel between Grotius and Salmasius was drawn by D'Argonne, and adds a farther illustration of our author's character.

" Salmasius had a lively genius and a prodigious memory. All his books are extemporary. But he did not digest the subjects which he treated. Whatever he gave the public, he gave with disdain, and as if he was in a passion. He seemed to throw his Greek and Latin, and all his knowledge, at people's heads.

" Grotius, on the contrary, considered every thing, digested every thing, and arranged it judiciously. He pays respect to his reader. His erudition is like a great river, which diffuses itself far and wide, and does good to all the world. Every work of Grotius is a master-piece in its kind ; a thing unexampled among the ancients and moderns. Never did an author make better choice of subjects. He grows great with them, and they grow great under his pen. ' Crescit cum amplitudine rerum vis ingenii.' "

There was something in the temper and manners of Salmasius which made him enemies ; yet the most illustrious critics, as I have already hinted, are warm in his praise. Vossius calls him, " Virum nunquam satis laudatum, ingens literarum columen." Casaubon says of him, " Est profecto dignissimus quem omnes boni ament." Grotius characterises his learning with the epithet consummatissimam. It was the poet of Paradise Lost who addressed him by the names of fool, blockhead, and rogue. Such is the virulence of party rage! The present times can furnish similar instances, especially in contro- versial divinity and politics.

EVENING LXVIII.

ON A DULL STYLE IN SERMONS.

THE man who preaches well, and turns many from the error of their ways, is a better divine than the greatest orientalist, casuist, linguist, controversialist, that ever spent his days in solitary libraries, caused the press to groan with folios of dull dissertation, or sat with all the heavy dignity of silent self-importance in a professor's chair. The latter, like an oyster with a pearl in it, may have great internal value; but, in the eye of reason, he is subordinate to the active divine, who reduces theological knowledge to practical use, the end for which the other's learning is but a preparatory mean ; and a mean, very often, totally superfluous. The world judges otherwise, and the dull S. T. P. who never converted a sinner, visited the sick, comforted the desponding, promoted piety, charity, and peace, is honoured, and preferred to the parish priest, whose life has been spent in active beneficence, in giving instruction, in alleviating misery, in teaching contentment and resignation.

The dull divine either communicates nothing, or communicates in a style or language unknown to the

people ; they therefore suppose him, after their manner of judging, to possess something of more value
than any thing which they see, or can approach with
familiarity.   An air of mystery secures to him a degree of veneration. " Omne ignotum pro magnifico
est."   The good rector, vicar, or curate, residing
among his flock, is seen every day, and, by familiarity, loses that great respect which the other, like
Eastern monarchs, possesses in concealment.   But
the latter is as much more extensively useful than the
former as a guinea in circulation than a coin of an
equally intrinsic value locked up as a cusiosity in
the cabinet of a virtuoso.

The respect paid to dull divines has introduced,
among respectable preachers, a dry style of discourses from the pulpit, which, though subtle and
learned, yet, as it defeats the very purpose of preaching, and is totally inefficacious, in a large and mixed
congregation, ought to be disapproved.   It is, however, in a secular view of it, the safest mode of preaching and writing ; as, being little attended to, and
less understood, it cannot give offence, nor subject
the preacher or writer to imputations of intemperate
zeal, heterodoxy, or any other of those lets and hin-
drances which might impede the progress of those
who are taken by the hand by Borough-mongers, in
order to be installed and mitred.

Of such preachers the first care seems to be the
preservation of their own dignity.   I will not say it
is the sole care ; but the consequence is as bad as if
it were ; for some of the congregation will not listen
for want of attraction, and the rest receive no more
information, no more impulse to virtue and religion,
than if they had sat at home and read a tract of speculative divinity in the silent recesses of their book-
rooms.   The dull matter is usually accompanied

with a dull manner; and the whole effect of the *viva voce* is lost by the pride, the indolence, the affectation, or the dulness of the preacher. Think of a preacher haranguing from the pulpit a parish like that of St. James, St. Giles, Whitechapel, or Shoreditch, in the style of writing and utterance which he would use in reading a divinity lecture in the Theological Schools of Oxford and Cambridge.

Sermons before the universities may, indeed, be considered as exercises in theology, intended for the improvement of both preacher and hearer in the theory of religion. If they are in the style which rhetoricians call *exilis*, the meagre and jejune, perhaps it may be excused, as being merely didactic, designed (*docere*, non *persuadere* et *movere*) to teach doctrines, and not to persuade the will or move the affections. And yet when it is considered that the greater part of the audience, in the university churches, always consists of very young men and of the common parishioners, I know not whether this apology can fully justify the languor of a pulpit dissertation. The truth is, that on most public occasions, and before a learned audience, the preacher ascends the rostrum to display his own attainments and ingenuity, and that the edification of the hearers is but a secondary purpose. Human nature is prone to vanity, and let him who censures it in others set the example of a total exemption from it himself. But I cannot help thinking, that vanity might be more effectually gratified by a livelier and more energetic address to the hearers. The impression would be deeper, and the preacher's eloquence more honoured: but eloquence is less aimed at in academical pulpits, than ingenious, erudite, and inoffensive disquisition. Politics regulate the pulpit.

The dull, dry, torpid, languid, soporific style

displays itself in all its academical grace, in sermons at Westminster Abbey before the Houses of Lords and Commons. These are commonly printed, and few things ever came from the press more insipid; mere watergruel, or rather mere chips in porridge. You may read several of them, and not find the name of Jesus Christ once inserted. The name of God is sparingly admitted. A passage from scripture might spoil a period, or give the discourse a vulgar air. No attempt to strike the imagination or move the passions. The first aim of the preacher seems to be to give no disgust to a fastidious audience; to go through the formality, with all the tranquillity of gentle dulness, neither ruffled himself, nor rudely daring to disturb his hearers. He is sometimes before his maker, in a temporal sense, on these occasions, and must therefore carry his dish very upright, and be upon his good behaviour, or he may hinder his preferment, and retard his translation. A bold rebuke, a spirited remonstrance against fashionable vice, against vain babbling, against reviling each other in the senate, might fix the preacher in his place for life, as the frost congeals the stream. It is safer to talk about good old King Charles and King David, the Jews and the Samaritans, the Scribes and the Pharisees, the Greeks and the Romans.

Dulness seems to be considered as a constituent part of dignity; and when a great man is desired to preach an occasional sermon, he assumes something of an owl-like heaviness of manner, to preserve the appearance uniformly majestic. If his discourse is not understood, so much the better. It may then be supposed to contain any thing, and every thing; and, as imagination exceeds reality, the preacher's fame is likely to gain by the artifice.

I have often lamented, that at assize sermons, the same dulness has been adopted. Such occasions furnish a very desirable opportunity, to strike the minds of the common people with an awe of justice, with a fear of offending, with a conviction that the wages of sin are death. But the preacher, who means to show his parts before the judge and the lawyers, commonly talks about jurisprudence, Roman and Justinian codes, the origin of civil government, municipal laws, and similar matters, prodigiously edifying indeed to the judge, but to the vulgar, and to the jury and other persons concerned, no less unintelligible than if it had been written in Arabic.

Ordination and visitation sermons may, perhaps, claim something of the privilege of theological lectures, though a rhetorical peroration affecting the heart might be, on such occasions, equally creditable and more beneficial ; for, in truth, the student does not, at that time, require a theological lecture on abstruse subjects of divinity, but rather a persuasive exhortation which may strike his mind with an awful sense of the engagements into which he has entered, or is going to enter. He can read speculative theology in his chamber.

Sermons before inns of court have been remarkable for dulness and want of animation. You would almost suppose the preacher to be reading one of the statutes or a law instrument, like a clerk at the assizes. He seems to stand in awe of the gentlemen of the long robe, and would not be thought to insult their understandings by addressing their passions. But these gentlemen, however learned in statutes, precedents, and legal formalities, are still but men, and might be influenced like other men, by the operation of the Word, which is described as sharper than a two-edged sword, in the hands of him who is duly skilled in its use. St. Paul made Felix tremble on the seat of judgment.

The cold manner is not proper for the pulpit, and should be confined to the schools of logic and metaphysics. But do I mean to satirise the clergy, it will be asked, and to encourage a disposition to depreciate them and their services? It will be unjust and uncandid to suspect that I can have any such intention. On the contrary, I wish the learned, the rational, and philosophical part of the clergy, to possess all that authority and influence, and honour, which is due to their respectable characters, and to their attainments. But I have observed men totally different from them, certainly ignorant, almost irrational, and quite unphilosophical, engrossing the attention of the largest congregations of Christian people. If the better sort mean to do good in the most extensive manner, they will not despise that popularity which can alone enable them to do it. They will lay aside pride, false delicacy, affectation, and display their attainments and abilities in a popular manner, with a manly eloquence, and with the appearance of sincerity as well as the reality. Then shall I see their churches crowded; for the people will certainly give them a decided preference whenever they shall descend to the taste and understanding of the people. Then shall I no more see with pain, the gentleman and the scholar, who has had every advantage of education, neglected for the irregular mechanic and the pulpit demagogue.

I am aware that my interference in this manner, however good my motive, will be attributed, by those who are hurt by my animadversions, to an improper meddling with things of which the persons immediately concerned are, in every respect, com petent judges. Pride will spurn my hints; but, of much seed scattered abroad, some may fall on ground congenial to its nature, and adapted to its growth. I beg leave, however, before I dismiss a subject rather invidious, to refer the haughty despisers of popularity to a passage in the book of the Wise son of Sirach, where men who are wise and eloquent in their instructions, are at the same time praised for their popular manner; for it is added, that they were *meet for the people.*

Dr. Echard gives the following specimen of dull preaching in his day: " Omnipotent all, thou art only, because thou art only, and because thou only art: as for us, we are not, but we seem to be, and only seem to be, because we are not; for we are but mites of entity, and crumbs of something;" as if, says he, a company of country people were bound to understand Suarez and all school divines; as if, say I, the company were idiots.

Bishop Butler seems to be the model of dry preachers in the superior order. Some of his sermons are, in every respect, excellent, and, as a philosophical disquisitor on theology, he is admirable; but his disquisitions are, upon the whole, fitter for the closet than the pulpit. People will continue to slumber in churches, unless the discourse of the preacher is level to their capacities, and unless he rouses them by a judicious address to their passions and imagination. I recommend nothing frothy, nothing puerile, nothing fanatical; but the manly force, the fire, the pathos of a *Chatham* transferred to the pulpit. Let dulness be left to doze among the cobwebs of the schools; lulled by the drowsy hum of dronish disputants in metaphysical theology.

EVENING LXIX.

ON A DULL STYLE IN GENERAL.

WRITERS of strong intellect are often without imagination and sentiment, and consequently dull. They syllogise admirably ; but they cannot impress ideas with force, they cannot paint images with the pencil of fancy in the shape and colours of nature. They know not how to use the figure which the ancients called *Enargeia*, and which consisted in representing the action or fact related in so lively a manner as to render the reader a spectator.* Their books are, therefore, approved ; and then laid up on the shelf, where they continue in very good condition for sale, whenever it shall be their lot to be placed in a bookseller's catalogue. Your dull style is an excellent preservative of books, so far as the binding and paper are concerned.

Metaphysical writers have greatly countenanced the dull style. Their topics are of such a nature as scarcely to admit of vivacity. Yet they are voluminous. They have no pity on their readers, who, if they mean to be acquainted with the recondite authors, are obliged to toil with a pick-axe through tomes of dulness, with as much darkness around them, and labour in their progress, as if they were at work in the lead-mines. I wonder that there should be any such writers ; but I wonder more that they should have any readers, except those invalids who labour under the want of sleep, and who find such pages wonderfully efficacious in promoting gentle slumbers.

There are many large works with pompous and specious titles which may be said to be written upon

---

* Τὴν ἀκρὴν ὄψιν ποιεῖ. LONGINUS.

nothing, consisting of mere speculation and fanciful reasoning, which, while it pretends to argument and solidity, is more airy and visionary than the wildest romance. It would be easy to enumerate many works, metaphysical, theological, sceptical, philosophical, and political, which are mere cobwebs, spun from the brain of inexperienced and unlearned speculatists, taking up much time in the reading, puzzling, confounding every thing they touch upon, and leading to no valuable conclusion. Their novelty, and the fame they sometimes acquire by the appearance of profound knowledge and wonderful refinement, has procured them readers, and introduced a taste for, or at least a patient attention to, dull thought in languid language.

Sceptical writers and abusers of Christianity are often men of disputatious tempers, with little sentiment and fancy, and consequently their works are, with a few exceptions, very soporific. Even Lord Bolingbroke, a lively writer on other occasions, displays, in his philosophical writings, a style and manner of writing which may be called a mere lullaby. Hume's metaphysics are also worthy to be offered up at the shrine of Morpheus, unless Vulcan should make a prior claim to them.

Few, I think, would wade through the dull and dry speculations of infidels and airy metaphysicians, if they were not supported in their progress by self-flattery. They please themselves with the fancied consciousness of great depth, subtlety, and acuteness; and are also not unwilling to be considered by those who know what they read, as very profound thinkers, men above the level of vulgar prejudice, free from the shackles of education, sitting like gods in the skies, and beholding other poor mortals blindly wandering in the regions below them. A little cloudiness, and even darkness, contributes to augment the dignity of both writer and reader.

It seems probable, *à priori*, that men who write against religion should be dull; for men of great sensibility feel devotion very forcibly. Their love, their gratitude, their hopes, and their fears, are all powerfully influenced by religious ideas. But the frigid philosopher allows nothing to sensations of which he is not conscious, but, at the same time, would bring every thing to the tribunal of his own reason, which he considers as infallible.

The taste for systematical writings, where every thing is forced to bend to an hypothesis formed in the writer's mind, contributes much to the prevalence of dulness. For systematisers indulge nothing to fancy, and admit no colours of rhetoric, but satisfy themselves with fabricating a chain of dry argument to lead up to the first link or spring, which they have forged by the *fiat* of their own authority. Men of geometrical and logical genius may be pleased with an ingenious system founded on the sand, but it will have few charms, and produce no good effect with the world at large. It is a pretty curiosity, and is to be laid up like shells and mosses in the cabinet of the curious, for the inspection of a few virtuosi.

The learned and philosophical are a small number in comparison of the rest of mankind, and, as they are already cultivated and refined in a great degree, want not the improvements to be derived from publications so much as the busy tribe employed in useful and honourable action in the living world. To address metaphysical works to them (though they might relish them) is, comparatively speaking, unnecessary; and, we may rest assured, that they will not be read by the men of business, unless by a few, who, from mere vanity and affectation, wish to appear deeper than their neighbours.

Of what kind are the works which have become the favourites of an admiring world, such as Homer, Virgil, Milton, Shakspeare? Homer is all life. He throws his narrative into a dramatic form, on purpose to give it an air of vivacity. A man who reads and tastes Homer, will not only be constantly awake and anxiously attentive, but elevated, fired, and enraptured. Virgil, Milton, and Shakspeare, are not quite so lively as their great model, but they are next to him in that quality, and follow him at no very long interval. Vivacity, spirit, fire, are the ingredients which embalm writers for eternity.

An affectation of great delicacy, softness, and gentleness, contributes much to dulness. An even, smooth, unvaried style, though it may be commended by the critics, and pronounced faultless, will yet infallibly cause the reader to stretch out his arms and yawn.

General terms, instead of particular, idle epithets, long and ill-turned periods, are in their nature dull.

A slow crawling style, jogging on like a broad-wheeled waggon, though it should be richly laden with sense, will not tempt many to accompany it for pleasure, who are able to enjoy a rapidity which resembles that of a post-chaise and four.

The anticipation of matter by a previous declaration of your method, as is frequently done in sermons, renders the whole languid and flat. Those formal divisions and subdivisions of the subject, which appear in many sermons, have a powerful effect in realizing the sleeping congregation of Hogarth.

In a word, whatever solicits attention, without

repaying it, either by striking facts, or beautiful language, lively imagery, and the splendour which genius, like the sun, diffuses over all it shines upon, must be irksome; and, because it is irksome, will in time be neglected, and therefore entirely cease to produce the effect which the writer intended.

Bad writers, as well as good, must abound in a country where the press is open, and many motives, besides genius, impel men to employ it.

Manufactures are, however, served and promoted by the making of books; otherwise, at least half that have appeared might as well have been suppressed; I mean not those which are calculated to do harm, but those which can do neither harm nor good, from their intolerable dulness and insipidity.

But I must refrain: perhaps I am advancing opinions which may weigh against my Winter Evenings. I believe I had better say no more, but leave the gentle reader to stretch himself after this narcotic. Already, perhaps, he will be tempted to say, that he finds I not only knew the theory of dulness, but also the practice.

EVENING LXX.

ON THE SPIRIT OF CONTROVERSY.

THE variety of opinions which prevails among mankind, like the wind blowing at different times from different quarters, and with different degrees of violence and temperature, is certainly productive of a salutary agitation. The languor occasioned by a constant Sicilian *sirocco* would not be more insufferable than the insipidity of universal consent. If all men thought alike on all subjects, their pursuits would flag, like fire, for want of opposition;

and that enlivening diversity which appears in human life, and is found to promote the ends of social union, by mutually supplying defect, and by stimulating to cheerful exertion, would sink into the dead repose of unvaried uniformity. An offensive stagnation would be the consequence of an exact and universal resemblance of sentiments, instead of that delightful vivacity which results from the apparent chaos, the discordant concord of taste, studies, sects, parties, principles, antipathies, and predilections. All the hues of the prismatic spectrum are intermixed to produce that beautiful result of the whole, the snowy whiteness of the swan's plumage.

But much evil also arises from diversity of opinions ; for here too appears that characteristic of every thing sublunary, the alloy of predominant good by partial commixture of evil. It too frequently happens that the understandings of men cannot be divided by difference of opinion, without a corresponding division of their hearts and affections. Pride intervenes with usurping insolence where the appeal was made to reason, and where reason only should decide. Men consider their personal importance intimately concerned in maintaining the sentiments which they have once advanced. To acknowledge themselves mistaken, and convinced by the arguments of an opponent, would be an humiliating confession of their own inferiority. The object of the controversy, ceasing to be truth, becomes the triumph of victorious disputation.

But since the reciprocal discussion of interesting questions is conducive to the discovery of truth, as the winnowing of wheat separates it from chaff; and since a difference of opinion appears to be in general salutary, and, from the nature of man, is likely also for ever to subsist, I think it worth while to endeavour the accomplishment of a purpose so valuable as that of preventing a disagreement in matters of opinion from violating the connexions of friendship, diminishing philanthropy, and souring the sweets of social intercourse.

Politics, in a free country like our own, have always been a principal cause of disunion. The politician feels himself so far interested in the conduct of a government in which he participates by his suffrage, as to be powerfully affected by it, independently of his private interest. He is not contented with barely approving or disapproving public measures according to the decisions of his judgment, but enters so warmly into the subject, as frequently to feel a conflict of violent emotions, seeking vent in violent language. If his decisive dictates happen to be opposed in company, angry and vindictive expressions arise in the warmth of collision. Pride is wounded on both sides by some random shaft ; and they who sat down at the hospitable board with all the cordiality of friendship, often rise with a considerable degree of indifference at least, if not with the rancour of a settled animosity.

If passion could listen to reason, it would surely be acknowledged by the disputants themselves, a disgraceful folly to permit a difference of opinion to disunite those whose opinions can never have the least influence on the direction of public affairs, of which they dispute. It is indeed most ridiculous to behold two poor mortals destroying private happiness, under the pretence of serving the public, or zeal for the government, when their insignificance as individuals renders them totally unable to control, in the smallest degree, the settled course of national transactions. It is like two flies on the pole of a coach and six, fighting for the privilege of directing

which way, and with what speed, the carriage
shall advance.

But, to the honour of the present age, it must be
allowed, that a disagreement on party and political
subjects no longer causes those irreconcilable ani-
mosities among families, which disgraced the manners
of the English, as they appeared in the last and in
the beginning of the present century.   Such is the
liberality of the age, that two families, who espouse
the cause of opposite parties, and think differently of
a new ministry, or a public measure, can now live in
the mutual interchange of neighbourly offices without a particle of enmity.   This gentleness and
moderation among a people whom the fury of
political rage has often enflamed to phrensy, is one
of the most remarkable as well as beautiful features
of the times, and reflects honour on the progress of
national humanity and unaffected refinement.

Religion, properly understood, inspires every thing
benevolent ; yet the Christian himself blushes while
he owns, that no subject of human concern has
raised more violent disputes and more inveterate
hatred, among its warmest and perhaps sincerest
professors.   In this respect also, the superiority of
the present age over the past is strikingly conspicuous.   A Church of England man, a presbyterian,
and a quaker, will now sit at the same table, and
discourse, not only on the common topics of the
day, but on religion, without jealousy, and with all
the affectionate attention of cordial esteem.   Re-
membering that they are united as men, they forget
the petty distinction of names. This liberality ought
not in candour to be attributed to a lukewarm indifference, but to the prevalence of that real charity,
which, whatever the satirist may allege, seems to
have increased with our improvements in real know-

ledge. Happily for mankind, in the fluctuation of modes, benevolence and liberality are now not only entertained from principle, but become the fashion and the boast of the times.

Books of controversy are at present less common, and less encouraged than in the preceding age. Scarcely any thing of consequence came out, at one time, without a numerous train of letters to the author, examinations, queries, answers, replies, and rejoinders. The abuse poured from men of letters, teachers of religion, professors of theology, was such as can only find a parallel in the schools of Billingsgate. The subject itself was perhaps insipid, and, like a tasteless dish, could not be relished by the majority of readers, unless it was highly seasoned with vinegar and pepper as well as salt. They who enjoyed it must have had coarse palates, and a stomach like the ostrich, by whom lead or dirt, it may be imagined, is no less digestible than iron.

I will trespass on my reader's patience while I give him a specimen of the controversial style of two most eminent divines writing on a most awful subject, the Holy Trinity. The combatants were *Dr. William Sherlock*, dean of St. Paul's and master of the Temple, and *Dr. Robert South*, prebendary of Westminster and canon of Christ-church ; both celebrated authors, both zealous, and, I think, sincere, professors of Christianity.

Dr. South says, that Dr. Sherlock had made use of such expressions as the following, with reference to him : " Ingenious blunderer, trifling author, wandering wit, wrangling wit, leviathan, one whose risibility will prove him a man, though he is seldom in so good a humour as to laugh without grinning, which belongs to another species, *videlicet*, a dog. A notable man, and one that can make shift

to read and transcribe." Of Dr. South's animadversions, Dr. Sherlock observes, that " They are
characterised by senseless mistakes, school terms
instead of sense, gipsy cant, perfect gibberish, ignorance and raving, an hundred absurdities and
fooleries, huffing, swaggering, and scolding, that it
is a great scolding book, remarkable for want of
sense, &c."

So far the reverend Dean against the reverend
Prebendary in a trinitarian dispute.   Now let us
hear the Prebendary against the Dean.   On the
above expressions of Dr. Sherlock, Dr. South thus
concludes his remarks :

" There are several more of the like Gravel Lane
elegancies."

Dr. William Sherlock, it seems, was born of
honest parents in Gravel Lane, Southwark ; and
the great Prebendary often throws the said Gravel
Lane in the teeth of his opponent, being, to be sure,
a circumstance of great weight in discussing the
doctrine of the Trinity.

Dr. South proceeds : " All these expressions have
such peculiar strictures of the author's genius, that
he might very well spare his name where he had
made himself so well known by his mark ; for all the
foregoing oyster-wive, kennel rhetoric, seems naturally to flow from him who had been so long rector
of St. Botolph's, with the well spoken, Billingsgate*,
that, so much a teacher as he was, it may well be
questioned, whether he has learned more from his
parish, than his parish from him."

" But, after all," proceeds the great South, "may
I not ask him this short question ?

---

* This famous school of rhetoric being in the parish of St. George,
Botolph Lane, of which Dr. Sherlock was rector.

" Where is the wit and smartness of thought?
Where are the peculiar graces and lucky hits of
fancy, that should recommend the foregoing expressions to the learned and ingenious? No—
Nothing of all this is to be found in this man's words
or way of speaking; but all savour of the porter, the
carman, and the waterman; and a pleasant scene it
must needs be to the reader to see the Master of the
Temple thus laying about him in the language of the
stairs. But what," continues the dignitary, " men
draw from their education (he means in Gravel Lane),
generally sticks by them for term of life; and it is
not to be expected that a mouth so long accustomed
to throw dirt should ever leave it off till it comes to
be stopped with it."

In one of his prefaces Dr. South interrogates,
" Was it the school, the university, or Gravel Lane
that taught Dr. Sherlock this language?"

In another place, he who was to teach us " to
return good for evil, and when reviled, not to revile
again," goes on thus :

" In requital of that scurrilous character of an
ingenious blasphemer, I must and do here return
upon him the just charge of an impious blasphemer;
telling him withal, that had he lived in the former
times of our church, his gown would have been
stripped off his back for his detestable blasphemies
and heresies, and some other place found out for him
to perch in than the top of St. Paul's *, where at
present he is placed, like a church weathercock, as
he is, notable for nothing so much as standing high
and turning round. And now, if he likes not this
kind of treatment, let him thank his own virulence
for it, in passing such base reflexions upon one who

* Dr. Sherlock was dean of St. Paul's.

he might be sure would repay him, and certainly will, though he has not yet cleared the debt."

And now let me ask my reader, whether he has not had a sufficient specimen of the spirit with which a trinitarian controversy has been conducted by two of the most celebrated divines of this country?

If he delights in such wit and such language, he may go in pursuit of his enjoyment either to Dr. Sherlock's "Vindication of the holy and ever blessed Trinity," (for such is the title), and to Dr. South's "Animadversions and Tritheism charged upon it," or else to the next alehouse, where porters, carmen, and hackney coachmen assemble to regale themselves with spirituous liquor and spirited debate.

But notwithstanding this unhappy dispute, Dr. Sherlock and Dr. South were most respectable men. Dr. South in particular, was an admirable wit, and a powerful orator in the pulpit. I venerate the names of them both, and lament that they should thus have exposed themselves to deserved reproach. Let them who are inclined to engage in paper wars observe, to what the spirit of controversy may lead; to the disgrace and injury of the controversialists, and of that sacred cause which they both originally intended to promote. A striking instance of human infirmity. Both these men preached, and I believe in the sincerity of their hearts, meekness and benevolence.

The little religious controversy which remains among us at present is usually conducted with candour. Abuse is seldom offered; and, whenever it appears, recoils upon its author. A polemic Christian divine is a contradiction in terms, if by polemic is understood, as both etymology and experience justify, a hostile soldier of Jesus Christ, contending, in the church militant, with the prohibited weapons of anger and violence, for the personal glory of conquest.

It is greatly to be wished that men could be satisfied with maintaining their own principles and opinions in a dispassionate manner, and living conscientiously according to the system or sect which they may have adopted, without anxiously endeavouring to compel all others to unite in their persuasion. The most violent zeal is too often the least honourable in its motives. The violence is not derived from an honest regard for truth and the welfare of others, but from pride, ill temper, self-interest, and secular ambition ; and it is as ineffectual in producing conviction, as it is in itself unreasonable, ungenerous, unchristian.

It is not inconsistent with charity to suspect (what the knowledge of the human heart strongly insinuates), that a love of distinction, and a desire to be looked up to as the founder of a new sect, are the true causes of many divisions and subdivisions which too often arise in religion. Far be it from man to pronounce decisively of the sentiments of the heart, which are only known with certainty by him who made it; but when we see one man opposing with vehemence opinions and doctrines which the majority, apparently endowed with equal sense, and equally improved by education, receive with humble submission, it is difficult not to conclude, that he forms an undue estimate of his own sagacity, or is endeavouring to procure distinction from the sinister motives of vanity and pride. But to make use of religious pretences in support of sordid purposes of any kind, is a sort of hypocrisy which deservedly excites the highest resentment.

I think the temper with which a religious controversy is conducted one of the best criterions of

Christian prudence; and those who are duly on
their guard against delusion will be cautious of en-
listing under leaders however plausible and eloquent,
who forget, in their zeal for religion, its distinguishing grace, Christian benevolence.

It has been apprehended by some, who respect
the characters of both the disputants, that there was
rather too much asperity and haughtiness beginning
to display itself in a late controversy between a dignitary of the established church and a philosophical
dissenter. The parties should certainly beware lest
that warmth, which I believe to be an honest one,
should deviate into the virulence of party rage, injure the Christian cause, and give occasion to the
common adversaries both of themselves and the
cause, to triumph over them. Spirit and magnani-
mity are certainly consistent with that forbearance
without which Christianity is but a name. In this
age the old question,

Tantæne animis cœlestibus iræ?   VIRG.

will always be applied by the laity to their teachers,
when their teachers treat each other with contumelious language. An offence is given by it, for
which no learning or ingenuity displayed in the contest can make a recompence. Intemperate warmth
greatly increases the number of gainsayers, though
it may obtain a mitre. It is a fortunate thing for
orthodox polemics when an audacious heretic arises.
A good hardy heterodox writer becomes an anvil on
which mitres may be fabricated. Practical doctrine
availeth little in this manufacture, in comparison
with polemical.

But I pass from religious to philosophical and
literary controversy. It might be supposed that
pursuits, which bear the name of philosophical,
would proceed with the most dispassionate mode-

ration. But here also victory, rather than truth, is often the object of the contest. Practical and theoretical philosophy are often divided; and many, whose understandings are highly cultivated, remain still subject to all the irritation of irascible affections.

Every scholar will recollect the virulent controversy between Bentley and Boyle on a book which was suspected of being spurious, but which, if allowed to be genuine, is of little value. Bentley displayed wonderful learning, and great wit and acuteness in the contest; and his acrimony is almost forgiven in return for his having enriched literature with the Dissertation on Phalaris. The parts of some writers appear to be drawn out and improved by spleen, which operates on them like the fabulous inspiration on the poets. Dr. Bentley is an instance of it, for, I believe, none of his works are equal to his controversial. Mr. Pope also, with every muse at hand, too frequently sought the aid of indignation; *facit indignatio versus.*

Those who are acquainted with literary history can remember controversies conducted with an excess of warmth on the metre of a comic poet, in which divines, high in character, and high in ecclesiastical honour, gave a lamentable example of charity superseded by the pride of erudition. So true is it, that knowledge puffeth up and charity alone edifieth. Every one knows of Bishop Warburton's learning; but where are the testimonies of his humility? It were easy to select from his works the bitterest expressions, the very venom, and quintessence of all malice.

The wranglings of Cambridge, and the disputations at Oxford, are apt to give young men a controversial turn, which afterwards influences them both in life and literature.   The disputations at Oxford are now indeed merely formal; but the wranglings at Cambridge still continue, and often infuse an acid into the mind of youth which turns the milk of human kindness quite sour.

In days of yore the logical disputations in Oxford were the cause of ebullitions of rage among the academics not less furious than any which have arisen in the world of politics.   In the warmth of syllogistic discussion, the ardent disputants have been known to rise from their seats, and terminate a dispute about *quiddities* by the exertion of muscular vigour, according to the manly system of the Broughtonian philosophy. This was certainly the stratagem of dunces; for, in these polemical altercations, the thickest sculls were most likely to gain the conquest. Black eyes and bloody noses were the trophies; and there is reason to suppose from their language, that the abovesaid dean Sherlock and prebendary South would have had no objection to pull off their pudding sleeves, and have it out, as the belligerent phrase is, amidst a circle of spectators, at the Temple Stairs, or in Gravel Lane.

There are, after all, no subjects either in literature or philosophy, notwithstanding the parade of professors, sufficiently momentous to justify, in a contest concerning them, the violation of the law of love. In the estimate of reason, employed in investigating what is most beneficial to society, as well as of sacred Scripture, charity is far more valuable than knowledge; than knowledge of the most dignified kind; much more, therefore, than the knowledge of trifles, mere matters of taste, abstruse learning, and curious speculation.

Whenever, therefore, a controversy arises, and it is to be hoped that liberal and candid controversies will always continue to arise, let each party be immediately on their guard, and resolve, whatever may happen, to keep in view the preservation of a respect for each other's personal happiness and reputation; a respect which constitutes a great part of that charity which never faileth, and which, universally diffused, will contribute more to the good of mankind, than the discoveries of a Newton.

A caution may indeed be necessary against indifference in the support of evident and useful truth; an extreme, into which some may lapse in the laudable endeavour to avoid intemperance of zeal; but I am doubtful whether it is right to insist much on this caution, as the proud and angry passions, under every restraint, will be likely to produce a degree of warmth and energy sufficient for every laudable and beneficial purpose. Where a plant, from its inherent vigour, deviates into a detrimental luxuriancy, the gardener uses the pruning knife, and leaves the acceleration of growth to the powers of unassisted nature.

Upon reviewing the misery occasioned by contention, one cannot help indulging the reflexion that the evils of man are great, without unnecessary aggravation. In the little journey of our life, why should we increase the inconvenience of rough roads and bad weather, by mutual ill humour? Why should we be wasps and hornets to each other; since the stings of outrageous fortune are so pungent as scarcely to be endured? let us not, by adding sharpness and venom to their point, increase the anguish of their wound; but rather learn to soften and sweeten society by that admirable precept of philosophy and Christianity, " Bear and forbear." *Veniam petimusque damusque vicissim.*

I will beg leave to call the attention of all controvertists to the vow of Dr. Hody, "a right good-natured man and an excellent scholar." Mr. Boyle quotes it for Dr. Bentley's benefit and Dr. Hody's honour, in the celebrated controversy on the Epistles of Phalaris.

" Faxit numen, ut vel æterno ego silentio inter non scribentes delitescam, vel semper, ut virum in-genuum, liberalis ac generosæ educationis veræque philosophiæ studiosum decet, scribam : Veritatis unicæ indagator, absque omni styli acerbitate, mitis, urbanus, candidus, ad id quod indecens est adeo non pronus, ut nec movendus : Nugarum denique con-temptor."

This vow is so good an one, that I shall endeavour to adopt it as a rule for myself in all the virulent attacks, which my " Parrhesia," or freedom of sentiment and expression, very naturally occasions.

EVENING LXXI.

ON SEEKING PREFERMENT WITHOUT FIRST LABOURING TO DESERVE IT.

Sicut Cervus anhelat, &c.	DAVID.
Cœlestium inanes !	PERSIUS.

IN many professions and employments the only object in view is the acquisition of money and advancement in the ranks of life. But religion teaches men to look above the profits and honours which the world is able to bestow; and when an official professor of it appears to be remarkably anxious for pluralities and accumulated dignities, it is difficult to believe that he is perfectly sincere. To the vulgar, at least, he seems to be one of those who follow Jesus Christ, not so much for the wonderful works which he did, as for the loaves and the fishes.

There is so much of hypocrisy, deceit, and avarice, in the mere preferment-hunter, that I shall not hesitate to stigmatise his character with the most opprobrious epithets. To the vices of a sharper and an usurer he adds those of the pretended devotee, who wears the robes of religion to conceal the deformity of avarice. Tradesmen who endeavour to obtain goods under false pretences are disgraced with the name of swindlers ; and why should not a term of infamy be appropriated to the preferment-hunters, who, professing themselves teachers of a sublime and religious philosophy, appear to seek nothing for themselves but the goods of this world, which they persuade others to despise ? Why should it be thought unjust or illiberal to denominate them, as a mark of distinction from better men, ecclesiastical swindlers ?

A clergyman of learning and abilities, who acts consistently with his profession, and many such there doubtless are, supports the most respectable character in society. But that the corruption of the best thing is the worst, is true also in this department. A sensible layman, however religiously disposed, and however candid and charitable, cannot view the ministers of Christ, as they call themselves, more eager in pursuit of a prebendal stall than in the salvation of souls, without disgust and indignation. When he sees them pay the most abject court to statesmen and rich patrons, who are able to recommend them at court, and procure ecclesiastical dignity, without any regard to moral character, he naturally concludes that they are worshippers of Mammon, and that their sermons are but the cold productions of official necessity.

True religion inspires a greatness of mind as distant from abject meanness as from empty pride; but how cringing is the demeanour of the preferment-hunter, how servile his conversation! He assents and dissents at the nod of his graceless patron. Many a footman is a man of spirit in comparison. And are such as these the servants of Jesus Christ, commissioned to rebuke vice boldly, and to teach others not to be conformed to this world? Themselves the slaves of vanity and fashion; looking upwards, not to heaven, but to preferment, and downwards with contempt on the inferior clergy, and all the poor? Are these the men that are to bear the cross, and teach us to follow their example? They know this world well indeed, and love it heartily; and if you wish to play your cards well, either in the literal or figurative sense of that phrase, you cannot find better instructors; but for religion, many a plowman is a saint in comparison. Divest them of their feather-topt wigs and their short cassocks, and they are only qualified to make a figure at a watering-place, a dancing and card assembly, or in Exchange Alley.

Nothing seems to satisfy their rapacity. From vicarages and rectories they rise in their aspirations to prebends, canonries, archdeaconries, deaneries, bishoprics, and archbishoprics, and thence to heaven as late as may be. Such is the edification after which they pant, like as the hart panteth for the water brooks; as to preaching the gospel to the poor, visiting the sick, clothing the naked, feeding the hungry, they have neither time nor inclination for such mean employment. Think ye that they entered the church to serve others? They have no such enthusiastic ideas. Themselves only they wish to serve, and in this world are contented to fix their residence, provided they can but lodge themselves in a palace, or fatten in a stall.

Did they ever rebuke the vice of their patron either in the pulpit or in conversation? Have these men, who think themselves entitled to the very first places of ecclesiastical dignity, devoted their youth to study, and their manhood to useful labours in their sacred profession? Have they been indefatigable preachers or irrefragable controversalists? By no means. They have studied the graces and the arts of pleasing, and the Letters of Lord Chesterfield have been unto them as a gospel. Contrary to the scriptural precept, they have had men's persons in admiration because of advantage. They have been neither men of learning themselves, nor inclined to encourage it in others. When they have been at last elevated to the wished-for pinnacle, they have still seemed to look down with contempt on the poor and the miserable, for whose sake Christ was born and died. To form connexions with titled personages, or men in power, is their first labour and their last.

Dr. Dean was born in the middle rank. He had a good person, and was not deficient in common sense, though he had no pretensions to taste in poetry or the fine arts, and very little learning. He excelled his school-fellows when a boy, rather in the accomplishments of music and dancing, than in grammatical knowledge, or skill in composition. He went to college with a character of decency, which he has retained through life, though he never rose above mediocrity in his attainments.

A certain lord wished for a travelling companion for his son, and young Dean was recommended as a well-behaved person, from whom the pupil would learn something of address and manners, which, it was agreed on all sides, were far more useful in the world than Greek and Latin.

The pupil was of a very vicious and extravagant turn; and Mr. Dean found that he should be entirely out of favour if he attempted to restrain him within the bounds of virtue. He therefore gave him one general caution, which was, to have regard to decorum in his vicious indulgences, and to conceal that conduct, upon which, if he saw it openly, he should be obliged to animadvert *ex officio*. The young man understood the nature of the restraint, and had cunning enough to regulate his conduct by it.

After running over the Continent in the usual manner, the young nobleman returned improved in the graces, and therefore to the entire satisfaction of his father. Several noblemen, who were intimately acquainted in the family, were struck with the easy freedom and disengaged air which marked the travelled pupil, and did not hesitate to attribute much of the merit to Dean. Some compensation must be made the tutor; but my Lord was too mean to expend any thing out of his own purse, and therefore used his interest to procure a Chancellor's living of five hundred a year, in which he succeeded.

Mr. Dean never saw his parish-church since he was inducted into it; but the revenue of it enabled him to make a respectable appearance in his patron's family; and he contracted many intimacies with persons in high life. His time was entirely spent in cultivating friendship with those who had interest.

In the list of his noble acquaintance, there was a Lord of great weight in politics; but of infamous character, and a professed unbeliever in Christianity. To this nobleman he attached himself by the most assiduous attentions. Jollity was excellence in his Lordship's opinion, and therefore Dr. Dean, for he had now taken his doctor's degree in divinity at Oxford, was jolly in the extreme.

Qualities so agreeable and useful could not fail to endear him to his patron, who not being deficient in gratitude, resolved to reward him, especially as he could do it without incurring any expense. A dignity in the church, of very considerable value, became vacant, and Dr. Dean was presented to it at the request of his Lordship. Thus great men pay their clerical toad-eaters!

The doctor now became a man of consequence in his own eyes, and in the eyes of those who are inclined to venerate external appearances. As he had ascended the ladder so highly and so easily, and began to form hopes of reaching the top of it, he pursued the same plan of flattery and accommodation with which he had set out in life, and which he had found successful. He had almost made a sure friend of one of those great men who make bishops, by a present of a brace of most excellent pointers, when death, whom no arts can render exorable, disappointed his ambition. He had been at an election, where over-fatigue in canvassing for the ministerial candidate, brought on a violent fever, that occasioned his dissolution.

In this instance we behold a man of very little learning, and no piety, exalted to a station in which none should be placed who are not remarkably distinguished for both. How does the instance operate on the clergy and the laity? The clergy it teaches to believe that their advancement in the church will not be promoted by virtue or learning; and the consequences of such an opinion among the majority are easily imagined. The laity it leads to entertain dishonourable ideas of the church, some of whose main pillars are so rotten and ugly, and perhaps of the religion which the church is established to promote. Whenever the clergy become contemptible, religion shares the disgrace.

The mere preferment hunter is certainly a very fair object of satire, for his conduct is base in itself, and very injurious to society. He brings every thing that is sacred, and every thing that is just and good, into disrepute, as far as the influence of his example is diffused. While such persons succeed by sinister arts, what chance have men of real merit, whose spirit can never submit to mean behaviour, if they were sure of a mitre? The preferment hunter has been studying the graces, and attending levees, while the modest man of merit was studying wisdom, and acquiring an ability to teach it others, in the recess of his library. While the preferment-hunter was conning the Court Calendar and the *Liber Valorum*, the modest man of merit was reading the Bible.

God forbid that any of these remarks should be misconstrued into a reflexion on the good man, who, in consequence of his merit, is advanced by the over-ruling direction of Divine Providence to high stations in the church. Many such there have been in this country, and many such there are at this time. Their penetrating and generous minds must have seen and loathed the character which I have just described, that of a professed servant of Jesus Christ, an ordained minister of the Gospel, making use of their profession merely to grasp riches and honours, and to gratify peculiar avarice and ambition.

I cannot but express a wish, that patrons of church preferment would consider their right of patronage as a sacred charge.

I beg leave also to add, that there are no personal allusions in this chapter. Nor let any one accuse

me of censoriousness or illiberal reflexion on a profession which I honour.   It is because I honour it,
that I would explode those characters which con-
trive to receive the secular rewards of it, while they
load it with disgrace.

Every honest, sensible, and unprejudiced man,
whether in a black or a brown coat, whether with
a mitre or a slouched hat on his head, must see
and acknowledge the justice and utility of exposing
characters which, with the grimace of religion, and
the false pomp of erudition, endeavour to engross
the highest sublunary honours and rewards, to the
exclusion of modest merit, unaffected piety, and
honest independence.   I have been reproached for
the freedom of this paper; and I neither expect nor
desire to be spared for a quality in which I might
glory.   The cant of candour and charity on such
subjects as this, is used by those only who wish to
palliate and accommodate all things for their own
selfish purposes.   It has always been the lot of
truth to be abused by those who were interested in
its suppression.   Who were more reviled in their
lives than the first reformers ?   No reproaches, no
slander, no opprobrious epithets were unapplied to
them.   They bore all with patience.   They perse-
vered with manly resolution ; they gained their
glorious cause, and are now remembered with honour, while their dignified persecutors are either
sunk into oblivion or condemned to infamy.

EVENING LXXII.

ON MAN AS DISTINGUISHED FROM OTHER ANIMALS.

To survey an object distinctly, to perceive the
beauties of its colour, and the symmetry of its

shape, it is necessary to place it at a distance from the eye. Man, therefore, it may be concluded, when he contemplates his own species, stands too nearly to it to be able to examine it with sufficient accuracy.* If indeed he were elevated to the rank in which we conceive an angel, he might investigate the nature of his fellow-creatures with a skill no less masterly than that with which he now anatomises a reptile, or analyses a plant; but in his present state, participating the nature which he undertakes to describe, the delineation must of necessity be incomplete; for though it may be said, that to do justice to the subject he has only to inspect himself, to examine that nature and those properties of which his own bosom is conscious, yet it must be remembered, that to the mind as to the eye, any exertion is more easy than self-contemplation.

What man, therefore, can know with certainty of himself is but little; yet that little, as it constitutes the whole of his knowledge on the most interesting of all subjects, is to him highly momentous.

It is obvious to remark that man, after all his boasted pre-eminence, resembles the brutes in his birth, in his growth, in his mode of sustenance, in his decay, and in his dissolution. In these particulars he must be numbered among the animals whom he has reduced under subjection, and whom he often despises as mere animated matter.

But man possesses reason, and is sufficiently proud of the endowment. Reason, however, alone will not confer that superiority which he haughtily assumes. Many among the tenants of the air, the water, and the grove, display a degree of sagacity which

---

* Ου γαρ εν τω θεωρουμενω θεωρειν.　　　PLOT.

resembles reason so nearly as scarcely to be distinguished from it but by the microscopical powers of metaphysics, or the partial medium of human pride.

The dog and the horse are the familiar companions and assistants of man, and every one may form an idea of their sagacity, to which the epithet half-reasoning scarcely does justice. There are many beings in the human form, and in a state neither of idiotism nor insanity, who yield to these animals in qualities allowed to be mental, such as quickness of apprehension, cunning in the accomplishment of a purpose, and in memory. Insects and birds in the structure of their nests equal the works of human dexterity; and in the provident care of their young, while their care is necessary, afford a model which man may imitate to advantage.

" But this is instinct," interposes an objector. I ask how instinct and reason differ, and whether the sagacity of man is not instinct, similar in species to that of the brutes, though in many instances infinitely superior in degree?

But to what point do these observations tend? The degradation of human nature? To a purpose essentially different. They lead to a conclusion that man is distinguished from the brutes that perish by something superior to reason.

Philosophers have defined man, a two-legged and unfeathered animal, and have found other distinctions from the bestial train, in his power of laughing and shedding tears. But the noble distinction of his nature is, in my opinion, his sense of religion, his idea of a God. He alone among the numerous tribes, into which life has been inspired, possesses the glorious privilege of recognising his benefactor. He alone looks up to Heaven as his home, and thence seeks comfort and support amidst the miseries of an humiliating exile.

EVENING LXXIII.

OF THE WORLD IN A RELIGIOUS VIEW OF IT.

THE vanity of the world supplies an ample topic for declamatory invective. But though the florid language of declamation may display to advantage the abilities of a rhetorician, and amuse the curiosity of an idle hearer, yet it avails little in producing permanent conviction.

General invective against the world and its inhabitants is indeed impiety; for they are both the creatures of God, and the moral as well as natural phenomena are conducted by his providence. Men feel that there is good in the world, and to argue against experience cannot persuade, but may provoke derision.

The world has in it much evil; but the good preponderates; and to suppose the contrary derogates from the Deity. Even pleasures, riches, honours, against which so much specious oratory has been vainly exerted, are good in themselves; and evil only in the excess, in the abuse, and as they engross that attention which is due to the duties of piety to God, and benificence to man.

Mr. Pope says, to enjoy is to obey; and it cannot be doubted but that the same benignant hand which reaches out a favour designed that it should be received and enjoyed. The rose was not taught to breathe fragrance, and man at the same time forbidden to inhale the sweets with those nostrils which are furnished with organs for their perception. External objects are furnished in great abundance and variety, and internal senses formed with exquisite sensibility to receive impression from them, as the wax from the seal.

But if the world is not contemptible, where is the truth of Solomon's emphatic sentence against it—" Vanity of vanities, all is vanity ?"

I answer, that the corruption of the best things is the production of the worst. The vanity of the world arises from the folly of man. This it is which has transmuted gold into dross, substantial blessings into misery. This it was which unparadised an Eden ; and, if it were not controlled, would rob even heaven of its felicity.

As this folly arises in great measure from the natural infirmity of man, and the depravity of his nature consequent on the fall, there is too much reason to believe that it will continue to operate, as it has always operated, in rendering the world a scene of vanity and vexation. God made the world, and saw that it was *good*, but man has made it *evil;* but since it is evil, it becomes man to seek a remedy or alleviation. And to whom can he fly for succour in his distress but to his Maker, who, though he is justly displeased, allows himself to be approached as a father, and has given man leave to hope and confide that, after all his offences, he shall be viewed not with an eye of justice but of compassion.

From a conviction of the vanity of the world, duly understood, arises not a censure of Divine Providence, but of our own folly ; and this leads directly to that humility and consciousness of dependence which constitutes the firmest foundation for the superstructure of piety.

Religion and virtue will restore to the world its primitive value and beauty. Man makes the world such as he experiences it, either a scene of vanity and vexation, or of such comfort and tranquillity as is reconcileable with a state of probation.

EVENING LXXIV.

OF AN EXCESSIVE ATTACHMENT TO THE WORLD.

WHEN a congregation hears their pastor declaiming from the pulpit, with all the vehemence of scholastic eloquence, on the folly and wickedness of loving any thing sublunary, and at the same time observes that he, like other men, has many objects of affection, is it to be supposed that he preaches to any useful purpose ? Do they retire to their homes, and renounce their amusements, their employments, their connexions, their pursuits ? Some indeed among them may be pleased with the preacher's performance as with the task of a schoolboy, or the recitation of an actor; but they will not feel such conviction as will influence their conduct. And is it not their fault that they will not be persuaded ? No; it is because the orator militates against common sense, and against that reason which has been placed in the mind by Providence, as a lamp whose radiance, like the sun, absorbs the light of every inferior luminary.

What! exclaims the voice of common sense, am I to love nothing ? Then why did God place in my bosom a heart vibrating with sensibility ? God has made a revelation of his will in forming my organs of feeling and powers of reflexion prior to, and clearer than any written manifestation.

I must love many things in the world, children, parents, friends ; comforts and conveniences, a good character, and various kinds of excellence, whether moral, physical, or artificial. Beauty is ordained by nature to excite love ; and if it failed, evil of a very pernicious sort would be the consequence. It is impossible to perform the indispensable duties of social life without such a degree of love to things and persons around us as stimulates to exertion. It is not easy nor usual to reach any superior excellence in the practice of any useful or ornamental art without a love of it. Extinguish love, and you blot out the sun of the moral world.

When divines therefore inveigh against the love of the world in terms so general, as prohibit the least attachment to the nearest and dearest kindred and friends, to the most beautiful and excellent productions of art and nature, who can listen with patience? Infidels and profligates are multiplied by the foolish zeal and declamatory rhetoric of professed teachers.

The passages of Scripture which forbid the love of the world must be understood with certain limitations. " Love not the world, neither the things which are in the world," is certainly a prohibition expressed in plain and strong terms ; but there can be no doubt but that the word love signifies in this place an excessive and misplaced eagerness of desire. It means such a love as excludes a love of all other things, and causes a neglect of duty. Experience often observes such a love of the world as devours all other affections, and fixes the soul to the earth ; acting in the moral world like the centre of gravitation in the natural.

Affigit humi divinæ particulam auræ.

Against such a love of the world too many dissuasives cannot be urged. It defeats its own purposes, and is the copious source of misconduct and misery.

The inordinate lovers of the world may be divided into three characters ; the voluptuary, the miser, and the ambitious man. I mean each of them existing in such a degree as to convey the idea of idolatrous veneration for the objects of their pursuit ; in

z 2

a degree so unreasonable as to exclude, in fondness for the creature, all ideas of the Creator.

EVENING LXXV.

OF THE VOLUPTUARY.

UNDER the denomination of the Voluptuary I describe the man who, from an excessive selfishness, cannot be satisfied with that share of satisfaction which falls to the common lot of human nature, but endeavours to render the whole of his existence one uninterrupted state of sensual indulgence.

The folly of such an attention, considering it only in a worldly view, sufficiently appears from this circumstance, that, such is the nature of man, pleasure of no kind can be uninterrupted. Though the external object should remain immutable, the internal organ of perception would contract insensibility from lassitude. The Creator has wisely provided, that so selfish and useless a design should be punished in the first instance by disappointment.

To be lovers of pleasure more than lovers of God, the giver of every comfort, argues a disposition either foolishly thoughtless, or basely ungrateful. It prevents all consideration of the causes for which, it is reasonably to be concluded, such a creature as man was placed in society. It destroys benevolence; for as soon might light and darkness co-exist in the same place, at the same moment, as sensual selfishness with Christian benevolence. In the pursuit of personal gratification, the true voluptuary regards not the injuries he does to others while he can do them with impunity. He chiefly ruins the innocent and unsuspecting; because they are the most easily ensnared. He feels no compunction if he can with, safety destroy the peace and comfort, the hopes and the fortunes of a family, in the gratification of a brutal passion. He destroys at the same time his own health, fortune, and reputation. But he thinks himself (and plumes himself in the appellation) a man of pleasure.

Let the frequenters of the tavern, the brothel, and the gaming-table, and all the tribes of fashionable votaries of selfish gratification, consider seriously whether they may not be comprehended among the voluptuaries whom I have thus imperfectly described. And if so, let them also think whether they are acting the part of truly reasonable and liberal men, whether their system is not contemptibly mean and narrow, and whether He, whom they are not used to think of, the God of purity, has not reason to be offended with them; whether, placing themselves for a moment in the place of Creator, they would not be provoked with creatures who should debase their nature so meanly, and, like them, think so little of their benefactor. Would they not require that the gifts of time and abilities should be employed in acts of beneficence, in self-improvement, in useful pursuits, and in promoting the general benefit of society. They are wont to be proud and insolent, and to despise the more sober part of mankind for want of spirit; but if they view themselves in a true light, they will appear mean, little, and objects of contempt or compassion.

But happily they have a power of raising themselves again to their native height and magnitude. Faith and repentance producing their genuine fruits, amendment of life and piety, will recover the favour of Him who, knowing the infirmities of our internal frame, and the power of external objects, offers pardon on repentance, and declares that the attribute in

which he delights is mercy.   What a ray of comfort
to the weary traveller in the path of vanity.

EVENING LXXVI.

OF THE MISER.

I COMPREHEND under the name of Miser, not only
him who denies himself the common comforts of life
for the sake of sparing the opulence in which he
abounds, but those also, in whatever profession or
employment, who devote all their time and attention
to the accumulation of money which they neither
want, nor can possibly enjoy, which they will not
communicate, and which they relinquish reluctantly
even when they resign their breath.

Men engaged in the busy occupations of commerce, early and late, and from their youth to old
age, commonly think themselves, and are thought
by others, laudably and honourably, as well as usefully employed.   Observe the Exchange, the Quay,
and the Bank, what anxious looks, what airs of
supercilious importance, what an unceasing din and
bustle!   You would think that man was created to
buy and sell stock, and that the happiness of human
nature depended on the price of Scrip and Consols.

Men thus ardently and constantly engrossed by
Mammon, cannot be supposed to have time or inclination enough remaining to serve God acceptably.
These, and they constitute a very numerous division
of mankind, may almost be said to have dethroned
the living God of heaven and earth, and raised a
golden image, in adoration of which they fall down
prostrate.

There is no passion so general as avarice. The
principles of it are implanted in human nature for

the wisest purposes; but they are suffered by neglect, and even encouraged by misconduct, to grow
up to vicious excess.

The education of boys in this country leads immediately to the encouragement of avarice. At the
most teachable age many are taught nothing but the
arts of keeping pecuniary accounts. Not only polite learning is despised in comparison with that
which teaches to secure what is called the main
chance, but religious instruction is also neglected,
either as a matter which may be postponed without
inconvenience, or as of little consequence, when
weighed in the balance with the art of thriving in
trade, and raising a family by making a fortune.

Before any principles of virtue can be formed, or
real and valuable knowledge obtained, the stripling
is often sent from the place of superficial education
to the banks of the Ganges, there to heap up enormous riches, honestly, if he can; but at all events,
to fulfil the ultimate end of his mission.

Rem—si possis, recte, si non, quocunque modo, rem.

Many are engaged in the servile employments of
a shop or warehouse, without a religious idea impressed by parents or masters, and without an allowance of time to compensate, by personal application,
the defects arising from their superintendent's neglect.

Can it be wondered, since this is the case, that
we are a nation of misers, or devoted, in the language of Scripture, to the lust of the eye, and to
covetousness, which is idolatry?

Those who fall into the snare from the defect of
education, and the powerful enticement of example,
are indeed to be compassionated; but let them believe it a friendly voice which exhorts them, amidst
all their pursuits after worldly wealth, to seek the

riches of divine grace; for " what shall it profit a man, if he gain the whole world and lose his own soul —and what shall a man give in exchange for his soul?"

You have spent your life in some laborious commercial engagement, you have borne the heat of the torrid zone, for the sake of acquiring treasure; and, in the activity of your pursuit, you have not had time to think of God, or of your own soul. But you succeeded in your pursuit. You are rich. You have houses, lands, carriages, servants, every thing which luxury and pride can demand and riches supply. But life is short, and death approaches every hour. Remember that the King of Terrors is not to be bribed by the largest fortune ever brought from the East Indies, and that gold is dross in the eye of Heaven. Think of these things, and amidst your pursuit of riches, learn to meditate on serious subjects, such as the shortness of life, the nature of man, and his chief good, the existence of a Deity, the possibility, at least, that Christianity may be true. You are not required to resign your property. A competency is certainly desirable; and I know no sin in possessing abundance. But I desire you to enlarge your views beyond the sphere of material things, beyond this world; and among the many ventures you have made to improve your fortune, I desire you to venture something in expectation of that, in comparison with which the empire of the Mogul itself shall appear contemptible—a happy immortality, and the favour of the Almighty.

Here is an interest, here a reversion, which may surely justify your expending a little time and a few thoughts to secure it, especially as you are safe from loss; for though you may have a probability of obtaining such advantage, you incur no danger of losing any thing valuable.

EVENING LXXVII.

OF THE AMBITIOUS MAN.

To minds not duly enlightened by Christianity, this world appears of such value, that there is no labour or danger which they refuse to undergo, however inconsistent with religious duty, for the sake of obtaining a conspicuous place in it.

If indeed this were our home, and not our inn, it would be desirable to be labouring after power and pre-eminence. But as we are only in our journey, and that a short one, it is not worth our while to contend with eagerness, or embroil ourselves in rivalries, for the sake of a little elevation above our fellow travellers. Death will bring us all to a level in a few years; and they who in an humble sphere shall have made their peace with God, will then be honoured with distinctions, in comparison with which earthly honours are but mockery.

Yet I do not deny that man has natural tendencies to ambition, as well as to pleasure and to avarice. And they may certainly be gratified with innocence while they transgress not moderation, else they would not have been implanted in the human heart.

The principle of ambition in man is a desire of power lest he should be oppressed, and of honour lest he should be despised; but the desire of power becomes the lust of dominion, and of respect, unbounded pride.

I mean to comprehend under the name of Ambition, not only the avidity of the conqueror, and the aspiring aims of the hero and statesman, but that love of distinction, in common life, which produces a restless and an envious pride.

A transient survey of the world evinces that a

great number of the human species place their chief
good in being admired by each other.   The fashionable world, by whom I mean those who follow fashion in all her extremes, seem to have no other
wish but to appear pleasing or great in the eyes of
persons honoured with the same denomination.
View the purlieus of a court, or a frequented water-
ing or bathing place, and you will easily see that the
first endeavour of the greater part is to be noticed
and admired. Scarcely any extravagance, or affectation in dress or behaviour, is so absurd as not to be
adopted if it contributes to obtain distinction.   Virtues, vices, religion, irreligion, charity, or selfish
parsimony, fluctuate in the degrees of estimation
and abhorrence in which they appear according to
the capricious decision of fashion; and many seem
not unwilling, for the sake of attracting notice, to
sacrifice their best hopes, their most indispensible
duties, at the shrine of this fanciful deity,

This is a love of the world which all who entertain any right sentiments must condemn as equally
forbidden by reason and religion.   In so great a love
for the admiration of mere mortals, and those too the
silliest of the race, there cannot be found the two
great virtues required in every good man, piety to
God, and beneficence to our fellow-creatures. Ambition creeps as often as it flies.   Its mean servility to
the great, and its contempt of the poor, are utterly
repugnant to the spirit of Christianity.   Its connivance at vice, and even compliance with it for interested purposes, its time-serving duplicity, are no
less inconsistent with moral virtue.   Its constant
attention to its objects, to courting the great, and to
seeking opportunities of access to the powerful,
occupy too much of the time and thoughts to permit
a due degree of attention to God, and to such duties

as our own personal frailties and the want of society demand.

Excessive ambition is chiefly visible in the political world and in the professions. The mercantile part of mankind are employed in amassing wealth; and seldom think of raising their families to rank and honour but by raising a fortune.

In the clerical profession ambition too often allures her votaries to a behaviour highly unbecoming as well as irreligious.

But I cheerfully turn from a tender topic. Let us examine the profession of the law. As by a strange abuse, civil and hereditary honours have been particularly lavished on this very secular profession, more than common ambition is found in the profession of the law. Such is the eagerness of pursuit in this profession, that the mind seems to be chained down, during the whole period of life, to worldly concerns. The professional business of itself is indeed entirely secular; and there is a private concern at the same time going on, the aggrandisement of a name and family, which, added to the public labours, leaves little time and attention for religion. The world admires the abilities and assiduity of the successful lawyer; and it would be surprising if the world did not admire its own ardent votaries. The title perhaps at last arrives, and the successful candidate dies worn out with the labours of courting this world. With respect to the other, he must offer as an apology for his inattention to its concerns, that he had not time to think of it. But in the eye of sensible and considerate men, what is the applause of the world, a coronet, and a family ennobled, in comparison with the objects proposed to our hopes and endeavours by Christianity? Many things are commonly done in the law, of which it may be candidly said, that they are hard and unchristian,-if not absolutely dishonest, even by the most celebrated professors of it, in the course of a long and multifarious practice. If Christianity be true, so long and warm an attachment to the world, its business, and its rewards, cannot be venial.

Those who engage in political concerns, and aspire at civil honours, usually pursue their objects with an ardour which engrosses the whole mind; and consequently leaves no room for attention to religion. How shall they work out their salvation with fear and trembling, whose days and nights are given to the study of politics, and the paying court to patrons in power? Ability in the senate, and success attending a long course of exertion, appear objects of such magnitude, that every thing which religion has to offer is diminished on comparison, and too often esteemed only the contrivance of priestcraft co-operating with the arts of government.

I all along proceed upon the hypothesis that Christianity is true ; and that being the case, all the ambitious in excess, that is, all who pursue fame and grandeur without attention to the King of Kings, are in a deplorable state, though they may shine with stars, ermine, ribbons, and coronets.

EVENING LXXVIII.

OF THE MAN OF THE WORLD.

THE lust of the flesh, the lust of the eye, and the pride of life, are the scriptural names for voluptuousness, avarice, and ambition. I have already considered them separately, and I now consider them in union, and constituting that admired character, the Man of the World.

The man of the world is a composition of lust, covetousness, and pride. Ugly names indeed! and he is therefore particularly solicitous to varnish them with graceful manners, ornamental accomplishments, and all the plausibility of affected elegance and virtue.

The man of the world founds his system on two hypotheses, both of which are erroneous; the first, that this life is the whole of man's existence; and the second, that, such being the case, the chief good of man consists in gratifying lust, avarice and ambition.

This life cannot be the whole of man's existence, on the supposition on which I proceed, that Christianity is true; and the experience of man previously to revelation, had determined the question, that health, virtue, and temperance, were more desirable than any external advantage.

But Christianity being true, vicious gratifications cannot for a moment be supposed to constitute the felicity of man. They are, on the contrary, snares which lead to perdition; and to beware of them is the very essence of Christian Wisdom.

The man of the world, notwithstanding all arguments from reason and revelation, gives himself up, at the various stages of life, and in various circumstances and degrees, to the lust of the flesh, the lust of the eye, and the pride of life. The man of the world then, however admired in the private circle, applauded in public, honoured with titles, elevated in rank, and loaded with riches, is that unhappy man who is said in the Scriptures of the New Testament to be dead in trespasses and sins: And let him remember, that in the book it is written—

"Neither fornicators, nor idolaters, nor adulterers, nor thieves, nor drunkards, nor covetous, nor extortioners, shall enter the kingdom of Heaven."

He must see from this passage only, and many more equally in point might be cited, that it is impossible at the same time to be a man of the world and a Christian.

This is a plain truth, without disguise on one hand, and on the other without exaggeration; and with earnest affection I entreat every man of the world to retire a little from the gaudy and deceitful scene, from admirers, from flatterers, from seducers, to the death-bed scene, to the house of mourning, and there endeavour to view his own condition in its proper colour. Happy will it be if he shall see the things which belong unto his peace in this his day, and before death terminates the golden opportunity.

EVENING LXXIX.

OF THE DANGER OF BEING LED BY IMITATION WITHOUT PRINCIPLES OF RELIGION.

It is thought the safest mode of advancing in the journey of life to follow the footsteps of others, who, from pre-eminence of rank and reputed abilities, may be supposed to possess the least fallible knowledge. To derive instruction from books, time, attention, and judgment, are necessary; but to tread where others have trodden before, little more direction is required than to use the eyes. The greater number, therefore, from mere indolence, give themselves no farther concern in settling their moral and religious conduct, than to observe the behaviour and sentiments of those to whom wealth and civil honours have given a superiority of condition.

But, unhappily many of those who are thus selected as models for imitation, are themselves under the influence of the most fatal delusion. They have

arrived at the pre-eminence which gives them the
authority of guides, by pursuing those objects which
are merely secular ; and the artful pursuit of which
constitutes them truly men of the world ; who, instead of being guides to happiness, might often be
considered as beacons, rendered conspicuous, to admonish the traveller of danger in the vicinity.

There cannot be a more pernicious mistake than
to suppose wisdom or right conduct the necessary
attendant of splendour of appearance and elevation
of rank, and, in consequence of so weak an opinion,
to follow the example of the rich and great in affairs
which essentially concern the happiness or misery of
life. It is safe and proper to imitate them with
judgment and moderation, in the indifferent modes
of dressing, entering a room, dancing, or external
behaviour ; but to renounce religion, conscience,
virtue, health, and peace, because some leaders of
the fashion seem to have renounced them, deserves
to be stigmatised by a harsher name than folly.

Truth is immutable. Whether the majority is for
or against her, she remains unaltered. Let all therefore who seriously wish to reach as much happiness
and perfection as they are capable of, employ their
reason with humility and patience in the pursuit of
her ; and when they have found her, which on a
faithful inquiry they will easily do, let them follow
her guidance with a firm attachment, uninfluenced
by the false, though brilliant lights of fickle fashion.

I mean not to insinuate that all the votaries of
fashion are either irreligious or profligate. Many,
I am convinced, from a false modesty, and a respect
for the world which it does not deserve, appear less
virtuous and less religious than they really are. But
it is the appearance which seduces ; and the appearance of profligacy in those who are able to grace

every deformity with the tinsel of rank and riches, is apt to allure the unthinking herd into an imitation, fatal to their virtue.

Too much precaution, therefore, cannot be used in guarding all who hope to be proficients in Christian philosophy against that influence, which seduces more to vice, folly, and infidelity, than any books of the most ingenious sceptics, I mean the influence of grandeur and worldly power, operating on the thoughtless by a bad example.

EVENING LXXX.

OF A MORAL LIFE WITHOUT RELIGION.

" I PAY my debts. I take care to injure nobody. I amuse myself as I like, without intruding on the amusements of others. I am temperate, for I find temperance conducive to health, comfort, and long life. I am an obliging neighbour, a constant friend, a peaceable subject ; but, after all, I am not religious. Can I be easy without religion ? I trust to a good life ;

> " For modes of faith let graceless zealots fight,
>   His can't be wrong, whose life is in the right."

Such is the soliloquy of many a man who maintains a decent character in society, and at the same time values himself in a freedom from what he calls the shackles of superstition. But virtue without religion, since Christianity has appeared, is certainly of a questionable kind. The voluntary renunciation of a religion like the Christian, is at first sight a circumstance sufficient to render any virtue suspected. A truly good mind will not easily relinquish its hopes, its consolations, its friendly influence on human happiness and society. So that there is great reason to suspect, from the very pretension to morality without religion, that the virtue of the pretender is defective and spurious.

Such virtue, though specious in appearance, will be found, when duly analysed, nothing but pride; a vice the most repugnant to real goodness, the source of injustice to man, and impiety to God, of every vanity and of every folly, and a vice against which the displeasure of Heaven is particularly pointed.

Many causes of a worldly kind concur to make men adopt the appearance, and even the practice of various virtues. Reputation is in general necessary to success in the projects of ambition and avarice. A man is often temperate and just, because the character of intemperance and injustice would retard his advancement, or injure his interest; or because his habits of virtue have been early formed by the care of parents and the influence of example; or because he is little exposed to temptation, or is secured from many vices by constitutional aversion, indifference, or infirmity.

An inoffensive conduct, arising from any of these causes, is entitled to respect, or at least to an exemption from severe censure; but it cannot deserve the praise nor the reward of virtue proceeding from principle.

This irreligious virtue is in most instances little to be depended upon; for, as it respects nothing but this world, and the opinion of man, whenever the interests of this world can be served, or the opinions of others secured by secrecy, there remains little to preserve it inviolate.

Man is so weak, and so prone to fall into vice and misery, that it is certainly unsafe to resolve to walk without guidance and protection, when both are offered by an Almighty arm.

Whatever sophists, philosophers, metaphysicians, and witlings may say, on virtue being its own reward, on the fitness of things, and on many refined subjects totally unintelligible, and totally unregarded by the majority of mankind, I will recommend it to all, to strengthen the force of virtue by erecting round her the ramparts of religion.

EVENING LXXXI.

OF THE HONOUR OF MEN OF THE WORLD AS A SUBSTITUTE FOR RELIGION.

A sense of honour, as it is commonly understood in the intercourse of society, means a determination to avoid contempt, by avoiding whatever contradicts the prejudices or practices of people of fashion.

If vices are fashionable they become perfectly consistent with this sense of honour; indeed they seem ornaments necessary to complete the character of a fashionable man of honour. Experience proves, that some practices and opinions utterly inconsistent with virtue, are often fashionable, or at least not deemed disgraceful in the circle of fashion.

The following habits and practices are rather esteemed ornamental accomplishments to the modern man of honour: gallantry, in all its enormities, duelling, gaming, incurring debt without the power and inclination to repay, pride and contempt of others, however virtuous, who are without rank and riches, extravagance in all expenses, luxury, voluptuousness, ostentation, effeminacy; or, in the language of Scripture, every vice and folly which can arise from the lust of the flesh, the lust of the eye, and the pride of life, provided a certain appearance of external decency be duly preserved.

And this proud overbearing principle, which has every appearance of originating from the grand adversary of mankind, is to supersede the necessity of any other guidance. The dictates of the sense of honour are capable of directing those who possess it, if you will believe themselves, more safely and infallibly in the path of rectitude and happiness than any light derivable from philosophy and religion.

I fear that He who requires purity of heart will not accept even laudable actions when they proceed from evil motives; but I am sure that evil actions committed to please the world, presumptuously and boastingly repeated, in defiance of all the lights of conscience and revelation, must, in his sight, become singularly malignant and offensive.

How mean will appear that proud race who now strut about the earth with swords ready to shed the blood of any one who offends them, when the sentence shall be pronounced—"Depart from me, ye workers of iniquity."

I hope to leave it forcibly impressed on the minds of vicious men of honour, that, if Christianity be true, their conduct, under this principle, is repugnant to the will of God; and that their state, though admired by many, and perhaps envied and imitated by the thoughtless is truly dangerous and dishonourable.

When death approaches they will wish that in the season of health and youth they had been led by the sense of religion, instead of a sense of honour; a principle too often unconnected with common honesty, and invented and recommended by the pride and wickedness of the human heart in its unregenerate state. "The beginning of pride," says

A a 3

the Son of Sirach, " is when one departeth from God, and his heart is turned away from his Maker."

EVENING LXXXII.

OF THE KNOWLEDGE OF ONE'S SELF, THE NATURE OF MAN, AND OUR DEPENDENT STATE.

IF one can suppose a man never to have seen the face of the earth but in the month of May, one may conclude that he would scarcely be able to form an idea of its desolate appearance in December. So men in the midst of youth, health, seducing pleasure, riches, honours, flattery, and the obsequiousness of all around them, can with difficulty conceive the evil day which nevertheless awaits both them and all the sons of men.

The misery of man is a topic on which it is unnecessary to enlarge. All men are convinced of it at some time in their lives by experience, but all men do not sufficiently reflect upon it, nor prepare an antidote against it, nor alleviations under it.

Men ascend to the skies, and dive into the earth in pursuit of knowledge ; but they descend not into themselves, they examine not their own nature.

If they courted an acquaintance with themselves, they would find their own frailty and misery the most distinguishing parts of their character ; and they would be led by the sight to seek strength and comfort, where alone it can be found, in the favour of the Creator.

In a state in which we are liable every moment to be deprived of all our souls hold dear ; of relations, friends, fortune, fame, health, our senses, and our peace ; a religion which offers but a hope of comfort and support from an Almighty power, ought to be cherished as the most valuable treasure, far more precious than the Indies can bestow, far more desirable to a thinking mind and a feeling heart than the jewels of the brightest diadem in the universe.

Yet how little is this treasure valued in the busy walks of pleasure, avarice, and ambition! The most trifling allurements of the world will induce men to postpone or dismiss all thoughts of God and their dependent state.

But the evil day of sickness, or old age, or dejection of spirits, will come, and come in peculiar horrors to those who have made no religious preparation. Things will then appear in a shape and colour totally different from that which they deceitfully assumed in the hour of prosperity. Think, O man, before the evil day comes, and mitigate the evil by securing a retreat in the storm under the wing of the Deity.

Thou totterest, like the infant unable to walk without the nurse's aid, when thou venturest to walk alone; but God is thy nursing parent, and if thou wilt not, in the foolish pride of thy heart, reject his guidance, he will lead thee with all the tender solicitude of a parent, strengthen thy weakness, and console thy misery.

EVENING LXXXIII.

OF THE NECESSITY OF BEING AWAKENED TO A SENSE OF RELIGION.

In a busy intercourse with the world, and especially in the season of health and prosperity, man is wonderfully prone to fall into such a degree of insensibility in all that relates to religion, as is characterised in the forcible language of Scripture by the appellations of Sleep and Death. If any man gives himself the trouble to recollect the time in which he has scarcely thought of his spiritual state, or thought of it with great indifference, he will find it a very large portion of his existence.

An habitual insensibility becomes very difficult to be removed. It often ends in a disease which may be termed a lethargy; a disease fatal to the spiritual life.

The symptoms of this disease may be easily understood. Men who are seized with it appear totally immersed in the pursuits of worldly objects, either think not at all of religion, or think of it as beneath their serious notice, as the contrivance of policy and priestcraft, as fit only to awe fools, or women and children, as an interruption of real and important business in life, by which they always mean the pursuit of pleasure, money, or advancement. They consider the Sabbath Day as an injurious loss of time, seldom attend the church, but settle pecuniary accounts at home, write letters, ride out on parties of pleasure, or travel. They are extremely apt to cavil at the Scriptures, and ridicule all pious people as weak or enthusiastic.

Other symptoms of this lethargy of the soul might be enumerated, but they are similar to those already specified, and are obvious to observation.

A life, indeed, led without faith and repentance, is a scene of darkness and delusion. To live without God in the spiritual world, is like living without the sun in the natural. When the soul is turned away from God, a thick darkness overspreads it, and night comes on; but artificial lights are supplied by the world, whose brilliancy is deceitful, and of short continuance.

There cannot be a greater misfortune than this

spiritual insensibility; and God Almighty suffers it not to become extreme but by man's own voluntary presumption and pride. He sends some affliction, which speaks with a warning voice. It is heard for a moment. It is silent again. The world approaches once more with all its allurements, and the unhappy patient relapses into a fatal security.

Extreme sickness, and the evident approach of death, usually awaken the dull spirit at last; and few, however thoughtless they may have been in life, die without a pious ejaculation. Sickness, and the dread of dissolution, though efficacious, are painful remedies; how much better to be prepared by reason and reflection; to arise from sleep voluntarily, and without a call, so loud and so alarming to the human ear.

The obvious means of resuscitating the sleeping soul are prayer and attention to exhortation. The word of God preached in due season, and attended to with faith and humility, has had wonderful effects on the most obdurate heart. Happy, where the love of the world has not precluded all affection for things sacred and divine.

But the death of some dear relation, some beloved of the soul, is perhaps the most awakening scourge of Providence. Then the feeling heart is exceedingly sorrowful, and learns to look up for comfort to the source of all consolation. Whoever has not worn out his sensibility in the practices of vice, must, on such occasions, receive a deep impression. Let it be every one's care to watch, lest the deceits of the world efface it too soon.

And here I cannot help lamenting the fashion of the age, which, on the departure of a parent, a child, or a wife, drives all the relations from the house of mourning, and from the side of the grave. No

sooner has the heart of some beloved object ceased
to palpitate, than the family, which ought to mourn
over the poor monument of mortality, and receive a
due impression from the melancholy scene, is hurried
away to some distant residence, there to seek in
dissipation, as soon as decency will permit, a total
oblivion of the dear departed.

Providence gave feelings to man on such occasions
productive, when permitted to take effect, of great
improvement in all that concerns the state of the
soul.   These are the things which, if not prevented
by our own perverseness, would awaken us from
sleep—the sleep of death.

In the entertaining voyages of a late great circum-
navigator, we read, that in ascending a mountain in
Terra del Fuego, a tendency to sleep seized the travellers, almost irresistibly.   But if the tendency
was indulged, the consequence was death.   This
remarkable effect bears a great analogy to what
happens in our spiritual journey, our pilgrimage
through the world ; and all who are wise will avoid
that sleep, from which they may wake no more in
this world, and wake only at last to misery.

I cannot do a more beneficial service to my fellow-
creatures than to admonish them of the danger of
falling insensibly, from a love of the world, into this
dreadful stupor of the soul.   Thousands and tens of
thousands feel themselves perfectly at ease on the
subject; but let them beware lest their want of
feeling be found the numbness of a mortification.
The surgeon pronounces the limb safe while pain
is felt ; but immediately prepares to amputate, or
gives up hope of life, on the discontinuance of sensation.

A total freedom from solicitude on the subject
of religion is certainly a most alarming symptom ;

and let us beware in time, lest that wretched permission may be given us,—Sleep on now, and take your rest.

EVENING LXXXIV.

OF NEGLECTING RELIGION, AND AVOIDING RELIGIOUS OFFICES THROUGH THE FEAR OF BEING DEEMED GUILTY OF HYPOCRISY.

UNDER the false but specious appearance of singular piety and righteousness, to promote the mean purposes of secular interest, is a deceit which justly deserves the contempt of man and the vengeance of heaven. The peculiar deformity of hypocrisy has given so general and cordial a disgust to it, that most men are fearful of exhibiting any appearance of religion, lest they should be suspected of hypocrisy.

The aversion to hypocrisy is just; but transgressing the proper limits, it has been a fruitful cause of irreligion.

He who habitually neglects the various external offices of religion, which were wisely instituted to preserve a regard to its essence, will insensibly become less attentive to it than he ever intended. And he who, fearing the imputation of over-righteousness, and the appellation of a saint or methodist, treats things sacred with affected levity, will in time lose all proper awe of every thing that is worthy of religious veneration. He will be in danger of losing the substance when he disregards the genuine and unaffected appearances resulting from it.

To be ashamed of Jesus Christ, and his religion, is, to carry the abhorrence of hypocrisy to a dreadful extreme. To be a Christian, indeed, is to be a greater character than was ever possessed by the renowned heroes and philosophers of all Pagan antiquity. And he who, on proper occasions, is unwilling to show that he is a Christian, and that he duly esteems all the ordinances necessary to preserve a sense of religion, has not an adequate idea of the dignified character he claims, and the value of the religion which he professes.

Let us manfully avow what we sincerely believe, and not presume to insult the great King of Kings by showing that we esteem the external insignia of his service badges of disgrace. The cause of Christianity would flourish more than it has yet done, if all who feel its truth would, under the guidance of discretion, let their light so shine before men, that they might glorify their Father which is in heaven.

There is no occasion to proceed to any extremes, to affect an appearance of being righteous overmuch, or better than our neighbours. Such appearances are usually suspicious. But it is certainly unmanly and disgraceful to a Christian to fear to avow his principles whenever the occasion requires the avowal; or to be ashamed of such conversation and behaviour as becomes the professed disciple of Jesus Christ. It is a mean compliance with the vicious part of the world; a desertion of our post from mere cowardice; a behaviour in a subject which would justly provoke an earthly potentate.

Let it be our first care to be sincere, and in acting as that sincerity, under the direction of a manly prudence, shall urge us, let us be totally regardless of the imputation of hypocrisy. The imputation may arise only from the ill nature and envy of incompetent judges; but God knows the heart, and the persecution of the wicked will only tend to render our obedience to him more acceptable.

Dare to be what you are, and be more solicitous to be than to appear. Truth indeed may be secure, that though for a time she may be misrepresented, she will at last be known and honoured; for there is a feature in her face which, like light, strikes the organ with irresistible force, whenever the artificial obstacles to the view of it are removed. She has no occasion to be uneasy at the malice of those who bestow on her the name of hypocrisy.

It is certainly right to seek to please our fellow-creatures by every instance of behaviour consistent with honour and conscience; but to stand more in awe of them, of their opinion, of their representations of us, than of our common Lord and Creator, is at once a most irrational conduct, and an insult offered to the Majesty of heaven.

EVENING LXXXV.

RELIGION ORIGINATES NEITHER IN PRIESTCRAFT, NOR WEAK-NESS, NOR SUPERSTITION ; BUT IS FOUNDED ON THE EVIDENT SUGGESTIONS OF REASON, AND THE NATURAL FEELINGS OF THE HUMAN MIND.

MEN who study this world only, and value themselves on a subordinate wisdom, which deserves only the name of cunning, are apt to conclude that religion, and all its salutary restraints, are derived from the policy of civil power erecting its fabric on the basis of the people's superstition. The priesthood is suspected of having been called in to add a main pillar to the massy pile of political architecture.

While this idea prevails, and great ingenuity has been exerted to disseminate it, every attempt to recommend the doctrines of religion in general, or of Christianity in particular, becomes ineffectual.

It is considered either as a crafty co-operation with power, or as the foolish enterprise of a zealot's infatuation.

But it is evident, from the deductions of reason, and the native feelings of the heart, that religion owes its origin to causes far more respectable than either policy or folly.

To enter the lists with the Atheists would be to engage in more than, in these short chapters, I have been able to undertake.   Indeed, after all the attempts of libertines to attribute religion to policy, it has been justly doubted whether a real Atheist ever existed.

If any other proof is necessary than the visible works of the creation, every thing we see and feel around, I must refer to the fine arguments produced at the lecture founded by Mr. Boyle.

I will only desire my reader to consider what he has himself felt, and what he has observed others feel, under the pressure of affliction, in the hour of sickness, and at the supposed approach of dissolution.   In opposition to all that wit, or malice, or misapplied ingenuity have advanced, in those circumstances he has found in himself, and observed in others, an irresistible impulse to seek comfort and assistance from that Supreme Being, in whose hands are the issues of life.

Could this feeling, I will ask him, arise from priestcraft, worldly policy, or mere folly and infirmity ? Was there not something in his bosom which told him, in language awfully convincing, Verily there is a God ?

And if that sentiment is founded on truth on a death-bed, since truth is immutable, is it not founded in truth throughout the whole of our existence, in the day of youth, health, and prosperity ; and is it not wisdom to be influenced by it before the evil day arrives, when there is danger, lest it should be too late for piety to atone for past omissions, and the long continued errors of pride and presumption ?

Death has been called the great Teacher. Few approach him without learning the most important truths. Wits, sceptics, minute philosophers, bow at last to this sovereign instructor, and acknowledge the vanity of their own imaginations when weighed in the balance with the lessons of Death.

I request then the scoffer at religion, the sceptic, and the professed libertine, to permit the ideas concerning the truth of religion which arise in extreme sickness, the loss of those we love, the apprehension of immediate death, or any other alarming situation, to influence his principles and practices through life.

They will then be far from employing their abilities in the malignant office of depriving others of that religion which affords solid comfort under every circumstance, but will rather most cheerfully and gratefully seek their own happiness in faith and piety.

EVENING LXXXVI.

OF ATTRIBUTING RELIGION TO THE PREJUDICES OF EDUCATION, AND THE UNDUE INFLUENCE OF PARENTAL AND SOCIAL EXAMPLE.

AMONG the many groundless causes assigned for the prevalence of religion in the world, one of the commonest is the prejudice of education, and the influence of example.

The pretended philosophers are fond of asserting that man is rendered, by the restraints of education, an animal totally different from that which he was originally formed by nature. They allow no argument to be drawn in favour of religion from the universality of religious sentiments, because, they urge, that this universality arises from the crafty or foolish suggestions of parents, who teach the doctrines of religion as the most effectual means of enforcing and securing filial obedience.

But does a tendency to religion appear in those only who have been religiously educated ? The most neglected sons and daughters of Adam, those who, like the wild ass's colt, are left to themselves in their infancy, are found to be as strongly impressed with an idea of a God as the most cultivated disciples of the most refined philosophy. They cannot give a rational account of any system; but they fear God, and depend upon his support in their afflictions.

I was much pleased with hearing a remarkable instance of piety in the very outcasts of society, in those whom nobody instructs and nobody knows, the vagrants distinguished by the appellation of Gypsies. A large party had requested leave to rest their weary limbs, during the night, in the shelter of a barn ; and the owner took the opportunity of listening to their conversation. He found their last employment at night and their first in the morning was prayer. And though they could teach their children nothing else, they taught them to supplicate in an uncouth but pious language, the assistance of a friend in a world where the distinctions of rank are little regarded. I have been credibly informed that these poor neglected brethren are very devout, and remarkably disposed to attribute all events to the interposition of a particular providence. But can their piety be attributed to the influence of education and the prevalence of example ? They have no education, and they are too far removed from all intercourse with society to feel the seducing power of prevalent example.

Whoever is conversant with the relations of voyagers and travellers, must know that the principal employment of many savage nations is the due observance of religious ceremonies, and that all, with not a single exception fully ascertained, are convinced of the existence of a God, and of his actual, though invisible government. But in savage nations there appears to be no education, and there is not, it may be concluded, political cunning or wisdom sufficient to have rendered religion a fashion, with a design to diffuse it by example, and facilitate civil obedience.

The truth is, religious sentiments rise in the heart of man, unspoiled by vice, and uncorrupted by sophistry, no less naturally than sentiments of love, or any other affection.

All that education effects in the countries of Christianity is to direct the natural tendencies to religion to that revelation of the divine will which constitutes Christianity. Early education, or subsequent instruction, is certainly necessary to teach this; for a man is not born a Christian; but the knowledge of any science taught in infancy might as well be called the prejudice of education as the knowledge of Christianity.

LIBERAL EDUCATION;

OR,

A PRACTICAL TREATISE ON THE METHODS OF ACQUIRING USEFUL AND POLITE LEARNING.

FUNGAR VICE COTIS.

Hor.

PREFACE.

THOUGH a conductor of a school may be qualified by his experience to write on the subject of Education; yet there are circumstances arising from the nature of his engagements, which render the undertaking extremely delicate. While he recommends any particular mode, it will be supposed that he is obliquely recommending his own plan, and consulting little more than his own interest. If he suggests a hint derogatory from the merit of any new and fashionable method, or places of instruction, he will appear to some to be actuated by envy, and artfully inviting pupils to his own roof. Many can see and attribute to selfish motives a passage which has a tendency to promote the writer's advantage, though they may be incompetent judges of the propriety of the sentiment, or of the advice which it conveys.

It is indeed a truth to be lamented, that few of us are so improved by philosophy, though we study and admire it, as not to feel the influence of interested motives. Interest insensibly blinds the understanding, and often impels the judgment to decide unjustly, without the guilt of intention. I will not arrogate so much, as to suppose myself exempted from one of the most powerful principles of action which stimulate the human heart. But I will say, that I have endeavoured to divest myself of every improper prepossession, and to write the dictates of my conviction and the result of my experience. To some share of experience he may without arrogance pretend, whose life has been spent with little inter-

B b 2

ruption in places of education ; at school, as a learner; at college, as a student; and again at school, as a master.

That I have notwithstanding frequently erred, is but too probable ; and I should have profited little from observation, if I had not remarked the folly of presumptuous confidence. I am ready, therefore, to acknowledge my mistakes upon conviction. Useful truth is my object; and if I have not yet discovered it, it is still equally desirable in itself, and will be welcomed whenever it shall be pointed out by more successful inquirers.

Some apology may be thought necessary for the number of quotations in the notes. All I can advance in my defence is, that they were not introduced from ostentation, but to confirm my opinions. I was indeed desirous of securing some elegance and some authority to my book, by giving them a place in it.

I have, from the same motive, made additions to the notes, in this and every new impression : and, in consequence of a particular request, the mottoes, and most of the citations from the ancient writers, are now translated. That some are not so, I must acknowledge to be rather the effect of accident and indolence than of design.

One volume having increased beyond the due size, I was advised to divide the matter into two; but to this I could not consent, without making some additions. As the state of the universities is of great importance to liberal education, I have made many free remarks on them, relying on the protection of the generous Public at large, against the pride, prejudice, and resentment of those who may think their dignity sullied by the freedom of my censure.

It is but justice to acknowledge, that in speaking

of the universities, I chiefly, though not entirely,
allude to that of Oxford, of which I am an useless
member;

——— tanquam

Mancus, et extinctæ corpus non utile dextræ. Juv.

As this part of my work cannot fail of giving
offence to some, I hope I may be permitted to declare, that my animadversions on the universities
arise from pure motives. I have nothing either to
hope or to fear from any university. I am attached
to that of which I am a member, on many accounts,
and esteem all universities as institutions which, in
their original design, redound not only to the honour
of the nations in which they are encouraged, but of
human nature. Do I act the part of an enemy in
endeavouring to recover their lustre, and to remove
the abuses which length of time has gradually introduced? I censure no particular persons in them; I
honour many. I lament, as I believe many resident
members do, that the academical magistrates are so
embarrassed by useless forms and customs, and so
entangled by antiquated statutes, that they cannot
act according to their better judgments, in rendering
the places efficient for the purposes of a virtuous and
learned education. I have reason to believe, that
those who possess most power and reputation in universities, think as I do on the subject of their defects
and corruptions, and that they would readily co-
operate in producing the reformation, if they were
not unwilling to incur the odium which attends the
character of an ostensible reformer. But though I
am persuaded that my attempt will meet with secret
approbation from the most respectable persons, yet
at the same time I cannot but expect to excite in
others an implacable enmity; for what is it to oppose
old establishments like the universities, with which

dignified persons and great families are intimately connected, but to contend against power, riches, pride, and prejudice ?

Defendit numerus junctæque umbone phalanges.   Juv.

It is somewhere observed, that it is particularly imprudent to offend public bodies of men; that individuals forgive or forget, or if they should not, that their resentment dies with themselves ; that their power of revenge is circumscribed within narrow limits: but that public bodies become immortal by perpetual succession ; that they render their resentment traditionary, and that their collected power is able essentially to injure every single antagonist.   Of this I am convinced; but having engaged in the cause, whether rashly, or from good motives, let events determine, I am not inclined to shrink, from a fear of any consequences, however formidable. The improvement of education, and the reformation of the universities, are great national objects; and to have been instrumental in any degree to their accomplishment, will furnish a source of satisfactory reflection.*

---

* Τὰς ἐπιδόσεις τῶν τεχνῶν, καὶ τῶν αλλῶν ἀπάντων ὁρῶμεν γινομένας οὐ διὰ τοὺς καθεςῶσι ἐμμένοντας· ἀλλα διὰ τοὺς ἐπανορθοῦντας, καὶ ἀεὶ τολμῶντας κινεῖν τι τῶν μὴ καλῶς ἐχόντων.   ISOCRATES.

It is by continual efforts that human affairs are preserved in a state of tolerable perfection.   They have a natural tendency to degenerate. It becomes necessary, in the revolutions of ages, to point out errors and correct them ; but he who undertakes the office, is in danger of incurring peculiar dislike.   The censure which he insinuates, though general, will be applicable to many individuals ; and all who fear a disturbance of their indolent repose, or a prohibition of their improper conduct, will naturally unite in persecuting the writer who attempts the reformation.

The fear of this odium causes a connivance at abuses and errors which are too obvious to escape notice.   Evils long allowed, like

The universities certainly claim particular attention in every book on the subject of a Liberal Education; for as rivers flow into the ocean, so schools are emptied into universities; and it is of great consequence to the collected youth of the nation, the hopes of the rising age, that universities should be preserved in a state proper to receive them. A conviction of the importance of universities, has led me to pay them particular attention; but the general scope of my book is to promote good education, independently of particular places or establishments, an object far superior to the concerns of any single university, however celebrated.

I cannot suppose but that both they who educate, and they who have been educated in methods which are represented in this Treatise as erroneous or defective, should feel themselves displeased with it. Their displeasure may probably rise to resentment. I lament the probability. I most sincerely wish it had been possible to have pleased them, and at the same time not to have concealed what appeared to me useful truth. I mean to give offence to no man. I have no personal enmity. I speak plainly, but not malevolently.

I am aware that he who endeavours to promote an universal advantage, by opposing errors widely diffused, must meet resistance. I am also convinced, that he ought to disregard both the mistaken and the malicious animadversions of the interested and the ill-informed. Every reader has indeed a right to make remarks : but his alone will deserve

---

some noxious weeds, strike root so deeply, that they can scarcely be removed. If, however, the odium consequent on the attempt, or the difficulty of succeeding in it, were utterly to preclude it, the advances to corruption and ruin must at length become rapid and irresistible.

attention, whose judgment is not influenced on one side by partiality, nor on the other by favour.

Little good would have been produced by the works of the best writers, if the voice of Truth, and the genuine feelings of Independence, had been suppressed by the fear of personal or of party resentment.

In the Pamphlets of the Writers who have done me the honour to animadvert on my Book, I do not recollect that there is any argument which demands a particular refutation.

Upon the whole, if from mistake and precipitation I have advanced a single opinion injurious to any good man, or any good institution, I beg leave, in this place, to retract it, and to say with Grotius, " Id pro non scripto habeatur." But after many years experience, and the opportunities of reviewing my opinions afforded by the numerous editions that have been printed, I have discovered nothing that deserves retractation.

INTRODUCTION.

Ego multos fuisse homines excellenti animo ac virtute sine doctrinâ, naturæ ipsius habitu propè divino fatur;—sed idem contendo cum ad naturam eximiam accedat ratio quædam et conformatio doctrinæ tum præclarum quid et singulare solere existere.——*I allow that there have been many men of an excellent spirit and virtue without learning, merely by their extraordinary natural endowments approaching to divine;—but yet, I maintain that when to this extraordinary nature are added the advantages of regular discipline and education, then at last something remarkably eminent, and singularly great, is usually produced.*   Cicero.

ONE of the first ideas which will occur to a reader of my Treatise will be the multitude of books which has appeared on the subject of education. The multitude indeed of books on the subject evinces its importance, but supersedes not the necessity of an addition to the number; for, however the most celebrated pieces on education have amused the speculative reader in the retirement of his closet, I venture to affirm, that they have afforded but few valuable directions to the real student and the practical instructor.

For the names and abilities of Milton, Locke, Rousseau, and of others who have written on education, I entertain all the respect which is due to them. Their systems are plausible, and truly ingenious. The world has long placed them high in the ranks of fame, and with respect to their general merit as writers they indisputably deserve their honours. But, when they wrote on education, they fell into the common error of those who attend to speculation more than to practice. In the warmth of the innovating and reforming spirit, they censure modes of treatment which are right, they recommend methods which really cannot be reduced to practice,

and which, if they could, would be useless or pernicious. It is indeed easy to censure things already
established, and project new institutions. The world
is commonly tired of that to which it has been long
accustomed, and fondly attached to novelty. It is
then no wonder, that visionary writers on education
are greatly admired, though their directions can
seldom be closely pursued.

Innovation in plans of instruction is indeed found
to be so agreeable to the human mind, and is received
by the inexperienced and injudicious with such avidity, that it becomes expedient to stand up in defence of those established practices, which, besides
that they were originally reasonable, have been countenanced and supported by the uniform decisions of
long experience.

I mean then, in the following Treatise, to speak
in favour of that ancient system of education, which
consists in a classical discipline, and which has
produced in our nation many ornaments of human
nature. Its own excellence has hitherto sufficiently
recommended it ;* but the observers of the times
have remarked, that a mode more superficial, and
more flattering to idleness and vice, has of late begun
to prevail.

I am the rather induced to defend that discipline
which lays the foundation of improvement in ancient
learning, because I think, and am not singular in the
opinion, that not only the taste, but the religion, the
virtue, and I will add the liberties of our countrymen, greatly depend upon its continuance. True
patriotism and true valour † originate from that en-

---

* As Luther said of theology, *ulscicitur sui contemptum*, it revenges
itself on those who despise it.

† Αλεξανδρος πλειονας παρά Ἀριϛοτέλους τοῦ καθηγ̑ητοῦ, ἤ παρα φιλίππου τῦ
πατρὸς, ἀφορμιας ἔχων, διεβαινεν ἐπί Περσας. "Alexander made his expe-

largement of mind, which the well-regulated study of philosophy, poetry, and history, tends to produce; and if we can recall the ancient discipline, we may perhaps recall the generous spirit of ancient virtue. He who is conversant with the best Greek and Roman writers, with a Plato, a Xenophon, and a Cicero, must imbibe, if he is not deficient in the powers of intellect, sentiments and notions no less liberal and enlarged than elegant and ingenious.

Indeed, this enlargement, refinement, and embellishment of the mind, is the best and noblest effect of classical discipline. Classical discipline is not only desirable, as it qualifies the mind for any particular profession or occupation; but as it opens a source of pure pleasure unknown to the vulgar. Even if it were not the best preparation for every employment above the low and the mechanical, which it confessedly is, yet it is in itself most valuable, as it tends to adorn and improve human nature, and to give the ideas a noble elevation.

The possession of an elegant, enlightened, and philosophical mind with a competency, is greatly superior to the possession of a superfluous fortune with gross ignorance;* and I do not consider his lot as unhappy, who enjoys a small though sufficient income, and has received the benefits of a liberal and philosophical education. I will point out an instance taken from a department in life where instances abound. The country curate, though his pittance is small, yet if he adheres to his cha-

---

dition against the Persians with better supplies from his master Aristotle, than from his father Philip." PLUTARCH.

* ' Ο' τον ἑαυτοῦ ΠΑΙΔΑ ΠΟΛΛΟΥ ΑΞΙΟΝ ἀποδείξας, κἂν ὀλίγα καταλίπῃ, πολλὰ ἔδωκε. " He who hath rendered his son a very valuable man, though he should bequeath but little, hath already bestowed a great deal." XENOPH.

racter, and affects not the man of fashionable and expensive pleasure, but has formed a taste for the classics, for composition, and for the contemplation of the works of nature, may be most respectable and happy. The passions will sometimes ruffle the stream of happiness in every man ; but they are least likely to discompose him, who spends his time in letters, and who at the same time preserves virtue and innocence, which indeed have a natural connexion with true learning and taste.

Yet whatever may be advanced in favour of classical education, they who censure it will always find a willing audience. The ignorant and illiberal, those who have not had an education, and who are often not on that account deficient in low cunning, will endeavour, like the crafty animal in the fable, to persuade others, that the ornaments which they possess not, are of little value.

But I will venture to assert, that classical learning tends most directly to form the true gentleman ; an effect of it which men of the world will scarcely allow. The business of forming the gentleman they arrogate to themselves, and are too apt to separate that character from the idea of a scholar. But it is not a fashionable dress, nor a few external decencies of behaviour, which constitute the true gentleman. It is a liberal and an embellished mind. I will not indeed assert, that a man who understands Virgil and Horace must, from that circumstance, become a gentleman ; because it is possible that he may be able to explain the meaning of every word in them, without tasting a single beauty ; but I cannot help thinking, that no man can taste their excellencies without a polite and elegant mind ; without acquiring something more pleasing than the mere graces of external behaviour. Is it not reasonable

to conclude, that he who has caught the spirit of
the polite writers of the politest ages and cities,
must possess a peculiar degree of polish and com-
prehension? He shines with native lustre, like the
precious stone, while others owe their false glare to
paint and varnish.

An objector may perhaps urge, that there are
reputed scholars who have no appearance of this
superiority; and I will allow the assertion to be
true; at the same time, I believe it is easy to assign
a probable cause. Such persons are perhaps reputed, and only reputed scholars; or, it is possible
they may have attended only to the less elegant
pursuits of literature, such as are abstruse and not
ornamental. Many have gone through all the forms
of a learned education, and have assumed the appearances of learning, who possess not enough of it
to render the possession valuable. Such persons
bring learning into disgrace, since they discover the
pride of it, and profess to have pursued it, yet are
able to display no such fruits of it as are genuine
and truly desirable. Others have been engrossed by
verbal criticism, and the asperities of controversy.

We every day meet those who have been placed
at great schools, and who are said to have received
a classical education; but who, at the same time,
not only exhibit no peculiar advantages resulting
from it, but are also very ready to confess, that they
have found it of little use. In all such cases I must
observe, what I have before suggested, that, though
they are said to have had a classical education, they
really have not. It is true that they have been
placed at the schools where it might have been had;
but they have not received it. Either they had no
parts, or they were universally idle, or they were
taken away too early. One of these circumstances

will be applicable to all of those (and I believe, in the present age, there is a great number) who have been placed in the classical schools without receiving any advantage from the classical mode of education, and who endeavour to bring it into disrepute, by alleging their own examples of its inutility.

There are, I think, two kinds of education; one of them confined, the other enlarged; one, which only tends to qualify for a particular sphere of action, for a profession, or an official employment; the other, which endeavours to improve the powers of understanding for their own sake; for the sake of exalting the endowments of human nature, and rendering it capable of sublime and refined contemplation. This last is the kind of education which it is the primary purpose of the subsequent pages to recommend. It constitutes a broad and a strong basis, on which any kind of superstructure may afterwards be raised. It furnishes a power of finding satisfactory amusement for those hours of solitude, which every man must sometimes know in the busiest walks of life; and it constitutes one of the best supports of old age, as well as the most graceful ornaments of manhood. Even in the commercial department it is greatly desirable; for besides that it gives a grace to the man in the active stage of life, and in the midst of his negociations, it enables him to enjoy his retreat with elegance, when his industry shall have acquired an ample fortune.

Supposing for a moment, that a truly classical education were not the best preparation for every liberal pursuit, as well as the most efficacious means of exalting and refining the mind; yet, as the greater number are still trained in it, who would choose to be totally a stranger to that kind of learning, in which almost every gentleman has been in some degree initiated? A man, however great his natural talents, appears in some respect inferior in truly good company, if his mind is utterly destitute of that species and degree of liberality, which a tincture of the classics is found to bestow.

I will not, however, injure the truth by insisting on too much. There are cases in which classical education may be properly dispensed with; such is that of a very dull intellect, or a total want of parts; and such is that of the boy who is to be trained to a subordinate trade, or to some low and mechanical employment, in which a refined taste and a comprehensive knowledge would divert his attention from his daily occupation. It is certain that money may be acquired, though not liberally enjoyed, without either taste or literary knowledge. And indeed the good of the community requires, that there should be grosser understandings to fill the servile and subaltern stations in society. Some of us must be hewers of wood and drawers of water; and it were happy if those could be selected for the work; whose minds have been rendered by nature little capable of ornament or extension.

But, after all, if taste, which classical learning tends immediately to produce, has no influence in amending the heart, or in promoting virtuous affections; if it contributes not to render men more humane, and more likely to be disgusted with improper behaviour, as a deformed object, and pleased with rectitude of conduct, as beautiful in itself; if it is merely an ornamental appendage, it must be owned, that life is too short to admit of long attention in its best periods to mere embellishment. But the truth is, that polite learning is found by experience to be friendly to all that is amiable and laudable in social intercourse: friendly to morality. It has a secret,

but powerful influence in softening and meliorating
the disposition. True and correct taste directly tends
to restrain the extravagancies of passion, by regulat-
ing that nurse of passion, a disordered imagination.

Indeed, however highly I estimate knowledge,
and however I admire the works of a fine fancy;
yet I will not cease to inculcate on the minds of
studious youth, that goodness of heart is superior to
intellectual excellence, and the possession of innocence more to be desired than taste. At the same
time I cannot help feeling and expressing an ardent
wish, that those amiable qualities may always be
combined, and that the noblest of all sublunary
objects may more frequently be produced, an all-
accomplished man! a character, perfectly polite, yet
neither vain, affected, nor superficial; elegantly and
deeply learned, yet neither sceptical nor pedantic;
that a graceful manner and a pleasing address may
be the result, not of artifice, but of a sincere and a
benevolent heart; and that all the lovely and valuable qualities, whether exterior or internal, may
operate in augmenting the general sum of human
happiness; while they advance the dignity, and increase the satisfactions, of the individual.

It is certain that religion, learning, and virtue,
have sometimes worn a forbidding aspect, and have
appeared, by neglect, unamiable. Elegant and ornamental accomplishments have also sometimes lost
their value, because they have been unaccompanied
with the solid qualities. The union of polite learning with useful and solid attainments, will add a
lustre and a value to both; and it is one of the
principal ends of the following Treatise to promote
their coalition.

SECTION I.

ON ELEMENTARY DISCIPLINE.

Istiusmodi res dicere ornatè velle, puerile est; planè autem et perspicuè expedire docti et intelligentis viri. To affect ornament on such a topic as this, is puerile; but to dispatch it with plainness and perspicuity, is the part of an intelligent and well-informed man. CICERO.

A DIVERSITY of opinions has prevailed concerning the time at which education should commence. Many suppose that it is usually begun too early. To determine the question with accuracy, discernment must be exercised in discovering the different degrees of expansion which different minds display, even at an infantine age. Upon the principle, that the earliest impressions are the most durable, and with a view to save time for future improvements, a child should be taught all that it can comprehend, as early as possible.

To acquire the art of reading, is certainly difficult to a very young boy; but we daily see the difficulty surmounted at the age of five or six. If it is not acquired about that time, we know that the difficulty increases with increasing years. Many boys, neglected at this age, have written a good hand, and have made some progress in the Latin grammar, before they have been able to read with fluency. Their inability in this respect has dispirited them, by rendering them objects of derision to their juniors; and this has given them an early disrelish of books, and led them to seek employment in dissipation. Early inferiority has had a fatal influence on all subsequent proficiency.

Education should begin even in the nursery; and the mother and nurse are, in the first stage, the best instructors. The task of teaching an infant the alphabet, is too painful for a man of a very cultivated understanding. It is indeed, in the present age, not unusual among the rich, to solicit the care of some ingenious persons in teaching the very letters; and the reason assigned has been, that children acquire from the matrons, who have commonly held this province, a disgustful monotony. This indeed is often true : yet the greater expedition with which a child will probably learn to read, under the females who are always with him, who have been used to manage him, and who can stoop to his infirmities, than under a learned tutor, to whom the labour must be irksome, and therefore often ill-performed, is a sufficient reason for adhering, during a few of the first months of instruction, to the old and established method of our forefathers.

A sensible and good-tempered mother is, in every respect, best qualified to instruct a child, till he can read well enough to enter on the Latin grammar. I have indeed always found those boys the best readers, on their entrance on Latin, who had been prepared by maternal care. Neither let this office be considered as degrading.* Boys, thus instructed, have seldom had vulgar tones,† but have read with unusual ease and elegance. But even they who have been taught to read by the more illiterate, by nurses and by aged matrons, and have acquired disagreeable accents, have soon lost them again, on receiving

---

* The Gracchi were educated, non tam in gremio quàm in sermone matris. *Not so much in the lap, as in the conversation of a mother.*

† Ante omnia, ne sit vitiosus sermo nutricibus ; has primùm audiet puer, harum verba effingere imitando conabitur; non assuescat ergo, ne dum infans est, sermoni qui dediscendus est. *Before all things, let not the nurses have a faulty manner of speaking ; them he will first hear, their words he will endeavour to imitate closely. Let him not therefore be accustomed, not even while he is an infant, to a mode of speaking which must be unlearned.*

QUINTILIAN.

better instruction, and on hearing better examples. And these early proficients in reading have always made a more rapid progress in their grammar, and in all classical learning, than boys who were kept back by fanciful parents, lest they should be injured by too early application, or catch the inelegant enunciation of an illiterate woman.

Let then the child be taught to read, as soon as the infant faculties begin to exhibit symptoms of improveable expansion. His attention, active in the extreme, must fix on a variety of objects. Let his book be one of those objects, though by no means the only one. Let no long confinement, and no severity of reprimand or correction, attend the lesson. A little will be learned at the earliest age, and with the easiest discipline. That little will infallibly lead to farther improvement; and the boy will soon, and with no great pain to himself or others, learn to read; an acquisition, considered in its difficulty and in its consequences, truly great. He, on the other hand, who is retarded, by the theoretical wisdom of his friends, till he is seven or eight years old, has this burdensome task to begin, when habits of idleness have been contracted, and when he ought to be laying the foundation of classical knowledge.

It is much to be lamented, that mothers in the higher ranks of life, who are usually best qualified for the task, seldom have time or inclination to take an active part in the elementary education of their own children. The happiest consequences would flow from their immediate interposition. But it must be confessed, that the employment, though maternal tenderness and a sense of duty may render it tolerable, is by no means pleasurable; unless, indeed, under the particular circumstances of a remarkable docility, and an amiable disposition in the pupil. It may not, however, be irksome to super-intend the child's improvement under the governess or servant of whatever denomination, to whom this charge may be allotted.

To facilitate the acquisition of the art of reading, various contrivances have been invented. The letters have been made toys, and the whole business of learning to read has been converted into a game at play. The idea is pleasing and plausible; but I never yet saw any great success attend the attempt. Loose letters cut in ivory are apt to be inverted, and to puzzle the child by the different appearance they make in different positions. Reading, if it was a game, was still such a game as the child liked less than his other diversions. It was, indeed, a game at which he would never play if he could help it. I am not quite sure, that it is right to give him a notion that he has nothing to do but to play. Let him know, that he has business of a serious kind; and, by at-tending to it periodically, let him contract a habit of application. A temporary attention to something by no means tedious or laborious, but which, at the same time, he is not to consider as play, will make his diversion more agreeable. Indeed vicissitude is necessary to render diversions pleasing. They be-come painful business, when continued without variety. We all come into the world to perform many duties, and to undergo many difficulties; and the earlier the mind learns to bear its portion of them, the less likely will it be to sink under those burdens which will one day be imposed upon it. To lead a child to suppose that he is to do nothing which is not conducive to pleasure, is to give him a degree of levity, and a turn for dissipation, which will certainly prevent his improvement, and may perhaps, at a future period, occasion his ruin.

It is surely not rigid to explode those fanciful modes of instruction which injure, while they indulge, the inexperienced pupil. But it would be rigid not to unite the agreeable with the useful, whenever the union can be effected. Books therefore, written for the use of children, should be rendered pleasing to the eye and the imagination. They should abound in cuts, and be adorned with gilding, and every attractive colour. The matter should be not only intelligible to the weakest mind, but interesting. Fables are universally used, and with great propriety. No one wants to be informed how many, and how various, are the books in our language adapted to the use of children. Even the common spelling-books, though they exhibit no great ingenuity in their compilation, are sufficiently well calculated to teach the art of reading, and have been instrumental in teaching by far the greater part of the nation, from their first appearance. A poetess of our own times, remarkably distinguished by her taste and genius, has condescended to compose little books for the initiation of children in reading, and they seem admirably adapted to effect her laudable purpose.

The greatest objection to the very early instruction which I recommend is, that, when injudiciously directed, it may injure the health of the tender pupil. But it may certainly be so conducted, as neither to injure health,* nor to preclude that lovely cheerfulness which marks and adorns the vernal

* " There is nothing to hinder a child from acquiring every useful branch of knowledge, and every elegant accomplishment suited to his age, without impairing his constitution ; but then the greatest attention must be had to the powers of the body and the mind, that they neither be allowed to languish for want of exercise, nor be exerted beyond what they can bear." DR. GREGORY.

season of life. All corporeal punishment,* and all immoderate restraint, must be prohibited. Praise, caresses, and rewards,† are the best incitements to application, If these will not operate, the point must for a while be given up. A more favourable season will soon arrive, under proper management. These motives, however, will seldom fail, when applied by the parents, or by those who, with the real interest of the child at heart, have also integrity and diligence to promote it. Such qualities are certainly more desirable in the first instructors, than learning and great abilities.

SECTION II.

ON DISCOVERING WHETHER OR NOT THERE EXISTS A NATURAL PROPENSITY TO LEARNING; AND ON FIXING THE DESTINATION, ACCORDING TO APPEARANCES, AT AN EARLY AGE.

Ut sæpe summa ingenia in occulto latent!
How oft the greatest genius lies conceal'd!   PLAUT.

MUCH has been said on the necessity of studying the natural propensity of the pupil, and of directing

---

* 'Ου λυπῶντα δεῖ ΠΑΙΔΑΡΙΟΝ ερθῶν· ἀλλα και πείθοντά.
  Correct your little one by winning arts
  Of soft persuasion ; but forbear to grieve
  His tender heart.   MENANDER.

† Kindness in words and looks effects wonders in children, who are governed more by what they feel and see than by reason. The French, when they speak to a little one, say " mon ami," with the utmost famliarity and appearance of affection ; and they are excellent instructors of early youth, merely from their condescending affability. How terrifying severe looks, rods, and canes, to infants ! If they have sensibility, no culprit ever suffered more than they do, when he sees the wheel, the axe, and the executioner by whom he is to be tortured.

Children should not be punished for mere accidents, little noises occasioned by high spirits, lapses of the memory—forbid it humanity: forbid it, ye mothers ! who have sent your smiling pledges from your breast ; forbid it He who took the infants up in his arms, laid his hands upon them, and blessed them !

him to those peculiar studies to which he appears
particularly adapted by nature. Masters have been
censured for giving their instructions without a due
discrimination, and for training a great number of
boys, of different tempers and destinations, exactly
in the same method. The censure is often misplaced; for it seldom happens that the opinion of
the master has any influence in determining either
the future profession of the boy, or the particular
modes of preparation for it. The parent, for instance,
who has friends in the church or in the state, or
possesses an advowson, sends his child to the grammar-school, where he is to be qualified for the university. Perhaps chance, or the caprice of the child,
or an opinion that he is not likely to make his way
in any other road, determine the father in selecting
him for a learned or a clerical life. The master
receives him into his school. He can seldom have
a competent trial of him, previous to admission. To
refuse him, even if he despaired of his succeeding as
a scholar, would perhaps, in many respects, be imprudent; and very likely, if the school is an endowed
foundation, it would be unjustifiable. In this school
there usually is, and there ought to be, a regular
plan of study. According to this plan, every scholar
must, for the most part, proceed. There cannot
possibly be adopted as many different methods of
instruction, as there are diversities of genius among
the numerous individuals who fill a school. The
parent is commonly apprised of the uniformity of
the plan, and not easily convinced that his son is less
fit than others to submit to it. At least, the previous determination, that he shall be brought up to
some preferment which may be made a sinecure in
the law or the church, makes him careless about
literary attainments, provided the boy is enabled, by
a superficial improvement, to pass from the school

to the university, and to go through those forms,
without which he cannot obtain the lucrative appointment which awaits his acceptance.

Even where interest is not in view, the parent,
without experience or examination, often chooses to
dictate the general plan of study in which his son
shall proceed ; and would be not a little offended,
were a master to refuse to admit, or advise to remove
from his school, the boy who is placed under his
care, however unlikely to profit by it.   Indeed, in
the present state of things, masters are unfortunately
necessitated to consider themselves under an obliga-
tion to the parent, like a tradesman to his customer,
and consequently to suppress or submit their own
judgment, when it does not coincide with the decisions of paternal authority.

But supposing that masters were appealed to, and
their judgment followed, in determining whether or
not a boy is fit for a learned life, and in pointing out
the means which are the likeliest to lead to success
in it : and also that, after a long trial, they were disinterested enough to acquaint a parent with a
son's inability ; yet there would be many mistakes
committed in this important decision.   For though
masters, from their general experience, and from
their particular knowledge of the boy placed under
their inspection, are indisputably the most competent
judges ; yet, from the nature of things, they must
often be mistaken.   The appearances, from which
they must judge, are deceitful.   A boy, during three
or four years continuance at school, will appear
stupid, and will make little proficiency.   Keep him
there another year, and perhaps his parts break
forth on a sudden ; his emulation is strongly excited ;
he feels a pleasure in his progress, and soon outstrips
those who went before him.   This revolution in the
young mind often takes place.   On the other hand,

he who is cried up as a prodigy of infant genius, sometimes becomes dull, contracts an aversion to learning, and at last arrives at no solid and lasting attainment. The mental faculties, in different constitutions, display themselves earlier or later, according to some internal organization, as difficult to be observed as explained by human sagacity. The parent, therefore, must follow the dictates of common sense and prudence in the disposal of his child, and leave the result to Providence.* Supposing him divested of all parental partiality, he cannot form such a judgment of a child, at that early period at which his future profession is often fixed, as can fully be relied on; but he may see clearly the fairest prospect of temporal advantage, and he may pursue the usual methods of qualifying his son with a degree of constancy, vigilance, and industry, which may, in some measure, supply the defects of nature, if any really exist. This will be the wisest conduct, notwithstanding what has and will be said, by those whose wisdom originates in theory uncontrolled by practice, on the necessity, and the possibility of discovering in childhood the predominant defects or excellencies which point out the intention of nature.†

All human creatures, not in a state of real idiotism, are capable of making some advances in knowledge; and it is desirable to proceed even a little way.

---

* Ἑλοῦ βίον ἄριστον, ἡδὺν δὲ αὐτὸν ἡ συνήθεια ποιήσει.
Choose the best life, and custom will render it agreeable.

PLUTARCH.

† The marks of a proper disposition for a scholar are these, according to Socrates, in Plato de Rep. He must be, εὐφυής, μνήμων, φιλομαθής, φιλόπονος, φιλήκοος, ζητητικ⊙, φιλεπαιν⊙. "Of a kindly nature, of a good memory, fond of learning, fond of labour, fond of hearing, inquisitive, and a lover of praise."

This passage is taken from Ascham, who has not quoted it faithfully from Plato, though he has made no material alteration.

Idiotism however, and all very near approaches to it, are visible to a common observer ; and he may be suspected to be in that state himself, who should select a son under this misfortune for a studious life. But there is no good reason, why all who possess a common share of common understanding, should not have a fair probation.* At any rate, it is probable they will make some improvement. It is possible they may make a great one. For no one can foresee, to what extent that share of understanding may be dilated, by the co-operation of a secret and internal vigour with favourable circumstances.

I wish to guard parents against a common mistake. They are apt to think early vivacity and great loquacity marks of genius, and consequently to dispense with application. I would despair of none but ideots ; but I would sooner despair of a remarkably vivacious child, than of one whose reserve and silence exhibit to careless observers the appearance of dulness,† but are in fact the result of thought and reflection.

---

* Besides, there is a mediocrity of excellence, which is very desirable ; Οὐδὲ γὰρ Μίλων ἔσομαι, καὶ ὅμως οὐκ ἀμελῶ τοῦ σώματος· οὐδὲ Κροῖσος, καὶ ὅμως οὐκ ἀμελῶ τῆς κτήσεως· οὐδ' ἀπλῶς ἄλλου τινὸς τῆς ἐπιμελείας, διὰ τὴν ἀπόγνωσιν τῶι ἄκρων, ἀφισάμεθα. *I shall never be Milo, and yet I do not neglect my body ; nor Crœsus, and yet I do not neglect my property : nor do we decline any other care, through a despair of arriving at the summit of excellence.*   ARRIAN. Ep.

Exigo itaque a me, non ut optimis par sim, sed ut malis melior. *I require of myself, not that I should equal the best, but be better than the bad.*   SENECA.

† Illud ingeniorum velut precox genus non pervenit ad frugem . . . . Placent hæc annis comparata, deinde stat profectus, admiratio decrescit. *That early ripe kind of understanding does not come to much . . . These things please us when we compare them with the boy's age ; then improvement stands still, and admiration gradually decreases.*   QUINTILIAN.

" Nothing is more difficult than to distinguish in childhood real dulness and want of capacity, from that seeming and deceitful dulness, which is the sign of a profound genius."   ROUSSEAU.

SECTION III.

ON THE QUESTION, WHETHER A PUBLIC OR A PRIVATE EDUCATION IS TO BE PREFERRED?

Non enim vox illa præceptoris, ut cæna, minus pluribus sufficit; sed ut sol, universis idem lucis calorisque largitur. *For the master's instructions do not become, like a dinner, insufficient for more than a certain and limited number ; but, like the sun, dispense a like degree of heat and light to* ALL.

QUINTILLIAN.

FROM the time of Quintilian to the present day it has remained a question, whether public or private education is the more conducive to valuable improvement. Quintilian approved of public education, and has supported his opinion, as indeed he usually does, with reasons which carry with them irresistible conviction. From the arguments which he has used, and from the dictates of much observation, I am led to prefer public to private education,* unless under the particular circumstances which I shall presently enumerate.

Though, upon the whole, I prefer the education of schools, yet I know that much licentiousness has often been found in them. The prevailing manners of the age, and of the world at large, are apt to insinuate themselves into those seminaries of learning, which, by their seclusion from the world, might be supposed exempted from its corruption. The scholars often bring the infection from home; and certainly increase it by contagion. From whatever cause it proceeds, it is certain that schools often degenerate with the community, and contribute

---

* By private, I mean only domestic and solitary education ; I do not mean the education of those schools, which, though they are called private, have all the advantages of public schools ; such as a number of boys, emulation, &c.

greatly to promote, by diffusing at the most susceptible periods of life, a general depravity.　The
old discipline is relaxed in schools, as in families,
habits of idleness and intemperance are contracted,
and the scholar often comes from them with the
acquisition of effrontery alone to compensate his
ignorance.　When I recommend public schools,
therefore, I must be understood to mean places of
education where the intention of the pious founder is
not quite forgotten, and where the practicable part
of the original discipline is still retained.　Such, I
trust, may be found, and such will increase in number,
when the general dissipation, which, it is confessed,
has remarkably prevailed of late, shall be corrected
by public distress, or by some other dispensation of
divine providence.

　　The danger which the morals are said to incur in
schools, is a weighty objection to them.　I most cordially agree with Quintilian, and with other writers
on this subject, that it is an ill exchange to give up
innocence for learning.　But perhaps it is not true,
that, in a well-disciplined school, (and it is only such
an one which I recommend,) there is more danger of
a corruption of morals than at home.　I am not unacquainted with the early propensity of the human
heart to vice, and I am well aware that boys contribute greatly to each other's corruption.　But I
know, that the pupil who is kept at home cannot be,
at all hours, under the immediate eye of his parent
or his instructor.　It must happen, by chance, necessity, or neglect, that he will often associate with
menial servants, from whose example he will not
only catch meanness of spirit, but vice and vulgarity.
Yet, supposing him to be restrained from such communication, the examples he will see in the world,
and the temptations he will meet with in an inter-

course with various company at an early age, will affect his heart, and cause it to beat with impatience for emancipation from that restraint which must be removed at the approach of manhood. Then will his passions break forth with additional violence, as the waters of a stream which have been long confined. In the course of my own experience, I have known young men nearly ruined at the university, who attributed their wrong conduct to the immoderate restraint of a domestic education. The sweets of liberty never before tasted, and the allurements of vice never before withstood, become too powerful for resistance at an age when the passions are strong, reason immature, and experience entirely deficient.

After all the confinement and trouble of a domestic education, it is probable that the boy will at last be sent to the university. There he will find the greater part of his associates, consisting of young men who have been educated at schools; and if they have any vices, he will now be in much greater danger of moral infection, and will suffer worse consequences from it, than if he had not been secluded from boys at a boyish age. He will appear awkward, and unacquainted with their manners. He will be neglected, if not despised. His spirit, if he possesses any, will not submit to contempt; and perhaps he will imitate, and at length surpass their irregularities, in order to gain a welcome reception. From actual observation I am convinced, that this voluntary degeneracy often takes place under these, or under similar circumstances. That happy conduct which can preserve dignity and esteem at the university, without any blamable compliances, must arise from a degree of early wisdom and experience, as well as of moral rectitude, rarely possessed by him who has been educated in a closet. It is not enough, that the mind has been furnished with prudent maxims, nor that the purest principles have been instilled into the heart, unless the understanding has itself collected some practical rules, which can only be gained by actual intercourse with others of the same age, and unless that degree of fortitude is acquired, which perhaps can only arise from frequent conflicts terminating in victory.

With respect to literary improvement, I think that a boy of parts will be a better scholar, if educated at a school than at home. In a school many circumstances co-operate to force his own personal exertion, on which depends the increase of mental strength, and consequently of improvement, more than on the instruction of any preceptor.

Many of the arguments in support of this opinion must be common, for their truth is obvious. Emulation cannot be excited without rivals ; and without emulation, instruction will often be a tedious, and a fruitless, labour. It is this which warms the passions on the side of all that is excellent, and often counterbalances the weight of temptations to vice and idleness. The boy of an ingenious mind, who stands at the head of his class, ranks, in the microcosm of a school, as a hero, and his feelings are scarcely less elevated. He will spare no pains to maintain his honourable post ; and his competitors, if they have spirit, will be no less assiduous to supplant him by generous exertions. No severity, no painful confinement, no harsh menaces, will be necessary. Emulation* will effect, in the best manner, the most

---

* Some moral refiners disapprove of emulation as a spur, because it leads to envy and other unchristian passions ; but there is a generous emulation free from envy. Fanciful philosophers would deprive us of all motives ; for there is none to which captious ingenuity cannot object.

valuable purposes; and at the same time cause, in
the bosom of the scholar, a pleasure truly enviable.
View him in his seat, turning his lexicon with the
greatest alacrity; and then survey the pupil in the
closet, who, with languid eye, is poring, in solitude,
over a lesson which he naturally considers as the
bane of his enjoyment; and concerning which he
feels no other wish, than how to dispatch it as soon
as he can with impunity. It is true, a private tutor
may do good by praise; but what is solitary praise
to the glory of standing in a distinguished post of
honour, the envy and admiration of a whole school?

The school-boy has the best chance of acquiring
that confidence and spirit which are necessary to display valuable attainments. Excessive diffidence,
bashfulness, and indolence, retard the acquisition of
knowledge, and destroy its due effect when acquired.
They are the cause of pain to their possessors, and
commonly do injustice to their real abilities, and
hurt their interests. It is one circumstance in public
schools, which tends to give the scholars a due degree of confidence, that public examination or election days are usually established in them; when,
besides the examination, which, if undergone with
credit, inspires courage, orations are spoken before
numerous auditors. This greatly contributes to remove that timidity, which has silenced many able
persons brought up to the bar and the pulpit. The
necessity of making a good appearance on public
days, causes a great degree of attention to be paid
to the art of speaking; an art, which, from the
defect of early culture, has been totally wanting in
some of our best divines; many of whom never gave
satisfaction to a common audience, in preaching
those compositions, which, when published, have
been admired in the closet.

The formation of connexions* which may contribute to future advancement, and of friendships which cannot easily be dissolved, has always been a powerful argument in support of the preference of public schools. Such connexions and such friendships have been, and may be formed. The opportunity which public schools afford, is certainly an additional circumstance in recommendation of them. But I cannot omit expressing my disapprobation of the practice which has sometimes prevailed, of sending a son to school merely to form connexions and without any serious solicitude for real improvement. One reason is, that a son, in such cases, has been usually instructed, at home, to pay a servile deference to those of his school-fellows who are likely to be distinguished by future rank or fortune. By this submission, he has acquired a meanness of mind, a sordid attention to interest, highly disgraceful to a man of liberal education. He has entered into a voluntary slavery, the self-abasement and inconveniences of which no emolument can compensate; and after all he has not unfrequently been frustrated in his expectation even of profit; for it so happens, that the servility which accommodates the great man, often renders the voluntary dependant contemptible in his sight. After many years servitude, the greedy expectant is often dismissed, as he deserves, unrewarded. But let him gain what he may, it will, in my opinion, be dearly purchased at the price of the conscious dignity of a manly independence.† On the other hand, those disinterested

---

* Μέγα πρὸς φιλίαν και τὸ σύντροφον. " To be educated together contributes much to friendship." ARISTOT.

† Prandet Aristoteles quando Phillippo lubet; Diogenes, quando Diogeni. *Aristotle goes to dinner when Philip pleases; Diogenes when Diogenes.*

friendships which are formed at public schools, from a real congeniality of sentiments and taste, will certainly contribute much to comfort, and perhaps to advancement. Experience proves, that they are more durable than the intimacies contracted at any subsequent period, when the heart is less susceptible and the attention distracted by a multiplicity of objects.

A great degree of bodily exercise is necessary for boys. Nature has taken care to provide for this necessity, by giving them a propensity to play. But they never enter into the puerile diversions with proper spirit, but with boys. He then who is placed at a school, has the best opportunity of answering the intentions of nature, in taking that constant exercise and lively amusement which at once contributes to strength of body and vivacity of mind.

I may add to the many arguments in favour of school-education, the pleasure and enjoyment of the pupil. Placed in a little society of members like himself, he finds ample scope for the exertion of his various powers and propensities. He has friends and playfellows constantly at hand; and the busy scene passing before him, is a never-failing source of amusement. Why should the happiness of any period of life, even the earliest, be neglected? The boy may never reach manhood or old age. Let him be happy then while a boy.

The private pupil languishes in solitude, deprived of many of these advantages, or enjoying them imperfectly. He feels but little emulation; he contracts diffidence; he makes few friendships, for want of opportunity; he is secluded from the most healthy exercises; and his early youth, the pleasant spring of life, is spent in a painful confinement.

But yet there are a few circumstances which will

render private education the most proper. These are, uncommon meekness of disposition, natural weakness of understanding, bodily infirmity, any remarkable defect of the senses, and any singular deformity. Boys in these circumstances should be treated like those tender plants, which, unable to bear the weather, are placed under glasses, and in the shelter of the green-house. The oak will flourish best in an open exposure.

SECTION IV.

ON GRAMMARS, AND INTRODUCTORY BOOKS TO THE LATIN.

Plus habet operis quam ostentationis. *This business has more of labour in it than of show.* QUINTILIAN.

Of no books has there appeared a greater variety than of grammars. Almost every master of eminence seems, at one time, to have thought that he could improve or facilitate the elementary introduction to the Latin language. Many of their productions were really ingenious; but the multiplicity of them tended to retard, rather than to promote, a general improvement.

An uniformity of grammars in all grammar-schools is of great importance to public education; and so it appeared to King Henry the Eighth, and to succeeding monarchs, who strictly enjoined the universal use of that excellent compilation which passes under the name of Lily, though he was not the only composer of it. Of such material consequence was this uniformity esteemed, and such were the pains taken to preserve it, that bishops were obliged to inquire at their visitations, in the reign of Elizabeth, and since, whether there were any other grammar taught in any school within their respective dioceses, than

that which was set forth by king Henry the Eighth,
and has since continued in use? Other grammars
have, indeed, occasionally been used during the lives
of their authors, and in the schools for which they
were intended; but none of them have remained
long, or become general. I may confidently recommend a continuance of this grammar, because
the experience of more than two centuries has
evinced its utility, and because I am sure there is
none better accommodated to schools. Time has
decided on it; and it is often no less injurious than
presumptuous to controvert his decisions.

In the old editions of Lily's grammar, there were
a few mistakes; such as tend to prove the remark,
that nothing is begun and brought to perfection at
the same time; yet such as do not mislead the learner
in any truly important article. But every thing
should certainly be rendered as perfect as human
abilities can render it; and therefore the ingenious
Dr. Ward very properly published a new edition of
Lily, with notes and corrections. Although boys
do not often attend to notes in the grammar, and
usually the text is sufficient, yet it is right that where
there are errors or omissions, there should be notes
to correct and supply them. They may do good,
they can do no harm: and therefore it is proper to
advise the general reception of Ward's edition of this
ancient grammar.*

The Eton Introduction† is an useful abbreviation

---

* There are, however, it must be confessed, some superfluities in
this grammar.

Minutiæ ought not to be attended to in first going over the grammar. Many masters compel their boys to study the little niceties
of grammar so long and so closely, that one would think they were
teaching the science of grammar only, and not a language, to the
attainment of which the grammar is but an instrument.

† I call this Lily's Grammar, for it is only an epitome of it, with a

of Lily, and perhaps very justly preferred, upon the whole, to the more prolix original. Nothing militates against the universal reception of it, but a wish to preserve the uniformity of grammars ; and Lily's has hitherto prevailed with good success. For the same reason, I would not adopt in England Ruddiman's Rudiments, nor any of those introductions, which are used in some seminaries. I do not in any respect censure them ; I know them to be highly meritorious ; I only think them unnecessary, and avoid them for the sake of preserving uniformity.*

Nor is this regard to uniformity founded on caprice, but on many solid reasons. Among others, it may be remarked, that boys are frequently removed from one school to another. If they change their grammars, the injury they receive by removal is great. They must inevitably lose time. Happy if that is the worst consequence ! A perplexity of mind often ensues, fatal to their farther advancement. That master has had but little experience, to whom the ill effects of a change in grammars are unknown, when boys are removed from one school to another.

But whatever grammar may be used, I would not have the attention of the young scholar confined during a very long time, to the grammar only. I mean, that as soon as possible he should be introduced to the parsing and construing of some easy Latin author, in order to exemplify, by actual reading, the many rules he every day commits to memory. This not only enables him to understand

---

few alterations. See, in Chalmers's Life of Ruddiman, a curious dispute concerning an uniformity of grammars, in the High School at Edinburgh.

* In parsing, and taking places in the classes, all the boys of the same class must quote the same rules, or confusion and loss of time must be the inevitable consequence.

them more clearly, and to remember them better, but renders the study of grammar, which to a young mind is of necessity dry, less unentertaining. I have known boys quite wearied and disgusted with learning the grammar, for a whole year, without any variety, and without opportunity of learning its use and application. Neither were they so well grounded as others who had opportunities of applying the rules, by reading lessons in some easy and diverting author.

Yet the grammar is by no means to be neglected or deferred. If a grammatical foundation be not laid deep at an early age, it will not often be laid in such a manner as to bear a large superstructure. Let me then be clearly understood. The grammar should be daily studied ; but in order that it may be studied with more success and more pleasure, I wish the easiest and most entertaining Latin author, that can possibly be found, to be read with it. This reading should commence as soon as the nouns, pronouns, and verbs are perfectly learned. It is certain that a boy will improve much faster by these means, than by labouring invariably in the same course, till he shall have passed through the grammar in all its parts ; a method, however, not uncommon.

I know it is a frequent objection to the received grammars, that the rules are in Latin. It has been called absurd to begin, as it were, with the end, and to learn Latin by those rules which presuppose a knowledge of Latin already acquired. The objection appears plausible to those who are not practically acquainted with the subject. But it must be remembered, that there is subjoined to the end of the Latin grammar a literal translation, and that, by learning the rules in Latin, the meaning of many words is discovered to the scholar, which would be unknown to him if he learned them in English only; that he is initiated by these in the art of construing; and, to sum up the whole in a few words, that more good scholars have been formed in this method than by others, which, indeed, have generally been invented and practised by the vain or the visionary. The long duration, the universality, the success, and the reasonableness, of the practice of learning Latin rules, will probably continue it, notwithstanding the attacks of those who derive their ideas chiefly from speculation.

Parents, indeed, who have not had a classical education themselves, and who are unacquainted with the true means of obtaining its advantages, and perhaps with the nature of them, are apt to be impatient in the expectation of their appearance.* When a boy begins to learn Latin, they immediately expect him to show some evident superiority over others in all the puerile studies. Perhaps he appears inferior to them. His attention to his grammar may cause a temporary neglect of less important, but more shining attainments. What he is learning has nothing of show in it. It makes no appearance in the eyes of the superficial. It is, as Quintilian observes, like the foundation of a building,† which, though the most important part, lies

---

* There are not wanting those who are ready to take advantage of credulity in this, as well as in other very important matters. They generally produce wonderful stories of premature improvement. But "those who tell or receive those stories," says the solid Johnson, "should consider, that nobody can be taught faster than he can learn. The speed of the best horseman must be limited by the power of his horse. Every man who has undertaken to instruct others, can tell what slow advances he has been able to make, and how much patience it requires to recal vagrant inattention, to stimulate sluggish indifference, and to rectify absurd misapprehension."

† Fastigia spectantur, latent fundamenta.—Non sunt contemnenda

concealed under the earth. Parents must not expect the crop in the season of planting. They must form an analogical argument, from considering the nature of vegetables. Those are seldom the most valuable, durable, or beautiful, which emerge from the ground, or expand their blossom, at a very early season, or soon after their plantation. But others, which are scarcely seen at the first approach of spring, are often, during their apparent inaction, spreading their roots deeply and widely, in order to display, at a maturer period, a profuse luxuriance.

At great grammar-schools, little attention can be paid to this impatience of the injudicious parent. A regular plan is usually there established; such an one as, from the earliest times, has been attended with success. The great and leading principle of that plan is, to lay a firm and durable foundation in grammar. I hope no parental indulgence, and no relaxation of discipline, will avail to bring into neglect this less splendid, but indispensably necessary, attainment. When the grammar is learned inaccurately, all other juvenile studies in polite literature, if prosecuted at all, will be prosecuted inaccurately; and the result must be, imperfect and superficial improvement. The exercise of mind, and the strength of mind acquired in consequence of that exercise, are some of the most valuable effects of a strict, a long, and a laborious study of grammar learning, at the puerile age.* At that age, grammatical studies

---

quasi parva, sine quibus magna constare non possunt.—Nec si quid discere satis non est, ideo necesse non est.

The roofs of buildings are seen by every body, while the foundations escape notice.—Things are not to be despised as little, without which great ones cannot be produced.—Nor are we to reject any thing as unnecessary, because it is not of itself sufficient, and is only conducive to some other purpose. QUINT.

* A study absolutely necessary, but absolutely disgustful to a riper

must be difficult; but the difficulty is every day conquered, and the conquest has given additional strength and confidence, and facilitated the acquisition of farther victories.

SECTION V.

ON SCHOOL-BOOKS, DICTIONARIES, &c.

Pueris quæ maximè ingenium alant, atque animum augeant, prælegenda.
With boys, those things which tend most to nourish the genius, and to enlarge the mind, are proper to be read.   QUINTILIAN.

IN the more celebrated schools, the proper books are already chosen; because the masters of them are, and have been, men of judgment and learning. But as I wish to comprehend every thing that appears useful in real practice, I trust it will not be presumptuous to make a few remarks on school-books, and the editions of them which are best calculated to accelerate the improvement of classical scholars.

The choice of a dictionary is not quite unimportant. I need not say that Ainsworth's, and the Abridgement, or Young's, are the only dictionaries to be used in the higher classes; but it is certain that one of their excellencies, their copiousness, is an objection to them in the lower. When a boy, just out of his accidence, begins to read the Latin Testament, he is under the necessity of looking out almost all the words in his dictionary. He searches for them in Ainsworth's; a book which, even abridged, is, from its bulk, very inconvenient to a very little boy; and there, after much labour and loss of time, he finds the Latin word be sought.

age; therefore more proper for childhood, which cannot be better employed.   Father GERDIL.

Under it he finds twenty meanings, besides phrases and authorities. He reads them all as well as he can, and when he has done, he is as much at a loss as at first. To avoid this very great obstacle to improvement, I recommend, for the first two or three years, the use of a little portable dictionary, compiled by Entick. Since it has been improved and augmented, the English-Latin part is become, from its convenient size and conciseness, the best calculated for very young scholars of any extant, I must repeat, lest I should be misunderstood, that this should only be adopted during the two or three first years, and that Ainsworth's is the proper dictionary to be used by the senior scholars. The Abridgement of Ainsworth is undoubtedly better adapted to schools than the original work. If any prefer Young's, or Cole's, there is no objection to the use of them; though, perhaps, no good reason can be given for the preference.

Schrevelius's Lexicon is, with great propriety, every where used. It is particularly adapted to the Greek Testament, and to Homer; and is well suited both to the beginner, and to the proficient in Greek. Hederic's ought, however, to be always provided in the school, for the common use of all the Greek scholars; for sometimes a word will occur in reading, not included in Schrevelius. Scapula's Lexicon is justly disused in schools, since his method is perplexing to a learner, though his book is excellent. Stephans's Thesaurus is too voluminous for this purpose, and must be reserved for the library.

I would banish all Nomenclators, Parsing Indexes, Synopses, the Clavis Homerica, and the Clavis Virgiliana. The dictionary, the grammar, and the living instructor, constantly near, are the only allowable auxiliaries. The other contrivances generally serve either to confuse the young student, or to increase, by encouraging, his idleness. The revivers of learning, who had none of these assistances, have never been excelled in the knowledge of the ancient languages. They dug their treasure out of the mine, and learned to value and preserve it by the labour of acquisition.

I have already mentioned the grammar most commonly approved. I have preferred Clarke's Introduction for beginners, because the Latin is furnished on one side of the English. Perhaps that circumstance is an objection to its use among the higher classes. Let then the Eton Exempla Moralia, or Wyllimot's Particles, be substituted in its place.

With respect to choosing the Latin and Greek books proper to be read in schools, and adapting them to the age and class of the scholars, no judicious and experienced master will want directions. But I will beg leave humbly to offer, and not to obtrude, my sentiments on this subject, as it is a subject of importance.

Suppose then the school to be divided, as it often is, into eight classes. In the first or lowest class, the accidence or grammar only will be used ; in the second, let Cordery's Colloquies and the Latin Testament be introduced ; in the third, let the books consist of Cornelius Nepos, Phædrus, and the latter part of Cordery ; in the fourth, of Ovid de Tristibus, Erasmus's Dialogues, and Phædrus continued ; in the fifth, of Ovid's Fasti and Metamorphoses, Virgil, and Cæsar ; in the sixth, let Greek be commenced, and let the books consist of the Greek Testament, Virgil, and Cicero's Letters ; in the seventh, of the Greek Testament, Lucian, Virgil, Cicero de Officiis ; in the eighth, of Homer, Demosthenes, Xenophon, Anabasis, Virgil, Horace, Juvenal, Cicero's Orations, and his golden treatises De Amicitia and De Senectute. The books may certainly be varied with propriety, according to the judgment and taste of the teacher; and I only enumerate these, because I think it right, as I have elsewhere said, to descend to particulars in a practical treatise.*

General removals should take place throughout the school twice a-year. The best scholars should be promoted to the next class, and the others remain where they were, another half year. The books should be read in regular rotation, and with the most scrupulous regard to method and regularity.

The editions of school-books in Usum Delphini, are almost universally received. I confess I do not entirely approve them. I know that the interpretation is always more attended to than the text. The eye and mind of the young student are confused with a page crowded with that, and with annotations. The master should, indeed, have a comment before him, to assist and facilitate his business of

---

* The reading books at schools in too small portions, and at long intervals, is the cause why they are so little understood and relished. "Uno tempore legendi sunt libri, quorum argumentum cohæret et continens est.——Non est mirum si omnis fere lectio in scholis frustra sit, quia nimis parva pensa sunt. Leguntur simul Cicero, Cornelius, Cæsar, Virgilius, Horatius, Ovidius. Per totam hebdomadem impenditur una hora, et absolvitur una particula; et illa particula est tam parva, ut planè non possint videre quomodo cohæreat."

Books, whose subject is continued, should be read without interruption. It is not to be wondered, if what boys read at school is of little use to them, since their tasks are short. Cicero, Nepos, Cæsar, Virgil, Horace, Ovid, are all read at once. . . Through the whole week one hour is bestowed on each, and a little portion of each is gone through, and that little portion is so very inconsiderable, that boys cannot see how it is connected with the context. GESNER.

The master may, however, obviate this inconvenience by recapitulating, at every lesson, what preceded it, and thus preserve the links of the chain unbroken.

explanation; but I wish the scholars to have editions
without notes, or with very few. The type and
paper cannot be too beautiful. These allure and
please the eye. With such editions, let the boy discover the meaning of his lesson, *proprio Marte*, by
his own efforts, and the use of dictionaries. It *will*
be difficult at first. The master will have additional
trouble. But the scholar will derive great strength
of mind from being obliged to exert himself, and
will infallibly improve much faster, and retain his
improvements longer, than if he were assisted with
those inventions, which, though they were designed
to introduce the student to his books with greater
ease and success, are always abused to the gratification of indolence.

I will not close this section without declaring,
that, in pointing out books, or editions of books,
I mean only to give advice, and not to dictate. I
write what I think, and I offer directions on this
topic, unnecessary indeed to the profoundly learned,
but such as may possibly suggest some useful hints
to the inexperienced instructor.

SECTION VI.

ON WRITING EXERCISES.

Stylus optimus magister.
The pen is the best master.   CIC.

To ensure improvement, it is not enough to
be passively attentive to instruction. Opportunities must be given to the student to display his
attainments. He must learn to reduce theory to
practice. He must exemplify his rules. He must be
exercised in thinking. He must be accustomed to

solitary study, and a habit must be formed of literary labour.*

For all these reasons, it has been the custom of our best schools to exact from the scholars a written exercise, to be brought every morning on entrance into the school. Under proper regulations, and duly attended to both by the instructor and the pupil, this practice has been productive of effects greatly beneficial. I therefore recommend it to be universally pursued, as soon as the pupil shall be capable of writing easily and legibly.

. From the age of eight to ten, no exercises can be done with more propriety than those of Clarke's Introduction. I think it would be superfluous to go through the whole of that book, and that the most successful method is to make use of a page or two only of each chapter, in order to exemplify the rules of Syntax; and to repeat them three, four, or five times, according to the boy's capacity and improvements. This method, I am convinced by experience, will give the scholar a clearer idea of his business, than a regular and laborious application to the whole book, in the order in which it is left by the author. Care should be taken that the rules prefixed to the chapters be carefully read, and fully explained before the chapter is begun. Half the usual labour, and half the usual time, will produce more than double the improvement, if such methods are practised from the first as tend to give the scholar clear ideas, even though they are few.

. After the age of ten, provided the boy's improvements are adequate to his age, I advise that he shall begin to compose nonsense Latin verses. I wish to begin this exercise early, because it will insensibly,

---

* φύσις, μάθησις, ΑΣΚΗΣΙΣ. To complete the work, there must be united nature, instruction, and exercise.

and in a very short time, acquaint him with the
quantities of Latin words, without a knowledge of
which he will not be able even to read Latin with
propriety.   It is not, however, necessary that this
should be done every night, but alternately with
exercises adapted to the age and acquirements.
Clarke's introduction, or some other exercise book,
must still furnish the exercise once or twice a week.
Indeed, it is not to be entirely relinquished till a very
considerable progress is made in Latin composition.

At the age of thirteen, supposing, as I did before,
that the abilities and improvements of the pupil are
adequate to the age, I would gradually introduce
him to compose in English.   If it should be asked,
why not before ?   I answer, That if the boy have
parts, he may begin at ten ; but, generally speaking,
it will be found that boys have not collected ideas,
or language enough, to compose any thing before
twelve or thirteen.   His first effort should be, to
write from memory some of Æsop's fables in his own
words, grammatically correct.   When he can do
this tolerably well, let him compose for his exercise,
once or twice in the week, a letter on a familiar subject, to a parent, a brother, a sister, or an acquaintance.

At fourteen, and long before, if he possess parts,
let him enter on English themes.   But in order to
facilitate this business, to gain *copia verborum*, and a
collection of ideas, he must be directed to read every
day, as his private study, the Roman History, Plutarch's Lives, and the Spectator.   Other books may
be adopted in proper succession.   But I would begin with these, because I have found them peculiarly
useful.   Plagiarism must be discouraged.   And in
order to discourage it, I think it best not to be too
severely strict in remarking and punishing the many
and egregious mistakes which will appear in the first

attempts. When a boy finds that no fault is forgiven, he will be tempted to steal from authors, to avoid correction, And when this practice is become habitual, it will defeat all our intentions of promoting his improvement in English composition. For the mind, naturally indolent, will not bestow the labour of invention, when it finds it can escape with impunity without such labour, and that it incurs punishment by offering to the eye of the master its own imperfect, though laborious, productions.

From fourteen to eighteen or nineteen, (and I would by no means advise, that the student, who is to make a solid improvement in learning, should leave his school till he is about that age,) I recommend that the scholar's week shall be thus employed; Monday evening, in Latin theme; Tuesday evening, in Latin verse; Wednesday evening, in English or Latin letters; Thursday evening, in English verse; Friday evening, in Latin verse, or in translating English into Latin; and the interval from Saturday to Monday, in a Latin or an English theme. The days and the exercises may indeed be changed at the discretion of the judicious master; and I only prescribe this plan for the sake of precision. I repeat, that in a practical treatise, such as this professes to be, it is proper to descend to particulars, which I do without the least intention to dictate.

It must be remembered, as we proceed, that the books selected both for private reading and scholastic study, in the course of this progress, must be such as have an immediate relation to the exercises to be performed. The best models of composition must be placed before the eyes of the student at all times, but more particularly while he is engaged in the work of imitation. And to imitate well a Virgil, a Cicero, a Pope, and an Addison, indicates a

mind which has imbibed a portion of their mental
excellence.* No method is so likely to cause this
most desirable participation of their spirit, as repeated and continued efforts to exhibit, in juvenile
exercises, some resemblance of their sentiments and
their style.

This assiduous and unremitted attention to exercises, will, I apprehend, be considered by the superficial as too great a task, and as too severe an exaction. To such I can only say, that if they will
not suffer their sons or scholars to submit to it, they
must not expect any great and lasting effects from
that which is commonly called a good education.
How few, indeed, do we see bring a knowledge of
the ancient languages from their schools, sufficiently
extensive or profound to be useful in any great degree, or even to be retained by them throughout
their lives! What is the cause? Undoubtedly, an
indolence in themselves, and a too great indulgence
in their superintendants or parents, who will not let

---

* Many modern writers have renounced imitation as beneath their
genius. But there is one excellence, as there is one truth and one
sun. They who have discovered this excellence, and exhibited it in
their writings, must be imitated by those who wish to partake of it.
To deviate from the standard, when it is once acknowledged, is to deviate into absurdity. " What has been the consequence," says an
ingenious author, " of leaving the beaten path of the ancients? Have
we not plunged ourselves into affectation, antitheses, playing with
words, into bombast, into all the defects which other ages have always
experienced when caprice has been substituted for imitation? . . . In
vain has the graceful, the smiling Fontenelle strewed his elogies with
the flowers of rhetoric. They cannot cover his quaintnesses. He sur-
prises us at the first reading, but fatigues at the second. He seems
more attentive to display himself, than explain the subject ; whereas
the great talent in writing is, that the work should so much engross
our ideas, as to make us forget the author . . . It is however true, that
a finical style may have its admirers in a crowd of busy people, who
read merely to amuse themselves.'' Father GERDIL.

them submit to any degree of application which is at first painful. But I will venture to repeat a truth, which has been collected and confirmed by revolving ages : and it is, that such is the appointed condition of human affairs, that no object, really and durably valuable, can be gained without labour and difficulty. This is the price at which Providence has decreed, that the satisfaction and advantages arising from the possession of any extraordinary degree of excellence shall be purchased.

But, indeed, the labour of composition is not always painful. I have known boys of parts take great delight in composing themes and verses. The natural pleasure of invention, and the consciousness of increasing strength of mind, alleviated all the labour of the work ; and the praises and encouragement they received, gave their ingenuous minds a glow of delight, which none of their usual diversions could confer. When once a boy feels an emulation to excel in his compositions, his improvement is secure.

SECTION VII.

ON WRITING LATIN VERSES.

Det primos versibus annos.
Let him devote his first years to verses. ARBITER.

SOME writers on the subject of education have expressed themselves against the general practice of composing Latin verse at schools, with a degree of acrimony, which has led their readers to conclude, that they themselves were ignorant of the art, and without a taste for its beauties. I should imagine, too, that some of them never had a truly classical education at a public school, or were members of either English university ; for both our schools and universities are often the objects of their pointed,

but oblique satire, where they do not deserve it,
and particularly for requiring from students exercises in Latin verse.

However they may have gratified their spleen, or
promoted their interest, by censuring in general the
methods of public schools, they have acted, in this
instance, without candour, and in opposition to experience. Mr. Burgh is one of the writers who have
attacked, with great freedom, the plan of public
schools. I respect his memory greatly, as that of a
man of sense and virtue, and of one who promoted
the cause of virtue, by his " Dignity of Human
Nature." But I think, that in his censure of the
practice of composing Latin verse and Latin prose
at schools, he appears to be under the influence of
prejudice. He has, indeed, declaimed against it
with plausibility, and in a manner likely to please
and convince a certain class of readers. It is easy
to produce many arguments against what he has
advanced; but I would only refer those who are his
converts, to the decisions of long experience. Let
them read Wood's Athenæ, and the Biographia Bri-
tannica. They will there find, that the ornaments
of our nation, of letters, and of mankind, were instructed according to the usual methods; that is,
were early tinctured with the classics, accustomed
to compose in Latin verse and prose, and sent from
their school to the universities. They will be led to
conclude, from these and from many living instances,
that the classical mode of instruction received in
public schools, is the best foundation for future improvement in every department of learning. Science,
properly so called, may be afterwards acquired.
Classical learning opens an avenue to this, and every
object of liberal pursuit; and he who sets out without
it, will find many obstructions in his passage. I

think myself divested of prejudice, when I declare
that I never yet knew a writer who appeared to
great advantage in his style, or who was well received by persons of allowed taste, whatever might
be his scientific attainments or natural powers, if he
were totally ignorant of classical learning. Such an
one might write an useful, but seldom an agreeable,
book. The graces are certainly related to the muses,
and the muses have been most successfully cultivated
by the ancients.

It appears then from the observation of real facts,
that there is no reason to suppose the long-esta-
blished methods of public schools unable to produce, as they have hitherto produced, the most
accomplished characters. Indeed, when I see many
among the great, and among others, who have been
educated according to the schemes of innovators,
exhibiting an ignorance of ancient learning, and
scarcely retaining even the superficial qualifications
which they acquired under innovating instructors;
I am inclined to attribute much of the levity of the
present age, to a preference which has been given,
by those whose example is seducing, to an education totally unclassical.

It is certainly safest to adhere, for the most part,
to the established methods, rejecting nothing but
evident abuses. As a part of the established methods, I wish to retain the practice of teaching boys
to compose Latin verse. But let me not be misunderstood. I agree with those who say, that, when
a boy is designed to fill a subordinate sphere in
commercial or active life, to trouble him with Latin
versification, is to waste his valuable time. Such a
mode of gaining an intimate knowledge of the classics, is desirable to those only who are to assume a
profession or adorn a fortune.

To persons in such circumstances, and with such
liberal views, I strongly recommend an adherence to
the plan of instruction which includes Latin versification.   I am not so unreasonable as to recommend
the practice, merely because it has been long established ; but I derive a solid argument for its excellence, from its long establishment.   And I will add,
that I know, from actual experience, that it is the
best method of giving a student a refined taste for
classical expression.*   The necessity of composing
Latin verse, renders him more careful in remarking
and selecting elegancies of expression, than he
would be, if he were only to read, without imitating
and emulating, a Horace or a Virgil.

After all I am ready to allow that, they who think
differently from me, may very likely be right, though
they appear to me to err.   But on this subject I
believe the greater part of the regularly-educated
think as I do.   I have, however, found, upon inquiry, that in some of our most popular schools,
Latin verse is attended to as an exercise, rather too
early, too constantly, and too indiscriminately. †
For the sake of gaining prizes, and for other less de-
fensible reasons, it is made the first and the last
object, which it certainly ought not to be.   Boys
who happen to have no taste for it, however excellent their understandings in other respects, have, at
those schools, little encouragement.   But, omitting
to expatiate on a subject rather invidious, I proceed
to specify that plan which I judge most likely to

---

* Cowley, Milton, Addison, Gray, Jortin, and a great many other
men, of fine taste as well as profound leaning, were eminent in Latin
verse.

‡ It is absurd to confine a dunce, who can hardly compose a prosaic sentence grammatically correct, to the *ligata oratio*, to metrical composition, where the difficulties are greatly increased.

facilitate the acquisition of this elegant, though subordinate attainment.

A common method is, to suffer boys at first to write verses formed of words combined, without regard to meaning or grammatical construction, but, at the same time, with a close attention to the rules of prosody. This method certainly contributes to facilitate the pursuit, though it is not universally approved. It should not, indeed, be continued very long ; but it is certainly an excellent mode of introduction to an art which is confessedly attended with some difficulty.

Instructors differ much in opinion respecting the propriety of allowing their pupils the *Gradus ad Parnassum*. I am one of those who think, that the facilitating methods often contribute to retard advancement by indulging indolence. But this is certain : if you forbid the use of the *Gradus* in a place of education, the prohibition will be frustrated by the clandestine introduction of it. It is a book easily procured, and boys in the senior classes will not be without it. It is generally permitted, and I have known it used with judgment, by boys who have received great improvement from it. When the pupil possesses an uncommon share of parts, he will ascend Parnassus without this step to help him. I have seen excellent copies of Latin verses composed by boys who were never openly indulged with the use of the Gradus ; and I think that the improvement made without it will be more permanent and solid. The misfortune is, that the art appears so difficult at first, that the greater part of boys are likely to be deterred and disgusted, if they are denied this assistance.

When the quantity of syllables is pretty well known, it is a very good method to place the words

of one of Martial's Epigrams, or of any beautiful
passage in the Latin poets, out of their metrical
order, and to require the scholar to form them into
verses. Literal English translations from a Latin
poet, written in lines corresponding to each line in
the poet, may be given him to translate them into
Latin verse. When this is done, the original may
be read, and compared with the pupil's own production.*

But the utility of exercises consisting merely of
translations is comparatively little. It is best to exercise the boy's invention. As soon, therefore, as
he can write hexameters and pentameters, let him
have a subject given him. Let him be made acquainted with the nature of an epigram. Let him
be told, it is to consist of one thought. The search
after this thought is attended with many collateral
advantages. The mind in pursuit of it often ranges,
as well as it can, through the moral and physical
world. Men, manners, and things, whatever the
student has read, heard, or seen, come under his
consideration. A great improvement is derived to

* It has been made an objection to the practice of writing Latin
verse, that the moderns never can attain to ancient purity. But
Muretus deceived the great Scaliger, by publishing some verses of his
own under the name of an ancient; and if the moderns do not quite
equal the ancients in this particular, they come very near them. I
appeal to the writings of Fracastorius, Sannazarius, Vanier, Vida,
Bourne, and many polite scholars educated in the grammar-schools
of England. Dr. Johnson says, rather strongly, " that the Latin
poems of Milton are lusciously elegant ; but that the delight which
they afford is rather by the exquisite imitations of the ancient writers,
by the purity of the diction, and the harmony of the numbers, than
by any power of invention or vigour of sentiment." Ut transeundi
spes non sit, magna tamen est dignitas subsequendi. *Though we
have no hopes of getting before these great men, (the ancients,) yet
there is a great merit and honour in following closely after them.*
QUINTILIAN.

the mental faculty from this practice, and, at the same time, a habit of reflection gained, and knowledge of various kinds extended and confirmed. Let any one impartially examine the Lusus Westmonasterienses, Musæ Etonenses, and several other publications as well as manuscripts of this sort, and he will see the justness of my observation. The composers, like bees, sought sweets from every flower in the wide range of a most extensive excursion. Epigrams, odes, and various poëmatia, should alternately constitute exercises in the higher classes. Accuracy, copiousness of invention, a depth of thought, an elegance of style, and many other advantages, I have known derived from this method to every kind of writing in which the scholar afterwards employed his ingenuity. I have seen it; and therefore am not induced to alter my opinion by the declamation of those, who, from a defect in their own education, are not competent judges on this question. Neither am I deterred from continuing the practice of exercising boys in poetry, by the trite remark, that a poet is born, and not made. No one knows the genius of a boy till he is tried. The most unpromising* have often succeeded best, when called forth by opportunity or necessity. It does

---

* Dr. Isaac Barrow's father used to say that if it pleased God to take from him any of his children, he hoped it might be Isaac, as he was the least promising. For three years, say his biographers, which he spent at the Charter-house, he was remarkable for little else but fighting, negligence of his clothes and of his book. "So vain a thing is man's judgment," they observe, "and so unfit our providence to guide our own affairs."

I remember once, when I was a school-boy, and happened to be in the company of Dr. Goldsmith, to have heard him say, that he never was particularly attached to the Belles Lettres till he was thirty. Poetry had no peculiar charms for him till that age; and he believed, he said, that his genius, when a boy, was rather unpromising.

not follow that a boy must be professionally a poet, who has acquired a skill in poetry, or a taste for poetical composition.

SECTION VIII.

ON WRITING LATIN PROSE.

Scribendum quàm diligentissimè et quàm plurimùm. *Let the future orator compose with the utmost care, and as much as possible ;—i. e. rather than declaim only extempore.* QUINTILIAN.

AMONG many established practices in public schools, which the lovers of innovation wish to abolish, is that of composing in Latin prose, as well as in Latin verse. When they assert that they know not its use, they will readily be believed ; for such innovations as this commonly proceed from those who either have not had the opportunity of a truly liberal education, or who, from idleness or from dulness, have not availed themselves of its advantages. Persons under these circumstances cannot form an adequate idea of the utility of classical instruction in all its parts and consequences. Their ideas are usually confined to commercial objects, or to those

---

These remarks are offered with a view to prevent parents from hastily giving up their sons upon very early unfavourable appearances. Many a child has been sent to sea, or put out as an apprentice, to some subordinate trade, who might have shone eminently in letters, if his parents had not been inclined to despair too soon, from their ignorance of the nature and the operations of the human mind, and from their inattention to the biographical accounts of eminent literati.

On the other hand, parents must not consider early profligacy and idleness as symptoms of genius ; for this is a most fatal mistake. Bad boys have sometimes become good men ; but the instances are rare, and therefore taken notice of ; while by far the greater part of bad boys go on from bad to worse, and, at an early age, are ruined and forgotten.

which have little in them of a refined and a purely intellectual nature. That accomplishment which has no apparent tendency to an immediate and lucrative advantage, or which makes not a conspicuous figure in busy life, they cannot understand, and they consider as contemptible.

But the composition of Latin prose, considered merely as an exercise, naturally contributes to increase, and to confirm, an intimate knowledge of the language. He who can write a language, will not often be at a loss in reading the authors written in it. He will completely and accurately understand the delicacies and the beauties of the language, both when he considers it in its single and separate words, and when he views it in construction. When words and ideas pass immediately under the pen, in the act of composition, they are considered more distinctly and maturely than when they are only perused in a volume.

Besides this advantage, to be able to write Latin, qualifies the student to correspond with the learned in all countries.* Latin has long been the universal language of learning. The books which, from their extensive subject, seem to interest mankind at large, have usually been written in Latin. Indeed they are not so commonly written in Latin in the present age; a circumstance which plainly indicates a less degree of attention to that learned language, than was paid to it at the revival of letters. Yet scientific subjects of all kinds are still often discussed in Latin; and it is unbecoming a scholar to be unable to express his ideas in a language, in which learned foreigners not only write, but frequently converse.

---

* Latin letters should form one of the evening exercises in the highest classes at school; for which Cicero affords admirable models.

Add to this motive, that if the student proceeds
to either of our English universities, and really wishes
to appear and be a scholar, and not merely a man of
fashion and pleasure, he must acquire the habit of
composing in Latin. Latin themes, Latin declamations, Latin lectures, are constantly required of
academical students. It is true, that the idler usually procures these exercises, either from friends,
from books, or from collections of old compositions;
but, though he may pass through the forms of an
university by such mean subterfuges, he cannot
acquire credit, or acquit himself to his own satisfaction. Indeed, if he take the degree of master of
arts in one of our universities, he is bound by his
oaths to recite publicly in the schools Latin declamations of his own composition.

Nor is the practice of exacting Latin exercises in
the universities, to be considered as originating from
prejudice in a dark age, and continued by a fond
attachment to ancient customs; but as producing,
and as intended to produce, valuable effects. It
contributes greatly to keep awake an attention to
the classics, and consequently to all ancient literature. Many a lively young man would neglect his
studies in Latin, if he did not see that his neglect
would expose him to contempt or trouble, by dis-
abling him from performing those public exercises
which must be performed for the attainment of academical honours. Many members of the university
are induced to keep up, by constant application, the
habit of reading and imitating the more elegant
classics, because they may be required on some occasion to speak publicly in Latin. If the exercises
were required only in English, I am sure that the
study and knowledge of the Latin language would
greatly decrease. Indeed, all who wish to innovate

in this particular, indicate a design to render the university a place of education merely for men of the world, and to banish the Muses, that the Graces may reign alone; yet it is certain, that, without the Muses, the Graces will lose much of their beauty. Every scholar ought to be a gentleman; and, indeed, I can hardly conceive a true gentleman, by which character I understand a man of an elegant, a liberal, and an enlightened mind, who is not, in some degree, a polite scholar.

It is another argument in favour of the Latin exercises in our seminaries, that it has a natural tendency to improve the student in English composition. He who has been accustomed to make Cicero his model, will insensibly exhibit something of Cicero's beauty in his own language, and in whatever language he can compose with facility. That habit of accuracy, and that care in the collocation of words, which is required in Latin works, will insensibly extend its good effects to every production. To write Latin in youth, is an excellent preparation for that vernacular composition, which some of the professions indispensably require.* It ought, therefore, to be continued in our schools; but it will not often be attended with success, unless the pupil remains there long, and applies closely under the inspection of an experienced instructor. Much practice and long habit are necessary, to give excellence and facility.

There is no argument brought against the practice, which is not founded in that prevailing aversion to difficulty of all kinds, which is injurious to society in general, and particularly hurtful in the course of education. But while I insist on its general utility, I must allow, where boys are intended to acquire

---

* "It always gives perfection to have the exercise harder than the ordinary use."   BACON.

only a superficial knowledge, and to be removed early from their seminary to the warehouse and accompting-house, or to be introduced into any mode of active life incompatible with contemplation, that, in such a case, they will not be able to acquire an ease in Latin composition, and that it will not be necessary.

About the time of the revival of learning, every scholar was early taught to compose in Latin; and to excel in it was one of the first objects of his literary ambition. Many most honourable testimonies are extant, of the success of those indefatigable students; and I believe, if a taste for the manners and pursuits of that age were adopted, it would be a circumstance equally favourable to virtue and to letters. Simplicity, and a most ardent love of learning, excluded many vices, and debilitated many fatal passions.

With respect to the style which is chiefly to be imitated, I shall not hesitate to recommend that of Cicero.* The imitation of Cicero has, indeed, been often carried to a ridiculous excess; and a student deficient in judgment may sometimes resemble him, without displaying excellence. His more diffuse and Asiatic manner is not to be imitated. But the style of his Letters, his Offices, his Philosophical Conversations, his book on the Orator, his treatise on Friendship and on Old Age, with a few of his Orations, abound with sweets, from which the industrious bee may load himself with the purest honey. I am aware that some of the learned, wearied with the uniformity of the Ciceronian period, have imitated, and recommended as models, the

---

* Ille se profecisse sciat cui Cicero valdè placebit. *Let him be assured that he has made a great proficiency, who is much pleased with reading Cicero.* QUINTILIAN.

styles of Quintilian and Tacitus. These are excellent in their kind; but they have not the grace and sweetness of Cicero. They excel rather in the austere. They please and strike a mature taste, but they are not well adapted to allure a young student to the labour of imitation. Sweetness best pleases the young and unvitiated palate.

The practice in our old schools and universities, of exacting Latin themes and declamations on subjects of morality and history, is then attended with many useful consequences; * and I hope it will be continued in all places of a truly liberal education. Many modern schools have very properly bestowed, or professed to bestow, much attention on teaching the English language. I may venture without presumption, to suggest to their institutors and managers, that a judicious study of Latin composition will greatly facilitate the acquisition of an elegant style and of an intimate knowledge of English. I believe I may say, though not without danger of offending the conductors of English academies, that no man who does not understand Latin, can understand English. Almost all the polysyllabic words in our language are of Latin or Greek extraction. Classical grace may in some measure be transfused, from the elegant writers of Greece and Rome, to the less harmonious languages of northern Europe, by a

---

* Among others, it tends to keep up an intimate knowledge of Latin in the nation; which would not be preserved in perfection, if all were contented merely with understanding authors.—Cæsar, Cicero, Virgil, Horace, Livy, Sallust, have kept their rank, as standards for imitation, during eighteeen hundred years; and a careful imitation of them has produced such writers, in Italy, as Dante, Boccace, Petrarch, Ariosto, Casa, Galileo; in France, Racine, Moliere, Boileau, Bossuet, Fenelon; in England, Milton, Dryden, Addison, Pope, and a thousand others, who, altogether, have improved and innocently delighted myriads of the human race.

student who has been used to imitate the classics,
and whose ideas are strongly coloured by the channel
in which they have flowed. The improvement of
the English language,* therefore, as well as of the

---

* No man understands his own language better than Cicero did
his; yet he adhered to Greek exercises till he obtained the prætor-
ship: ad Præturam usque Græcè declamavit. SUETON. When a
boy, he was kept from a celebrated master who only taught his own
language: equidem memoriâ teneo, pueris nobis primum Latinè docere
cæpisse Plotium quendam, ad quem quum fieret concursus; dolebam
mihi idem non licere. Continebar autem doctissimorum hominum
autoritate qui existimabant Græcis exercitationibus ali melius ingenia
posse. *I remember when I was a boy, one Plotius first began to
teach the Latin language; and as it was the fashion to attend his
lectures, I was uneasy that I was not permitted to go too. But I
was prevented by the authority of some very learned men, who
were of opinion, that the understanding might be better cultivated
by exercises in Greek.* CIC. ad M. Titinium.

It has been said by persons who have not a proper idea of the grace
and elegance of the Latin language, that it is learned in a better, as
well as more compendious manner, by speaking than by writing it.
I think differently, and am happy to coincide with the opinion of the
celebrated Sanctius.

Quis porro ludimagister grammaticus non subinde pueris crepat;
vel male vel bene loquere? Tanta est stultorum hominum ignorantia,
perversitas et pertinacia. At ego, apud quem pluris est rectæ rationis
pondus, quam multorum præscriptum, assero, nihil pestilentius posse
juveni linguæ Latinæ cupido evenire, quam aut verbis Latinis effutire
cogitata, aut loquentium profluentiæ interesse . . . Non discimus
Hebræa, vel Græca, ut loquamur, sed ut docti efficiamur. Cur igitur
in Latinis non idem efficiemus? quandoquidem jam nulla natio est,
quæ Latinè aut Græcè loquitur. Stylus exercendus est diligenter:
hic enim, ut M. Tullius ait, est egregius dicendi magister; hic verè
nos docebit, communi sensu illos carere, qui linguam in Plateis aut
etiam in Gymnasiis, miris modis conantur dilacerare. *What schoolmaster is not for ever ringing in the ears of his boys this command:
Speak Latin, it signifies not whether ill or well, speak it? So great
is the ignorance, perverseness, and obstinacy of these foolish persons.
But I, with whom right reason has more weight than the injunc-
tions of the many, assert, that nothing can happen more injurious
to a young man who aims at a skill in the Latin language, than to
spout his thoughts in Latin words, or to be conversant with the*

scholar, greatly depends on the continuance of Latin composition as a scholastic exercise.

SECTION IX.

ON USING TRANSLATIONS.

Cum hæc ignaviæ subsidia simul et incitamenta in promptu habeat, parcius viribus ingenii utetur sui ; nullum porro in re grammaticâ, nullam in lexicographis impendet curam ; opibus alienis adjutus nihil de suo promet ; nihil demum marte proprio sibi elaborandum esse censebit : et velut in regione ignotâ hospes inelegans ducem secutus aliquando falsum, sæpe fallacem, huc, illuc temerè circumvagabitur. *When the boy has these helps and incitements to idleness at hand, he will make less use of his own powers of understanding. Henceforth he will not attend to the grammar or lexicon. Assisted by the wealth of others, he will bring nothing from his own store. In a word, he will think it no longer necessary that any thing should be done by his own personal exertions; and, like an inelegant stranger in an unknown country, submitting to be led by a blundering and treacherous guide, he will wander about without knowing whither he is going.* JOANNES BURTON.

IT may perhaps appear paradoxical to assert, that many of the modes which have been devised to facilitate the acquisition of learning, have contributed to retard it.* Yet, there are proofs, and those very

---

prattling effusions of Latin talkers . . . We do not learn Hebrew or Greek in order to speak them ; but to become learned in them. Why should we not do the same in the Latin? Since there is now no nation which speaks Latin or Greek, the pen is to be diligently exercised ; for it is this, as Tully says, which is the best instructor in the art of speaking ; but this will teach us to discover that they are destitute of common sense, who attempt to tear the language in pieces, in the streets and schools, in so strange a manner. SANCTIUS.

* ——— Pater ipse ———
Haud facilem esse viam voluit ———
——————— Curis acuens mortalia corda.
Nec torpere gravi passus sua regna veterno.
The father of mankind did not choose that the way should be easy ; but designed to sharpen the wit of man by cares, nor would he suffer his subject world to grow torpid through sloth. VIRG.
The following is the opinion of archbishop Markham on the subject of the facilitating methods. His opinion deserves attention, as he was a schoolmaster, and therefore speaks from experience.

numerous too, which might be adduced to support the opinion. There was, it will on all sides be confessed, a very small number of auxiliary books at the revival of learning ; but there were scholars, who, in the accuracy and extent of their knowledge in the ancient

---

" It is natural, indeed, for common minds to look to those things which are obvious and superficial.   It is natural also to avoid labour, and to seek for compendious methods. We may, with very little appli · cation, acquire the opinions of those who have gone before us ; and if our pursuits are mean, they may serve our purpose.   But no high point of excellence was ever attained, but by a laborious exercise of the mind. I do not say, that abridgments, systems, and common-places, with the other assistances, which modern times have so abundantly furnished, may not have their use.   At the same time, it can scarcely be denied, that they have contributed very much to languid and inefficient studies. The advantages of rational mathematics have, perhaps, been much abridged by the useful invention of algebra.   And in divinity, physic, and law, whatever promises to save us trouble is generally a corruptor, and leads us only to superficial attainments.   The same it is, in the inferior professions.   Whatever facilitates the art tends to the decay of it.   To obviate these corruptions, our best security seems to be in a liberal education ; in which, by frequently conversing with those great authors of antiquity, who are distinguished for just and clear concep- tions, the mind acquires the habit of thinking as they did, and is tempted to try its own powers.   The profession of physic is one of the most liberal and useful ; it has a connexion with learning and science of every kind ; it has great opportunities of adding to the common stores of knowledge, and has usually been particularly conversant in, elegant letters; without the aid of which, it can neither use its best sources, nor communicate its discoveries with any advantage.

" It is to be lamented, that many attend only to the technical and vulgar kind of education : useful, indeed, as the rules of arithmetic are to the tradesman, they facilitate the process of his business, but never apply to his sentiments or manners. It is to be lamented, that so many in the practice of physic have looked to this part only ; and have con- tented themselves with those mechanical acquirements, which a per- son may easily possess, without having the least tincture of any thing that deserves the name of education.   A small acquaintance with lan- guages, enough perhaps for common currency, with a few courses of lectures in the medical branches, are thought to form a sufficient stock."
Sermon before the University of Oxford.

languages, have not been equalled in any subsequent period. The conquests obtained in the regions of learning at that period, were obtained with difficulty; but a degree of force was acquired and exercised in the conflict, which extended and secured the subjugated domain.

In common life a remark has become obvious, that the fortune which is bequeathed, or acquired at an easy rate, is more likely to be dissipated than the fruits of laborious industry. It is so likewise in learning. Ideas collected without any great effort, make but a slight impression on the memory or the imagination. The reflection, that they may be recalled at pleasure, prevents any solicitude to preserve them. But the remembrance, that the degree of knowledge already acquired has cost us dearly, enhances its value, and excites every precaution to prevent it from being lost. I would compare the learning acquired by the facilitating aids of modern invention to the vegetables raised in a hot-bed; which, however precocious they may become, never acquire that perfection, which is gradually produced by the slow process of unassisted nature.

For these reasons, and indeed from experience, I am led to disapprove those translations, which, in many schools, are constantly used. I believe that few causes have contributed more to impede the scholar's progress, than the general adoption of translations. The human mind is naturally indolent, and particularly so at the early season at which education is commenced. At all times it is averse from unnecessary labour, and rejoices to facilitate the means of arriving at its end. When, therefore, a translation is presented to the eye on the same page with the original, it is not likely, that for the sake of a remote advantage, the mind should neglect present ease; that it should turn from the meaning which is offered to its notice, and willingly pursue it in the mazes of a lexicon. The boy learns to construe his lesson by the English printed at its side, and takes care to remember it during half an hour, when he will probably have said it to his instructor; and after which he will let it slip away without reluctance, conscious that his collateral translation will enable him to go through the same business on the morrow, without punishment, and without the pain of recollection. I hope it is not uncandid to suppose, that translations have often been used to save the trouble, or conceal the ignorance, of the instructor.

Instances have occurred to me, as they must to others, of boys who came from schools where translations were used, and who have been advanced to the higher classes with translations; but who, without those assistances, were totally ignorant of the rules of construction, and, in order to make any solid improvement, were compelled to begin at the very elements of the Latin language. If they have been so unfortunate as not to have been removed from the injudicious discipline which allows translations, they have generally deceived the expectations of their friends, and brought grammatical instruction into disrepute. The knowledge they have gained of the classics has been little and superficial; seldom sufficient to enable them to taste the beauties of the ancient authors, and never extensive or profound enough to distinguish them as men of letters. When neither pleasure nor advantage has been derived to them, it is not to be wondered at, if the unsuccessful students have condemned that classical education in general, which they never rationally pursued.

The exertion of mind necessary in learning to construe a lesson, without a translation, is one of the most desirable consequences derivable from the lesson. A habit of attention is acquired by it; conjectural ingenuity called forth; and a degree of penetration, and patience of literary labour, a most desirable acquisition, insensibly produced. Whatever difficulty it may be attended with, will be overcome by the boy who possesses parts; and he who possesses none will never make any valuable proficiency with or without these indulgent assistances. He may indeed be allured by them to throw away his time, and reap nothing in return but disgrace.

The use of translations is not, however, destitute of advocates in its favour. Mr. Clarke, the author of the Introduction to making Latin, is a very warm one. I hope his zeal in their defence arose from a more honourable motive than the wish to promote the sale of those editions with translations, of which he had published a considerable number. It might arise from a sincere conviction of their utility; for Mr. Clarke was one of the first who recommended their general use; and the introducer of an innovation is commonly enthusiastic in his recommendation of it. His arguments, though urged with vehemence, carry little intrinsic weight with them, and are abundantly refuted by experience.

I believe it will not be controverted, that good Greek scholars have seldom been so numerous as good Latinists. What shall we affirm as the cause? Greek is not more difficult in its elements than Latin. Its authors are equally, perhaps more, inviting. It is usually entered on at a less puerile age than Latin, at an age when the understanding has acquired strength enough to overcome any grammatical difficulty. Nothing has impeded the equal advancement of Greek studies, of late at least, but the universal practice of publishing all Greek books with a Latin translation.* Some candid editors have been sensible of this truth, and have added transla-tions with apparent regret. Their conviction has been over-ruled by a species of argument very forci-ble on these occasions, and which I shall name the Bibliopolian. The bookseller has urged, with great truth, that without concomitant translations, Greek books have ceased to be a saleable commodity. When Greek scholars were scarce in Europe, a few translations contributed to facilitate the introduction of the language ; this expediency introduced the custom, which is not likely to be abolished, though

* " The study of the original text can never be sufficiently recom-mended. It is the shortest, surest, and most agreeable way to all sorts of learning. Draw from the spring head, and take not things at second-hand. Let the writings of the great masters be never laid aside : dwell upon them, settle them in your mind, and cite them upon occasion : make it your business thoroughly to understand them in their full extent, and in all their circumstances : acquaint your-selves fully with the principles of original authors ; bring them to a consistency, and then do you yourself make your deductions. In this state were the first commentators ; and do not you rest until you bring yourself to the same. Content not yourself with these borrowed lights ; nor guide yourself by their views, but where your own fails you, and leaves you in the dark. Their explications are not yours, and will give you the slip. On the contrary, your own observations are the product of your own mind ; where they will abide, and be ready at hand upon all occasions, in converse, consultation, and dispute. Lose not the pleasure it is to see that you were not stopped in your reading but by difficulties that are invincible, where the commentators and scholiasts themselves are at a stand, and have nothing to say ; those copious expositors of other places, who, with a vain and pompous overflow of learning, poured out on passages plain and easy in them-selves, are very free of their words and pains where there is no need. Convince yourself fully by thus ordering your studies, that it is nothing but men's laziness which hath encouraged pedantry to cram, rather than enrich, libraries, and to bury good authors under heaps of notes and commentaries ; and you will perceive that sloth hath acted, in this instance, against itself and its own interest, by multiplying reading and inquiries, and increasing the pains it endeavoured to avoid."

BRUYERE.

it is most inimical to Grecian literature, and, for that
reason, to the prevalence of a good taste. The Greek
poets, as well as the philosophers and historians, have
been read and criticised by those who could only read
them in the same style of a literal translation, who
acquiesced in so wretched a substitute for the original,
but who, probably, would have studied the Greek,
and understood it, had they not been led astray in
their youth by that powerful incitement to indolence, a collateral translation.*

To the use of translations, and to the various
modes of facilitating puerile studies, I may venture
to attribute the decline of solid learning, and of that
just taste which the ancient models tended to estab-
lish. Together with translations, I wish it were possible to banish those editions in which the order of
construction is given on the same page with the text.
I am convinced, that to the order alone the boy's
attention is usually given; and that consequently

---

* Omnibus versionibus de lingua Græca in Latinam, de utravis in
vernaculas, quibus hanc cum doctorum incredibilem paucitatem, tum
semi-doctorum et sciolorum multitudinem præcipuè, ni fallor, de-
bemus, capitalis hostis sum, et hunc ridiculum morem adjungendi
libris Græcis Latinas interpretationes Græcarum literarum labem et
perniciem extitisse semper existimaverim .... Compendii Bibliopolæ
habenda ratio erat; qui confirmavit, Græcum codicem, incomitatum
versione Latinâ, omnium malorum mercimoniorum longè indivendi-
bilissimum; quare se magnopere mihi auctorem supplicemque esse,
ut pestiferum illud consilium abjiciam, &c. *To all translations from
Greek into Latin, from either into English, to which I think we owe
the wonderful paucity of the truly learned, and the multitude of the
half learned and of sciolists, I am a declared enemy : and I have
always been of opinion, that this ridiculous practice of adding Latin
translations to Greek books is the disgrace and destruction of
Grecian literature..... But I was obliged to have a regard to the
bookseller's profit ; who assured me, that a Greek book, without a
Latin translation, was of all bad commodities by far the most un-
saleable ; for which reason he most earnestly begged and prayed me
to lay aside that ruinous intention, as he called it.*

THIRLBÆUS, in Prefat. ad Justin Mart.

all the beauty of an elegant disposition of words, one of the most striking in the classics, must pass unnoticed. It tends also to enervate the mind, by rendering exertion unnecessary. The most unexceptionable method of rendering the classics easy to the younger scholars, is to subjoin, as is sometimes practised, a vocabulary at the end of the volume. Even the interpretation in the editions in Usum Delphini, which are universally used, tends, in my opinion, to corrupt the style, and to vitiate the taste, by drawing off the attention from the elegant language of a Virgil to the bad Latin of a modern commentator.

The young student cannot too early be taught to exert his own powers, and to place a modest confidence in their operation. This will increase their native vigour, and give him spirit to extend them as far as they will go on every proper emergency. Accustomed to depend upon himself, he will acquire a degree of courage necessary to call forth that merit which is often diminished in value to its diffident possessor, and totally lost to mankind. The little superficial learning of him who has been used to the facilitating inventions, may be compared to a temporary edifice, built for a day; while the hard-earned knowledge of the other resembles a building, whose foundations are deep and strong, and equally to be admired for dignity and duration.*

---

* Οὐδὲν τῶν μεγάλων ἄφνω γίνεται. *Nothing great is done on a sudden.* ARRIAN.

END OF VOL. III.

Check Out More Titles From HardPress Classics Series In this collection we are offering thousands of classic and hard to find books. This series spans a vast array of subjects – so you are bound to find something of interest to enjoy reading and learning about.

Subjects:
Architecture
Art
Biography & Autobiography
Body, Mind &Spirit
Children & Young Adult
Dramas
Education
Fiction
History
Language Arts & Disciplines
Law
Literary Collections
Music
Poetry
Psychology
Science
…and many more.

Visit us at www.hardpress.net

CPSIA information can be obtained
at www.ICGtesting.com
Printed in the USA
BVHW061344160819
556068BV00021B/2112/P